OUR MUSIC
WITH

THE STORY
OF THE CREATION

SEAN EGAN

This edition published in Great Britain in 2004 by
Cherry Red Books Ltd, 3a Long Island House,
1–4 Warple Way, London W3 0RG.

Copyright © 2004, Sean Egan.

ISBN: 1-901447-22-7

ABOUT THE AUTHOR

Sean Egan's first professional writing work was a brief stint providing scripts for the television soap opera *EastEnders*. He is currently a journalist specialising in popular music and tennis. He has written for, among other outlets, *Billboard, Billboard.com, Classic Rock, Discoveries, Goldmine, Record Collector, RollingStone.com, Serve And Volley, Sky Sports, Tennis World, Uncut* and *Vox*. He also writes CD liner notes. He is the author of books on The Verve, The Animals and Jimi Hendrix, as well as the critically acclaimed rock'n'roll novel *Sick Of Being Me*.

CREDITS

My grateful thanks go to those who agreed to be interviewed for this book. First and foremost among them, of course, are the three surviving original members of The Creation, Bob Garner, Jack Jones and Eddie Phillips, who all granted several lengthy and no doubt patience-exhausting interviews. Grateful thanks also go to the following for talking to me:

Tony Atkins, Andy Bell, Johnny Byrne, June Clark, Gail Colson, Glen Colson, John Dalton, Stephen Friedland aka Brute Force, Joe Foster, David Garrick, Keith Grant, John Iles, Paul Kahan, Damon Lyon-Shaw, Alan McGee, Alan O'Duffy, Tony Ollard, John Pantry, Dave Preston, Roman Salicki, Rod Siebke, Ed Strait, Shel Talmy, Mick Thompson, Pete Townshend, Ken White and John Wonderling.

In addition to the original quotes generated by the above interviews, I have included in the text many quotes from the few major articles that have been published on The Creation down the years, something that was made particularly necessary by the wish to represent the points of view of those Creation members no longer with us, Kenny Pickett and Kim Gardner. I have endeavoured to credit the source of the quotes when reproducing them but am happy to also acknowledge here the debt owed in this respect to *Blitz* magazine, which carried interviews in 1982 with Kenny Picket and Eddie Phillips, both conducted by W Lynne Aldridge, *Ugly Things* #15 (1997), which contained a special of almost 30 pages on the band mostly written by Mike Stax and *Record Collector*, for its July 1995 Creation feature by John Reed. Also of significant help was the Eddie Phillips interview on the website http://www.sixtiespop.com

I am humbled by the enthusiasm of fans of The Creation who have shown unstinting enthusiasm in their help with the project. I am particularly indebted to Rod Siebke for cuttings, videos, CDs and a bottomless pool of information and suggestions, Greg Weatherby for provision of recordings and cuttings, Mike Griffiths, also for recordings and information, as well as spreading word on the project through the Eddie Phillips and Creation discussion group he runs: http://groups.yahoo.com/group/theWorldof _EddiePhillips_and_The Creation/; Syd Kreft for videos, cuttings and information about German chart placings; Mark A. Johnston for song lyrics, information and suggestions; Mike Stax for providing back issues of his excellent magazine *Ugly Things* http://www.ugly-things.com and information.

The following also provided much appreciated assistance:
Frank Allen, Mick Avory, Keith Badman, Dave 'Digger'
Barnes, Denis Blackham, Ken Blaikley, John Briggs, Matt
Bristow, Mick Capewell, George Chkiantz, Bob Clifford of
EMI Publishing, Don Craine, Jools Devere and Keith
Phillips of Advance Graphics, Daniel Diezi, Roger Dopson,
Russ Garrett, Andy Gray, Douglas Hinman, Ken Howard,
Tony Jasper, Mick Liber, Judy Lipson, Zeke Lund, Jim
McElwane, Tim Madgwick, Antion Meredith, Don Mudie,
Wendy Ellison Mullen, Andy Neill, Sharon O' Neill of EMI
Publishing, Andrew Loog Oldham, Jackie Payne, Martin
Payne, Mark Paytress, Aaron J Poehler, Alan Robinson,
Mike Ross-Trevor, Marc Skobac, Malcolm Stewart, John
Timperley, Richie Unterberger, Chris Welch and David
Wells. And a big thank-you to all the wonderful Aussies
who assisted me in my (sadly fruitless) search for the
elusive 'Digger': Bazza, Peter Bruce, Paul Culnane, Ian
McFarlane and Bruce Sergent.

FOREWORD BY ALAN McGEE

n the mid Nineties, my record label Creation began to take off. The taste of success was very nice, of course, but for me every one of the records we sold by the likes of Oasis and Primal Scream and Teenage Fanclub came with an extra little pleasure: spreading the name of The Creation, the band whose name I had taken for my label, around the world. Despite the fact that they recorded a whole load of classic tracks, The Creation sold very few records in the UK and the US when they were together (1966-68). By the late Nineties, Creation was arguably the biggest record label in Britain. Tens of millions of people who bought records by Oasis alone were seeing The Creation's handle whenever they glanced at the sleeve of their purchase. I made sure to drive the connection home by mentioning the band every time I could in the many interviews I was doing at the time. I even made a sort of fairytale transition from fan to benefactor when I financed a comeback album by The Creation in 1995, 27 years after they'd split.

I'd first heard of The Creation in 1979, at the age of eighteen. In fact, I was introduced to their name via a process similar to the one I've just mentioned. Closely inspecting the inner sleeve of the album 'All Mod Cons' by one of my favourite groups, The Jam, I noticed a mention of them and one of their songs, 'Biff Bang Pow'. My introduction to their actual music came about three years later in the shape of a compilation that Edsel had put together called 'How Does It Feel To Feel'. I was amazed by what I heard. Tracks like 'Making Time', 'Painter Man', 'Through My Eyes', 'Nightmares', 'How Does It Feel To Feel' and many others were not only brilliantly written, brilliantly arranged and brilliantly played, they were also – it seemed to me – a fantastic style of music I didn't even know existed: psychedelic punk. It was love at first listen.

Though I would have liked The Creation to have achieved the success they truly deserved in the Sixties, in a way I enjoyed the fact that they didn't. It's difficult to describe the delight you get when you're young in telling people your favourite band is someone they've never heard of. While kids my age were saying 'The Three Johns' (the hip ones) or 'Kajagoogoo' (the not so hip ones) when someone asked them who their top group was, I could stand there feeling sooo cool when replying with the name of a group that would just make people scrunch up their noses in bewilderment. If you knew who The Creation were, you were a member of an elite. In time, I would find a few other people in that elite and form a band with them. Of course, we named it after a Creation song, 'Biff Bang Pow'.

I mentioned psychedelic punk. I doubt if that exact phrase actually popped into my had when I first heard The Creation's stuff but by the time I was setting up my own independent record label in 1983, it definitely had. Psychedelic punk was a neat concept. Psychedelia without the airy-fairyness and lack of crunch that often spoiled the wonderful surrealism of it. Punk without the lack of tunefulness that sometimes ruined that fabulously raw style of music. As I'd decided that my label was going to put out records that were a mixture of punk and psychedelia, the name for the label was pretty obvious: the same as the name of the band that had – without meaning to or knowing it – invented the whole genre and then gone back to their day jobs when it turned out no-one was interested. Thankfully, the world had moved on by the Eighties and people did seem to be interested in my label's records.

It's long overdue for somebody to write a book about The Creation. Their best records were as good as the best by the Beatles, Hendrix, Sex Pistols and anybody else who has had heaps of books written about them that you want to mention. They were just one of those great bands that slipped between the cracks. Sadly, it happens sometimes in the music business. I've managed to convince the public perhaps more times than most that a band I think are great are worth spending money on but at the end of the day you can't frogmarch people to the checkout and force them to buy a band's single or album no matter how good you yourself consider them to be.

There's been a process of change in The Creation's fortunes since being a fan of theirs put you in an elite that was so small as to be almost non-existent. Their catalogue is back in print in several countries, their songs have been used on film soundtracks and they – or a couple of them – play sold-out gigs today. In my own way, I think I've helped to ensure their name lives on, whether it be by giving them the chance to do a new album or by naming my record label, publishing company and recording studio after them. Sean Egan's book is kind of the final stage of that process. Though we all know that there's no correlation between being great artistically and fame/commercial success, we still can't help replying – in contempt – 'Never heard of 'em' when someone swears they've just seen the next superstars-in-waiting. The same thing applies to biographies: you shouldn't do it but you sort of think that if a band were really that important, why has no-one ever done a book on them?

Well, you're holding it in your hands. I don't need a book to make me realise the importance of The Creation. I knew that long ago. But it's fantastic that one has now been written. It will help convince those people who can't quite admit to themselves what their ears are telling them when they listen to their records: that the Creation were one of the greatest bands in the history of popular music.

Alan McGee

INTRODUCTION

Their songs have been covered by acts as diverse as Ride, Boney M and the Sex Pistols; they impressed Pete Townshend so much that he asked their guitarist Eddie Phillips to join the already successful Who; said guitarist pioneered the use of the violin bow on guitar strings (an innovation subsequently appropriated by and credited to Led Zeppelin's Jimmy Page); they inspired the name and original musical direction of Creation Records; they have been cited as an influence by Paul Weller, Alan McGee, Ride, Pete Townshend, John Lydon and others.

Yet The Creation never had a bona fide hit single in either Britain or the US, had a recording career of no more than two years, experienced endless changes in personnel which ensured that at their death only their drummer had been a consistent factor since their original incarnation and never – before their 1990s reunion – released an album on either side of the Atlantic. So why write a 100,000-plus-word book about them? Well, read the first paragraph again. For a Sixties band to so inspire subsequent generations of musicians (as well as ones from their own era) without troubling the hit parade is almost unprecedented: in the age before albums superseded singles as the most important way of disseminating rock music, only the Velvet Underground spring to mind as a band who profoundly affected fellow artists while remaining a secret from the wider public.

Quite why The Creation never achieved significant commercial success – at least outside West Germany and a couple of other Continental countries – remains a mystery. Their compositions 'Making Time', 'Painter Man', 'Biff Bang Pow', 'Nightmares', 'Can I Join Your Band', 'Life Is Just Beginning', 'Through My Eyes', 'How Does It Feel To Feel' and others are incontrovertible classics. They were also utterly innovative, a unique hybrid of pop, rock, psychedelia and the avant garde. Additionally, they were able – almost unbelievably – to continue creating great art no matter how many different permutations of the personnel they experienced. Yet their career never really got going, with even the commercial success and teen idol status they achieved in countries like West Germany seeming almost like a sick joke: a melancholia-inducing reminder of their failure in their home country and America, the territories which every rock'n'roll band considers to be the ones that truly matter.

Despite having made great records through each different line-up, by the end of their tumultuous existence, the band were reduced to putting out Continental-only cover versions of 'Bony Moronie' and 'Mercy Mercy Mercy' that were a world removed from their previous barrier-shattering art. Exhausted by their inability to find a replacement for their lead guitarist/creative genius Phillips, they dribbled to a close in April 1968. One of their ex-personnel, Ronnie Wood (a short-term member) found fame with the Faces and the Rolling Stones and another, Kim Gardner, achieved moderate success with Ashton, Gardner and Dyke. For the rest, however, ordinary life and the necessity to come to terms with shattered dreams beckoned.

In the early Seventies, being a Sixties has-been (or indeed a never-was) was not easy. Well before the nostalgia boom gave stars a virtually limitless career span, musicians who were no longer able to make ends meet in their chosen profession faced only the bleakness-tinged life that is the lot of those who had tasted screaming fans, limousines and adoring girls but have nothing to look forward to but humdrum jobs and suburban uneventfulness. Eddie Phillips – one of the greatest and most innovative guitarists of his generation – started driving the 38 bus from Leytonstone to Piccadilly five days a week. His fellow London Transport staff had no inkling that their colleague had supported Cream, The Kinks and The Rolling Stones on stage nor that one of the occasions he had appeared in the pop papers was when a story had broken that Pete Townshend has asked him to join The Who. One can't help but feel that something sadder than a desire not to be seen to boast was behind Eddie's taciturnity about his previous life.

Then something strange happened. As rock music grew in age and respect, and as its audience matured with it, it started to acquire its own biographers, annotators and historians. Music once dismissed as disposable trash was increasingly cherished and documented by its devotees. Proper analysis of rock music turned from rare to commonplace and books on popular music figures were now less likely to be exploitation fluff than the type of serious, in-depth studies that the world had previously thought only 'proper' artists like painters, authors and classical composers deserved. In such a climate, chart positions began to be seen as fundamentally less important than artistic merit. Correspondingly, great artists who had not achieved commercial success began to be perceived in some quarters as just as respectable as those who had had strings of chart toppers.

They were also deemed just as worthy of having articles written on them as the superstars – in a way more so, for who wanted to read yet anther article about artists like the Beatles or Dylan, who had already been the subject of several millions of words? Like many great, neglected bands, The Creation began to acquire a cult status. Their records – which shops had not been able to give away in the Sixties – now became collector's items, fetching increasingly inflationary prices. Their records began to be reissued as record companies were taken over by a new generation who had grown up in the Sixties and to whom art was just as important as commerce.

By 1987, Eddie and Creation vocalist Kenny Pickett were so aware of the cachet status their ex-band's name had that they were planning to issue a new album under that sobriquet. (By then, by one of those lovely instances of good karma that can happen to songwriters, they had experienced an unexpected windfall when ultra-successful disco group Boney M had released an unlikely hit cover of the Creation's signature song, 'Painter Man'.) The decision in the mid-1990s by Alan McGee – the defining British music mogul of his era – to finance the very first proper Creation studio album was the ultimate acknowledgement of The Creation's worth.

Our Music Is Red – With Purple Flashes (the immortal quote coined by Phillips to describe his band's records) can't turn back the clock nor put right the injustice of their failure nor undo the fact that Pickett died in 1997 an unfulfilled and disappointed man. What it can do is take part in and hopefully help consolidate the process in which various rock journalists, reissue labels and celebrity fans have been involved over the last couple of decades: giving one of history's great neglected bands their due.

CHAPTER 1
IN THE BEGINNING

The story of the band who became The Creation begins with an ensemble called Neil Everett & The Vibros. This group was one of a surprisingly high number on the music scene of the Cheshunt/Waltham Cross area on the outskirts of North London, in the early Sixties. That Cheshunt had the kind of throbbing music scene more usually associated with an urban area than a suburb is probably attributable to the example of Cliff Richard, a local boy who in 1958 became Britain's first proper indigenous rock'n'roll star with his hit 'Move It'. (Tommy Steele's hit of two years earlier, 'Rock With The Caveman', doesn't count on the grounds that it was intended as a parody of the genre.)

It was in the Vibros in the early Sixties that a young Jack Jones began his career in music, albeit on a singing basis, rather than in the role of drummer that he would fill with The Creation. Jones had grown up if not alongside then adjacent to Cliff Richard, or Harry Webb as he was then. "(I wasn't) a mate of his but I went to the same school," says Jack. "He was a couple of years older than me. Cliff was a prefect. Didn't like 'im much! No, he was all right. He was a good guy. He actually had a band there. He played at our school concert."

The Vibros are of no particular significance in rock'n'roll history but marked the first point at which the professional paths of two future Creation members bisected: after Jones' brief stint in the band ended, he was replaced by one Kenny Pickett, future Creation frontman. Explains Jack," "I think I was Neil Everett number two and I think Kenny was Neil Everett number three. I left because I just loved playing the drums and I didn't really feel right as a frontman out there at that particular time. Never met Kenny at the time."

Jack Llewellyn Jones was born in Northampton on 8 November 1947. One of three children, he has an older brother and sister. "My dad was a painter and decorator," he says. "He was an old Welsh miner one time and he got one of these old Welsh miner diseases so he had to pack it in. He couldn't go underground any more 'cos it would have killed him so he come up to find some work – 'cos there was nothing about in them days – to London and that's where he met my mum. Her mother and father had a grocery shop in Bethnal Green and my mum was the oldest in the family so she was like a manager and she used to spend a lot of time looking after the shop. When she met my dad they got married and off they went."

Educated at Cheshunt Secondary Modern, Jack's original job was that of cabinet maker. Like many of his musical generation, though, he continued to show symptoms of the rock'n'roll bug that had bitten him in the late Fifties via playing in amateur bands in his leisure time, a bug that the once unbelievable global success of a British band called the Beatles naturally did nothing to counteract. Ray Vincent and the Raiders was the setting for Jack's drumming skills but he would also occasionally dep for a more proficient local group known as Jimmy Virgo and the Bluejacks. As well as the titular vocalist Virgo (real name James Hayford), the Bluejacks featured a guitarist called Norman Mitham. Mitham had grown up, attended school and played in a band with Harry Webb/Cliff Richard.

Unfortunately for Mitham, the guitarist with whose name Richard's would become synonymous was not him but Hank Marvin. "He only got rowed out when Hank came along," explains John 'Nobby' Dalton, Mitham's colleague in the Bluejacks. Dalton, like Richard and Mitham, had attended Cheshunt Secondary Modern School, although was a few years younger than them. Dalton was asked to join the Bluejacks just after leaving school himself although not on his preferred instrument of guitar. "In those days – this was about '59 – there wasn't any bass players about," Dalton explains. "The first bass player I ever heard of was Jet Harris from The Shadows. I actually had a six-string guitar, a Hofner Club 40. I couldn't really play. The first thing I learnt was a Jet Harris number called 'Jet Black'. They liked that and said, 'Join us?' I said, I can't really play'. They said, 'Well, we'll teach you'. That's when Norman Mitham taught me the rudiments of it all." Mick 'Spud' Thompson was the Bluejacks' rhythm guitarist.

Pete Wilson and Bobby Henrit would occupy the drummer's stool in the Bluejacks but, Dalton recalls, "It wasn't until we actually got Jack that we had a regular drummer." Jack had no difficulty in accepting the offer made by the Bluejacks sometime in 1963 to move from the status of dep to permanent drummer. He says of the Raiders, "It wasn't going anywhere. A couple of the guys wanted to pack it in." The Bluejacks, on the other hand, "were quite a decent band for their time."

"It suited it, what we was doing at the time," says Dalton of Jack's drumming. "I've had this all along in me musical career: you know of better drummers but it doesn't mean to say they're better suited for the band. An example, Ringo Starr – far from the best drummer in the world but he was exactly right for the Beatles, his style of playing and everything. Jack was the same really... Later on, his vocals were a great asset as well." Dalton also recalls Jack being an asset as a person with a "dry sense of humour."

Like almost every semi-professional British group at that time, the Bluejacks served up a diet of classic rock'n'roll and current chart hits for audiences who were concerned not with watching the performance of the band but with having an appropriate sonic backdrop to dancing, drinking and attracting members of the opposite sex. Not that the band members were apt to agonise about this: they were supplementing the income from their 'real' jobs by having fun. At that stage of UK rock history, that was all most British musicians could imagine asking for.

"We used to do okay," says Jack. "We used to work regular. We had all the American air force bases and clubs. We did a little tour down in Wales once which went really well. It was good fun." Playing US air force bases – then thick on the ground in Britain – provided a glimpse into what seemed almost a different universe to the natives of country whose perennial weather-dictated greyness was then exacerbated by the post-war austerity that still stubbornly lingered following the ending of rationing in 1954. "There were loads and loads," says Dalton of the bases, "and for us they were totally different – to play the officer's mess and things like that. You'd never seen anything like it. They just knew how to live and dance and the first American hamburger we tasted, we thought, 'Blimey – this is unbelievable'."

Small-scale their ambitions may have been but The Bluejacks even did some recording, albeit in the form of an acetate. The one copy of the acetate pressed, which is still in existence, contained versions of Gene Vincent's 'Say Mama' and Vince Taylor's 'Brand New Cadillac'. Both are uncanny facsimiles of American rock'n'roll but essentially characterless, unless you count Virgo's patently Hertfordshire accent on his cry of "Let's rock!" before the guitar break.

"I think that was done in Regent Sound," says Dalton, referring to a studio in Denmark Street, London that saw the recording of many tracks at the time both of the complete lack of significance of the Bluejacks' and of the importance of the Rolling Stones' classic debut album. "We didn't get anywhere with that. I think we just done it for ourselves. Perhaps we thought it wasn't really quality enough." The very success of the Bluejacks on the live circuit was what led Jimmy Virgo to decide in mid-1963 to leave the group that bore his name. "We were trying to get a bit bigger and we wanted to do more work," recalls Dalton. "There was a lot more work coming along with the American air bases. At that time as well, most of us were working and playing of an evening. Getting home two or three in the morning and up for work next morning."

As a postman, Virgo had to get up earlier than most. Dalton: "We were all single but him being a family man with kids, it was getting too much." Following Virgo's decision, Jack, Dalton and Mitham had a meeting at Jack's house to discuss what they were going to do next. They decided on the obvious answer: to continue with a new name and a new singer. A man from Welwyn Garden City whose name is lost in the mists of time performed vocals for a few gigs before a permanent frontman was recruited. Dalton: "People used to come and watch us, Roy and Margaret Morris. They lived on the same estate and they used to come and watch us with Jim in the band. They come to see me and said, 'We got a friend who sings'." The singing friend in question was Kenny Pickett. "Kenny was a plumber and Roy's a plumber and I think they used to work with the same firm in Hertford," says Dalton. Kenny was given an audition at the Tudor Rooms in Hoddesdon. Dalton: "He come along and sung 'Don't Be Cruel'. We thought, 'He's quite good'. He got the job straight away. I think Ken had been in bands. I don't know what ones but I think a local band. He wasn't doing anything at the time apart from plumbing. We desperately needed a singer and he looked good. You could tell straight away: he could sing. So that was it."

Kenneth George Pickett was born in Ware, Hertfordshire. His earliest published date of birth was 3 September 1942. However, his true year of birth was 1940, making him easily the oldest of all the future Creation personnel, and the only one of them to have done National Service. He told *Blitz* magazine in 1982, "At the time you didn't dare tell anyone how old you were. I was 26 when I was in the Creation but I didn't tell anybody." As well as being the only Creation member to have been conscripted, he was also the only one to have received a grammar school education. In the days before comprehensive schools, the fate of British schoolchildren would be decided by the 11 Plus examination that dictated whether they went to a school which assumed they would become blue-collar workers (secondary modern) or white-collar workers (grammar). It was, perhaps, this extra degree of intelligence that led Kenny to possess a character that was notable for supreme confidence bordering on arrogance.

"There was nothing shy about him," says Dalton of his new colleague. "He was very outright and said what he had to say. Most of the time that's good for a lead singer, 'cos you've got to have the courage to stand out front and project your image across. It doesn't really help if you're a shy sort of person. He was very forthcoming." However, Dalton recalls drawbacks to Kenny's confident personality: "Ken would jump into something both feet without thinking anything about it." Despite being educated at Hertford Grammar School, Kenny was working as a heating engineer/plumber at the time of his recruitment to the band in late 1963 and Dalton says he saw no sign of the academic bent that would, in later years, see him try to embark on a career as a novelist. Kenny had at this point roadied for Neil Christian, whose band The Crusaders included a young Jimmy Page.

As was then still the custom, despite the Beatles' example, the singer's name would be in the group's new title. As was also something of a custom, the singer would not go out under his birth name. In the new group, Pickett was Kenny Lee. It's possible Kenny alighted on 'Lee' as a nod to rock'n'roll hero Jerry Lee Lewis, but more convincing is the idea that it was an allusion to the Lee Valley, in which Cheshunt and Hertford are both located. The rest of the band were christened the Mark Four. Nobody seems able to recall how the name came about or what it means. Kenny Lee and the Mark Four were completely unrelated to two British groups with similar names: the Liverpool-based Mark Four – who, like Kenny Pickett's, would eventually record for Mercury – and the Mark Five, who recorded for Fontana, another future Kenny Pickett-Mark Four label.

The latter recorded a 1964 single called 'Baby What's Wrong' b/w 'Tango' which has erroneously ended up on at least one compilation purporting to feature only material recorded by the Pickett Mark Four. "We had never heard of them for ages," says Dalton of the other groups, "cos you're only in your little old world there. You don't go up to anywhere like Liverpool or anything like that." There was also an American group in the Fifties called the Mark IV (with a Top 30 *Billboard* hit to their credit): again, the name was simply coincidence.

The original line-up of Kenny Lee and the Mark Four didn't last long. By early 1964, the members had decided that Norman Mitham, local legend or no, was surplus to requirements. "We had to get rid of Norman 'cos where he started off as a fine guitarist, I don't think he progressed," reasons Dalton. "He stayed on the same level as a guitarist but everything was changing around him." For the hapless Mitham, who had already narrowly missed one boat to stardom, it must have been sickening. However, his replacement was the musician who would ultimately make The Creation the revolutionary band they were: Eddie Phillips.

"The last I heard, (he was) a milkman," says long-term Creation fan and friend Rod Siebke of Mitham's fate. "That's 15 years ago. I saw him one time in the late Eighties. Freddie Wilkinson from the Bluejacks died, there was a benefit gig put on and Norman couldn't even play. Eddie played behind the stage and Norman just mimed. He'd totally lost it, I think. He was quite a good guitarist." Eddie Phillips was a delivery driver by day (he had also been an insurance clerk) and at the time had recently finished a long-term stint as lead guitarist with a band called Bobby Lee and The Travellers who had been managed by Ian Swan, also the manager of Kenny Lee and the Mark Four. An audition was arranged for the band-less guitarist to rehearse for the Mark Four at Joe's Bar in the Salisbury Arms in Hoddesdon, a venue occasionally played by the group which they borrowed for the evening.

Though Eddie was at this point far from the violin-bow wielding, feedback-invoking innovator of future years, he was clearly a cut above the rest. In contrast to Mitham's staid, Fifties-rooted style, Eddie was on the cutting edge of guitar technique, even if that didn't mean too much in those musically basic times. "He come along and he could bend a string," marvels Dalton. "We went, 'Oh, blimey! Ooh, that's great'. Like Joe Brown was doing at the time and Jim Sullivan. He was straight in after that."

Edwin Michael Phillips was born in Leyton in the East End of London on 15 August 1945. Eddie was the middle of three children, having an older sister and a younger brother. His father was an electrical engineer and his mother a housewife. Eddie's first instrument was the family piano. Picking out the popular tunes of the day from the age of about seven on the keyboard of the instrument that happened to be in his house was a grounding that Eddie considers to have been invaluable in his future musical adventures. "You'd figured out what music was and how it all worked," he says. "Press that note and it went like that and press that note and it went like that."

Eddie was another willing victim of the rock'n'roll bug, mesmerised at the age of 13 by this new form of popular music which for the first time emphasised rhythm over (but not to the detriment of) melody and whose practitioners were awe-inspiring, glamorous creatures like Elvis Presley, Jerry Lee Lewis, Buddy Holly and Chuck Berry. "We was absolutely mad for it," recalls Eddie. "We lived for it, really. We was going to school and going to work but the music somehow was, like, so, so important. It was because the rock'n'roll thing was just breaking in this country, it was a teenage revolution almost. I always think there was two really good times for British music. One was that sort of '56-57 time when it was just breaking."

The other golden age in Eddie's opinion was the summer of love of 1967, to which psychedelic season he contributed so much with his work with The Creation. Back in the late Fifties, though, with no conception of what he would later achieve artistically in the medium, Eddie was lapping up the sounds and images of rock's first wave of heroes. Eddie: "When you saw Elvis for the first time (you went) 'What?' And Buddy Holly with a Strat. And you was hearing that Duane Eddy guitar. We used to go up to the caff, (me and a) friend of mine Stuart who later played bass in a band I was in, which had a big Bel-Ami jukebox and we'd sit there with a Coca-Cola and doughnut and just feed this thing all night. Just fantastic. We loved it."

Unlike affluent America where kids could afford instruments, rock'n'roll in Britain went hand-in-hand with the skiffle phenomenon, whereby teenagers would try to emulate the sounds made by their heroes with instruments put together from household fixtures. "One person would get a guitar, then someone else'd get one, then you'd see pictures of the old tea chest bass with a broom handle and a bit of string," recalls Eddie. "Then one of the other guys made a bass and we used to go round each other's houses in the evenings, just muck around with this. Didn't know how to play."

Although Eddie had had the luxury of living in a house where a piano happened to be present, his hankerings for the main instrument employed in rock'n'roll were not so easily satisfied. His first guitar was actually handmade. "We used to go to a youth club after school to play records and stuff and one of the guys there was pretty handy with wood," he says. "He cut me up a solid body. I don't know to this day what I did for a neck. I got a neck from an old acoustic, I think. We just put some strings on it and it worked, in actual fact. It was just basic. It just had a pick-up. It didn't have any tone controls."

The guitar was cut in the shape of a Fender Stratocaster, the guitar made famous by Buddy Holly, the sleek, thin, classy appearance of which seemed to epitomise space-age modernity just a much as rock'n'roll itself. "Up to that point we'd only ever seen pictures of Buddy Holly with the Fender," says Eddie. "That was pre-Shadows so nobody we knew or who was around on the English scene had a Strat. You'd look at this guitar, and think, 'My God, what is that?' It's got the tremolo arm. Just looked so fantastic. And great sound as well." Eddie's home-made instrument wasn't quite up to the standard of Holly's model. In contrast to the way that the Strat's revolutionary double cutaways enabled access up to the 21st fret, when Eddie attached the neck to the body his friend had provided he found he couldn't play past the fifth fret. "It was impossible," he laughs. "The strings were about half an inch away from the fingerboard."

Tightening the strings merely caused the fingerboard to curl up. Eddie: "Nothing like a Strat in reality. It just was a solid-body guitar." Similar naiveté attended Eddie's first adventures with amplifiers. After having got over his initial shock that one couldn't just plug an electric guitar into a light switch, he sent off for a mail-order amplification kit consisting of a self-assembly chassis and valve for which the customer was expected to provide his own case. Eddie constructed a box which he covered in red leatherette and added screw-in legs similar to coffee-table supports.

Nonetheless, he had made a start as a guitarist. "From that I bought an f-hole acoustic for four quid, which seemed much more playable," he says. "I could actually hear it without plugging it in. That was a nice little guitar, actually. Paid four pound for that. That was a fair bit of money in those days, the equivalent of about fifty quid now." Eddie's journey on the path to guitar hero initially went down a cul-de-sac. "I played for six months having the guitar tuned up completely the wrong way," he says. "I had it tuned to an open chord and I'd just barre the positions on the fifth and the seventh fret when I needed to change – 'cos it was all three-chord stuff. I bumped into someone one day and he was tuning his guitar up and I said, 'What you doing?' He says, 'Tuning it up.' I said, 'No, you don't do it like that – you do it like this.' He said, 'No – you do it like this'. I'd wasted six months playing this way."

Asked if he was thinking of music as a career at this point, Eddie says, "It never really happened like that. It was just this wave of music that was going on and you kind of got swept along with it. I never dreamed for one minute in those days that I'd ever make a career in music. Even when we was doing it in the Sixties, like with The Creation that was never a thing; it was just playing the music. If you'd said in 30 years' time they're still going to be remembering these songs, I wouldn't have believed it then. Some people go into it in a different way, as a business, I dare say, but with us, a lot of the bands that I've been involved in, it was just like, 'Let's just do it'.

"In those days, if you could play anything, it was the greatest thing you could ever do. The nicest thing as well. The possibility of doing it instead of doing a day job and getting paid for it – wow! Probably didn't ever get better than that." Eddie's inaugural public performance came when he was around 15, although his parents weren't in a position to celebrate this momentous occasion: "I couldn't even tell my parents where I was going 'cos I was gonna play in a pub and my mum wouldn't have liked that. I think it was the Lion And Key in Leyton or something like that. I can't remember the band. The guys were a lot older than me. I don't even know how I was actually playing with them. I did a few sort of local things with them."

Eddie modestly denies the precocious talent his playing with older musicians implies. "I suppose I could play a bit – and don't forget in those early days of rock'n'roll, this is pre-Sixties, nobody was a fantastic standard. The most prominent guitar player at that time in the real early days would probably be Bert Weedon. He'd do 'Guitar Boogie Shuffle' and you'd think, 'Wow, that's fantastic'. If you knew half a dozen chords, you were well on the way. And a lead break was very, very simple, maybe just barre-ing the first and second strings and then when the chord changed you'd just move up to the second and third fret, past that, get that sort of classic rock'n'roll solo. Things like 'Whole Lotta Shakin'. The guitar break in that was one I used to listen to – and, of course, Chuck Berry. To hear that 'Johnny B Goode' intro, was like, 'How *did* he do that?'"

The first band of which Eddie was a long-term member was Nick Taylor and the Breakers, which became Bobby Lee and the Travellers upon a change of singer. The bathroom of bassist Stuart Salter (a previously-mentioned ex-schoolmate of Eddie's who remains a friend to this day) was the location for skiffle jams for its good acoustics. The Travellers, with the usual repertoire of covers, began making a name for themselves in and around their area. "We lasted about four years," Eddie recalls, "from 1958 'til I joined the Mark Four about '62. If you were doing gigs you were playing the charts. Whoever bought out a song, you'd try and cover it so you could play it that weekend.

"There was five of us in The Travellers; bass, rhythm, lead, drums and singer. I was lead player. Locally, we worked a lot. We all had day jobs but would work most Saturday nights."

One of their regular gigs was Leyton Baths, a swimming pool which, in winter, had a cover pulled over it and was converted into a dance hall. The primitive nature of the live circuit in those days is illustrated by The Travellers' experiences in playing this venue. "It was massive, and the only amplifier I used then was a small Vox," recalls Eddie. "About 15 watts, I believe. Stuart's bass amp (was) something he'd made himself, a big cabinet with a Linear 15-watt or 30-watt amp. Mike, rhythm guitar, he had a small amplifier and the PA was something like a couple of little WEM cabinets with two tens in each side. Yet we didn't feel it wasn't loud enough.

"It was weird, really. If you did that venue now, you wouldn't feel right going in there without a whacking great big serious rig, but everybody had the same gear then. You either had a pair of WEM or Vox PA columns. This was pre-Marshall days."

In 1961, the Travellers made an acetate record, just as the Bluejacks had done. In a day and age before the widespread availability of tape recorders, this was the musician's equivalent of vanity publishing: a fee would be paid to the owner of a recording space/recording equipment whereupon the band would be given the opportunity to preserve their sound for posterity. An additional little thrill was provided by the fact that this would be in the form of an acetate record that, at a glance, looked like a record that you might find in the selfsame shops as stocked the product of your rock'n'roll heroes like Elvis or Buddy Holly. It's doubtful, though, that those two icons encountered the kind of semi-comical conditions as The Travellers did at Radcliffe Recording Services.

Eddie: "You'd go to this place and you'd give them something like 15 quid – a week's wages – and you could go in and set all your gear up. This guy was like a Frankenstein bloke, (with) all these knobs and that. It was eerie. It was a proper business but (in) this big old house, like the Addams Family house. Imagine like Igor to open the front door for you." There was no multi-tracking or overdubbing involved. "You'd record and you'd play it like a gig." Nor was there opportunity for multiple takes. "Pretty much one hit unless it was something diabolically went wrong." As with the Bluejacks, there was no thought of using the recording to attract the interest of record companies: "It was just to have. For the buzz of it: you'd made a record. Kids did that then." The acetate featured two or three numbers, amongst which were a Phillips-penned instrumental and (possibly) 'Pointed Toe Shoes' by Cliff Richard.

By '62, Eddie was looking for another band. "The Travellers slowed down and we decided to pack it in. Ian asked me if I'd like to join the Mark Four. Just went along there with my amp and met the other guys and Kenny turned up in his Mark Two Zodiac, very impressive. Played a couple of hours together and went on from there." (Dalton remembers him rehearsing "a couple of numbers" . He also recalls that Eddie was now playing a Futurama electric guitar.) "He could be quite jovial at times," says Dalton of Eddie as a person. "The funniest person in the band was our rhythm guitarist Spud Thompson but Eddie had quite a good sense of humour. Always helps to have a few light-hearted ones like that."

Initially, the band's repertoire remained as cover versions, despite the presence of a rather special guitarist. A prosaic attitude was the key to the era, as Dalton explains: "People say to me now, 'Was you a mod or a rocker?' And I say, 'Well, I was totally different 'cos I was in a band and you went with the times'. In the very early days you were playing rock'n'roll, 'cos it was all that was around, so you had your quiff in your hair and I suppose you were labelled a rocker. And then you become a mod. We was just playing covers.

"We really started doing a lot more work," continues Dalton. "We didn't have that many days off each month. It was a nightmare at the start though 'cos we were still working. It weren't too bad for Eddie 'cos a lot of our work was through a promoter called Billy Smith. He ran a lot of pubs in South London and we did a lot of work for him. Eddie was always the last pick-up on the way down there and we'd go and do the gig in Catford and Lewisham, places like that. He would get dropped off first." As mentioned, Eddie was then working as a delivery driver. "Kenny was a plumber still," says Dalton. "I was a carpenter. Spud was a builder. I think Jack was a factory worker."

Mark Four manager Ian Swan secured the gigs but the band's busy schedule did not inspire any particular gratitude on the band's part. Swan was also the manager of another local band called Group Five, whose lead guitarist Tony Atkins gives an idea of Swan's abilities. Atkins: "He loved traditional jazz. In fact he used to run trad clubs in the Fifties. That's when the old pop stuff came out, electric guitar bands, then he booked a couple of them into some of his clubs and moved on to become a promoter. He wasn't a very active manager. He was acting more like an agent than a manager, to be honest. I don't really want to knock the man too much – he did his best, he really did – but there was quite a few late-night telephone calls where people had been double booked and a fair bit of confusion going on.

"Poor old June, his wife, used to take the flak a lot of the time. He was harmless inasmuch as he wasn't a crook, he wasn't a cheat. He was just inept. He promised a lot and not a lot happened. We used to talk about him a lot, between the two bands. The only thing Ian did for us – and I think the Mark Four were a bit peeved at this – we did a gig with the Beatles in '63. That was at Salisbury Civic Centre. I suppose we were a better type of band to be with them than the Mark Four were at that time. We were probably a bit lighter, a bit less aggressive – Kenny was a pretty aggressive sort of bloke at times."

In early 1964, Kenny Lee and the Mark Four recorded an acetate at the City of London Recording studio consisting of Larry Williams' 'Slow Down' and Johnny Otis' 'Crazy Country Hop'. By the same kind of miracle as ensured the survival of the Bluejacks' and Travellers' acetates, this record still exists. Both recordings were competent but unspectacular versions but some sources have suggested that this acetate secured the band a deal with Mercury Records. Certainly, both of the tracks would later be re-recorded by the band for Mercury.

Despite their increasing rhythm and blues orientation, it wasn't to be 'Dimples' or anything so credible that the Mark Four laid down when they achieved every musician's dream of getting a record deal. The deal, such as it was, was strictly short-term. Although they ended up releasing two singles under Mercury's aegis, it's possible that the band were only signed on a record-at-a-time basis. Furthermore, when the band actually turned up at Mercury's recording studios in March 1964, it was under the impression that they were there only for an audition. "Ian Swan got it," says Dalton of the audition. "Ian Swan kept applying to people. They hadn't heard us. They just got us to go in. They said, 'Well let me hear you'."

The man supervising the session was one Dennis Berger. "We run through two or three numbers and he said, 'Yeah, that's fine. You got anything to record?'," recalls Jack. "So we looked at each other, said, 'Not really'." Thompson: "We hired the studio for an hour, I think, and after we'd been there about twenty minutes, Ian Swan came in and said, 'Look, we got another three quarters of an hour – do you fancy doing 'Rock Around The Clock?' He used to run a couple of dance places. He said, 'It's going well, all the kids keep asking for it.' I don't know if he had discussed it with the company or it was his idea."

Jack: "We looked at each other and because we were so thrilled about actually making a record – because we thought we were just going for an audition – we went along of it." The lack of enthusiasm Jack's comments imply was understandable. Even only nine years after it was a smash in Britain and despite its status as the record which kicked off the entire rock'n'roll revolution, 'Rock Around The Clock' was not only a hoary old chestnut but utterly old-fashioned. (In point of fact, it had become a little old-fashioned just a year after its release, when 'Heartbreak Hotel' by Elvis Presley proved there was real musical gravitas behind this new form of music.) In an age where the British beat-group sound had swept all before it, what place was there for a revival of a clunky, slightly characterless and overrated relic from the Fifties? Additionally, there was the issue of it being a song so strongly associated with one artist that anybody else attempting it on record would look absurdly presumptuous. As Eddie puts it, "Who else can do that apart from Bill Haley?"

However, hope springs eternal for a group of callow youths who, half an hour previously, had merely been hoping that in a few weeks time an envelope might drop through their manager's door inviting them to record yet had been instantaneously transformed into recording artists. Dalton: "Everybody had heard the number, so we sat down for five minutes and wrote the words down and then just run through it." The band got the same number of takes its personnel had been allowed when recording acetates for their various previous bands. That one take featured a fluffed drum part. "It's just awful," says Dalton. Dalton is too harsh. Nobody would ever be bothered if they never heard the track again, but at the same time it's a perfectly game (and brisk) run-through of the number. It certainly sounds nothing like a first take. 'Slow Down', the other number recorded that day, is also not a disgrace.

Before the record could be released, another significant development occurred in the career of Kenny Lee and the Mark Four. "Ian Swan phoned us up one day and said, 'I've been offered to open this brand new club in Wilhelmshaven, Germany. Are you interested?'" recalls Dalton. Swan's question could not have been more rhetorical. A well-known part of the legend of The Beatles – whose career was the fantasy template of every working British band at that time – was that they had learned their chops at Germany's Star Club. "It was like a dream for us 'cos you'd heard of the Beatles and that in Hamburg," says Dalton. There was more stardust fluttering down onto the proposal. Dalton: "He said, 'The chap who's opening it is an ex-bouncer from the Star Club, Hamburg – he's opening his own club and he wants you to be the first band on there'."

The residency was to be for a month, so if the band were to accept it, maintaining semi-pro status was not an option. Kenny Lee and the Mark Four duly turned professional. "We weren't that old," says Dalton. "It was like a dream for us. So we all packed our jobs in and went to do that." The Wilhelmshaven club in question had a British theme every bit as clichéd as the habitual British portrayal of Germans wearing lederhosen. Titled the Big Ben, the exterior bore a massive painting of the Houses of Parliament. An English band was clearly needed to get the club rolling.

Kenny Lee and the Mark Four became something of a sensation in the northern German seaport town of Wilhelmshaven, adored for their music – not difficult for an audience who in many cases had never seen a live rock act before – and notorious for their 'long' hair (just above average length in Britain for the time) which caused them to be nicknamed The Mushroom Heads by the local newspaper. "They really used to stare in the streets if we walked past," Eddie told *Good Times* magazine in 1992.

The Big Ben residency saw the band working harder than they ever had before, performing eight 30-minute sets a night to ever more appreciative audiences. The vocal casualty count for such gruelling conditions was high. "One by one, the voices were going," says Dalton. "So everybody really had to take a turn in singing because a few nights we went down from a five-piece to a three-piece because two of the members were in bed." Even the drummer had to muck in, and when he did his colleagues were surprised at what a confident singer Jack turned out to be. Dalton: "He wasn't that forward. He was a bit quiet and shy. When he decided to start singing, we all thought, 'Blimey, he's got quite a good voice'." Returning to England, the band received a fine send-off from the fans they had galvanised. Though they couldn't expect as rapturous a reception from residents of their home country – who had far more bands to choose between than did the Wilhelmshaven crowds – they were still kept in work in the UK for almost every day of the month of April 1964.

Inevitably, they returned to German shows for another residency – this one for around a fortnight – within a month of two. The club's owner had been disappointed by the performances of The Roadrunners, the Liverpool band who had taken over from Kenny Lee and the Mark Four. Ironically, Mick Thompson credits The Roadrunners for helping to turn the Mark Four into a more substantial, R&B-oriented act. Rhythm and blues was something many musicians (and audiences) of the era turned to in desperation at the way the once earthy rock'n'roll had become the domain of pompadoured legions of clean-cut singers seemingly all called Bobby.

In many ways, the band's Big Ben residencies was as significant a factor in their development as stints in Germany had been for the Beatles, although memories differ on this. Both Jack and Mick credit the residencies for moving the group into a more hardcore R&B direction. In addition, Jack and Kenny cite Wilhelmshaven as marking the start of Eddie's experiments with feedback.

Feedback is the term given to the high, shrieking sound that results when an electric guitar set to a high volume is placed too close to its amplifier and causes the guitar's sound to enter the guitar and get amplified again (which in turn feeds back in a continuous loop). Though Pete Townshend has received credit for being the first to employ feedback creatively, Eddie Phillips is one of a couple of other candidates for being the true pioneer in this area. "There was a band there (on the second residency) who had two nights to go by the time we got there, so we just hung around," recalls Jack. "One night we listened to them and the guitarist was a good player – I don't know his name — and he used to use just a little bit of feedback to lengthen his chords and that. We looked at it and we thought, 'That's interesting' and Eddie started experimenting with it and took it on from there. We liked it and we encouraged him: 'Open it out, man, really go for it'."

Kenny Pickett, talking to *Record Collector* magazine in 1995, had identical memories. "Their guitarist used controlled feedback and his solos sounded like an organ," Kenny said of the Roadrunners. "We were open-mouthed." Dalton, though, doubts Kenny's and Jack's recollection: "I remember The Roadrunners but apart from accidental feedback I wouldn't have thought they'd have done it 'cos they were a real crash-bang-wallop outfit. I think he was doing it himself before then. I remember where he needed to do it first. I can remember doing Hertford Corn Exchange and 'House Of The Rising Sun' by The Animals had just come out. We didn't have an organ so Eddie used to play the chords and feed back with it. That's how I remember it coming into action."

'The House Of The Rising Sun' was released in June 1964, several months after the Mark Four's first Wilhelmshaven engagement, but memories are cloudy as to whether the second residency was pre or post-June. "I remember The Roadrunners," says Eddie. "I weren't sure if we were doing that sort of thing then or not. I can't really recall the sequence of things then." However, his instinctive feeling is that his journey into the world of feedback started by accident. "I used to use a Futurama guitar which was solid-bodied like a Strat, and I used that with a Vox AC30 treble boost (amplifier). Then in the early Mark Four days I bought a Gibson 335. It was a new guitar. They only came out in '62, I believe, and I think I was the first British guitarist to use that model."

At first, Eddie didn't like the sound he got from the Gibson with a Vox amplifier: "So I changed my amp and went over to a Marshall, but the 50-watt Marshall wasn't as loud as the 30-watt Vox so I went on to a 100-watt Marshall with two cabinets . That's when I first experienced the feedback, the Gibson being a semi-acoustic. First of all, I thought, 'Oh God – what am I going to do with this? This is like, every time I stand in front of the amp, the guitar starts howling'. But then I figured out that you could actually play a shape and, according to what pick-up you was using, the feedback would be in tune with the shape you're playing and you could get a note feeding back. I thought, 'This is quite handy, really'. I figured out how to (use it)…

"That's how I first stumbled across it. When The Animals brought out 'House Of The Rising Sun', we wanted to play the song so I put this vibrato thing on, then turned the volume up on the guitar after hitting the chord shape – never struck the chord – and got this weird organ sound out of the guitar. That was all done on feedback and sustain from overloading the amp and hammering on the chords. I could play the whole song without ever playing the strings with my right hand. We all went, 'Yeah! That's alright'. And from that, we used it here and there."

Though a trademark of the Mark Four's act, the band wouldn't put this technique onto a record until 'I'm Leaving', the B-side of their third single, released in August '65. For Eddie, there is an art to feedback of which too many practitioners aren't aware: "It's not just a case of turning the guitar up and just standing in front of the amp. I've seen people do that and it's just a racket. Sometimes it's a bit hit-and-miss but if you really work at it you can actually use it to a degree where it (fits) in with what you're doing." As to who invented feedback – or, rather, turned it from a technical drawback into a form of artistic expression – Eddie points out, "It was probably some old blues player in the Forties. Probably got too near his amp and went 'I don't like that!'"

In modern pop terms, the first record to feature feedback was The Beatles' 'I Feel Fine' (November 1964), although nobody claims that the Fab Four were doing anything other than putting on vinyl a technique that others had been doing before on stage. The question is, who was the first? At the time, Eddie thought he was the only guitarist on the scene utilising this strange new feature he'd discovered about his instrument. Unbeknown to him, across London, another guitarist in a group uncannily similar to the Mark Four was doing the same thing. This group was the High Numbers and their guitarist was one Pete Townshend. "It is ironic the way it worked out," says Eddie. "We worked mainly in the Mark Four in north London and east London and the High Numbers were doing a similar kind of thing in west London and we never really knew about it until someone said to me one day, 'There's this band called the High Numbers and they do all that sort of thing that you do.'

"I felt really pissed off at the time 'cos I didn't think nobody else was doing it. Didn't think that much more of it really 'cos then we wasn't really aspiring to anything, we was just doing our thing really. But history shows that was that and that was that." He adds, "It was ironic that we ended up with a producer who previously recorded The Who." Townshend himself says, "I know for a fact that Dave Davies, Eric C(lapton) and Jeff Beck all happened on feedback at the same time. I have never claimed to be first. My claim is that I was the loudest."

"I did see the High Numbers as well so it was something we knew about," says fan Rod Siebke. Interestingly, asked who had greater mastery of feedback out of Townshend and Phillips, Siebke opines, "Eddie, definitely. His control was better." However, it didn't seem to Siebke that the Mark Four and the High Numbers had any other similarities: "I don't know about later on, I don't know about the '66 band. I would imagine maybe things got a little bit more Who-ish then but really I would say the '64-65 band were a rhythm and blues band really."

The similarity of the guitar styles of Townshend and Phillips would increase when the Mark Four became a four-piece in late '65. With Eddie now covering both rhythm and lead parts, he developed a similar rhythm-lead style to the one for which Townshend would become famous when The Who achieved commercial success. The similarity between the two didn't stop there. Eddie observed to Dave Barnes of <Sixtiespop.com>, "The weird thing was with Pete we actually did a couple of gigs together and I don't suppose he realised, but I did, how alike we were in off-stage things. I remember at the time we were both into slot-car racing and things like that."

Nor did it end there: footage from the Sixties shows Phillips and Townshend were both skinny, black-haired axe-wielders with a similarity in the nose department. The two bands into which the High Numbers and Kenny Lee and the Mark Four respectively mutated– The Who and The Creation – were also comparable, each featuring a four man line-up with a non-playing singer purveying explosive but melodic music that has come to be termed Pop Art, a nascent form of psychedelia inflected with performance art usually associated with the mod movement.

Because the Who secured a record deal before The Creation, they were generally perceived to be the originals and The Creation the copyists. Perhaps because of this, journalists drawing parallels between the groups was something that infuriated Kenny Pickett. In his interview with *Blitz* in 1982, he said, "The only thing that the press used to do that I didn't like was compare us to The Who. We weren't anything like The Who. We were a totally different band. We did the same circuits and I suppose we made the same sounds. But we'd get to a gig and the adverts said, 'The band with the Who sound' and people didn't come because of that."

Even as late as 1995, interviewed by *Record Collector*, when asked if The Creation were influenced by The Who, Kenny spat "No, we weren't" and did so – according to interviewer John Reed – "angrily". "He used to get really pissed off about it, 'cos he knew where we came from," says Eddie. "It all started from the Mark Four and the Mark Four really did their own thing and didn't even know about The Who – what was then the High Numbers." Nonetheless, Eddie acknowledges that of all the guitarists he has seen, Townshend is the one with the closest style to his own and that there were similarities between The Creation and The Who: "That was really – I say that to this day – a strange kind of fluky coincidence."

If the story of the Roadrunners putting the idea of feedback in Eddie's head is true, they would seem to have made quite an impact – at least on Kenny Lee and the Mark Four – for a band who achieved precisely nothing in commercial terms. Dalton, too, recalls the Roadrunners as being the catalyst for a change of style which saw his band move over to music with a bit more grit. "When we first went over there we was playing all Beatles numbers," Dalton recalls. "We went from the Beatles (to) R&B – totally different band. When we saw The Roadrunners, they went down so well we thought, 'Oh well, we better change a bit' and did Jimmy Reed stuff and stuff like that. If you listen to the track we made called 'Try It Baby', that's an R&B number we copied."

Not that the Roadrunners were the only band to be credited with influencing the Mark Four in an R&B direction . Kenny Pickett, speaking to *Blitz*, said, "The one biggest influence on our band was a north London band nobody had ever heard of called Four Plus One... Steve Howe was one of their players. We were doing a gig at the Club Noreik in North London and Four Plus One came on, doing American rhythm and blues. We'd never in our lives seen a band like this because they were so loud! All they did was Chuck Berry and Bo Diddley, but they did it their own way. They were leaping around the stage and going absolutely bananas! That night, we dropped everything we'd ever done and we didn't do any gigs for a month of two. Then we totally changed and became a rhythm and blues band."

"We was influenced a bit," Jack says of Four Plus One, "because at the time we were doing rhythm and blues by now, moving into that style of stuff, but we were still basically a band, we just stood there and played our stuff." He recalls the venue for the first night the Mark Four shared the bill with Four Plus One not as Club Noreik but as Watford Town Hall. However, his other recollections chime with Kenny's: "They had all these movements and really were quite a good band, a good show and everything. Their movements were weird for a start. A couple of them were racing around the stage – it was probably a throwback to the old rock'n'roll stuff – and jumped up in the air, all this stuff. They sold themselves to their audience rather than just standing there and saying, 'This is the music'. Nobby then decided he was going to move around like that a bit and somehow the band just seemed to wake up after that. We seemed to have a bit more movement, a bit more vitality."

Tony Atkins of Group Five recalls a marked difference in the abilities of the band after their German sojourns. "When they came back they were much, much tighter and they really had evolved," he says. "They were doing fairly similar stuff to us – pop stuff, cover versions and not too much R&B – and they changed their image quite a lot. There was a lot more leaping around on stage as well." The band were obviously proud of their Wilhelmshaven stint as the group's van – to be seen parked outside John Dalton's house – was emblazoned with a handwritten sign declaring 'The Big Ben Club, Wilhelmshaven, Germany'. Through the windows, incidentally, could be discerned the gold lamé suits they wore on stage.

"We was looking for things other than the pop-chart stuff of the time," says Eddie. "That's how we got on to our version of rhythm and blues, the Jimmy Reed stuff. I picked up the harmonica and learnt how to play that a bit 'cos we wanted to do stuff like 'Dimples', the John Lee Hooker song." Not that any musical style was set in concrete for a band who, then, were fundamentally populist. Dalton: "We was even at one time going through a stage of playing Tamla Motown. We went through different stages so we were never just an R&B band. We just used to alter with the swing. Whatever was in at the time."

On their second visit to Germany, the group had their minds projected further forward. Their debut single had been scheduled for a May release by Mercury, so stardom was therefore possibly just around the corner. "It was going to be released while we were away," laughs Dalton, "so we said to Ian Swan, 'We better not take any gigs for when we get back because obviously if it's a hit record, the money goes up a hell of a lot'." It was on this second German trip that the band dropped their Kenny Lee prefix because, for a very brief period, he was slung out for deserting his comrades. "He actually went into Hamburg with the governor, the bloke who owned the club," recalls Dalton. "Without saying a word, they just disappeared. We were having to do eight sets a night, and for your lead singer just to go missing without telling you was really hard."

However, Kenny was almost immediately given a reprieve. "We needed him, to be quite honest," says Dalton. "Although we all did a small piece of singing, he was the lead singer." However, the band insisted that the shortened name they had adopted be retained. It no longer made sense – Kenny Lee and the Mark Four had added up to five, reflecting the number of personnel – but a gesture had to be made. (Jack also suggests another reason for the shortened name: "While we were out there, The Beatles and the Mersey stuff was really starting to happen and we decided we'd be better off with one name. That would have been a bit dated then, that style of name. So we just dropped the Kenny Lee bit and called it the Mark Four, 'cos we couldn't think of anything else.")

Kenny would always have an somewhat uneasy relationship with his colleagues in the Mark Four and The Creation. "I think he was always a little bit aloof from the rest of the band," says Rod Siebke. "Even in more recent times, just before he died, he was one on his own, as such. Even on stage, he was the frontman, the band was the backing band. Kenny was that little bit older which probably made him a little bit more aloof. He'd already been out there working with other bands and been a roadie."

'Rock Around The Clock' b/w Larry Williams' 'Slow Down' appeared in May 1964. Perhaps due to the fact of the sheer novelty – or, in some eyes, impertinence – of them covering the song, it actually received some media exposure. Not only was it advertised in the music press – with the band wearing the black leather waistcoats and black trousers they had adopted around this time in place of the gold lamé image – but at least one music paper reviewed it. "Sooner or later, someone had to revive 'Rock Around The Clock' ," said the *New Musical Express*. "In fact, I'm surprised it's taken so long! New Mercury group the Mark Four are the ones to do it, but regrettably they make no attempt to change or modernise the original styling. The treatment is just the same as Bill Haley's. Still, if you're too young to remember Mr Haley, this won't bother you. In any case, you'll have a ball to the swinging, rocking beat. The title 'Slow Down' is rather inapt for this medium-twist ditty, with its insistent driving beat. Again, good material for dancers."

The band were also treated to the thrill of hearing themselves on radio for the first time. "They tried," Dalton says of Mercury's promotion department. "I think they got it played on *Family Favourites* on Sunday morning." However, the riches the band had envisaged as rolling in from their new status as recording artists did not materialise. "I don't think it sold anything at all," says Dalton.

Sometime in the middle of 1964, the Mark Four were supervised at a recording session by Bobby Graham, producer of one of the sensations of the moment, the Dave Clark Five. The connection was made because both the Mark Four and Graham were clients of the Starlight Artists agency. The Five's chart smashes 'Glad All Over' and 'Bits And Pieces' had been propelled by a colossal rhythm track and it would seem that Graham was trying to reproduce that big beat with the Mark Four when they entered the familiar environs of Regent Sound. Jack: "I noticed that Bobby put a lot of emphasis on the drums and he kept sitting down and saying, 'Do it this way Jack, do it that way Jack, bang bang bang', and I was just looking at him thinking, 'That's *awful*'. It was very difficult to equate what he wanted to do and what I wanted to do."

The tracks the Mark Four were recording were Ray Charles' 'You Be My Baby' and Fats Domino's 'Sick and Tired' (written by Dave Bartholomew and Chris Kenner). "That was just one of my whims I had," says Dalton. "Funny enough I got the idea from The Kinks, 'cos I'd heard 'You Really Got Me' so I thought, 'That's what we want to do: something like that'. I'd heard this Ray Charles number, a very similar sort of thing." There is a certain resemblance in 'You Be My Baby' to the Dave Clark Five, though more in the hoarseness of the vocals than the rhythm track. 'Sick And Tired' is an adequate uptempo 12-bar blues. The tracks were never released. "It was pretty crappy, what I remember of it," says Jack, "and we weren't happy at all. We thought about going in the studio and trying something on it but in the end it was dropped."

Instead, it was Marvin Gaye's 'Try It Baby' that became the Mark Four's second single, a suggestion by a band friend named John Nutt (who had also been the first to introduce them to the record's B-side, 'Crazy Country Hop'). "That's when we was just heading a bit more towards Tamla Motown (which was) just hitting the charts so we said 'Let's try something different'," says Dalton. "We heard that one and we thought 'Ooh, that's a good one to cover'. Totally different for us."

'Try It Baby' b/w 'Crazy Country Hop' appeared on Mercury in August 1964. Though both tracks have that archaic patina that afflicts so many records of their era, they are both perfectly easy on the ear. 'Try It Baby' was a strange hybrid of old-style rock'n'roll and what would soon be widely known as soul and had a sweet and forgiving air. Meanwhile, the continuing advance in the group's abilities was underlined by 'Crazy Country Hop', a far more knowing and confident rendition of the song than was heard on their acetate with a lot more bite, if a lesser velocity. Despite the advances, though, the record, like its predecessor, went nowhere .

Sometime around either the end of 1964 or the beginning of 1965, Eddie Phillips added another string to his bow. Or, rather, he added a bow to his repertoire. Long before Jimmy Page made a bowed electric guitar famous with Led Zeppelin, Eddie was experimenting with a violin bow on the strings of his Gibson. Dalton: "I remember Jack getting the idea from somewhere and saying, 'Ed, why don't you try it?'. Obviously at first, 'cos violin strings are curved where guitar strings are flat, it was awful. But as far as I can remember it was Jack Jones' idea but Eddie perfected it." Kenny told *Ugly Things* magazine in 1997, "Jack got the idea of playing the guitar with a hacksaw; then he said, 'Why not use a violin bow?' and Eddie said, 'Oh no, that'll never work'. So that's how that came about, all Jack's idea really, although Eddie gets credit for being the first exponent of it."

Eddie recalls that he got the idea for the violin bow on his own through browsing in a music store in Leytonstone but also admits, as with other subjects, he has problems recalling the sequence of events and ideas. Eddie: "When I first got the Gibson 335, that was pre-fuzzbox. I just had this idea in mind of having a long, sustained note and the first idea I had was playing a sustained note on the bottom E but with something and then being able to play pull-offs on the E and the D while that's going on. I never really achieved that but then I thought, 'Well how do I get this long sustained note?' And I first got a hacksaw and I took the blade out of this hacksaw and put a guitar string in it – it was an E string, with the thick windings – with the idea that the windings going opposite ways to the string on the guitar would create a kind of rasping effect. It didn't really work that good and the end of the hacksaw was catching on the guitar as I was playing it. I always remember these kids pointing at my guitar and having a laugh. While I was playing I seen these bits of sawdust flying off it. I'd virtually worn a hole through the bottom cutaway of the guitar. I hadn't even started paying for it: 250 guineas, which was really expensive, the equivalent of a two grand guitar these days."

Neither was the violin bow a success until, Eddie recalls, "Someone said, 'You've got to put this rosin stuff on it'." Rosin – a hard, pine-tree resin – is applied by violinists to their bow's horsehair strings in order to increase sliding friction. "I got the rosin and it really worked well...you could actually be a little bit musical with it," says Eddie. "We used it through the Mark Four. By the time it got to The Creation, I'd been doing it for quite a while but never actually put it on record." Eddie's new accessory became a fundamental part of his guitarist's psyche, and would become even more important when The Creation started: "It was always in my guitar case. As important as the guitar strap or a plectrum. I couldn't do a gig without it."

A gig's end would see multiple strands of broken horse-hair hanging untidily from the bow he held: "Used to be more like a whip than a violin bow at the end; I might get through two or three violin bows in one evening." Eddie had to make a sacrifice for his adventurism. "It used to really dull the strings, the rosin," he laments. "I had to live with that. It's nice when you get new strings on a guitar and they sound really crisp and clean, but rosin kills that. It's just one of those things." Tony Atkins recalls, "I thought it was more visual than it was from a sound point of view to be honest. It didn't over-impress me musically. A gimmick innovation that looked good."

Thompson disagrees. "Absolutely brilliant," he says of his colleague's new gift. "Such a novelty. He's such an adaptable man. He'll pick an accordion up, pick a mouth organ up, he'll play a banjo and then he'll play a piano. He's quite an accomplished musician. He didn't seem to struggle with it at all. On stage it was brilliant. There were no fluffs. He just done the business and that was it. Very exciting."

Though the violin bow was not as fundamental a part of the Mark Four's act as it would be The Creation's, it was used on a lengthy version of Bo Diddley's 'Mona (I Need You Baby)', which became the centrepiece of their set. Dalton: "Eddie used to get the bow out, I used to get the guitar, do a big thing where I'd hold it above my head, then throw it off stage and hope the road manager was there to catch it. Then I used to jump on the drums with Jack. While Eddie was feeding back, Jack and I used to do a double drum solo. There was all this feedback thing going on with two drummers. It was just part of our act that we were trying to perfect and it ended up we had to do it every night. That's what we got known for. Used to go down a storm."

In the autumn of 1964, the Mark Four appeared on television for the first time. Recalls Mick, "We'd just come back from Germany for the last time and we done a gig and they was doing a play and they said, 'Would you mind if we filmed you'? So we said, 'Okay'. We did 'Glad All Over' by Dave Clark Five and they filmed us. We asked 'em when the play was coming on, which was like the end of the year time. We obviously watched the play and they didn't show us playing, just the music in the background. As the two actors come into the hall, you saw 'em dance a bit and talk a little bit and you heard us but you didn't actually see us. We were a little bit choked. We were filmed while we was doing it, with close-ups and all the lights and everything but perhaps we was too ugly, I don't know."

The failure of the Mark Four's second single ensured that Mercury did not ask them for another record and there was a gap of an entire year before their next release. Asked if the band started to worry that their recording career seemed to be faltering, Jack says no: "There's such emphasis these days, band gets together and they immediately go into the studio. Now in them days you basically went out and you got work and you could work five or six nights a week, just playing the gigs, earning a living. The recording bit, that was the second part. We wouldn't have been too concerned there was a big gap between releases."

Eddie, too, wasn't worried. "We were probably a bit frustrated about it. It's hard to think now what you felt then. I think we were probably a bit pissed off because nothing sort of fantastic happened to that band. Mark Four was a good band and it deserved success. We used to have a good stage show as well. But there again that's not the sole criteria of success. Success is good management, good investment, having the right song at the right time, the right producer. All those things falling into place. And if one of those things is not present then success is very hard to find. But we didn't know that then." All members agree that the Mark Four were a fine live act. A couple of the more notable gigs they played in this period were their 9 October 1964 appearance at the Pill Social Centre, Milford

Haven where they were one of the acts supporting Little Eva (of 'Loco-Motion' hit fame) and their 19 May 1965 appearance at the Ritz, Potter's Bar where they were on the same bill as Them, who had hit big with both 'Baby Please Don't Go' and 'Here Comes The Night' that year. (Screaming Lord Sutch also appeared).

The excitement of the Mark Four's stage presentation is, for Dalton, underlined by the fact that their appearances on the same bill as The Who were a meeting of equals: "Used to support The Who a lot. They never used to blow us off stage, although we were just an unknown support band. The good thing about it is we'd still go down ever so well, so that was very encouraging. We (worked with) a lot of bands at the time: Spencer Davis and people like that and never once got shown up." Dalton remembers the Mark Four having a "big argument" with The Who one night when the two bands were playing a ballroom above Burtons in Uxbridge "They was trying to get rid of Roger Daltrey," he says. "They were saying, 'What do you think? He's a right arrogant bloke. He's this and that.' We didn't know him. All we could say is, 'Yeah, he's a bloody good singer, though, isn't he?' His stage presence was faultless."

The Mark Four began to unravel when they decided they would like the Starlight Agency to take over from Ian Swan. "They got us a lot of work, and we said, 'Would you take us over, management side?'," says Thompson. "They said, 'If he agrees'. So we asked Ian Swan. He said, 'No, no, no, no, I'm keeping you'. And I think we'd just signed to (him) for another year or 18 months." Following this incident, the band noticed they seemed to more and more be playing the kind of venues from which they thought they'd graduated. Thompson: "We'd done all the hard gigs, doing a full month of gigs every night, and then doing records, going to Germany. We thought we'd done out apprenticeship. After we asked Ian Swan if we could go to the others and he said no, he just seemed to put us in pubs then, the pubs we done when we first started. We thought, 'We've done all this'. As if to say, 'Well I'll teach you, try and get away', that sort of attitude. Probably wasn't but that's what you felt. We was getting disillusioned then."

Dalton dismisses Ian Swan as "a liar and bullshitter". He recalls, "I think we could have done better and I think our manager held us back. The gigs weren't as plentiful as before. Our manager had lost a bit of interest in us, so it was hard. That was half of our thing. I thought, 'I just can't live on this so I am gonna actually have to go back to work'." Dalton became so disillusioned that he may have made up his mind to leave the group – and music – even after the band secured another record deal, one which would result in their third single, 'Hurt Me If You Will'. For Dalton, the fact that the single would be released on a different label to the first two was symptomatic of Swan's deficiencies: "He'd keep telling you that things were happening and things like that and nothing was. I don't think he pushed us hard enough or anything so we didn't really know what was going on or why."

Though Jack admits that the band were stumbling from record company to record company (a third different label would release the band's fourth single), he is more forgiving. "Ian operated from his house in Wanstead," says Jack. "He was a solid working bloke all around north London but he wasn't a national manager. Of course, when the Mark Four broke up and we found Stratton-Smith, that was a whole different ballgame." 'Hurt Me If You Will' – and the number that would be its B-side, 'I'm Leaving' – marked another milestone for the band: the first self-composed Mark Four numbers. "Up to that point no-one even thought about writing," says Dalton. "It was just doing covers." The band members who decided they would have a crack at devising their own material were Eddie and Kenny. This bespeaks an ambition that Dalton admits he and the others didn't possess: "Spud and I, once we finished playing, preferred to spend the weekend down the pub with our mates. They would do a bit of work on the music."

Thompson: "None of us really wanted to do anything like that apart from them two. They had an idea and they just got together. I was quite envious. You've got to have a bit of talent to write songs. Eddie was definitely the driving force, although John Dalton was the man who got the bookings and took the money." "Pretty quick," is how Eddie recalls his and Kenny's writing gelling. "I don't know to this day why it was Ken and I that got together as writers, 'cos there was five in the band. It was probably a natural thing. I knew I could probably write melodies and things and put chord sequences together. Ken was really artistic with the lyrics. I can't remember how we got started on that but we just did it one day. Got together and had a go."

In all probability, the song started in the way all Pickett/Phillips collaborations began. Eddie: "I would kick the thing off with a melody and perhaps half of a chorus and I'd say to Ken, 'Well, it goes something like this and you need to do this and this' and he'd get the outline of it. A couple of days later he'd come up with a lyric. I don't think I could write with lyrics first. I had to work out the chords. All of a sudden you see the song in your mind and you know what it's got to be like – then Ken filled it all in, sort of painted a picture."

The melancholy picture Kenny painted on this occasion about the end of a love affair was set against a musical backdrop provided by the band that was typical of British R&B of the day, especially the generic thin, echoey guitar. However the wistful and poppy middle eight indicated something more going on here than merely the common ability amongst UK musicians to create accurate rhythm and blues pastiches. There is also something arresting about the utter resignation of the song from beginning to end. "You just thought to yourself, 'We'll give it a go'," recalls Dalton. Referring to The Kinks, of whom he was later a member, he says, "It's like any new number: 'til you've played it a few times, you've got no idea what you're doing. Like with Ray Davies: he knew what it was in his head but all we were doing at first was playing some chords and notes and trying to work something round it."

By the time the Mark Four booked into a studio, 'Hurt Me If You Will' had been worked through many times and was sounding substantial. The same could not quite be said for the song that appeared on the flip. "We done the other one just 'cos we needed a B-side," says Dalton of 'I'm Leaving'. "We come up with the idea from that Them number 'Baby Please Don't Go'. That's what I was trying to do on the bass. We thought it was such a good number, so we just changed the bass very slightly!" The fact the Mark Four were 'inspired' by the gritty composition that had been a hit for Them in January '65 was not just made transparent by Dalton copping the track's descending, rumbling riff almost note for note: even the Mark Four's song title seemed a nod to the part of the Them record where vocalist Van Morrison declares "My baby, leaving on that midnight train".

Nonetheless, even this blatant piece of plagiarism contained a significant artistic step forward. During the instrumental break, Eddie put on record the controlled feedback with which he had now been experimenting on stage for many months. "It was part of the stage show, our trademark, so you put it in to remind the fans what we do," explains Dalton. Mick: "Eddie just come out and done it. There was no talk about it."

Although Pete Townshend had already put The Who's feedback proclivities on vinyl on 'Anyway Anyhow Anywhere' the previous May, the notion was still alien to engineers. Memories are mixed as to the reaction of the studio staff to the feedback that Eddie induced. "I don't think it got anywhere near what it should have sounded like," says Dalton. "The engineers thought, 'What the hell you doing?'" However, Thompson insists, "I can remember them saying what a great sound it was. They were all for it." Whatever the truth, neither dispute that what resulted was in reality a rather puny approximation of the howling that had made the Mark Four such a compelling live spectacle. Yet, there is still something revolutionary about it. The extraordinarily long for the time (more than a minute and 20 seconds) instrumental break features Eddie coaxing gentle feedback like a snake charmer and creating a murky, subterranean atmosphere that must have been bewildering to the very few who would ultimately buy the disc.

'Hurt Me If You Will' b/w 'I'm Leaving' appeared on Decca in August 1965. Dalton: "Once we recorded it, I thought to myself, 'Let's see how it goes'." At first, things looked promising, the single acquiring a healthy amount of play on the pirate stations then proliferating in response to the monopoly the BBC had of domestic pop broadcasting. The group were championed by Tony Windsor, a DJ at pirate Radio London. Dalton recalls, "He used to come down to Cheshunt and see us, have a drink with us. He liked it but it never really done anything... A lot of people were interested in it but it didn't make major waves."

It was the final nail in the coffin for Dalton. "Nobby had had enough," says Jack. "We were skint and somebody pinched his car or something and he was so browned off, he'd had enough. He wanted to get married as well, so he said, 'I've got to put some money together.' We were getting crap money and basically going nowhere." When Dalton announced his resignation, Thompson – the colleague to whom he was closest – decided that he too had had his fill. Dalton and Thompson played their last gig with the Mark Four on 31 October 1965 at the Witchdoctor Club, Hastings. "I think he may have had a change of heart shortly afterwards," says Dalton of Thompson, "but it was all too late then. The wheels in motion had gone. They went a different way with no rhythm guitar at all and just made a more basic sound, like The Who were doing."

"I thought, 'Well perhaps I was a bit hasty' , confirms Thompson, who subsequently became a roofer. "After being professional for about 18 months, I thought, 'I don't really want to go back working'. I did regret it for a while. Not immediately. A few months after." He also confirms he did ask if he could come back. Thompson: "At one time, they was playing in London and I did sort of mention it but I think they said they was quite happy how they were." Dalton, though, never had cause to regret his decision. When he became the bassist for The Kinks in June 1966, he was joining one of the most successful chart acts in Britain. Furthermore, it was a gig that lasted – with one break – for a decade.

Of the Mark Four, Dalton says, "The records are bad and the band was a live band – something to watch, rather than just listen to." The something to watch though was something special. Dalton: "It's just a shame that we never made it a bit bigger than we did 'cos it was a well respected band. Everybody said we were absolutely brilliant. I can't say it 'cos I didn't really watch us! But so many reports afterwards." Kenny, Eddie and Jack filled the vacant bass player's slot with one Tony Cook, an acquaintance of Eddie who was a veteran of a band named The Leroys.

As indicated by Dalton's comments above, the rhythm guitarist's role was only filled insofar as Eddie now opted to cover both roles. Jack: "Eddie had expanded his style a lot. When he joined the band he was very much a lead guitarist, playing Chuck Berry solos and this sort of thing. But as we moved along, Eddie started bringing in big chords and using a bit of feedback and this and we found that we had a good sound and we didn't need anybody else. Also, it left Eddie free-er in a funny sort of way to expand on what he was doing. We just sat down, the three of us, and decided we just needed a bass guitar."

"It was different and, at first, a little bit strange," says Eddie of the change in technique necessitated by his new dual role. "But that was about the time when amplifiers were getting bigger and better. You began to realise you could cover two things. If the bass player had a good, fat sound and you were all loud enough – not deafening but loud enough – you could cover it. That's from a sound point of view. From a technique point of view it did feel a little bit strange at first when you were playing rhythm and had to break off for the guitar break but I got used to it and was fairly happy with that."

Eddie's style changed as a result of these responsibilities. In order to create a bigger sound – and so as to not leave a gaping hole in the music when he broke off to go into a song's solo – he had to abandon the classic lead guitar picking style. "You started figuring out other ways of doing a solo," he says. "You'd sometimes play it within chords. A lot of those Creation songs were chord shapes rather than individual notes. Like 'Making Time': the main thing is a chord shape and I was playing big chords but then I'd break off and do some kind of a solo."

Having mastered that rhythm-lead style, Eddie never went back. "A couple of times in the last 10, 20 years I've sat in with bands that have got a rhythm guitar player," he reveals. "I found it really hard. Found myself covering too much ground. It's a lot easier for me really to play the rhythm and lead style. I'm happy with that." Dalton went to see the new-look, slimmed down Mark Four a couple of times after his departure and was impressed. "Doing totally different types of music," he says. "Very good. You could tell they had rehearsed at it. It takes something like that. It takes a new project to give a band a kick up the bum and say, 'Right, come on, let's get our fingers out and sort something out here'." Asked if he was surprised at how the Mark Four then developed into something that sounded as radically different to its own past as The Creation, he says, "No not really. It's just completely something else. Although the Mark Four was a good stepping stone for them, taught them all to play together properly, they just put finer touches on it and turned into a good band."

New boy Tony Cook must have imagined that he'd secured his lucky break for February 1966 saw him appearing on a single. 'Work All Day (Sleep All Night)' b/w 'Going Down Fast' appeared on Fontana. The A-side was a gritty cry of class solidarity – albeit with a slightly unfocused lyric – in the mould of The Animals' similarly proletarian hits 'We've Gotta Get Out Of This Place' and 'It's My Life'. "That was my Eric Burdon phase," Kenny later admitted to *Record Collector*. Eddie's musical backdrop was an appropriately anthemic affair. "That record weren't bad," says Jack. "Kenny wrote that and he based it a bit on one of The Animals' numbers 'cos he'd written it originally with them in mind. He said, 'We can do this, this will suit us'." The B-side was possibly even better and certainly more articulate in its denunciation of the lot of the workers.

As is something of a tradition for these types of songs, in 'Going Down Fast' Kenny seems to have as much contempt for the ambitionless oppressed as for their uncaring oppressors. Overall, it was a powerful single and an indicator of a band who were truly developing a personality (such social commentary then being still relatively rare in popular music). This subject matter would become something of a theme for Kenny's songs right into the Nineties. In the Sixties, it was utterly in tune with the social climate in the UK. As Glen Colson, Kenny's lifelong friend, notes, "Basically they're all very classic English kind of (songs) – like *L-Shaped Room*, plays and films, *Billy Liar*. He loved that English sort of thing."

The band even secured a prestigious appearance on TV's *Thank Your Lucky Stars* to promote the record, lining up alongside such luminaries as Billy Fury, Lulu and, ironically, The Animals (who would probably have been promoting their current single 'Inside Looking Out'). The Mark Four dressed up for the occasion, sporting suits with alternate black and white arms and legs. "We were on our way to a gig when it was being broadcast," recalls Eddie, "pulled in at this radio and TV shop and asked the man if he could put the television on so we could watch it! And he did. That was in South London somewhere. We thought we looked great then. We probably looked a bunch of idiots."

Though this single again failed to chart, it certainly seemed the Mark Four were gathering some sort of momentum, both artistically and – if media exposure was any barometer of future prospects – commercially. However, the Mark Four as a band would shortly be finished. Some time in the first quarter of 1964 – possibly as soon as March, the month after the release of 'Work All Day…' – the Mark Four's road manager Bill Fowler recommended the band to Tony Stratton-Smith, with whom he was sharing an office. Stratton-Smith would shortly become the Mark Four's manager, tweak their personnel, oversee a change of name and administer a transmogrification into The Creation.

Tony Stratton-Smith was born in 1933. A native of Birmingham, his first career was that of a sports reporter, a job he practiced for 11 years. He had done well enough at that profession to have retired by the early Sixties, despite still being in his late twenties. His initial foray into the music business saw him try his hand at being a publisher but he was unsuccessful in this field. He returned briefly to writing before deciding – after an inspirational meeting with Brian Epstein – to be a pop manager. He signed Paddy, Klaus and Gibson, The Koobas and Beryl Marsden, Liverpool natives all.

Like many pop managers of the time, Stratton-Smith was gay. However, as with people like Simon Napier-Bell and Brian Epstein, this manifested itself not so much in camp behaviour but in a certain suaveness. Indeed, this led to many people with whom he interacted on a day-to-day basis not even being certain he was homosexual. "None of us were really sure," says Eddie. "There was this thing between being gay and camp. You could 'camp it up' and that was a way of being a bit over the top in terms of dress and attitude. We used to do it all the time in The Creation and the Mark Four. It was a way of being extravagant in dress and attitude but it wasn't a gay thing. I never really knew if Tony was gay or just really liked to camp it up. But it was never a problem whatever it was. None of us ever thought twice about it."

"He certainly didn't come on to any of us, I don't think," says Bob Garner, shortly to join The Creation. "When you see the different amount of types of presenting yourself as a gay person, it wasn't noticeable. He wasn't camp. He never said anything. 'cos if he had, one of the others would have said, 'Hang on, he's just come onto me' and I never heard that in any conversation. The only hint of anything – and whether it's true or not I've no idea – I think he had a thing for the bass player with The Koobas. That was the one they wanted to replace and they asked me to join but Tony Stratton-Smith said no and maybe that was one of the things on the line there. That was the only thing I can remember that gave any hint."

Jack says, "We never see him with a girlfriend or anything. I remember once he came out to Germany with us, spent the night with some bird and was sort of bragging about it. I don't know whether he was gay or he was just shy of women but I never really thought of Tony as gay. There was never any vibes. Gay guys never fancied me anyway. A few of 'em used to go after Bob 'cos he was a pretty boy. But if Tony was gay I'd be surprised. I thought he was just one of these guys who's a bit shy of women, but of course back in the Sixties being gay was a bit harder than it is today 'cos if you started putting it about you'd have the police after you. It wouldn't have mattered anyway – take people as you find them."

Almost hilariously, while the men-of-the-world who comprised The Creation were not quite sure as to the true nature of Stratton-Smith's sexuality, June Clark – a teenage schoolgirl who befriended the band in their early days and eventually became their fan club secretary – was fully aware of his homosexuality. "Strat managed The Thoughts," Clark recalls. "I knew The Thoughts really well. (Guitarist) Pete Beckett and I were quite close friends and Strat was really heavily after Pete and Pete was quite frightened of it. I saw that quite easily as a naive teenager. Because homosexuality wasn't spoken of back then very much, it was still quite Victorian in the way it was thought of."

She adds, "I think Strat was well respected by the guys in the band and I don't think he really made a pass at any of them. I think if he liked any of them it would have been Eddie because Eddie was very youthful, so friendly and the most outgoing of all of them – apart from Kenny, but Kenny had an arrogance about him that was offensive." Jack: "We'd never heard of Tony Stratton-Smith before then but we went and went over and met the guy and we liked him." The Mark Four, of course, already had a management contract with Ian Swan. "We had to break the contract," says

Jack, "but what I gather was that they worked out an agreement and I think Ian ended up with a little percentage. It was just to keep it nice."

However, Stratton-Smith did not agree to simply sign the group wholesale. At the same time as he informed them (or perhaps their representative: Jack remembers Kenny as being the one most involved in discussions) that he wanted to manage them, Stratton-Smith also dropped something of a bombshell: he wanted them to get rid of Tony Cook and had a bassist in mind to replace him named Bob Garner. The reason that Stratton-Smith gave was somewhat brutal: Cook wasn't good-looking enough to be in a band who he saw as chart prospects. It is one of the moral dilemmas with which many rock bands are faced: cutting loose a fellow human being and comrade-in-arms like so much ballast in order to effect a move upwards.

Usually, the reason for this is musical deficiencies. Sometimes it is because the rest of the group find the individual objectionable as a person. In either case, dismissing the member doesn't usually present a huge psychological obstacle: musicians know the score about getting sacked if they can't cut it and nobody is going to agonise too much about getting rid of a personality they find obnoxious. But when that person is well liked and technically proficient and has been deemed superfluous because of his looks, this presents an entirely different scenario.

"We were all tall and skinny and Tony was a lot shorter than us," recalls Eddie. "Visually, I suppose you could say it didn't fit. In those days that was really, really important, Tony (Stratton-Smith) saw that and that's why we had to make the change. Tony (Cook) was a really good bass player. Great singer as well. I can't imagine these days in a band someone had to leave it because they're too short but in those days that's how it was." Jack: "Tony was a really good bass player and he sung great falsetto and I liked him as a man. Trouble is, he was a small dumpy guy and he didn't have a good image. Which for me didn't matter, 'cos I just worried about the music. But at the time image seemed to be everything with a lot of these people and (Stratton-Smith) had seen Bob Garner over in Germany playing with his band. He thought Bob was great and he'd fit our band perfectly, even to the point where we were all brunette and Bob was blonde, all this sort of stuff that comes into it.

"He said, 'If I'm going to manage the band, you're going to have to let me manage it' and he said, 'I want this Bob in the band because I think that it'll set the four of you off perfectly: different characters and all this stuff'. Stratton-Smith insisted on it and we thought, 'Well we're going to go now or never'. So we went along with it, which was a bit tough on Tony 'cos he hadn't done nothing wrong." Cook seems to have taken the decision with a stoicism that would probably be beyond the average person. Jack: "We just sat down, had a chat, explained exactly to him what was going on and he said, 'That's okay, I understand'. He was that sort of guy. He knew showbusiness. He'd been in the Leroys a long time and he knew what the game was all about. One of the little regrets I have, because he was such a nice guy."

Robert Anthony Garner was born on 15 May 1946. Although he had served as an apprentice engineer upon leaving school at the age of 15, he had ultimately embarked on a career as a jobbing musician and had already built up quite an impressive CV by the time the Mark Four's new manager informed him his services were required. "I'm from Warrington, which is bang in the middle of Liverpool and Manchester," says Bob, the only child of a wire-drawer father and a mother who did various jobs including usherette and public baths employee before taking up nursing. "So that's where I grew up: *Coronation Street*... I got into music when I was 15. I left school at fifteen and I just liked Little Richard, Chuck Berry kind of stuff. A friend of mine, who I suppose (was) the equivalent of Jimmy Savile of the day – I don't think they were called DJs then – he managed to get hold of all the American stuff which I liked and that's how I got into it."

Unlike many bassists, Bob was never a frustrated lead guitarist forced onto the instrument because, in the time-honoured fashion of rock bands, he was the least able of a band's three guitar players: "I always played bass when I started. I saved up and I went for some guitar lessons but the man who was teaching the guitar lessons, he was teaching classical Spanish guitar. That wasn't of interest to me and I said, 'Well could you teach me how to play the bass parts?' I took my *Play In A Day* bass guitar book and he taught me from that book. I did eight half-hour lessons and went on from there. I enjoyed doing that."

Though not a Merseysider, Bob was located close enough to Liverpool to sample the throbbingly healthy Merseybeat scene: "We went and saw up in Liverpool groups then, which would be the Undertakers, the Swinging Blue Jeans and Rory Storm And The Hurricanes. They were playing out-and-out British rock'n'roll really. I saw the Beatles at The Cavern. Then I met the Beatles in Warrington – because I was in a little local group called The Brokers. 1961 or '62 that would be – and I think they were on 25 quid and we was on six. The Brokers was preceded by

Seth and the Sounds. That was exactly the same (line-up) apart from the drummer. That was Seth. Seth left."

Inevitably Bob became part of the Merseybeat scene. In 1964, he replaced founder member Billy Kinsley in the Merseybeats. "I went down to The Cavern on a lunchtime and the Merseybeats were appearing there," he recollects. "They had a bass player on stage with them. He was a lead guitar player with a Widnes band and he didn't want the job. When I went round the back it was like a doctor's surgery: there was about another 10 lads all there waiting to see if they could have the job as well. They came back and went 'Eeny, meeny, miny, mo', looked at me and said 'Do you fancy coming with us tonight?' I got in the van, went to my house, picked me guitar up and that was it. They then informed me that they was getting Johnny Gustafson in later – he was over in Germany – so I stayed 'til Johnny joined." Bob's brief stint in the Merseybeats saw him performing on *Top Of The Pops* and playing on the group's live EP 'On Stage'.

After his stint with the Merseybeats ended, Bob was invited to play with the Shubdubs, a band led by Jimmy Nicol who, for a few fleeting weeks, was one of the most well known drummers on the planet when he replaced a hospitalised Ringo Starr on a Beatles foreign tour. Nicol received a similar stroke of a luck when Dave Clark of the Dave Clark Five was taken ill and the Blackpool Opera House, where his band had a residency, urgently required a fill-in ensemble. Bob: "Harold Davison – the impresario of the time – got in touch with me and said would I go down to London. That was on the Thursday night and on the Friday me father drove me down to London, we got kitted out at Cecil Gee's with suits."

Bob admits he has no idea of how or how Harold Davison had heard of him. "I'd left The Merseybeats and it was creating something of a band from people who'd been with other people," he says. "Just somebody's inspiration." He continues the story: "So the five of us got to Blackpool on the Friday evening, met on the Saturday morning, rehearsed and were top of the bill at the Opera House on the Saturday. We did about three weeks, maybe a month, to replace Dave Clark Five. There was Red Price, a lad from Lancashire called Tony Allen, great singer, and a couple of other musicians. And no guitars. It was like two brass sections, Hammond organ, bass guitar and drums. I was completely out of my depth. I only knew about three guitars and drums."

In a friendly gesture, the Beatles invited The Shubdubs to support them on their late 1964 UK Tour. "That's when I met the Beatles properly and we did a few dates on that tour," recalls Bob. "I remember McCartney standing at the side, coming up and talking. Everything was just ordinary. There was no sort of, 'We are, we are.' It was just, 'How you doing?', one thing and another. The amazing thing was, each venue that we went to, at least three or four streets before you got to the theatre, all the fans were waiting for any sort of vehicle that might be carrying the Beatles. I remember sitting in the back of the van and the whole thing was rocking and rolling. It was frightening. It's not an exaggeration: it was swarming with people trying to get access to whoever might be inside."

After the Nicol gig came to an end, Bob took his anecdotes about sharing a bill with the world's four most famous musicians back to Blackpool where he was offered a job with the Midnighters, house band of the Ciador Club. Their drummer was future bandleader Keef Hartley, while their frontman was Freddie Starr, who would become famous in the Seventies as an anarchic stand-up comedian and television personality. After the season ended, the Midnighters backed Starr for several months on his UK gigs. "But that was horrendous because you never know which side of the bed he gets out on. He's crazy now, he was crazy then. We got an invitation to go to Germany in December '64. We did a month in Kiel as the Ice Blues. That was my first trip to Germany.

"Lee Curtis, who was resident in Hamburg, came to the club to do three nights just by the Christmas period. The music was changing from out and out rock'n'roll and getting a little bit more bluesy-jazzy, and that's what we were doing. We didn't have a guitar player, we just had a tenor sax, keyboard, bass and drums, and when he heard us he said 'Would you like to join me? I'm gonna change me backing band'. (I said) 'We're going home at the end of the month', which we did." Upon his return home, Bob had a spare six or seven weeks in the early part of '65. During this period he was offered a job in the Kinsleys, a spin-off of former band The Merseybeats who featured a powerhouse drummer called Dave Preston, someone who would pop up in an acrimonious episode in the story of Bob's future band The Creation. "We did do about two gigs I think," says Bob of the Kinsleys.

In the first couple of months of 1965, Bob and saxophone player Dave McShane took up Lee Curtis' offer to join his band, the All Stars, in Hamburg: "I played with just about all those sort of Hamburg names that crop up: Tony Sheridan, people like that. Then there's the visiting artists again: Chuck Berry, Little Richard, and all that kind of thing – it was great." Bob appeared on the Lee Curtis and the All Stars album 'It's Lee', released in 1965.

His next musical adventure was playing in the backing band of the aforementioned Sheridan, like Nicol another name familiar through his connection to the Beatles. Sheridan had been the man the Fab Four had backed on 'My Bonnie' (1961), their first appearance on a commercially available record. Things didn't go too well. "We were in Switzerland, Zurich, and the man who had organised the tour disappeared," recalls Bob. "We did a venue in like a cafe restaurant and they had a stage. We said, 'We're a bit stuck for cash here, we'll just play the week out and if you give us accommodation and food we'll do it for that, 'til we sort ourselves out'. He agreed, because we was filling the place every night."

While playing these dates, Bob was approached by the manager of a Swiss group called The Slaves, now revered in some quarters as great lost freakbeaters. Bob: "They were on tour in Switzerland and their bass player was ill. They came into the cafe – I remember we was having our meal – and said, 'Could you play with us tonight?' I looked at the other lads and they said, 'Yeah, okay'. So I left my instrument with them – the guitarist probably played bass – and I went with them on this show. It was almost like a Beatles-type hysteria for this group. I finished the gig and they said, 'Would you like to join us?' The Tony Sheridan thing had come to an end so I asked the lads. They said, 'Carry on, do what's best'. So I joined them. I was with them for three months when I got a letter off a friend of mine saying, 'There's a little advert in the *Melody Maker* and it says 'Will Bob Garner contact this number?'."

The ad had been placed by Tony Stratton-Smith shortly after having had his first meeting with the Mark Four. Bob and Stratton-Smith had never met but Stratton-Smith was aware of him through The Koobas, who had tried to recruit him to replace their bassist/vocalist Keith Ellis when The Koobas had been playing in Hamburg at the same time as Lee Curtis and The All Stars. "They came there for a month," recalls Bob. "We were the resident house band and The Koobas saw me and we made friends for the month, like you usually do. But I had no idea (that) when they got back they said to Tony Stratton-Smith, 'Could we get Bob Garner?' He said 'No', because this lad's voice was on the single – 'Any Day Now' – and they had the Beatles tour (December 1965) in the bag and everything. So that was in the back of Tony Stratton's memory. When he saw the Mark Four, he said, 'Yes, I'll take you on but change your bass player. I've got a bass player somewhere.'

"I rang up and was on the plane the next day. Got to London and I went into an office in Denmark Street and that was the first meeting I had with

Tony-Stratton-Smith and the three left out of the Mark Four. I met them and the first thing I said was, 'You're not one of those Who groups, are you?' (Laughs) Which I don't think went down really well. I'd been playing Ray Charles and Georgie Fame stuff, that was my thing. But they said, 'We're just trying to be a little bit different.' So I said, 'Okay, I've not been at home for over 12 months. Would you mind if I had a few days home and come back?' So I did." Bob's recruitment to the band was announced in the issue of *Record Mirror* cover-dated 21 May 1966.

Before his return home, Bob took the opportunity to see the Mark Four live. "A bit naughty, really, because the original bass player was there with them on stage," he admits. Nothing Bob saw that evening – or at the one gig he played with the band before their first recording session – made him think that the group he was joining was anything other than another of the conventional, journeyman covers merchants he'd played with in his career thus far. Bob: "They said, 'Do you think you can do that?' Well when I got there, they wasn't doing the psychedelic thing at all. They were doing songs like 'Barefootin'', regular numbers. I said, 'Yeah, that's not a problem'. But the first tune that we rehearsed was 'Making Time'. Went into the studio with them and we did 'Making Time' and 'Try And Stop Me' within the first week or two weeks of me joining."

For Bob, Stratton-Smith was an enabler of the band's music rather than an influence, and an only semi-interested enabler at that: "When I first met him, he had The Koobas, he had The Krew and a few others. Beryl Marsden. He'd had a little bit of experience but not a lot. I think he was fascinated with showbusiness, wanted to get into it but he only knew about the publicity side of things. I think he was interested in young people being progressive in an art form, whatever art form it was. He liked people who were prepared to move boundaries and things and help them along. He could see that somebody was trying to strive away from the norm and I think that's what he was into. I don't think he was a melodic sort of a person, he couldn't clap his hands in time. Tony really just let it free-flow. I think he liked what he saw." And was he a rock consumer, the kind of person who would go out and buy, for instance, the latest Beatles record? Bob: "No, not at all."

Stratton-Smith's placement of Bob within the band, purely it seems for the sake of image, was ironically the crucial piece of the musical jigsaw which made The Creation the band they were. Bob's Merseybeat bass style and Eddie's Southern powerchord playing created a unique noise. "The mish-mash came in when I joined because – just by the style I was playing and what Eddie was playing – it worked out that little Creation thing," says Bob. He elucidates: "The style I grew up with was playing along with the bass drum. Just simple really: whatever the bass drum did, the bass guitar would play most the same thing so there's a thicker sort of thump. If you listen to 'Love Me Do', I think that sort of just about says it really. The London sort of thing was perhaps a little more melody on the bass, more riffs if you like. They didn't really thump the beat out. Mine was more like one-note type rhythms.

"The thing is, it was always a problem for a lead guitar to play the individual notes and not have a rhythm guitar there. I think this is what happened with the powerchord-type thing, and the distortion helped to fill out that sort of gap, but the thing which helped it even more was the simple bass line. The single notes. Two notes at the most and a chord. Status Quo do it quite well: filling out of the bass, just: thump, thump, thump. The Brokers was just three and that was the same thing. it helped to fill that out."

The sobriquet 'The Creation' seems to have been adopted before Bob joined. Bob recalls, "I think it was decided that that's what they were going to be called as from that day I arrived." A reference to the band as the Creation in the 16 April issue of *Record Mirror* – almost certainly weeks before Bob joined – supports that recollection.

Whenever he was asked about the origin of the name The Creation, Kenny always insisted that he was responsible for it. For example, talking to Jud Cost in 1994 for an interview that would be published in *Ugly Things* magazine in 1997, the vocalist said, "I was going through a book of Russian poetry and saw a poem called 'The Creation'. I thought that looked good written down, especially for a band that was trying to be totally new." However, none of the other members remember it that way.

Jack: "The Mark Four wasn't a good name. There was actually a Scottish band called the Mark Five so the name had to be changed. Tony Stratton-Smith come up with the name The Creation. We said, 'It's a bit bible, innit?' And he said, 'That's alright. The Creation – we'll create'. So we went with it." Eddie: "I think it was Tony Stratton-Smith. I think it was there was this name which conjured up something new and with the style of the music we was into at the time – 'Making Time' was a little bit off the wall – and it all fitted."

Bob: "That was Tony Stratton-Smith as far as I remember." Of course, it could be the case that Kenny did come up with the idea in the way he suggested and then recommended it to Stratton-Smith and the other members simply assumed it was Stratton-Smith's own idea when he in turn mentioned it to them. Certainly, while Kenny seems to have had a healthy ego and an intensely self-justifying nature, nothing about him seems to suggest the capacity or propensity to come up with elaborate falsehoods, which the Russian poem would be if Stratton-Smith had devised the name. Whatever, we will now probably never know. The name certainly captured the way a relatively staid (if developing) R&B act with its roots in the Fifties blossomed overnight into something that was altogether more adventurous and modern. As Mike Stax of *Ugly Things* superbly summed it up, "The Mark Four was a staunch, traditional rock 'n' roll type name; The Creation reeked of art, intellect and modernism."

Stratton-Smith's patronage of Merseyside musicians had caused Bill Harry – founder of the *Mersey Beat* newspaper – to dub him an "honorary Liverpudlian" in *Record Mirror*, so it was appropriate that what was almost certainly the first ever mention of The Creation in print was in Harry's Up North column in that paper's 16 April 1966 issue. Harry reported: "Tony Stratton-Smith, manager of several Liverpool groups, tells me – "I've taken on a brand new group, nothing to do with Liverpool, called The Creation." The last line of this short piece was an illustration of just how different a league Stratton-Smith operated in compared to Ian Swan. Mentioning a name that was already responsible for overseeing several hit singles, some classic songs and more than one journey from obscurity to stardom, Stratton-Smith casually added, "They'll be recording with Shel Talmy."

CHAPTER 2

MAKING TIME

That Shel Talmy was a friend may have influenced Stratton-Smith's decision to engage him as producer of The Creation but there is no doubt that Talmy's track record would have justified the decision to employ him as producer of his new group on a purely objective level. By mid-1966, Talmy had produced a string of Top 10 UK hits, with more to come. Moreover these hits were not merely chart smashes. Talmy seemed to have a knack that was something more than the hit-making prowess of contemporaries like, say, Mickie Most who was as happy – and likely – to create a smash via the artistically negligible Herman's Hermits as he was by the very worthy Animals. Talmy, in contrast, routinely supervised epoch-marking classics, singles like the Kinks' 'You Really Got Me' (1964) and The Who's 'My Generation' (1965). A similar sense of *gestalt* would attend 'Friday On My Mind', the anti-work ethic hit he produced for The Easybeats in the latter quarter of 1966.

Yet Talmy was not an *auteur* producer in the mould of Phil Spector. Some might suggest this meant his impressive record was just a matter of luck. Asked if he was merely in the right place at the right time, Talmy says, "I don't know how to answer that. I suppose partly. I suppose partly it's because of what I do. I kind of assume that any producer who has a track record, has a track record because they choose what the public wants." Was he aware that the records he was recording were in some cases revolutionary? Talmy: "Revolutionary? No. Hits? Yes. They sounded like hits. Did I think that 'My Generation' was going to become an anthem for the teens? No. And anybody that tells you that they did know is lying to you."

Damon Lyon-Shaw, who engineered for many sessions Talmy recorded at London's IBC studios, half-supports Talmy's view of himself. "I don't know whether he knew a hit," he says, adding, "The thing about Shel was he actually knew how to get the best out of people, which is quite important. But you've got to remember that most of the stuff he did were good acts so they knew where they were going, they knew what they wanted. And then you had the engineer; if they were good then they were also putting their bit in towards the production, the sound and the ideas. So really, Shel wasn't a great ideas man but he was very good at getting stuff together and getting a good finished product.

"I'll never knock Shel. He was a clever lad and he did a lot of really good stuff but whether or not he was inspirational, I don't know. But there were too many people: that's why bands went on and dropped the idea of a producer and did it themselves."

Talmy's initial ambition was to be a film director. This ambition was thwarted by the fact that he was diagnosed in his late teens with retinitis, a condition which leads to incrementally and permanently deteriorating eyesight. It's one of the most remarkable facts about Talmy's life that he has managed to carve out very successful careers as record producer, literary agent and publisher despite literally being barely able to see a yard in front of his face. Now legally blind, even in the mid Sixties his visual capacity was so impaired that people who walked into the same room as him would feel compelled to announce themselves to him.

"I went round to his flat," Lyon-Shaw recalls, "and it was (the time of) one of the early moon missions. He actually had his face against the TV screen – and it was a big screen – trying to see what was going on, so even then he was pretty blind."

"I got diagnosed when I was about 17 and at the time I was seeing pretty well," says Talmy. "I was told it was going to deteriorate and eventually I'd pretty much go blind. I think I ignored that for the next couple or three years or so until I realised this was what was gonna happen so I acted accordingly." Realising that being a movie director would be beyond him, he opted to go into record production, which he describes as "the next best thing." Talmy began his recording career as an engineer at Conwell Studio in Los Angeles where he was trained by an Englishman named Phil Young.

Infused with the wanderlust of youth, Talmy decided to journey to Europe for a month or so. Hoping to secure some studio work to pay for his trip, he brought over to England a selection of lacquers of sides produced by friend Nick Venet – a producer at Capitol Records – and walked into the London offices of Decca Records, where he proceeded to claim he had been the producer of a string of Stateside hits that included the Beach Boys' 'Surfin' Safari' and Lou Rawls' 'Music In The Air'. Decca's

Dick Rowe – who is probably sick of being referred to as the Man Who Turned Down The Beatles – was so impressed that he started Talmy the following week.

The lie worked for as long as it needed to. "By the time they found out it was all bullshit, I'd already had my first hit" , Talmy later told journalist Richie Unterberger, "and they were very gentlemanly, never mentioned that they knew that I knew that they knew." That first hit was 'Charmaine' by The Bachelors, a UK top tenner in 1963. Unusually for Britain, though Talmy was initially working exclusively for Decca, it was as an independent producer, a concept he had brought over from his native country where it was normal. This meant that, unlike staff producers who were mere record-label wage slaves, he received royalties for every record sold. He would later refine this concept with The Who and The Creation, whose recordings he funded and therefore owned outright and was able to release through record labels on a lease basis.

In 1964 Talmy was approached by Robert Wace, co-manager of a London band called The Ravens. He was impressed enough to agree to work with the band and helped secure them a deal with Pye Records (his exclusive deal with Decca ended when he found they were turning down acts on his behalf like Manfred Mann and Georgie Fame, whom he would have liked to produce). The Ravens' name did not last. Their records would be released under a different sobriquet: The Kinks. To his eternal chagrin, The Kinks' string of Talmy-produced hits over the following two years were just about the only exception to his now usual policy of owning and leasing master tapes.

The first of those hits was 'You Really Got Me', a magnificent hard rock number with a guitar riff whose fearsomeness was then unprecedented and which is startling even four decades later. Nothing breeds success like success and before long managers were approaching Talmy to see if he could confer his magic touch to the efforts of their charges. Kit Lambert and Chris Stamp were one such pair of managers. The Who, the band they co-managed, were urged by Stamp and Lambert to write a song in the style of The Kinks' recent hits specifically in order to appeal to Talmy's ear. The ploy worked and The Who signed to Talmy's production company Orbit (which he co-owned with Arthur Howes, a leading promoter of the time) for five years.

'I Can't Explain' and 'Anyway, Anyhow, Anywhere' were very good records and minor hits for the re-named Who, with the latter featuring startlingly novel washes of feedback, but it was with 'My Generation' that the band truly found its character and started their ascent to their status as one of the most important half-dozen acts in rock history. With this record, Talmy managed to capture just about every important aspect of The Who: their brutal but melodic style, their pulverising rhythm section, their inclination to innovate (John Entwistle's bass solo was probably the first on record) and their propensity for using feedback. The very *blitzkrieg* nature of the record was as much as declaration of new values as its unforgettable first verse conclusion: "Hope I die before I get old!"

'My Generation' was an instant classic and a UK hit. It should have been the start of a long and beautiful friendship but relations between The Who – or at least their managers – and Talmy soured not long after the recording of the band's debut album, also called 'My Generation'. Lambert and Stamp weren't impressed by Decca, to whom Talmy was leasing their records in both the UK and the States and in order to effect a move to different labels told Talmy that he would be producing no further Who records. Talmy was outraged, probably justifiably considering the money he had invested in the band, and legal action ensued.

Although he would never mastermind any more of their recordings, Talmy did very well financially from the outcome, securing royalties on Who records for the next five years, including the staggeringly successful 'Tommy'. Asked if he would have liked to continue producing the band, he responds: "Of course I would've. I think I would have done a much better job than they wound up doing. With all the stuff. You may call that ego if you like. I really don't care. But I think my productions are a hell of a lot better than what they wound up with afterward. Most other people did too. I think 'Tommy' would have sounded a lot better if I'd done it."

When Tony Stratton Smith approached him about the his new band in 1966, Talmy had recently added another couple of strings to his already remarkable bow. Stratton-Smith was engaged in some writing projects that Talmy was supporting, the first such venture by Talmy and one which would eventually see him running a parallel career as a literary agent and publisher. His other new venture was as a record-label owner. Planet Records, which he had set up in December 1965, was one of the very first independent labels in the UK.

As Talmy now constituted the whole package – record producer and record company owner – it would have made perfect sense for Stratton-Smith to approach his friend about The Creation. "Heavy-duty rock band," says Talmy of how he recalls Stratton-Smith describing The Creation to him, "which is what I was looking for. Tony and I were very good friends so I took his word for the fact that they were good 'cos he always had good taste and I went to go see 'em."

Talmy remembers seeing The Creation live and in rehearsal and that this was possibly even before they were called The Creation and before Bob joined. This might be true – Stratton-Smith could have arranged for him to see a Mark Four gig without telling his charges – and something Bob says seems to go some way to confirming it: "I think he'd got Shel Talmy interested in the band before I got there because Ronnie Fowler was knocking around then. Ronnie had done something with The Who and Shel was probably interested in looking at another type of Who thing."

However, Talmy only seems to have registered on the band members' radars at a specially convened private performance. Kenny told *Ugly Things* in 1997, "We first met Shel Talmy in a recording studio in Denmark Street called Regent Sound. That's where Shel used to audition his bands." Eddie and Bob, however, remember the event taking place at the Astoria on Charing Cross Road, literally about a minute's walk from Regent Sound.

"It was a Saturday morning," Eddie recollects, "and there was about five or six bands there set up around the floor. On a given signal we all had to play a couple of songs each and Shel was sitting upstairs somewhere listening. Bit weird really. Bit like *Pop Idol*." "I remember there was a bit of a stage there and Shel was there with Tony Stratton-Smith," says Jack. "He liked the sound of 'Making Time'. He thought he could do something with it." "The first time I heard them I was sold on them," says Talmy. "They were great. The moment I heard 'Making Time', the first four bars of it, I said, 'That's what I want to do". It was very obviously the first single."

Talmy admits that, up to a point, part of his attraction to them was a certain similarity to The Who: "I was still I suppose steeped in American rock'n'roll and power rock, which was still pretty much of a novelty in England. They certainly were on the same wavelength as The Who were. When I first got to England, the first two, three or four years, the rock was 'polite' rock. It was not raucous, it was not raunchy, it was terribly played – which includes The Beatles. The Stones are the ones who started a departure in the other direction. Certainly The Who did. The Kinks were really polite rock. The Creation were very much in the mould of what eventually got called psychedelic and all that sort of stuff."

However, he says that the assumption of many that, having been forcibly removed from The Who equation, his work with The Creation was a manifestation of a desire to finish – or continue – with them the job he had started with The Who is off-beam. "It never crossed my mind. I took each band individually and did not try to make any band try to sound like any other band that I'd done. The correlation, if you're looking for one, is that I have certain tastes in music and so consequently I worked for bands who appealed to those tastes. If there were similarities between them – well, that's because of my musical taste, not because I was trying to make one band sound like another band."

Talmy signed the right to record The Creation's music, which he would do at his own expense. In return, he would own the recording master tapes outright and thereby have the exclusive right to exploit them commercially, which of course at this stage meant releasing them on his own label. When his label ceased to exist – which was within around eight months of signing The Creation – Talmy was still free to lease The Creation's masters to other labels. "It seemed like we were going to do something," says Eddie of the emergence of Talmy into the band's lives. "Big shot producer. You thought it could go a bit further."

Perhaps it was their excitement about Talmy that blinded the group to what some of them now consider to be deficiencies in the deal that was signed with the producer. Eddie is profoundly sceptical about the way money ended up being split from this arrangement, despite having remained friendly with Talmy down the years. "I dunno about the deal," Eddie says. "I have the original contract here and it's 50 per cent to him (Talmy) and 50 per cent between the four of us. (Laughs) That has actually been like that since the word go." Talmy also arranged to publish the band's original songs. Eddie: "He did a kind of sub-publishing deal with, I think, EMI where the writer would get fifty per cent and he would get a percentage of the publisher's share."

Talmy seems to have always been perceived by the band and their associates as more than a mere producer. Jack saw Talmy and Stratton-Smith as "joint managers" and assumed that "Shel had a small percentage of management." (Talmy says this isn't the case.) Jack: "Shel would take a back seat – just take care of the recording – and Tony would sell us. I think. Probably a financial thing more than anything but he took care of the recording side, and Stratters got us TV, radio and really got the band going." June Clark says Shel was "definitely involved in managing them in a strange way, although he wasn't management." The band's agency – the booking of their gigs – would be handled by Arthur Howes, Talmy's business partner.

If this sounds like Talmy doling out favours to a friend, it wasn't necessarily an example of nepotism the band would have objected to. As Gail Colson, then Talmy's secretary/personal assistant (and brother of Glen), points out, "At that time, Arthur Howes was the biggest promoter and agent around. He used to promote The Beatles."

The first Creation recording session occurred within, at most, a fortnight of Bob Garner's recruitment. "Everything was pretty quick in those days," shrugs Talmy. "We didn't screw around with going through tons of lawyers and all that bullshit." The session followed some band practice at their rehearsal space in Epping. Explains Jack, "I lived in Hertfordshire, Eddie lived in Leyton, Kenny was in Hertford and so it was a bit central and we used to go down there. I think it was Epping Community Hall. They had a cellar underneath." The Creation would always be an efficient unit in the studio. Jack: "We'd rehearse, not a lot but fairly regularly. If we had recording sessions coming up, we'd put some stuff down. They go in the studio now with nothing and start from there. Bloody hell, that's just throwing money down the drain. We used to go in, we used to have a fair idea what we were doing and then we'd add to it."

At these inaugural Creation rehearsals, the group were cooking up a new Phillips/Pickett composition, one that would make for a quite remarkable debut single. The song in question was 'Making Time', a track that would showcase perfectly the individual strengths of each half of The Creation's songwriting axis: Kenny's *zeitgeist*-encapsulating angry-young-man lyric writing and Eddie's innovatory guitarwork. Pickett had appropriated the title phrase from another record. As he told *Record Collector* in 1995, "I'd heard Dobie Gray's 'The "In" Crowd' and I liked the lines, 'Shoot the lines, making time." In fact the lyric – written by Billy Page and describing a man's pleasure in being part of a respected and stylish elite – says, "Dressing fine, making time" .

Unaware at the time that the phrase "making time" was slang for having success with women, Kenny decided it would serve as a nicely pithy description of the sort of grey, unfulfilled, existing-not-living working-class lifestyle he despised. Eddie, meanwhile, would exploit the occasion to bring his trademark bowing directly into the spotlight. "The song wasn't written around that," Eddie says, "but when it came to the solo I figured out it would be nice to use it as a way of getting that on tape."

The song seems to have slightly preceded Bob's entry into the group (although, for his part, Bob disagrees that it was played for Talmy at the Astoria audition). "We definitely rehearsed it," he recalls, "and it was almost like the other three knew it and I had to learn. Obviously, Kenny and Eddie knew it and I think maybe Jack was familiar with it and it was just for me to pick up the pieces. It didn't end up the way it started out. I don't think it was like, 'This is how we want it to be'. I think it was just a song that turned out that way."

'Making Time' and another Phillips/Pickett number 'Try And Stop Me' were recorded at IBC Studios in West London's Portland Place on or around 18 May 1966. (The original tape box is missing so the recording date can't be stated with certainty, but annotations by an employee of Talmy's indicate that this was the recording date). "Because I felt it was the best studio in town" is Talmy's explanation of why he chose to use IBC to lay down his new signing's first record. Possibly it was the best but it's an indication of how far the music business has come since then that the studio's environs now sound absolutely quaint.

The studio had an illustrious history of sorts in that parent company IBC (International Broadcasting Company) had set up Radio International to broadcast to mainland Europe during World War II, using Radio Normandy's facilities. "It was bombed during the Second World War," recalls IBC house engineer Damon Lyon-Shaw, "and it evolved out of the Second World War from a radio station into an independent sound studio. The half that was bombed was never replaced. It turned into a block of flats. Always a problem because of the sound. Tenants always complained of the noise of the studio late at night."

The building was divided into studio A and studio B but The Creation – and most other people – would record only in A. Lyon-Shaw: "Studio B was never very good and never functioned properly as a studio. We didn't have the facilities and eventually it became a mixing studio." Upon entering Studio A, the visitor would notice to the right a very steep and narrow flight of stairs that led up to the studio's control room. The control room was fronted by a large glass pane, beneath which giant letters spelt out 'IBC'. Directly underneath the 12-foot wide control room was a space which was utilised for recording, despite it affording no eye contact with the producer and engineer. Explains Lyon-Shaw, "That was the area we used to put the rhythm section when we did bands. We did all the (rock) stuff, The Who and the Small Faces, actually underneath the control room 'cos it was a low ceiling and a tighter sound."

To the visitor's left was a long room which ended on one side in a recess, meaning that Studio A described an L-shape. "It must (have been) 50 feet by probably 45," says Lyon-Shaw. "It was a good size. The L was around what used to be the tea-room and the lobby. If we did orchestras, we actually put them at the corner of the L so that the brass and strings were facing out from that and whatever else – vocals, whatever – were in the other part of the L." A curtain rail ran along the foot of the L (in which Bob Garner remembers a grand piano being situated) so that a drape could be pulled across it if acoustics required it. There was more clear evidence that the room was part of a converted house: "It had two huge Victorian fireplaces that were still there 'til its demise," says Lyon-Shaw.

Of the studio's facilities, Lyon-Shaw says, "The mixer was very basic in those days but good enough. The equalisers were nothing like nowadays." Separation was similarly basic, consisting of movable sound shields which would be lined along a wall when not in use. Lyon-Shaw: "We had very low screens, sort of hardboard screens with holes in them, fibre glass stuff inside. Very little separation at all – in those days we didn't have a lot of condenser mikes – but the separation was certainly good enough. The Irish showbands used to come over and we tended to do the whole thing live, including the vocals."

Though other recording methods were available, monaural recording was the predominant method. Lyon-Shaw: "When I came in 1964, just about all the bands were recorded on mono. Very rarely used three-track, which we did have. Four-track obviously came in after that. We didn't have that when I was around. We had a three-track sitting in the window but it was very rarely used. It was always mono to mono. Obviously with three-track you could separate a little bit, and have the voice separated, and we used to do three-to-threes and four-to-fours when we had four-track and then eight-track, but all the really good stuff in the early Sixties was definitely done on mono. I defy anyone to say that the ambience and the feeling on those early sessions wasn't as good as anything that happens now."

Although stereo mixes in this era were technically possible, they were usually inferior to the mono. "Even the days when we were doing the Bee Gees and they'd had at least two or three hits, we always mixed down to mono," reveals Lyon-Shaw. (Bee Gees manager Robert) Stigwood used to then say, 'Okay, now you've got to do the stereo for the States' and we would it on our own with nobody there at all. And that would be it. It was always the mono mix that was the important one in those days. Stereo was something thrown away for the States or just in an hour." Talmy confirms this: "I know I would have concentrated on doing mono mixes. That's what everybody wanted."

IBC was a place in which one could run into stars at any given minute of any given working day. "We used to do the bulk of the good stuff," recalls Lyon-Shaw. "The first session I walked in on was, I think, The Yardbirds and then I worked on a session with the Rolling Stones. So we were doing the top bands. Shel Talmy, who had a majority of the good groups, including The Kinks, used to work there. I took over working with The Who and they stayed there through the early albums and the 'Tommy' album."

In 1966, the working culture of the recording studio was very different from what it would start to be only a year later, when the fashion begun by the marathon recording length for the Beatles' 'Sgt Pepper's Lonely Hearts Club Band' album became standard procedure. A session for a single was still a three-hour affair, at the end of which one would emerge with finished masters of a single A- and B-side. Of course, the absence of multi-tracking facilities was partly responsible for this brisk, efficient methodology but, equally, before 'Sgt Pepper' people were apt to consider popular music more as commodity than art and the idea of spending more time and effort on it than three hours mostly didn't occur to people.

"It was usually an afternoon session," says Lyon-Shaw. "You started at two and finished at five and that was it. You really had to get it done so you were limited to getting a backing track down and then whatever overdubs, and it had to be a finished thing." This regimented culture – shortly to be swept away by the rebellious and libertarian spirit that had been building throughout the Sixties – was underlined by the fact that at the time he worked for The Creation, Lyon-Shaw was obliged to wear a blazer and tie.

Like Talmy, Lyon-Shaw considers IBC in recording terms to have been "the best". While that claim may be not unadjacent to the truth, frankly this is a familiar boast from London studio engineers from that era whatever the studio they were employed at: the same claims for ultimate superiority can be heard from people who worked at Pye, Olympic and Chappell. In any event, The Creation weren't in a position to judge.

As Eddie points out, "Quite honestly, we didn't know a good studio from a bad studio. It was a big studio and they had loads of gear there, so we thought it was probably a good studio. As time went on, . you got to learn about rooms and things and what felt good and what didn't. I liked IBC. It was alright. It was a good room. (It's) the people you're actually working with that depends if you're going to have a good session or not. You had to get a good engineer." Thankfully, The Creation could never complain about the quality of their production teams, even at the first session. Eddie: "Glyn Johns was the engineer for 'Making Time'. It was Shel, Glyn – that was as good as it got."

Glyn Johns would work on several Creation sessions at several stages of their short career. Now a world famous producer – responsible for bringing his universally respected producing skills to albums by the likes of The Who and the Rolling Stones and the producer in everything but name of the Beatles' 'Get Back' sessions, which resulted in the 'Let It Be' album – he was in 1966 only an engineer, although he would doubtless have quibbled at the 'only'. Lyon-Shaw: "Glyn was very good and he didn't suffer fools. He had a falling out with most of the people at the studio because he was a superstar in his own eyes and he alienated quite a few people, Shel along the way and certainly The Who with Kit. It was just how he was at the time. He was very successful and very good. He was full of himself but he did some good stuff and got the sessions done."

Johns was the very first freelance engineer in Britain. Lyon-Shaw: "He was the main engineer at the studio when I arrived but he was sort of freelancing, but even so he used IBC for all his sessions. I started off as tape op working mostly with Glyn. I learnt everything really from him." As if to underline his independence, Johns refused point-blank to wear IBC's regulation collar and tie.

"I think Shel was a hell of a good producer and Glyn Johns was a hell of a good engineer," says Jack. "They worked together – they knew each other – and Glyn was bending Shel's ear and vice versa and they knew what they were talking about. There was a team working there and they could put things together really good very quickly. We never spent long periods in the studio at all. I think probably, four, five, six-hour sessions at a time." Talmy is happy to acknowledge Johns as "one of the best engineers I ever used." Asked if he would have contributed ideas, however, Talmy says, "No. I was an engineer. What I always looked for was an engineer who was on the same page and I didn't have to explain everything to. Glyn was one of the best."

Talmy describes himself as "a hands-on producer. I'm there from beginning to end: I rehearse the band, I pick the material, help with the arrangements, do the sound, do the mixes, do the mastering." Yet two of the surviving members of The Creation do not seem to remember him having such an involved role, attending non-studio band practice or even acquiescing to much rehearsal time when in the studio. Jack says, "He used to be tight with the time. He never had a lot of time. You'd go in and do four-hour sessions so basically you got to get on with the recording, you can't just sit there wasting money and practising." He adds, "Shel just sits there and keeps an eye on things and he's more conscious of sound, I think, than the actual arrangements."

Bob has similar recollections: "I can't say that he did that much with the sound to enhance it or alter (it) because I think what's on the record is what we created in that room. It was just a direct recording. Wasn't played about with or anything like that... I think Shel was impressed by other people's ideas. Because he wasn't an outrageous person or anything like that. To him, I think it was a gimmick. It was like, 'This is a new angle. It's not The Beatles, it's not the Stones, this is a new thing'. It inspired him, other people's ideas.

"I can't remember him coming down and ever saying 'Change anything' or 'Do this'. I think once or twice on the vocals he may have said something to Jack, because Jack used to do this falsetto thing all the way through but I can't remember him coming on the floor and changing anything that we did. Most of the things were our ideas and he just grabbed 'em and said, 'Okay, I'll put it on tape for you." For his part, Eddie offered a dissenting voice about Talmy in *Ugly Things'* magazine: "He had this image in his mind of what he wanted to hear somehow. He'd come up with ideas and tighten the songs up a bit."

Bob recalls Jack being surrounded by baffle boards while he and Eddie were insulated by the studio's padded, movable sound shields. As indicated earlier, all IBC's rock band sessions would be recorded at the front of the studio. There is a difference in recollection, though, as to which Creation members were in the alcove beneath the control room. "I think Jack was sitting under that area," says Bob. Jack: "You was stuck in a cupboard almost. In an alcove." He adds, "It doesn't really matter. If the sound of the studio's good, that's all that matters."

Eddie, though, remembers things differently: "I was under there. Pretty sure I was. I think Jack and Bob was in the middle of the room but – could be wrong. A long while ago." 'Making Time' – produced by Shel Talmy, engineered by Glyn Johns and with probably Damon Lyon-Shaw in attendance as tape operator – was recorded in a small number of takes. The actual number will probably never be known again for the ledger that would have given this information was on the missing original tape box. Shel Talmy's vaults contain only later copy masters. Though Talmy was helpful in the assistance he provided for this book, he declined to allow the author to listen to The Creation's outtakes.

"I know that it wasn't a labour," says Eddie. "It was pretty much there. We might have done it twice, three times but nothing like take 15." Jack suggests, "Three or four" , while Bob says, "I think seven seems a good number to me." Talmy may have signed The Creation on the strength of 'Making Time' but this must have involved a degree of perspicacity if Bob is to be believed. "It was quite strange, really, because I don't think any of us really knew the song that well, what it was gonna sound like," Bob says. "The solo and all that, when they're going it was all pre-planned – it wasn't. I think it was a nice accident. None of us really knew what it was going to sound like."

Bob is convinced that there was no vision about what would be The Creation sound and that the band could just as easily have ended up making the relatively conventional sounds they had been practising before the 'Making Time' session. "Quite honestly The Creation – or the Mark Four before 'Making Time' – were not into playing that kind of music on stage," says Bob. "It was one of those nice accidents that happened. It was a great riff and the solo was unusual because of the violin bow. We did it, let's say, with innocence, listened to it and thought, 'Hang on, we've got something here'. And after that we traded on that and made more out of what we had from 'Making Time'. We weren't making that kind of music before. I'd only been with the band two weeks but I saw the set and I learned the set and that was not 'Making Time'.

"'Making Time' was a new thing to them and to me. It's only when we heard it, we thought 'Wow'. And you listened to other people saying, 'This is different'. And then you pounce on that and take advantage of it and the next time we went in – with 'Painter Man' and one thing and another – we carried on doing that." And the fact that Eddie had long been experimenting with feedback? "I don't think they were using it in their act that much because when they were doing those gigs then, they were there to do dance music for the kids," reasons Bob. "He may well have been experimenting but it was never a feature until The Creation brought those ideas out, but he had a free rein then to go on being the guitarist he is."

The solo Bob mentions is of course Eddie's seminal bowed guitar contribution to 'Making Time's instrumental break. Whether he was going to overdub the bow solo or record it live was going to be an issue. This was a day and age when the pressure was on to get as many sound elements onto the basic track of a recording as possible: there were a maximum of four tracks available before having to transfer the recording onto a new generation of tape for the addition of other elements, with the degradation in sound quality that entailed. This latter process was known as the reduction stage or 'four-to-four' (and later would become known as 'bounce-downs'): transferring the four tracks of the first part of the recording process onto a new tape, which itself provided an extra two tracks.

Alan O'Duffy, a tape op who worked with The Creation at Pye studios in 1967, explains the typical modus operandi of recording the first generation of takes, the 'basic track': "We would have recorded two tracks of backing track, so in other words we would have put down, say, drums and bass and piano on track one and on track two there'd have been guitar. Then what would have happened is that we'd have overdubbed the lead vocal on track three with the backing vocals at the same time, and then on track four we'd have done the lead guitar with the backing vocals at the same time, and also maybe handclaps." Of course, these elements would vary according to a band's set-up, The Creation – with only one guitar – being a case in point.

Four-to-fours were used if it was decided that extra elements were needed and would necessitate 'squashing' the elements already recorded to make room for them. O'Duffy: "You'd stick the four channels back onto another four track machine – in other words you're copying four-track to four-track – and on this machine you'd combine four of your channels down to two. So now we're on the second generation tape. You'd have mixed from the four channels of the original session and you'd have mixed the four tracks of tape information to a second machine where you would combine the four tracks to two tracks. So on your second tape machine you'll now end up with two tracks of information and we weren't at that point thinking in terms of stereo. Now if you wanted to overdub strings or a brass section or additional guitar or some other elements, you would then have two tracks free. There wasn't such an idea of you putting one instrument on one track. That didn't happen because you simply didn't have the scope."

There was a further element to this process, if one wished it, called mixdowns. O'Duffy: "Mixing the four channels to a mono but in addition to the mixdown you'd have the guitar player or the tambourine or a vocal out in the studio and the guy would sing along with the mix so you'd be mixing four channels of a tape plus a microphone from the studio with the guitar player or the soloist, whatever, singing along with the four tracks, making the mix. So the only point you'd hear maybe the counter voice or the alternative solo, the additional solo, the harmony solo perhaps, would be on the mono mix, where if you have an archive of a stereo mix or something you may find that that was done after the band went home and doesn't have this additional musical content."

Talmy insists everything was done live on this first Creation session: "He would grab the bow and do the thing and throw the bow down again, so we did it in one take. I didn't want to overdub. I could've, even with three or four track – I could have gone four-to-four – but I really wanted to get the essence of them live because they were for me the quintessential live band." Eddie's recollection about the 'Making Time' session is, "I thought we did it all in one hit." (This included, he thinks, the vocals.) "Pretty sure," he continues. "I always thought I had to do it live. I'm pretty sure I did because I was trying to figure out how I could get the bow. 'cos I played half the solo with a plectrum and then the other half with a bow and how I actually did that, I think I had the bow right on top of the amplifier, next to me, and being a Marshall I didn't have to bend down for (it), it was just there at arm's length.

"I can (remember) playing the solo so that probably the last couple of beats on the plectrum solo, I just played with my left hand and grabbed the bow quick and then went up. I'm sure it was live." "He overdubbed it," Bob says. "I think he did both actually. It may well he did it 'with' and then again on top." Jack also claims the bowing was overdubbed.

It's probably the case that the bowing was done live on the basic track – Eddie's memory seems distinct on this – but a listen to the finished record indicates that Talmy and Eddie are mistaken in believing there were no overdubs: during the bowed solo, there are simultaneous bits of guitar-picking, an impossible feat without overdubbing (or the presence of a second guitarist)."Musically it was pretty rough," says Talmy of the bowing. "It was probably a gimmick, I suppose. It's not something that even Jimmy Page is going to release a whole album on. It was fun. It was definitely different. I don't think it had all that musical merit."

The take of 'Making Time' used for the master was chosen despite featuring a mistake by Bob. "There's a key change in the solo and after so many bars, from A it goes up to B," says Bob. "We'd done it a few times, had a couple of takes, and maybe the third or fourth time, 'Here we go again' and I went up one bar too soon. So I went up to B, realised it and then went back to the A and then went up to the B in the natural time. But when you listen to it, it's still in there. It was kept in even though it was a mistake because it sounds okay. A nice accident, again. It sounded like a little cameo for the bass to play. Bass guitars weren't really used in any way apart from keeping time and rhythm. Here's a little burst of the bass."

This incident illustrates how Talmy was refreshingly inclined to let minor errors go if the overall feel of a take was good. Lyon-Shaw: "On quite a lot of the stuff that I worked with him he used to actually go for a specific track even if someone had played a wrong note. It was all a part of the ambience. He would actually accept the track if it had a good vibe, had a good feel. I think he went for the overall sound and feeling of the track. We used to did a lot of live stuff for Shel." Bob adds of the song, "'Making Time' wouldn't sound as good in any other key. You can change the key, make it lower, but because it's an open chord thing, it just wouldn't sound like it does.

"It's like 'Satisfaction' the key of E, if you play it in another key, it's not right. There's lots of songs like that. The songs that we played, I can't think of any key that isn't like an open chord. They're all open-chord keys. They're all in like G, A, E, D, so you get that real powerchord because once you start to barre it and go up the neck with it, you lose it. Those riffy guitar things are usually in the open keys, especially those powerchords. They just don't sound right in other keys." The keys chosen for Creation songs seem to have an additional reason. In the sleeve notes he wrote for 'Lay The Ghost', the album that documented The Creation's 1993 live reunion, Kenny wrote "Eddie Phillips raised the keys of the songs, making Kenny Pickett sing harder and tougher."

Jack confirms Kenny's comments: "I remember when we sorting something out once and Eddie said, 'Look, try it in that key 'cos you've got to go for it more, there'll be a bit more energy in it' and basically what we did, we got Kenny singing up a bit higher than he was comfortable with. When he started singing he was in the crooner mood, almost...blues or soul is a different ballgame and to get that sound you had to push him up a tone or two." Eddie explains, "I would write a song in A, for instance. I could sing it in A but if Kenny was to sing that same song, he would sing it in D probably, 'cos he had a real fantastic range. I always had to jack it up a bit 'cos Ken was great at the top end and at the bottom end he wasn't so good. Let's face it, he had a great top-end voice and that's where he was."

'Try And Stop Me' wasn't in the same barrier-shattering mould as 'Making Time'. An anthemic put-down of a clinging lover, it was catchy and pleasant enough – with some nicely asthmatic vocals from Kenny – but one could imagine it being performed by the Mark Four in a way that one couldn't envisage them performing 'Making Time'. Not that it was entirely conventional: in the Sixties, such was the long and disagreeable shadow cast by drippy and over-polite balladeering and media images of chocolate-box romance that songs such as this in which narrators displayed a contemptuous attitude to a lover seemed to chime with the anti-convention *zeitgeist*. Times have moved on, of course, and nowadays such songs seem like dated machismo.

Kenny's vocals on 'Try And Stop Me' were beefed up in places by Steve Aldo, a black Liverpudlian singer who was also managed by Stratton-Smith. "He was living with Tony Stratton-Smith," recalls Bob. "He was in one of his other little bands. He was trying to launch him as a solo act. That was the idea but I think he was playing (with) The Krew or something, depped with them, and singing around. He put one or two different bits on 'Try And Stop Me'. He made it a little bit more bluesy. He was quite a soulful sort of singer. We did the vocals separate and he was there so he joined in."

At the completion of the session, Shel Talmy had good reason to be pleased with his investment. The Creation had turned in a brilliant performance and revealed themselves to be an extraordinary unit. The fulcrum of that unit was, for the American, Eddie Phillips. "I think that Eddie is probably the best unknown guitarist in the rock business" , enthuses Talmy. "It's a great shame that more people don't know who he is and what he can do." Talmy claims to not see any particular resemblance between Phillips and Pete Townshend: "They're totally different guitarists. Pete is more a lead-rhythm guitarist. He is a fabulous lead-rhythm guitarist, best one I've ever heard. As a pure lead guitarist, Eddie for me is in the same category as Jimmy Page or Clapton or whatever. He's a true lead guitarist."

The affection and respect was mutual. "I liked him," Eddie says of Talmy. "He's a nice guy. He knew what he was doing. He had a good thing in his mind of what he wanted to achieve musically – the sound of the band." Despite Talmy's comments above about what he considers the dissimilarity between Phillips and Townshend, Eddie says, "I think with us he saw a kind of mixture between The Who and possibly something else." He adds, though, "He never actually said that and I think we always tried to have a bit of a little identity of our own."

Of Pickett, Talmy says, "Kenny was a very bright guy who can write stories and all kinds of other stuff as well as lyrics. He's an extremely smart guy. And he was great on stage.. Unfortunately he and Eddie battled non-stop, which is one of the reasons all this stopped happening, but (this) gave the band an edge. They were an edgy band because of it." However,

Talmy stresses that although disharmonious, The Creation co-operated where it counted: in the studio. Talmy: "All of them – and I got on extremely well with this band, probably better than any band I ever recorded – were open to suggestion. Regardless of anything else that's ever been written about the conflicts, we were all on the same page when it came to making the music."

Of the rest of the band, Talmy says of Jack: "He was not a great drummer. He was a good drummer. He was okay. I don't think Bob Garner was a great bass player. He was okay. And to be fair, Kenny Pickett was not the greatest singer I've ever heard but he could put over a song." So The Creation's brilliance came from their chemistry? Talmy: "That is exactly the word. They were greater than the sum of their parts." Damon Lyon-Shaw may only have been 18 but he'd already witnessed enough great bands in action and put in enough man hours (18-hour days were not untypical for IBC staff) to appreciate that he was seeing something special. " I thought they were a very good band," he says. "They were very tight. Very good backing tracks, they did. Very tight group and very professional. They got everything done, the vocals and everything. There was no messing. I was just impressed by that. From the initial impact when we did the mono sessions, because it's not easy, you've got limited time to get the rhythm tracks down so it's not easy but they cranked it out and they were very professional and very good. The guitarist certainly I was impressed with."

Lyon-Shaw didn't know in advance that the guitarist would be producing a violin bow: "That was a nice surprise," he laughs. He'd certainly never seen anything so outlandish from a guitarist. Lyon-Shaw: "Definitely not. The days of Jimi Hendrix was later, playing guitar with his teeth and things. I thought that was a pretty good trick. Certainly a good sound." He does add, though, that studio staff tended to take such innovations in their stride: "In those days, it was just part of creating hopefully a hit record, whatever people did. The guitar sound changed so much from whatever people did from the early Gibson sound and the very clean sound so it didn't really affect me that much. It was just another sound of a guitar."

In a pop paper lifelines feature Eddie, when asked "Own style of music", replied "Way out Pop – (with Feeling)". It was a pretty perfect description of 'Making Time' and of most other music the Creation would record in their short lifetime. 'Making Time' was pop with an abrasive edge that marked it out from almost everything else on the contemporary music scene. Yet though very little on the pop charts in 1966 was as raw, roaring and belligerent – musically or lyrically – as 'Making Time', not a single one of the principals when questioned about the results of the recording say that they experienced any fears about it being too radical for the market.

"Being a musician, you just want to do something you're really happy with," says Jack. "At the time, we didn't think, 'Oh we're going to record something and this could be a number one'. We wanted to record something that we really liked and then hoped it would be a Number 1 or just be heard or played on the radio so did the band good." "Sometimes you do things and you don't know what you're doing," Eddie says. "It was just like the mood you're in which reflects the mood of the time. I don't know. I think we felt good about it." Did a worry that this kind of music would be just a bit too difficult for the kids to understand enter the equation at any point? Eddie: "It did a bit, but we was the sort of outfit that I think would have preferred to have been like that rather than the other way where you just make a record that sounds like everybody else's records just because you want to get a hit."

Bob says he wasn't really aware of the fact of the track's radicalism: "It appeared more that way to other people than it did to myself." Not that it would have mattered much if he had been. "I don't think we were that business-minded," Bob says. "I certainly wasn't. I wasn't thinking 'Is this going to be alright in the market place?' I was 19, 20 years of age and I just wanted to play rock'n'roll and play in a band. I didn't think 'Is this going to sell? Is this going to please anybody? Anybody going to get upset by it? In forty years time, are people going still going to be talking about it?' Because I would have said, 'This is today'. And I've just lived long enough for it to come round again."

Asked if there was anything in pop that sounded quite like 'Making Time' at that point in music history, Talmy says, "I think probably nothing apart from maybe (The Who's) 'Anyway, Anyhow, Anywhere' – I suppose there are some similarities, it's got some feedback – but nothing else." And this didn't worry him? Talmy: "It never crossed anybody's mind. We didn't think any deep psychological thoughts. All we knew was that we were doing a new kind of music where there were no restrictions and there was no history, so we made it up as we went along. Innovation was what it was all about. Hell, I think if you spoke to any other producers from the era, they'd tell you they went out of their way to do new things because that's what we were doing. Obviously the object was to get a hit but it also included doing new things because we could."

Though probably as pleased with anyone at the result of the first session, Bob does add a caveat: "The only problem I see with those early Creation ones is the actual sound we produce on the stage, it was never on any of the records. Because Shel did want a two-and-a-half minute or 2:45 pop song. It was still down to, 'You can't bend all the rules'. The best you'll hear The Creation live is the gig that we did at the Mean Fiddler (in 1993). You will hear what The Creation sounded like. That is not on any single of The Creation – that noise." However, he doesn't put this entirely down to the compromise dictated by angling for a chart placement, acknowledging that The Creation were one of those bands about whose live performances there was something that it simply wasn't possible to capture on tape. "It's one of those crying shames," Bob says. "I've heard some of the blues singers. You hear them, you think, 'If you could only just really put it down like that'. One of those impossible things: can't be done."

Kenny expressed similar sentiments in his '82 *Blitz* interview, although his reasoning was slightly different. "We got a better sound live than we did in the studio" he said, "because we played so loud. None of The Creation's records give any indication of what The Creation sounded like live. We were phenomenally loud. I've worked with Led Zeppelin, Vanilla Fudge and The Who, all of whom were supposed to be loud, but they were never as loud as us. Not even Cream were as loud as us. My old lady keeps telling me it's impaired my hearing." "Well that's their opinion," says Talmy of Bob's and Kenny's feelings on this subject. "Certainly a lot of other dissenting opinions on that. I actually think – because, of course, the two are entirely separate and different entities – that with both The Creation and The Who the studio stuff captured the energy. There's no way to capture what happens live because it's an entirely different situation but I like what I got in the studio. I think I got the energy and that's what I was after."

"I would agree with Bob that the band were better live than on record," says Gail Colson, "but that goes for lots of bands. It's very hard to capture the excitement of live on record." Perhaps it's appropriate to give the last word on the subject to June Clark. As both fan and then fan club secretary, she felt it her duty to see every Creation gig she could and therefore almost certainly witnessed more Creation live performances than anybody else. When 'Making Time' was released, Clark says she did think it managed to capture the excitement she had felt seeing the band live. "It had an electricity to it and I don't think there was any other band around that had that sound," she says. "They just didn't."

And Bob's assertion to the contrary? "I think he's wrong," says Clark. "For instance, with the song that he sings, the ballad, 'If I Stay Too Long', that recording is just how it sounds on stage. And a lot of the heavier songs, I think are well captured. Because the band is also visual I could see how he might see that that's lacking. Production-wise, I'm not a musician but I think they are captured quite well on record."

June Clark first witnessed a Creation live performance in 1966 at the age of 16 at one of the small venues they were playing in their first few months of existence. That she was a schoolgirl doesn't invalidate how impressed she was by the group. Despite her youth, she was already a veteran of more gigs than she could remember – a consequence of the fact that at the time the venues played by rock bands were accessible to all ages. "When I first started going to clubs, they never served alcohol because they were discotheques," she recalls. "That was the new thing: records. Everybody played 45s."

Clark in many ways is the absolute epitome of the baby boomer generation and the reasons why pop and rock were so central in their lives. "For somebody that wasn't there when 45s were created, they can't imagine how it was just amazing that you could go out and buy one song, with a flipside to it. That was a new thing. It was on vinyl. It was small. It wasn't like this big 78 thing. It opened up a market because it was affordable." Clark began attending gigs at the age of 13 and was something of a pop connoisseur: "I used to go and see Georgie Fame at the Flamingo on Wardour Street. I was a huge Georgie Fame fan. I don't know how I did it: go out during the week and then get up the next morning and go to school. And my mum used to let me. My mother needs a medal."

Another of her favourites was The Who, nee the High Numbers, with whom she was friendly and whose fan club she helped with. Socialising with pop stars and would-be pop stars was not difficult: "Even when (pop stars) became well known, there was still a naivety and they were still at everybody's level. They weren't like royalty, like they are now. Now they're put on pedestals. It wasn't that way and I feel it was much more fun because the average person could be there with them." For Clark, The Creation compared more than favourably with The Who. "The Who was the closest thing to The Creation's sound but they were different," she says. "The Who were more poppy but The Creation weren't. They had a harder edge. When I saw The Creation, their material was unique.

Original. Every song sounded different. Very, very creative… They really were outstanding."

There was another reason why The Creation quickly became her favourite band: "They were mods. I was a mod. That was really important back then. How you dressed. What statement you were making. You could be what you call now a nerd. You were either a mod and really cool or you were in the middle like Freddie and the Dreamers. Whereas The Who were really stylised. I was a mod so I associated with them. Mentally, they had the same tastes as you, they wanted the same things as you, therefore you listened to what they had to say. (The Creation) had modern clothing but they weren't that stylised."

In fact, Clark had seen The Creation at the tail end of their mod phase, just before their move into outfits in the purple colour with which they would forever become associated. Though they had latterly adopted the modernist appearance, they were never true aficionados of the style the way that their contemporaries the Small Faces and The Action were. The mod style was defined by short hair and very smart, sharp and stylish clothing, a kind of conservative peacockery. The half-heartedness of the Mark Four's/The Creation's adoption of it positively drips from Eddie's recollections of its origins: "We followed the mod scene from Mark Four days. It was like a crowd, especially in London and Manchester, places like that. The crowd. in the early Sixties (had) changed from being rock'n'roll style to Italian style, through the mod thing. We was just part of the crowd. We was kids – young men – and kind of went along with the period."

Bob says bluntly, "People say (we were) mods. We weren't mods. It was just following fashion." Kenny elaborated to *Ugly Things* in 1997, "I think we were more progressive than mod. We never really thought of ourselves as a leader of mod bands. In London at that time, every band was a mod band, dressed like mods, looked like mods – even the Troggs, who were really from the sticks."

Clark spoke to The Creation at that first gig. "Because you just talked to them, just like if you were at a wedding nowadays," she says. "You just went up to them." She quickly became firm friends with the band and would attend every gig she could. She also began socialising with them.

"Small, small, small," is Clark's description of those very early Creation gigs. "So small. But then so was everybody else's gig. Not well attended. Just like when I used to go and see The Who in the early days when they were the High Numbers. Forget it. Me and my girlfriend were two of the 12 in the Greenwich Town Hall when I used to go and see the High

Numbers. At first, no-one was going to see them. And then you might have people going out really just to dance. And then people started taking notice. Same with The Creation. They were playing such small places. Watford Town Hall was one of the big ones. Everybody played the same venues. It was like a circuit. If you look at a gig list for some of the small bands like The Action and the Small Faces at that time and some of the local bands, they were playing a lot of pubs. Pubs were a big thing. Some pubs would have a hall at the back of the pub and they'd play in the hall. Maybe you could get 50 in there. But there wouldn't be 50 in there, I can tell you that. And they wouldn't be going to see the band – they'd be going to dance to music."

Even as late as the last quarter of 1966 – with at least one minor chart hit behind them – The Creation found themselves playing a gig at a school in Plumstead Common, London. By coincidence, it was the school Clark's father had attended. "Right round the corner from where I lived," recalls Clark. "I couldn't believe it when Bob told me he was playing this gig. They did the gig there and they did their whole stage act and they painted the canvas. It was just all local kids from Plumstead Common in the local school hall. But that was like a lot of gigs they did in these tiny little places, never really crowds of people. Usually full of mods, because that's what they'd attract. And everybody would dance."

For Clark, Eddie and Kenny were the best elements of The Creation's stage performances. "He was like a very, very subdued Pete Townshend," she says of Eddie. "He was skinny like Pete and really cool. Apart from excellent guitar playing, he had the complete image and was really good on stage." She felt that off-stage Kenny had a self-confidence that would overspill into egotism but that this self-confidence was exactly what was needed for a frontman. Though she was closest to Bob in the band, Clark saw no great stage presence about him. Instead, he reminded her of one of her old friends from The Who: "Bob used to just stand there. In fact, thinking of it, he was just like John Entwistle. Just like him. Never smiled."

The weakest presence on stage, she felt, was the drummer. "Jack was back there not doing anything," she says. "Not twirling his drum sticks, not throwing them up in the air, nothing. Just playing the old drums and looking bored. Jack always looked bored. Didn't even look like he was interested in it. Really weird image for this band. That's why I was glad when Jack left. Just because I (didn't) think he did anything positive for them image-wise. Just a pleasant, inoffensive, nothing sort of person."

Despite the 'small, small, smallness' of so many of their early gigs, The Creation did actually manage to rack up a prestigious concert appearance before the release of their first record. On 30 May '66, The Creation were one of a considerable number of bands on the bill at a pop festival at Sincil Bank, the stadium of Lincoln City Football Club. The Kinks and The Who were joint headliners. This event lasted from midday until approximately 10:45pm. The rest of the acts appearing that day (at least according to the programme: events such as this being subject to last-minute bill-tweaking) were The Brother-hud, The Children, The Dimples, Georgie Fame and the Blue Flames, the Small Faces, the Barron Knights, Crispian St Peters, Screamin' Lord Sutch, Dave Dee, Dozy, Beaky, Mick and Tich, Ray Northrop, The Ivy League, The Koobas, She Trinity, The Yardbirds and The Alan Price Set. BBC DJs Jimmy Savile and Keith Fordyce acted as comperes.

"The dressing rooms was the changing rooms," Jack recalls. "Big field. The place was packed. We had a great crowd in and I thought The Who that night were absolutely brilliant. Jimmy Savile was chatting to us in the dressing room." "Brilliant day in the sunshine," says Bob. "They built a fence from the dressing room into the centre of the pitch and there was a square area and everybody was stood on the pitch and you had to look through the fence to see the acts." This was one of the biggest crowds to which The Creation ever played. Bob: "It was massive, absolutely massive. I think we all got one side of our face sunburnt because of the way the sun was shining but it was quite a gig." Jack recalls The Creation taking the chance to catch up with The Who, who were now chart regulars. Jack: "We all had a chat. I used to like Keith Moon. He was a good lad. We were all London lads really and we'd played together before down at Burton's down at Uxbridge so we knew each other a bit." No doubt their mutual link in the form of Shel Talmy also came up.

Sometime before the June '66 release of 'Making Time', The Creation jettisoned their *faux* mod outfits and adopted a uniform: a formal, even military-looking shirt and trousers set in a thoroughly informal purple colour. The epaulettes of the shirts ran down over the shoulder to the upper arm. It was a sort of halfway house between the suited-and-booted styles sported by pop groups in 1963 and 1964 and the unalloyed outrageousness which 1967's Summer Of Love would usher in. That the purple uniform has become merged in The Creation's fans' minds with the quote with which Eddie came up to describe the band's music – "Red with purple flashes" – is appropriate from Jack's point of view because according to his recollection the origin of that quote is intertwined with the origin of the purple uniforms. Jack: "We were sitting round a table once with Stratton-Smith and he was looking for clues and that and he said, 'If you had a favourite colour, what would it be? Anything'll do, no matter how wild or whatever'. So Eddie come up with the phrase, 'Red with purple flashes'. So we based our clothes on the purple bit. The quote came first. I can remember Stratton-Smith actually asking about it. "

Jack is in a minority among the surviving original Creation members in recalling that the phrase "red with purple flashes" and the purple uniforms were jointly generated. Bob recollects the group being interviewed by a reporter from a newspaper at Shel Talmy's offices. Asked by the newspaperman what psychedelic meant, the band were unable to provide an answer. Asked then how they would describe the music, Eddie quipped "purple with red flashes" (this way round according to Bob's recollection.) Eddie – who can't remember whether the quote was "purple with red flashes" or vice versa – recalls, "I've got to say it was just something I said. We was having an interview with an American journalist who was talking about psychedelic and he said, 'If you had to say what your music was in colours, what would it be?' and I just said it." Was he being sincere or facetious? "I can't honestly remember. It must have been in my mind because the psychedelic thing, a lot of it was about colours."

Interestingly, both Bob's and Eddie's recollection points toward a *Sunday Times* Atticus column for which the band were interviewed. The column certainly addressed the subject of psychedelia but can't have been the source of the quote because it didn't appear until that October. The band's entrée 'Making Time' was accompanied by an advertisement that carried the quote "Red with purple flashes", attributed to Eddie but not sourced, in June '66. Says Talmy of Eddie's quote, "He just came up with (that) by himself. He came up with same great lyrics and great ideas." Was it a good description of the music he found himself producing when in the studio with The Creation? "On reflection, absolutely." At some point during The Creation's original incarnation, Eddie began writing a song with the title 'Red With Purple Flashes', although he didn't finish it for more than 35 years.

Eddie does remember Stratton-Smith as being the instigator of the purple look: "He had an image in his mind." It was an era when image was fundamentally important, as the unfortunate Tony Cook had found out. "It did give you a visual identity which I suppose was good," says Eddie of the new look. "In the Sixties it was a different world."

Jack recalls the manager "sending us down to a tailor, a little Jewish guy. He got our trousers going and our shirts with the epaulettes and the purple stuff and basically sorted out that early image we had." "I think we were going along with part of the fashion of the day," says Bob. "The kids in the street were buying army and navy jackets and such. What happened was, with those shirts, we went to Carnaby Street and we had those purple shirts made. They were made to suit and the epaulette thing came up. 'Well we want epaulettes on the top' and I can't honestly say who said it but (someone said) 'Could we have one coming down the side as well over a pocket'? 'Yeah you can do that, that's not a problem.' That's how that happened: more of an accident rather than somebody putting it on paper and saying, 'This is how the look is gonna be'."

Button-down shirt collars, wide white belts and purple trousers completed the outfit. Bob: "If you look at those photos, they were like hipster trousers but instead of us having denim we had mohair trousers. I remember they were really nice material. They didn't last long. Next record, we bought white jackets. When I saw the Mark Four, they had these trousers that were like one white leg and one black. I remember it so it must have been good. It was like a gimmicky thing. So it followed from there." June Clark approved of the new image. "They were doing their own creative fashion designs on stage and there's only so long you can wear something and then get bored with it. It did have a good impact on stage when they wore the same outfits, the same colour shirts and had a certain look. It did look good because nobody was doing that. It's a really bold colour. It was really a colour that the hippies wore. 'Cos mods were prior hippies. It was bordering hippie stage and all that psychedelic stuff and that's when everyone was using strong colours."

Despite his previous comments, Bob is not completely sure that this, or any Creation image, was a good thing. "I think one of the biggest problems with the band was we never looked like what we sounded like," he says. "The image, the way we looked, it's like trying to imagine The Beatles dressed in the Beatle suits and listening to 'Sgt Pepper'. That wouldn't fit. Now the noise that we were making and we were going out all dressed the same.

"We never had the right image for the music. I think we were young fellas all trying to be the best looking fella in the world. If somebody had choreographed it and said, 'Listen, why don't you just go a bit freaky?' I don't think any of us instinctively had that in us, to be able to dress down or dress towards something. With that kind of music, we should have been more outrageous.. Somebody should have said, 'Look, you've got to dress more outrageous, let your hair grow even longer', or whatever. We weren't a pop band but they were trying to make three-minute pop songs and I suppose that was a bit of a tug-of-war."

Bob doesn't limit his misgivings about The Creation's lack of outrageousness merely to dress. He laments the fact that none of The Creation, himself included, were sufficiently outlandish characters in the mould of The Kinks' Dave Davies, with whom he recalls a night out drinking could suddenly deteriorate – upon an explosion from the Kinks' lead guitarist – into a panicked feeling that it would be wise to leave the premises immediately. "We didn't do anything outrageous to suit what the image of the music was," Bob says. "I just read a little caption today on Noel Gallagher. Why am I reading it? Because I know he's going to say absolutely something outrageous: like, 'Everybody over the age of 30 is a load of crap. John Lennon's music's crap after he was 30.' He's saying that in the paper. I don't agree with him but I've read it and the fella's got his picture in the paper because he's said it. There's the bad side of publicity – you work on that one – or the Cliff Richard goody-goody and we were neither one thing or the other.

"I don't think any of us was mad enough to put a television through a window. I don't think any of us had that outrageous thing within us. When I first saw John Lennon, he had that edge on him, even then. He wasn't famous – I'm talking about before 'Love Me Do' – and yet he made me almost uncomfortable by his presence. And so did the others, but him more than the others. And I don't think any of us had that killer sort of instinct. If you just contrive – 'We've got to act bad when we get in here' – that doesn't happen either."

Making Time' b/w 'Try And Stop Me' was released in Britain in June 1966 as Planet PLF 116. It appeared in America in the same month, as Planet's US entrée.

The *Record Mirror* issue dated 18 June included a small feature on the record with quotes from Talmy. It also carried an advertisement for the single featuring a piece of a work by Keith Grant, a painter with whom Stratton-Smith had made a deal to use his artwork for the promotion of the band. The advert boasted a panel reading "'Our music is red with purple flashes' – Eddie Phillips, lead guitar" . That same issue carried the paper's verdict on the disc. Predicting it would be a Top 50 smash, it declared "Interestingly novel sound created by violin bow on lead guitar. Guitar figures are exceptional. Watch this one closely – it's good." A nice little plug to be sure – and no doubt assisted by Stratton-Smith's friendly relationship with the paper's scribe, Bill Harry – but it was as nothing compared to the general media blitz that The Creation camp were successful in arranging.

It's difficult to think of an unknown group of that period receiving the sort of exposure that The Creation did for 'Making Time'. In the first instance, the disc received a lot of airplay. "At that time you had Radio Caroline, Radio London, both pirate stations," says Eddie. "They were playing it and they were good radio stations because they would play songs that the BBC wouldn't." Then there was the television slots. Jack: "Stratton-Smith was brilliant on 'Making Time' because The Creation was an unknown band and he got us about five or six TVs in England and one in France and one in Germany. All on the first record. This was down to Stratton-Smith because he had a wonderful chat. We did *'Ready Steady Go!'* twice, I think."

Ready, Steady, Go! – or *RSG!* – was almost the TV equivalent of the pirate stations. Though not broadcast illegally, like the pirates it had a slightly hipper audience of kids and young adults who were prepared to grow up alongside a patently developing rock medium. Bob recalls that the band had to pass "a sort of gig-cum-audition" at London's Marquee club in order to get the *RSG!* gig. Because there was an element of miming, the band re-visited the backing track of 'Making Time' at the programme's studios. Jack: "Shel came and sat in the box to make sure we got it right." When it came to the live broadcast, Kenny was the only band member making a sound, or at last one that was broadcast. Jack: "We done the vocals live. And when we did the TV show, they played our backing track and we mimed to that. It had the feedback and stuff and it actually come across pretty good. We were well pleased with it. 'Cos Shel actually brought the bass up a bit. If you notice with a lot of TV things in them days, they used to sound a bit thin and tinny but Shel was in the box and he made sure the bass came up and we had a really good, full sound."

The leading act on the show that week was Little Richard, much to the delight of Eddie who promptly secured his autograph on the back of his Gibson. Like The Creation, Richard was singing live but against a pre-recorded backing track. "When he went to the piano, he couldn't get any sound out of the piano," remembers Bob. "'Cos I watched every move. (He said), 'Hang on, what's going on here?' Banged the keys and nothing happened. But then he looked under the (lid) – it was a grand piano – and blankets lay across the strings to deaden the sound. They just wanted to mime. He said, 'I'm not having that', took the blankets away and played.

"We did do a song with him at the end of the show – I think it was 'Long Tall Sally'. He sang three-quarters through the tune and then everybody that was on the show joined him singing 'We're going to have some fun tonight'." Eddie: "We later toured with Little Richard on one of these UK tours he did. I think we closed the first half. Great. What a performer." The support slot Eddie mentions were a string of gigs immediately after the *RSG!* appearance. Bob: "I think it was about five. I know we did Newcastle, Birmingham, places like that. We definitely did about five gigs with him." Did Bob take the opportunity to speak to Little Richard? Bob: "Yeah. He was my idol. All the silly questions that a young lad would ask."

Eddie loaned the guitar bearing the American's signature to Kenny in the Seventies. When Kenny's son cracked the instrument's neck, Pickett offered £100 to the guitarist in exchange for it, a sum Phillips accepted because he was strapped for cash at the time. The guitar is now whereabouts unknown.

"You really thought that that was going to do something for them," says Clark of the *RSG!* appearance. "Because if you were on *Top Of The Pops, Ready Steady Go!* or any show on television then, it was an amazing thing. You felt like you were almost there. If you were on *Ready Steady Go!*, you'd just made it. That was the coolest thing to be on. You couldn't get any better."

"We all thought it was going to go number one because everybody who heard it, although it was a bit weird for the time, seemed to like it," says Jack. "We thought we had a real chance." But 'Making Time' – for all its airplay and for all the attention-grabbing TV appearances of a purple clad ensemble with a violin bow-wielding guitarist – did not become a hit. At this point in time, there were several different charts in Britain, with the four main ones being those compiled by the music papers *New Musical Express* (now more commonly referred to as the *NME*), *Melody Maker, Disc* and *Record Retailer* (whose chart was also printed in *Record Mirror*).

The chart compiled by the *New Musical Express* was probably considered the most authoritative, partly because it was the longest-standing and because the *NME* had the highest circulation of any music paper. (The BBC's weekly *Top Of The Pops* chart show used an aggregate from the *NME, Disc, Record Retailer/Record Mirror* and *Melody Maker* to determine their chart.) 'Making Time' reached Number 49 in *Record Retailer/Record Mirror* and number 32 in *Melody Maker.*

For those in The Creation camp, there are two different reasons for the record's failure to go higher, neither of them to do with lack of public demand. For his part, Talmy insists that 'Making Time' – and every other record on the Planet label – was deliberately sabotaged by the label's distributor, Philips. The 18 June issue of *Record Mirror* with a review of 'Making Time' and an advertisement for it, also carried a mini-feature by David Griffiths that indicated problems simmering below Planet's surface. The piece had no headline but, beneath a picture of the band in their purple outfits in which Eddie is applying his bow to his Gibson were the words "The Creation – their hit produced by the man who was responsible for hits by the Kinks and the Who" . The article read:

"If The Creation are going to create a big impact on the pop scene, they've got a few difficulties to overcome: their first record is on a newish, small company label; the group craze is on the wane; the boys have been working together only nine months and they've only just changed their name to The Creation. In their favour: they are good-looking fellows and the 'A' side of their disc, written by two of the group, is an exciting, constantly building number.

"Also, Shel Talmy, who recorded them for his Planet label, is wildly enthusiastic. 'They came to me with this song, 'Making Time', and I immediately thought it was a winner,' said Shel. 'We had an easy, relaxed recording session with the four boys – guitar, bass, drums and lead singer. Everything went extremely well. Sure, it's becoming more and more difficult as groups are fading, but despite the trend, I think this disc will stand on its merits and – though I hate making predictions – 'Making Time' should provide Planet with its first hit.'"

All very bland so far, but Talmy was then quoted as saying something that was to prove a bad portent. "As usual with a new label we've had our problems of ensuring that the public can get to buy the records but we are being well distributed by Philips. I did my 'nasty American' bit with them – the shout-up routine I reserve for special occasions – and I'm sure Planet is getting excellent distribution. Incidentally, it's been a great help that Philips themselves have lately got very hot with their own productions – the Walkers, Dusty, Mindbenders, Spencer Davis and so on." If Talmy was convinced Planet was receiving "excellent distribution" , why did he say that he'd had to shout at Philips about his discs not making their way to the shops?

Today, Talmy says, "You're talking about a multi-billion pound company and a part of a huge conglomerate. I don't suppose they gave a shit. They had some political motives for not wanting to have an independent label. I wanted to have an independent label so they pacified me by giving one but they didn't want me to succeed. I had done some work for them. They were the ones who made the most noise about, 'Oh yes, we'd love to have your label and distribute it for you', which turned out to be a lot of crap. To this day, I don't know the reasons why."

Certain things said by band members seem to support Talmy's assertions. Eddie: "From our end of it, we'd go out and play this song on a Saturday night to the kids, who loved it. We couldn't figure out why nationwide it wasn't a success because everywhere we'd go it went down really good. We felt, 'Why don't they buy it?'"

Bob: "I didn't hear anything but my experience now I would say that's about right. Now whether Philips did it with intention I don't know, or whether it was misguided from Planet's end, I do not know. I'm not saying that the songs would have made it or the group would have made it big but certainly the records didn't stand a chance. We did enough television on 'Making Time' and 'Painter Man' for it certainly to stand a chance but (they weren't) on the shelves. People were saying, 'We would buy it if we could buy it' but they couldn't. That's where it went wrong as far as the records were concerned."

June Clark is not so sure. "I don't remember that at the time," she says. "Their records now from back then are very, very hard to find…but at the time I don't remember any of the fans saying, 'Can't get the record'. Everybody I knew was buying it. But you've got to remember: look at the (small) size of the fan club. The people interested. It's very strange that nobody was reacting to this band. I don't know why." However, Jack says that there is another reason for the record's failure to climb into the charts' upper echelons (although it is one that is not necessarily inconsistent with the theory of Philips sabotaging the disc).

Jack says that with 'Making Time' lodged in the lower reaches of at least one of the charts, Stratton-Smith was approached by a character when out drinking with an offer that The Creation's manager found attractive. Jack: (He said) 'I got a list here of all these shops that are returning to the *NME*. Now if you go around these shops and buy three or four records in each, those returns going back, that'll push your record on'. So Tony gives him a couple of hundred quid for the list and arranges some guy to go out and buy records all around the country."

Bob was vaguely aware of what was going on. "There was a fella involved in that, somebody called King," he says. "He was one of the payees. There were certain people he could pay and he gave them, I dunno, twenty quid or something to buy records in a certain shop and he would then send some money to Birmingham. Something like that and I remember this guy knocking about and his surname – whether it was his real name or not I don't know – (was) King. It wasn't Jonathan King. I just remember that."

Jack's recollection is that Stratton-Smith then undid his 'good' work. "The trouble was that Tony did like a drink and was bragging about how he hyped the song up the charts," says the drummer. "A few people heard it down (industry nightclub) the Cromwellian and the word got back to Maurice Kinn. He used to own the *New Musical Express* and he was really pissed off because it made his charts look phoney." It was feared by the Creation camp that Kinn was intending to expose the matter in his paper. This disaster was averted by the intervention of Arthur Howes.

Though more than one member of The Creation is on the record as not thinking much of his promotional capabilities, on this occasion the mere fact of having Howes as their agent quite possibly saved their career. An agreement was come to by Howes and Kinn. Jack: "(Howes) said, 'Listen, the lads knew nothing about it and they're only young guys and you're going to wreck their careers. So let's just back off. Let's drop the record quietly out of the charts and leave it at that'. So Maurice Kinn thought about it, thought about how much advertising Arthur did in his paper, and calmed down and agreed to do it."

'Making Time' in fact did not appear in the *NME* chart at all (although the paper only published a Top 30). "That was the reason," insists Jack. "It was deliberately dropped from the charts because Stratters had been caught fiddling it." "Well that's news to me," says Talmy. "I certainly don't know about it. I had somebody promoting it from Planet and he went out and promoted it. I don't remember it at all. If it happened, it certainly happened without my knowledge. But in any event, at the time virtually everybody was hyping records so it was not that big a deal – and I don't think it would have meant a damn thing if *NME* had 'blown his cover'."

Stratton-Smith decided to come clean after he ceased being the Creation's manager. In April 1967, the ex-journalist returned to his old trade for a one-off article for the Sunday newspaper *News Of The World*. Under a heading of "Why I Fixed The Pop Charts", Stratton-Smith explained that his chart-rigging had started earlier on in '66 with a record by Beryl Marsden, on whom he was initially losing between £50 and £100 a week. "At this point I received an offer from a man known to my office by a nickname," Stratton-Smith wrote. "He was a contact for one of the musical papers – whose other staff, I hasten to add, were quite unaware of his crooked activities. He told me that for between £100 and £150 a week a record could be introduced into the Top 50 and pushed week by week until it reached the Top 30. He spoke of other well-known 'clients'."

The unnamed fixer delivered, although Stratton-Smith admitted "suspicion had fallen upon him" . He went on, "My last dealings with him were when The Creation's record 'Making Time' was released. It showed Number 49 in one of the charts and sales were up again the following week. Then, to my astonishment, it dropped out of the chart and I discovered that a 'fix' was suspected because sales were restricted mostly to the London area. I was under suspicion for a 'hype' when it didn't exist. The fixer undertook to maintain the disc around the 40 mark for three weeks for a fee of £270, paid in advance. I gave him the money, ruefully, I admit, because I was virtually having to pay for the record to be maintained in its true position. But the record did not recover its placing."

Though this account differs from Jack's, it does support the claim that attempted rigging of some sort was going on, as does the recollection of, Stratton-Smith's right-hand woman Gail Colson, who says – without prompting – that she remembers 'Making Time' being bought into the charts. "In those days it was quite easy," she says. "You just had to pay the guy who compiled the charts in the newspapers. *Record Mirror* was the easiest with the *NME* next."

Though 'Making Time' didn't achieve the chart success its qualities merited, a trip to Germany – or West Germany as it was in those Berlin Wall days – to promote the record began to pave the way to the group achieving significant success there. The promotional visit was made in mid-May '66. 'Making Time' – issued on Hit-Ton (a subsidiary of Deutsche Vogue) – reached Number 10 in one of the country's music paper-charts, although it didn't register in the country's official listing. Stratton-Smith made sure that The Creation's continental visit received some exposure in the domestic press. The 23 July issue of *Melody Maker* (which also carried a small ad for 'Making Time') announced under the headline Creation Offers: "As a result of a successful TV show in Germany, last month, The Creation have received offers to visit Germany, Holland and Sweden. They will make a two-week tour in September."

In that very same July week, the Bill Harry Up North column in *Record Mirror* featured a summary of a very minor scandal involving The Creation's name. It had originated with another attempt by Stratton-Smith to acquire his charges some valuable publicity. Recalls Bob, "He wrote to every bishop, archbishop – you name it – around to say that this group was going to be called The Creation and they were going to be a little bit outrageous towards that name and had you any objections? I think two of them fell for it and wrote in. So straight away, he got an angle to put it in the paper. One thing Stratton-Smith did know about was the media, newspapers anyway."

In Sixties Britain – already a post-Christian society but with many in its elderly establishment steeped in religious doctrine – the idea that a group of mop-topped, outlandishly dressed purveyors of amplified electric music could boast a sobriquet which alluded to the first book of the Holy Bible could cause a certain amount of feather-fluttering. However, the outrage was muted, probably partly because the link was too nebulous – The Creation could just as easily mean the act of making art – but also because the old order was so clearly dying on its feet in a society where ostentatious rejection of long-held values was such an everyday public occurrence.

There is even a hint of self-conscious trendiness on the part of those who knew themselves to be considered fogies in some of the reactions reported in Bill Harry's column: "After Lord Hill of Luton, chairman of ITA (Independent Television Authority, watchdog of commercial TV in the UK), complained that The Creation's name could "possibly offend Christians" Tony Stratton-Smith approached Cardinal Heenan, The Archbishop Of Canterbury, Canon Collins and Catholic MP Norman St. John Stevas for their opinions. They all said the name couldn't possibly be construed as being blasphemous – and the *Catholic Herald* printed a story and pictures to that effect."

It was perhaps this desire to stir up a scandal that had motivated Stratton-Smith to approach Keith Grant with a view to incorporating his biblical painting 'The Creation' into the band's visual image. Grant was a 36-year-old artist who, though not a pop art practitioner, was considered to be a member of the new school in art. He had actually rendered several variations of 'The Creation', the first in 1965. "It was an illustration of the Creation myth, of course," explains Grant, "and had Adam and Eve in it and the serpent, but all the imagery really apart from the those classical bits came from the north of Norway and Iceland which I was visiting."

The first version of the artwork had been a charcoal drawing on paper with paint and ink but the one that had caught Stratton-Smith's eye was a circular colour oil painting around five-feet-eight in diameter. The deal involved part of the painting being used in an advertisement for the band's first record and the band using a portion of the painting on Jack's bass drum. Grant had not heard of The Creation before. "I wasn't a devotee of it," he says of pop, "but I knew about groups like the Rolling Stones obviously and I quite liked some of it. I never went to pop concerts." He doesn't think he saw the band in concert but adds, "I'm sure I went to rehearsal."

Grant was not particularly worried that the use of the painting might demean his craft: "No, not at all. But I do make a difference between what I call art as entertainment and amusement art and art which has got an aesthetic element which takes it not beyond that but makes it different from entertainment art. But entertainment art's always been very interesting to me." Jack was certainly impressed with the painting and Grant's efforts. "It was a very large circular painting and basically it was based on the biblical creation, The Creation of Man," he says. "And from the centre, everything was coming out: there was birds and animals and people. It was all coming out the centre of this painting.

"What Stratton did, he rung him up and said, 'We'd like to take a piece of that painting and use it on stage'. I took my bass drum skin round and he painted a piece of the painting and painted onto my bass drum and it was like a piece of 'The Creation' painting was on the drum there every night we went on stage. Quite good actually. I was quite happy with it." The Creation's association with Grant is the reason for music-paper reports in '66 that the band were set to play background music on a BBC-TV *Monitor* programme about British painters.

"I appeared on *Monitor*," Grant recalls, "and Huw Wheldon was the man who ran it. He's dead now but he became director-general of the BBC. I did quite a long interview with some other artists. It was to do with the young contemporaries I think and it probably was my suggestion that Creation provided the music. It was discussed most certainly and I remember discussing it with a man called Tony Rowland, who was making quite a lot of art films." This suggestion seems not to have been followed up: none of The Creation can remember their music being used on the programme's soundtrack and the press reports that did appear seem to be a matter of Stratton-Smith spinning a mooted arrangement into a done deal.

Grant got a peculiar mention in the Bill Harry Up North column in the *Record Mirror* of 20 August 1966. It read: "Will uncle Tony Stratton-Smith (affectionately known as Stratters) chastise The Creation? They deserve it, it seems. According to a reliable report from a publicist the group have been appearing onstage and displaying the expensive painting 'Creation' as a backcloth. 'Creation' is the Keith Grant painting that was used in the group's recent advertising campaign. It belongs to Dirk Bogarde and is insured for £500. One night recently at Great Yarmouth, Kenny Lee (sic) brought a huge piece of paper onstage and used an airbrush to create an abstract painting whilst the group were performing.

"He ripped it up and threw it to the audience. The girls went frantic, which perhaps explains why Eddie Phillips crunched up his violin bow and threw that to the mob of screaming girls. Further freneticism occurred and Eddie obviously overcome with passion commenced to rip up 'Creation' and throw it in the same direction as the other unfortunate mutilated objects. Hence even the insurance coverage becomes useless. Hence the little chat that uncle Stratters must have with The Creation in the near future."

The whole story seems to be a fabrication. Grant says that the British screen actor Dirk Bogarde never owned the painting and says of the alleged destruction of the backcloth, "It must have been a facsimile of it. They didn't destroy the original because it's in France now in somebody's house." Creation members themselves can't recall the Creation ever using a backcloth featuring the painting.

Though that *Record Mirror* piece was a tall tale, it was certainly not untrue that Keith Grant was unhappy with Tony Stratton-Smith. "I had to threaten legal action against him because they didn't pay me," Grant recalls. "He sent me a letter to say 'Bankruptcy wouldn't suit either of us' but of course I wasn't intending to go bankrupt. And I don't know how it ended but it ended amicably. I don't know whether I ever got the money. I know it was in the £200 bracket (which) at that time was quite a lot of money. I was a member of an organisation that protected artists' rights and they wrote to Stratton-Smith. I think he settled in some way."

Though things ended well for Grant, Stratton-Smith's initial unwillingness – or, more likely, inability – to pay him was a harbinger of problems that would ultimately sever the link between Stratton-Smith and The Creation.

In late July 1966, Dave Preston was sitting in the Giaconda in Denmark Street, London, waiting for fortune to smile on him. A drummer and native of Liverpool, Preston had come down to London from his home town following the chaotic dissolution of his previous band, The Kinsleys, of whom Bob Garner had briefly been a member.

The Kinsleys had been the ensemble formed by Billy Kinsley upon leaving the Merseybeats. However, Kinsley decided to return to his former band in late 1964. The Kinsleys decided to carry on, rather bizarrely retaining the name of their departed leader. Preston took them over to fulfil a residency at the Star Club in Germany. Like so many Sixties musicians who cut their chops at that venue (and in Germany in general), Preston credits it with teaching him much about technique. "I learnt to play left-handed then 'cos mainly when I play, I always sing," he says. "I used to have the mic between me legs so I used to play the hi-hat left-handed. I did learn a hell of a lot there myself. Even the manager of the Star Club said to me, 'You should be on your own, really'."

The Star Club's manager was not so impressed by Preston's colleagues: "Unfortunately they were young fellas and didn't take too well to it really. I think the oldest was about 17. It was a bloody nightmare. 'cos these kids, they were young, they were a waste of time really. They were going out and getting drunk and fighting and we got the sack from the Star Club. So when we got back I just said, 'I've had enough of Liverpool, that's it'. That was the reason I packed up and came to London."

Once in the capital, Preston was given a berth by some friends who resided in Victoria. Knowing he was looking for work, they suggested he make himself visible at the Giaconda, a cafe in Denmark Street. London's Tin Pan Alley, Denmark Street was such a throbbing hive of musical activity – boasting several musical instrument shops, at least one recording studio and within spitting distance of several others – that it effected the kind of scenario that would have been considered unlikely if it were to be depicted in a motion picture: engineers popping their heads round the doors of the Giaconda to enquire if there were any keyboardists in the house and, if so, would they be interested in playing on a session in progress around the corner was a commonplace event. As if to prove the fairytale qualities of the area, Preston's second day of nursing cups of tea in the Giaconda found him looking at a familiar musician's face.

Bob Garner's presence that day was probably due to the fact that Tony Stratton-Smith's office was located at number 23 Denmark Street. (Arthur Howes, meanwhile, was five minutes' walk away at 29-31 Regent Street, while Project Publicity – employed by Planet to promote The Creation's records – was also a stone's throw away in Dean Street; they would shortly move to the still nearby Gerrard Street.) "He was saying, 'This band I'm with, they've got a record in the hit parade'," recalls Preston of his meeting with Bob. "I think it was, 34, 35 at the time. 'Making Time' it was called. And I said, 'Oh, great. Pleased for you'.

"They'd just come back from Germany. They'd been promoting 'Making Time' or something. They'd been doing some sort of TV, just miming to it, no live gigs or nothing. He said, 'But the drummer's weak. Not very good'. He asked me what I was doing and I said, 'nothing at the moment'." A chain of events was being set in motion that would lead to Jack Jones being sacked by the band of which he was the longest-standing member. When Bob introduced Preston to Kenny, the two fast became mates. "We hung around quite a lot then," says Preston. "We used to drink quite a lot together and womanise together. I think Kenny said to Tony Stratton-Smith, 'Look, we want this guy in and Jack out'."

Jack sensed something was in the air. "Bob had a friend up in Liverpool and he was trying to get him in the band," he says. "Dave Preston. You imagine: every time you go to a gig, this guy's hovering in the wings." Says Bob of the plans being hatched by Kenny, "I've been blamed for that but all I did was introduce the two in a pub. Dave was a good laugh, always larking about, and Kenny fell for that really.

"To be truthful with you, I don't think Kenny had heard Dave Preston play. It was more like Kenny found something in Dave because Kenny is a very regular sort of guy. He didn't take too many chances, although he would have liked to have done; he had his feet on the ground. Dave was just the opposite, or appeared to be, because he was from Liverpool. He wasn't with a band, he was scallying round and pinching drinks and things like that...I could see the attraction."

Preston says it was Kenny Pickett who was behind the scheme to oust Jack from The Creation's drum stool: "It was Kenny who got me in. Bob approached me because we knew one another and he's obviously said to Kenny, 'Oh this guy, he's great' – whatever he said – and then Kenny approached me. He said, 'Would you be interested in having a rehearsal with us?' I said I felt a bit lousy because I just don't like that sort of thing. I'd hate anyone to do it to me. It's not nice for someone to not actually say to your face 'Well, look we've got this other fella and blah blah blah' – but to do it all behind their back..."

Jack has a different perspective on the situation: "I think Bob manipulated Kenny because you can push Kenny any way you wanted, he was so desperate for success. I think Bob was really trying to row the band in so he could be the singer. He had ambitions that way. Me and Eddie were in one camp and Bob and Kenny were in the other. A bit of how's-your-father going on. I think what it was: me and Bob, because he comes from Liverpool – which is a totally different style of music – and I come from London, we never really got on as a bass player and as a drummer. Me and Eddie used to get on okay. Couple of Londoners, I dunno. Kenny was always too impatient. He wanted to be a star tomorrow. He couldn't think like, 'Six months time, man'. And I think Bob was basically angling for himself. He saw himself as the star instead of the band. That's the way I always read it."

Eddie can't remember who the ringleader was but his gut instinct is that it was Kenny who was behind the coup. "He was unsettled in his outlook on people," he says. "My overall opinion of Kenny was that he was a nice guy and I did like him a lot – in fact I've missed him a lot – but he would have this thing where he'd get a bee in his bonnet about somebody or something and it was hard for him to shake it off. That's how the thing with Jack might have come about."

Whether it was Kenny or Bob or both behind the drum-related skulduggery, Kenny, Bob and Eddie were unanimous in agreeing that they wanted to hear Preston in action. Despite his moral qualms, Preston agreed to audition. "That's where I met Tony Stratton-Smith," the Scouser recalls, "and it all took off from there. It was only a few days (later). They set it up. I think it was Chislehurst or somewhere out in the sticks. They didn't want Jack to find out it was happening."

In his 1982 Interview with *Blitz* Magazine, Kenny was scathing about the quality of Jack's drumming. "Jack Jones was awful!" he said. "He was the worst drummer in the world! That's probably why we were so loud, to drown him out! Jack was a nice bloke, but a bad, bad drummer."

A listen to any Creation recording reveals no particular deficiency in Jack Jones' technique. Shel Talmy, who worked with Keith Moon – considered by many the greatest rock drummer of all time – says, "I actually wasn't as unhappy about him as they were. I thought Jack was okay. He was not Keith Moon but then again who was?" Meanwhile, Joe Foster, producer of The Creation's 1996 comeback album, has this to say of Jack: "Basically, a big part of the sound is Jack. We did routine tracks where Jack was sort of playing bits on the piano to show where the changes were and things and Tony (Barber) would just play 4/4 on the drums – and Tony's a pretty good drummer – but it just sounds nothing like The Creation. It just sounded completely rubbish. And Tony would go, 'Look, Jack, I think you better do this and I'll play the chords'. Jack would get behind the drums and it was The Creation. I think Jack is a really underestimated part of that sound. Once you got Jack playing, it's halfway there."

So why the sudden dissatisfaction among The Creation with their drummer's playing and their willingness to consider jettisoning a long-standing colleague? Both Eddie and Bob seem almost sheepish when asked about this now. "I wasn't so much dissatisfied," says Bob. "My opinion now is that it was probably the best for The Creation but for me as a strict tempo drummer it perhaps wasn't the best thing in the world, but that's what made The Creation. The way he played was all a part and parcel of The Creation thing.

"You must remember," he adds, "I'd only been in the band five minutes and I was just going along with things because these three people knew each for a good number of years and I really didn't stick my nose in too much really. I just said, 'Okay, if that's what you want, that's what you want'." Eddie offers, "I think we was beginning to notice around us drummers were quite powerful and Jack was probably never a powerful drummer but he was quite a clever drummer. I think we probably looked around and heard powerful drummers and probably thought it would be nice to have that kind of power pushing us along."

Of his audition, Preston recalls "I think we did 'Making Time' because I think this television was getting lined up, the *Rolf Harris Show*. We rehearsed for about half-an-hour or an hour or something." Preston describes his drumming style at that juncture as "Heavy. Very heavy...sort of like John Bonham, Keith Moon. Very busy, heavy, loud, active." He recalls The Creation being impressed by what they heard. "As soon as we started rehearsing, these fellas were blown away," says Preston. "They were all pleased with me." Preston was immediately offered the job – or, at least, a job.

It's interesting to note that at the time, not only did Jack not get the impression that he had been permanently sacked as such but it was not reported as that in the press. Jack himself talks of the period he was not in the band in these terms: "(Bob and I) had different opinions about things so in the end, I said to Eddie, 'I'm getting a bit fed up with this'. So Eddie said, 'Well leave things to me. I'll see what I can sort out with Stratters'. Anyway, I left the band for about two weeks and then I got a phone call saying, 'Jack, we've settled all the things, we'd like you to come back and put the original band in place again.' So I said, 'What's going to happen? Is everything going to be straight now?' He said, 'Yeah, I've got it all sorted out, everybody's got their head right and let's get on with it'.. So that was it. Sort of a storm in a teacup but at the time it was irritating."

Of course, it could conceivably be the case that the band had decided to sack Jack but couldn't face telling him so. Yet in the 20 August *Record Mirror* in which Bill Harry had written about Keith Grant's 'Creation' painting, Harry also included this snippet on the change in the band's personnel: "Drummer Dave 'Rave' Preston is now in The Creation. This Liverpool drummer is standing in for Jack Jones, who is ill. But he has given the group a bigger sound and it's rumoured they may keep him." As a confidant of Tony Stratton-Smith, Harry would presumably have been more *au fait* with what was occurring in The Creation camp than most other journalists. If his account was true, it would seem the band – or at least Stratton-Smith – were hedging their bets a little.

Bob: "I think maybe Stratton-Smith didn't like the idea of Jack leaving. I do think Stratton-Smith was of the mind, 'If it isn't broke, don't fix it'. Because when The Koobas wanted me to join them, the truth of it was it wouldn't have made any difference because I was a very similar sort of singer/player to Keith who I would be replacing." Asked if the band considered Preston a permanent replacement for Jack at the time, Bob says, "I don't really know. I think it was a bit whimsical myself. On Kenny's say-so, although he made contact with Preston through me."

Not that this was much comfort to Jack. Although he may not have known for a fact that The Creation would never be requiring his services again, he knew at least that the situation was uncertain. "I thought, 'What am I gonna do now?'" he says. "I didn't think about another band. It takes time to get back into that. I think it was the middle of summer. I think I went down the swimming pool and sat by the pool, got myself a tan." Preston, meanwhile, moved in with Eddie and his family and geared himself up for a schedule that included television appearances and a slot on a Walker Brothers package tour. "I didn't sign any contract," says Preston. "There again, it was such a long time ago."

He says of his new landlord, "Eddie was a lovely guy. He was very dedicated, Eddie. He was sort of the main faculty of the band. He was a nice fella, Eddie. Family man. He was more of the sort of Pete Townshend figure. He wanted to be the main man in the state of leading the band, which one does when you're lead guitar. He was the very quietest of them all." Of Kenny, he says, " I got on with (him) great actually and did become a great friend of his. I really loved that guy. I was upset when I heard about (his death) and it brought it all back to me. He was sort of laid back, Kenny. That's why I liked him."

Jack's last gig with The Creation before his departure was at the Cavern, which the band played on 2 August 1966. (The gig was advertised by the venue in the *Liverpool Echo* as: 'We proudly bring to Liverpool the group that is reputed to be more exciting than The Who.') It was something of a homecoming for Bob, who had played the legendary venue with the likes of Freddie Starr and The Merseybeats. Jack's abiding memory of the gig was that, because of its famous arches, it was like playing in a tunnel.

Bob has a recollection about the gig which, if correct, would indicate that Kenny's stage painting began weeks before its introduction has always previously been cited. "The Cavern (had) whitewashed walls at the back," says Bob. "Now when I see pictures of The Cavern they've got squares in the back. They originally weren't there, it was just whitewashed. Kenny went and sprayed all the walls and I'm looking at him thinking, 'Goodness me, you're going over sacred ground here!' I don't know what happened, whether they whitewashed them out again."

Nonetheless, Bob retains happy feelings about The Creation's performing at this venue: "Opposite where the original Cavern was, there's a wall there. It's quite new, just an ordinary brick (wall) but in every brick is the name of every group that's played at The Cavern. The Creation are on there but it's not got 'The', it's just got 'Creation'. It's really nice. It's where they've got John Lennon, the bronze statue, in the doorway opposite. Not where The Cavern was, it's on the other side. I went to see it a couple of years ago and I stood back and for probably the first time I really felt proud of what we did."

Jack had occupied the drum stool on a couple of Creation local TV appearances the previous week – ATV'S *Action* on 25 July and Rediffusion's *Five O' Clock Club* on the 26th – but on 3 August it was Preston who appeared with the band on BBC TV show *Hey Presto It's Rolf*. Though he was excited by his silver-screen debut, Preston – despite having only rehearsed with the band (he estimates) once at that point – wasn't particularly nervous. "I was playing in clubs when I was about 12 years old in Liverpool," he explains. "I've never been nervous of anything like that. I just love to get up there and do my stuff."

If the *Hey Presto It's Rolf* footage has not been destroyed, it will almost certainly be the only record of how the band sounded with Preston on drums: the programme saw the band performing 'Making Time' live (violin-bow solo included). To some extent the quality of what they were seeing was lost on the audience, both at the venue of recording and at home. Presented by the bearded, good-natured Australian Harris, the programme was aimed at pre-pubescent children. "There was a bear on there, he had some animal characters on there," recalls Bob, clarifying: "People who had costumes on. Yeah, it was alright. I can't remember whether Pete Murray was on that show or we did a Pete Murray show."

He admits that playing their innovative, high-quality music to such a young audience was weird: "The theatre situation for The Creation and that type of band – the young kids – it's a not a pop thing. We were trying to be different and it was a bit of a struggle." Even though Bob found Rolf Harris, to whom he spoke backstage, agreeable, the fact that Harris was someone who was used to presenting pop stars underlined the incongruity of it all. "I remember saying to him that the first time I saw him was on the south pier at Blackpool," says Bob. "He was the compere. Gene Vincent was on the show and Bert Weedon and people like that. That'd be about '62. He'd been around a while, that guy, and he was into the rock thing even though he wasn't rock himself. It's amazing. They had Max Wall compering a Beatles (show) one time, I think."

Preston, though, was thrilled. "It was really great to actually be on television and also playing live," he says. "It was fantastic. I didn't see it myself but my late mother saw it. Everyone was saying it was great, it was a great sound. I was made up because one didn't really think too clearly on the lines of us being televised – to me it was just a gig. It was a great experience." Preston was also thrilled by the amount of money he found coming his way over the following few weeks: "The money one was getting in the Merseybeat days was bloody awful to say the least... With The Creation I was earning money like I've never seen before. The money was just, like, incredible. I suppose today's terms it would be like winning the bloody lottery."

He adds an intriguing anecdote about Stratton-Smith and the remuneration for his own work with The Creation: "Funny enough, he used to pay us in the back of the van from the gigs and he used to get me to one side and say, 'You couldn't lend me £30, could you?' He didn't want the rest of the band to know. He always seemed to rely on me. He didn't want to ask the rest of the lads because they were his priority." Clearly, things were going badly awry with The Creation manager's finances.

Of live work, Preston says, "We were doing all the clubs around London at the time. I remember doing the Tiles in Oxford Street. There were all sorts on the outskirts." Bob was not impressed by the Tiles gig: "That was one of Shel's friends, that sort of thing. Just wasn't the right venue for us either. That was all the beautiful people. I don't mean hippie beautiful: Rolls-Royces and all the rest of it. It was a place to be seen." Bob adds, "There was a video made there. I think somebody might have that somewhere. I remember seeing a little bit of it. Where it's gone I don't know. It was just a personal thing, it wasn't professional."

Preston remembers The Creation working about five nights a week and playing to capacities of around 1,000. "Very big clubs," he says. "They weren't small clubs, because with that sort of amplification you'd blow the place out." He recalls Stratton-Smith as a regular attendee but not omnipresent: "Not every one. Most of the gigs in London. We did one up Manchester, I think he came to that one." The Creation were invariably the headliners. Preston: Once you've got a record in the hit parade, you get top billing and your money goes up, and that's what happens. I was making good money. I was spending it as quick as I was getting it."

Bob is amused by Dave's belief that The Creation were earning good money. "Dave's from a very rough part of Liverpool," the bassist says. "When Dave used to get hold of a fiver then, he would go out and spend it and enjoy life with it. And Kenny was like, 'Hmm, is that the right thing (to do)?' and that's what Kenny saw in Dave: this ability to just say, 'Live for today and tomorrow will take care of itself'. We were all trying to make our way, trying to make it and, I suppose, for Dave, having a drink in a pub and the next thing he was getting a fiver a night or whatever it was, was quite a jump. I would say it wasn't a lot of money." Bob also recalls a chaotic method of payment: "I think we were getting dribs and drabs really. Stratton-Smith would say – we'd sit in a coffee bar – 'How much do you need? A fiver?' and give us some money. I can never remember it being regular. Now, with Dave, to keep the thing going, I can imagine Stratton-Smith saying, 'I'm paying you your wages' and he may have got it regular at that time."

He also surmises that Eddie may have been on a different pay scale to his colleagues because an understanding Stratton-Smith knew that he was the only Creation member with children: "He realised that Eddie needed a little bit more money." Though his opinions about what is appropriate drumming for Creation songs may have changed since, at the time Bob admits that he felt Preston's recruitment had produced a discernible improvement in the band's sound. "I think there was more strict tempo and louder," he says. "Jack was erratic with his timing but Dave was a bit more rock steady."

Preston, though, was not as impressed with The Creation as they were with him. Though he describes them as "a nice gang of fellas," down the years, he has become increasingly bewildered at both the way they have acquired a legendary status and the impressed reaction that mentioning that he once played with them produces in people. "I've heard a lot of people, a lot of friends of mine, some of them go into history on a lot of big bands and they were saying what a great band The Creation were," he says. "They were sort of like the mod band thing. For example, Bob Garner, he used to do 'The Clapping Song' and I used to think 'What's that got to do with this mod-type band'? I used to do all that stuff years ago with black entertainers.

"They really didn't strike me as being something out of the ordinary. Kenny I wouldn't say was exactly dynamite for a lead singer. Sort of stage presentation. He's not the wild man of rock or whatever. He was just like a nice placid guy." And Eddie as a guitarist? "He was okay...presentable, I suppose. I've played with much better, in other words. Basically it didn't really prove anything, a violin bow on a guitar. 'cos all it was doing was sustaining a note which you could have done by just getting the feedback, turn the guitar towards the amp. It was a bit of showmanship I suppose. It wasn't impressive. I didn't think it added anything to any of the music. 'cos you're only using it once. I think it was in one number, only for a couple of bars, and that was it. They were good for what they liked. It was what they wanted, but to me it's a sound I'd heard before. I think they were trying to base themselves on The Who. I don't think it worked."

If Preston thought the TV appearance and the money he was earning from The Creation was a barometer of success, he really considered himself to have made it when that August The Creation joined a package tour headlined by the Walker Brothers. The tour was promoted by Arthur Howes and it was probably through their connection to him that The Creation got onto the bill. "That's when I hit it big time," Preston enthuses. "That was brilliant." Package tours have long passed into history but – in the days before different types of music consumers wouldn't be seen dead in the same building as other types of music consumers – they were an exciting proposition: a collection of different acts of varying degrees of success and styles all playing on one stage in one evening, with the star act allotted a reasonable time on stage and the supporting acts playing a handful of numbers or even the one song they were known for.

In the case of this tour, the acts ranged from the Walker Brothers – with five Top 20 hits to their name – through the middlingly successful likes of the Moody Blues (one Number 1 and three other moderate hits) to bands like The Creation with one minor chart entry and utter unknowns like The Quotations. The feast was not a fixed one. Although the 27 August 1966 date of the tour featured support by the Mindbenders, Jason Eddie, The Peddlers, Slade Brothers, The Quotations, The Centremen and Alan Field, Preston remembers an almost completely different set of supporting acts on the two or three dates he played: the Moody Blues, Amen Corner, Paul and Barry Ryan and Brian Poole and The Tremeloes.

As Preston explains, "You'd have like three nights of Brian Poole and The Tremeloes or something like that, then The Moody Blues. It was just like they kept adding a different guest every night." In one of those weird convergences of rock paths, the Quotations featured two recent flatmates of Dave Preston, one of whom was Billy Bremner. Bremner would, many years later, play in a band called Rockpile, for whom Eddie Philips and Kenny Pickett would write the song 'Teacher Teacher'. Rockpile also featured Dave Edmunds, who was by that time a close friend of Preston – although Preston remained unaware that Pickett and Phillips had had a song recorded by Rockpile until told so by this author.

The Creation were allowed four or five songs, which translated into a span onstage of 12-15 minutes. Asked how The Creation went down on the Walker Brothers' tour, Preston says, "Oh they loved it because of them having the record in the hit parade. That did a lot for them." Bob disagrees: "It wasn't the right venue for The Creation, it was such a contrast in style. But that used to happen in the Sixties. There was quite a lot of clashes. I don't think that was a real problem. I think it was the actual presentation, not knowing the songs. I don't think it was that well received. We didn't die or anything, but if the records had been on the shelves I don't think we would have sold any more."

The Walker Brothers specialised in string-drenched ballads like 'The Sun Ain't Gonna Shine Anymore', a recent UK Number 1. They weren't real brothers and often didn't play on their own records but could put on a good show. "They were brilliant," says Preston, before amending it to, "Scott Engel was." He adds, (Drummer) Gary Leeds – so-called Gary Walker – he used to mime. There was a London guy, I think his name was Brian, and he had two kits on stage and he used to mime. John, you couldn't hear him at all. The star was Scott Engel. He had a beautiful voice and moved dynamically on stage."

"I think there was only one time I actually got to meet the Walker Brothers," says Bob. "Scott and myself looked the same and we used to have a little bit of fun with all the kids outside. He'd go to the window and I'd go to the window. Just stupid, really." Although the incident Bob mentions probably happened after Preston had left the tour, The Creation's drummer did notice that Bob took a close interest in the headliner's frontman. "Bob had this big fascination about Scott," says Preston. "He always used to take him off and all this. That's why I couldn't make out what this band was about. He had his hair cut like him and used to always go on about every show, 'Oh wasn't he great, the way he did this and the way he did that? His movements here and his movements (there)?' And I was (thinking) he didn't know who he wants to be, this fella. Do you want to be a bass player in a band? Do you want to be Scott Walker? I think he's totally got his wish now if he's in cabaret. It was a little frustrating. That's why I wasn't really settled…I didn't know which way this band wanted to go."

Preston wasn't impressed with Bob overall. "He used to wear this bloody big Tam o'Shanter, six times the size. He loved to stand out in other words. And he used to have this big, long footballer's scarf on. It was like you were watching someone in bloody Hogmanay. He was doing 'The Clapping Song' with this big floppy hat. I just didn't know whether to accept it as a joke band." Asked if he thought Kenny was unhappy about ceding the mic to the bassist for his rendition of 'The Clapping Song' each evening, Preston says, "Well I would have guessed so, wouldn't you? If I was a frontman singing, you don't let someone try and have a (singer) who's got a two-bob voice. I just find that displeasing. It's just not done. Bob's a bit of an ego-tripper…he loved himself."

It was on the Walker Brothers tour that The Creation began an onstage gimmick that, like the purple flashes quote, is inextricably entwined with the band's mythology. They had recently incorporated a new Pickett/Phillips composition called 'Painter Man' into the set. Trying to come up with an attention-grabber for the song's instrumental break, it seemed appropriate to try something art-related. "We were all in a van and Stratton-Smith was as well," remembers Bob. "It was a Sunday morning, driving to Brighton or somewhere like that, and we were talking about different ideas. We stopped at a garage and bought some spray cans, different colours, and then we went out and we managed to get some lining paper – decorating paper – made a frame up in the theatre and we said, 'We'll paint that'."

The idea would become a permanent fixture in the band's set. "When the band is doing a big solo, there's nothing for the singer to do except stand there and look like a dick!" Kenny told *Blitz*. "We were doing a summer season gig in Margate and Tony Stratton-Smith said, 'Why don't you do some painting on stage or something?' I said, 'That's not a bad idea!'" Eddie: "It was just an added 'Why not?' We got this big screen and we used to go and buy aerosols from Halfords and spray the thing. At the end of it, the roadie or Ken would set it alight."

However, paper covered in cellulose paint creates bigger flames than unadorned paper. Eddie: "Sometimes we used to do real damage to venues, which we had to pay for. So we didn't make a lot of money." As with so many things about his current gig, Preston was not impressed. "I thought it was quite ridiculous," he says. "I couldn't see the point in it. It was like watching a kid with a big piece of paper. Like a graffiti artist today. Just spraying any old thing. If I remember rightly, Pink Floyd was the business for the psychedelic stuff and all that but I just couldn't make head-or tail of it.

"It seemed really embarrassing. One minute he's singing, then he's spraying this bloody thing, this big paper on a blackboard and all these aerosols, different colours. From the audience point of view, they bloody well couldn't have seen him anyway. It could have been anything. You know they've got these big screens today on gigs? It was like that but it was just an ordinary blackboard with a piece of white paper pinned on. I found it embarrassing, actually."

Preston wouldn't have to endure the embarrassment long as, on probably his third date on the Walker Brothers tour, events occurred which led to his dismissal from the band. Although he was with The Creation for possibly as long as three weeks, history has suggested the gig at which Preston was sacked was his sole performance with the band. This seems due to Eddie's memory having apparently compressed Preston's tenure. Those interviewing Eddie or reading his interviews, having seen no other recollection on the subject, naturally take his memories at face value.

Asked by this author about the incident, Eddie trots out this story: "We was on the Walker Brothers tour and we was opening up our set and Dave was on this massive great rostrum behind us. We started off I think with 'Biff Bang Pow'. I was driving it along and it got slower and slower. The next I know, a bass drum whizzed past my head. He'd got so out of it that he'd fallen off the rostrum and at the same time kicked all his drums off as he went. The bass drum just missed me. That was it. The curtains closed, that was our contribution that night and that was his one and only appearance with us. Then it was, like, 'Come back Jack – all is forgiven'."

No doubt that is Eddie's genuine recollection of both the incident and the length of Preston's tenure, but the truth is different – although just as funny. The fact that Preston had already played a number of dates with the band at this point has already been covered. Additionally, Bob's memories of the fateful Walker Brothers gig differ substantially from Eddie's.

"I can't remember whether it was Bournemouth or Torquay," says Preston. "We got there in the afternoon and we put all the equipment in the theatre. A couple of the guys on the tour said, 'We'll go down and get a few beers'. Unfortunately it wasn't beers, it was bottles of spirits as well…a mixture of everything. The pubs weren't open all day as they are now. We went down to the off licence and got a load of drinks."

Preston denies that he had any kind of drinking problem at the time, saying "It was only that particular incident." His denial is called a little into question, though, when he says of Stratton-Smith – with whom he got along famously – "Strat liked me in the sense that he liked a drink as much as me." Continuing the account of what happened that day, Preston says: "Obviously what with not eating and all, (we) just sat in the dressing room drinking and I passed out after that. Next thing is they were trying to get me round. I couldn't even move. And unfortunately that was that. They must have dragged me down there. Apparently I fell off the kit, which must have been a terrible bloody embarrassment, not only to the audience but for themselves."

While taking responsibility for his actions, Preston remains aggrieved by being put in an unfair position: "I thought to myself, 'It's a bloody stupid thing to do, not only on my behalf but to actually try and get me to play'. I've often asked myself why they didn't ask someone else on the tour to stand in. That would have been much easier, wouldn't it? You're only gonna do, like, two or three numbers and to drag me up there was stupid. I wouldn't have done that to anyone. If one's totally out of it, you're not gonna try and get them to perform when they're bloody well comatose."

"I honestly can't remember seeing him on the floor before we went on," says Bob. "That's not to say he wasn't, but my recollection of that was I only realised that he was incapable when we was actually on." Eddie concurs with Bob: "We didn't know he was pissed 'cos he disappeared just before we were supposed to go on. Nobody knew where he was and he appeared on the stage when we walked down to the stage. I didn't know he was pissed 'til he started playing. And it was too late. If we'd seen him legless, I doubt if we'd have even tried it ."

Bob's and Eddie's memories differ from this stage. (Preston, understandably can't remember a thing about what happened once the band started playing.) Though Eddie recalls not even finishing the first number, Bob's recollection – which is quite clear and detailed – is of the band playing a full set, albeit in chaotic circumstances. "It was that bad it became funny, if you know what I mean," he says. "It was like, 'Well, what can you do? You've got to make the best of this'. The one thing I do remember, I think it was the song 'I'm A Man' and no matter how many times Eddie and myself tried to end it, he (Preston) just carried on. Unbelievable. So we had to just keep going round and round."

Word quickly spread backstage about what was happening and the other acts on the tour began to congregate for a glimpse of the entertainment. Bob: "Even The Walker Brothers came out and realised there was something going on. They were all in the wings there absolutely in two with laughing. I think we had to bring the curtain down in the end or across, whichever way it was. Bring it to an end. But I don't know if the kids actually realised what was going on. I don't think they really noticed." The next day, the band drove back to London. "I was voted out," says Preston. "Which was the right decision, obviously. I suppose it was a day or two later. I accepted that. Fair's fair."

Preston recalls that Stratton-Smith explained that, of all gigs, this was the wrong one to screw up on: "They had this record producer or record label, some people from Planet Records, (who) came down to see me, this new drummer." Talmy doesn't recall being the person from Planet Records at the gig. He also says that if he had witnessed the incident, he wouldn't have been of the opinion that Preston should be sacked: "I was more tolerant in those days. Everybody was. Everybody got pissed and everybody fell over. I mean, hell, if that had been the criteria, there wouldn't have been any musicians left."

"It's a shame really," says Bob. "I didn't think he deserved the push then. If it hadn't been so early days after the changeover, if it had been a few months down the line and it was well established that he was in and Jack out, I think he would have stayed." Eddie, though, doesn't consider Preston's dismissal unfair: "Not really. If you can't rely on somebody… The worst thing a drummer can do is get pissed because it just ruins it for everybody and I've played with drummers since then who've been great when they're straight, but when they drink too much, it all goes out the window. You've got to enjoy your music but you've got to be serious about it and you've got to be serious to the point (where) you can't have a drummer whose timing's going up and down, slowing down and speeding up, that sort of thing, because it ain't going to go right. (He's) the foundation of the band and if he can't anchor it up and do a strict tempo..."

The aura of tragi-comedy hanging over Preston from that incident is misleading. Following his departure from The Creation, he worked live with soul band The Showstoppers of 'Ain't Nothin' But A House Party' fame. He was also offered a lucrative drumming gig which he turned down. He was invited in the Seventies to take over the drummer's stool from the incumbent in heavy rock outfit Uriah Heep in an identical situation to The Creation scenario the previous decade. This time, he walked away rather than take someone else's job.

Not that he seems to regret the circumstances in which he joined The Creation. "When they sacked me and they got Jack back in again, I believe he gave Kenny a hard time," says Preston. "(I heard this) from sources somewhere. They were saying when they took him back, he really gave him a hard time for getting rid of him in the first place. Personally speaking, I didn't think the guy was good enough."

In any case, drumming ceased to be Preston's musical activity of choice in around 1976 when he moved away from being an instrumentalist and into composing. "I've always written," he says. "Even when I was with The Creation. I was writing all the time in my head. I always knew what I wanted out of life and I've got it now. I've got my own studio and I've been writing and recording, play keyboards, bass, guitar. I've got a few good publishing companies over the years put some stuff out here and there and people have recorded it. I had one out with Madeline Bell".

At the time of writing, he derives most of his income from art: "I do a bit of painting and mix that with working with me songs and that. Couple of weeks painting and a couple of weeks working on my stuff."

"I never saw Kenny after that," says Preston of The Creation member to whom he was the closest. "I never saw none of them. Apart from Bob. I only seen him briefly." Bob, though, recollects of Preston after his sacking, "He was around in the usual haunts and that. He used to take us to the Cromwellian club, Tony Stratton-Smith. We'd see Dave there sometimes late on." (Bob also thinks that when Preston recalls Stratton-Smith borrowing money from him while keeping a wary eye out for Creation members, it may have been after Preston's stint in the band, not during.)

In any case, Preston remembers a meeting with Bob several years after his Creation stint fairly vividly. "I bumped into him in The Ship in Wardour Street and I said to him, 'What are you doing?'". "He was saying he's into this Georgie Fame stuff and he was thinking of getting a band behind him and he's going to be the front-line singer. And I said to him, 'Georgie Fame? Bloody hell'. I couldn't work it out." Preston had been unaware before being interviewed for this book that Bob ultimately became The Creation's front man. "Bob was always going that way," he says. "He always wanted to be the main attraction."

For Kenny, Eddie and Bob, an embarrassing necessity awaited them: asking Jack Jones to return to the fold. The very fact that they did not seek to recruit a different drummer rather than go through this awkward situation is another indication that there was nothing profoundly wrong with Jack's drumming. It is true that they had work in the diary, including the remainder of the Walker Brothers tour, but a fill-in drummer could easily have been found for these dates.

Jack: "Next thing, I know Stratton-Smith was on the phone (and) said, 'We've got to settle this argument, blah blah blah, the boys'd like you back in the band, Dave doesn't fit in the band' and all this crap. Eddie had really had enough of it. The idea of it was so stupid I couldn't believe, 'cos when I listen to Dave, he was a really good, strong drummer but he was absolutely totally wrong for the band. It was real Merseybeat sort of stuff he bashed out and the London stuff was totally different. It had a totally different feel. So I don't know what the hell Bob was on about."

Reconvening with his colleagues at the next gig, Jack says, "I can't remember where it was but we got up there and everybody was a bit embarrassed and all the rest of it. We did the gig and Stratters come after and he had a little chat: 'How you feeling? You all right? Blah blah.' I said, 'Yeah, I'm okay'. He said, 'Well let's try and put this all behind us and move on'. So that's what we did."

"I think Jack was back the next day," says Bob. "I can remember it was a little bit embarrassing at the time but everybody seemed to get over it but I think Jack had a chip on his shoulder. I think he's still got it." Talmy says, "It was definitely awkward and I don't think that Jack ever forgot it. I think he was probably pissed off from that point on and I suppose in a way I can't blame him." Of the affair as a whole, Eddie observes, "It wouldn't happen being like we are now, that experience of life and how everybody should treat each other. It's different now – you've lived and you've learnt."

Shel Talmy could be forgiven for worrying about upheavals in a band in whom he had quite a lot invested. However, he attempted to stay above the fray. "I felt I was trying to turn records out with a band I thought was going to be a superstar band. I did not make a stand and say, 'We've gotta have so and so or else I quit'," he says. "I wasn't managing the band. Tony was. It was up to him to sort all that stuff. I was looking for a unit that could make records. Also, I was involved in a lot of other recordings, not just The Creation, so I had a minimal amount of time to worry about band politics." Upheaval and personnel changes in The Creation were things with which Talmy would become more and more familiar over the following couple of years.

Jack enjoyed the remaining dates on the Walker Brothers tour and could see the logic of The Creation appearing on the same gigs with a band so very different to them. "They were pretty good actually for what they did," says Jack. "The Walker Brothers would be touring England and they'd be seen by a lot of people and so we tagged on as second or third on the bill and that meant we would be seen by a lot of people, so it was all about exposure really." Like Preston, he recalls The Creation as going down well with the tour's audiences: "The thing about the kids in them days is everything was new. The kids today, they've all seen and done it all but in the days it was new and if you got up on stage and made a noise, they liked it. We did okay, we held our own. There were some good bands on there. We used to go down well... (but) when The Walker Brothers came on at the end, the place used to erupt."

The tour's stop on 13 August at the Gaumont Cinema in Bournemouth saw a reunion between Eddie, Kenny, Jack and their old mate and colleague John Dalton, for this date found the Kinks on the bill. They were riding high, with their 'Sunny Afternoon' having just been Number 1 in Britain. It wasn't much of a pleasure for Dalton, though. "It was a real nightmare," reveals the man who was now the Kinks bassist. "I said, 'Oh that's great. Me old band. That's wonderful'. But as normal, we turned up and one of the Davies brothers – it was Dave this time – decided not to go. It used to happen a lot. One of 'em would say, 'No, I'm not coming tonight'.

"We still used to go to the gig. We went all the way down (thinking), 'Oh this is so embarrassing'. We used to get a doctor's certificate, pretend he was ill. (The Creation) done their set and all we done, we walked on stage and apologised for Dave being ill and we played half of 'Sunny Afternoon' and went off. It was so embarrassing for me to be playing with me old band and not even do a proper set. Went on there just to apologise, really."

Bob recalls the Walker Brothers tour as possibly being a two-leg affair and this seems borne out by the fact that before the tour's end, The Creation went into the studio to cut what would be the A- and B-sides of their next single. IBC studio A was once again the venue as, on 23 August 1966, the band laid down two new Pickett/Phillips songs, 'Painter Man' and 'Biff Bang Pow'. This time Johns and Lyon-Shaw were not in attendance and Talmy worked with engineer John Pantry.

'Painter Man' has usually been interpreted literally (including by Bob) as the lament of a great artist reduced to illustrating advertisements in order to make ends meet. However, Jack's and Eddie's recollections indicate that Kenny intended his lyric more as a metaphor. Eddie: "The song was about somebody that's got this idea to be a great artist or a great musician and instead of being able to do classic art and make a living at it – or play classical music and be great at it – he ended up doing art for adverts and commercial art."

"Kenny told me it was about the frustrations of the showbiz thing," says Jack. "Somebody trying to strive to get on as an artist, if you like. Like a painter man can be the greatest artist in the world but if he's unfashionable, he's got no chance. The silly nonsense that goes on in the human race, especially in the art word." A metaphor for the music business? Jack: "Absolutely. Kenny was serious about his lyrics." Bob, though, is not so sure about it being a clever metaphor. Bob: "No. it was a single (about) being an art student. Because, 'Went to college to study art/To be an artist, make a (start)' – no. Whether 'Paperback Writer' was out then, I don't know but it was that sort of 'work'-type (song)."

The Beatles' 'Paperback Writer' – a song about the trials and tribulations of a budding novelist and the first Fab Four single not to address romantic love – had been released on 10 June, so it is perfectly possible that Kenny had been inspired by that record. Bob: "That's the feeling I got, that it came from that. To be honest, although 'Painter Man' was a commercial song I didn't really get 'Who wants to be a painter man?' (sic) 'cos there was no connection. When Kenny wrote that, we weren't doing anything in connection with that song. He came up with the lyrics of that as like an art student, that type of thing. It was only later that the graffiti on stage, etcetera, came. We did the stage thing to suit the song. It wasn't that the song was written about what we were doing."

Eddie's music for 'Painter Man' was, when one thinks about it, incongruous, an anthemic affair that sat oddly with a lyric of ill-luck and dissatisfaction. Yet it works, the kind of Beautiful Loser anthem which wouldn't become fashionable until into the following decade. Also highly effective was Eddie's memorable, undulating, seven-note riff, first played as the introduction and repeated after each chorus. Meanwhile, the bowed solo – sounding like a buzzsaw going into overdrive and spinning out of its owner's hands – was stupendous.

Ten attempts at 'Painter Man' were made. Take one was a 'breakdown' in studio parlance, meaning proceedings were called to a halt before the song was finished, either because someone had made a mistake or the track plainly wasn't up to scratch. Take two was a complete take but takes three and four again broke down. Takes five and six were 'false starts' – recordings that broke down within a few seconds of starting. Take seven was a complete recording. This was followed by two more false starts. Take ten was another breakdown. It was decided that of the two completed takes, take seven was the superior one and this was chosen as the one from which to create 'Painter Man's master, the basic track upon which to add the overdubs necessary to make a finished record.

An indication of just how primitive recording techniques could be in those days is given by the annotation on the tape box containing the results of this session. 'Painter Man's mono master has one version marked 'With bass drum and claps' and one marked 'Straight' . Lyon-Shaw laughingly explains, "The bass drum and claps probably would have been because of the mono overdubbing. The bass drum and the drums became a mush because they got lost with everything that went on top. So people used to put claps on top to bring out the snare drum, and obviously the bass drum was because there was lack of bass drum."

The attentive listener who is also familiar with the work of Nat 'King' Cole will notice a little joke at the song's finish, one suggested by Bob. "On the end of 'Painter Man', you will hear 'Mona Lisa'," says Bob. "Listen to the fade out, you will hear 'Mona Lisa' on the violin bow and guitar. I said, 'Why not stick that in?'." Bob had an even greater role in the genesis of 'Biff Bang Pow'. "When I first joined the band I used to stay at Kenny's house," he reveals. "I was watching television and *Batman* was on and those cloudbursts you get where they were having a fight and it was 'Biff!' 'Bang!' 'Pow!' and all that kind of thing. I said, 'That would be a good idea for a song'. That's where it came from." (The Creation would also introduce a version of the theme tune to the same *Batman* series – written by Neal Hefti – into their stage act, which they would often play with 'Biff Bang Pow' as a sort of conceptual medley.)

Of course, there is a difference between merely providing a title and/or subject of a song and sitting down and weaving the actual composition but Bob – in what seems a non-bitter way – feels he should have received some credit for his contribution to this and other tracks whose composition was attributed to Pickett/Phillips. "I didn't realise the value of writing a song or what you were entitled to," he says. "I threw a lot of ideas in the pot and walked away. I wasn't thinking, 'I should have a contribution of that'. Little bits and pieces that are certainly enough of a contribution to say, 'Well hang on, I've a certain right to that title'. I'm not bothered now about what's gone by – I didn't worry at the time – but Eddie and Kenny had had the experience of (how) writing a song could be (of) value because they'd done things in the past. I'd never done anything like that before."

From what Eddie says, it appears that Kenny approached him with the idea of 'Biff Bang Pow', at which point he devised a melody into which Kenny could insert his idea: "The *Batman* series was on the TV, the one with Adam West," Eddie says. "That was great. Used to love it. It sounded like a good idea: biff, bang, pow. It had to be a kind of a song which was like biff, bang, pow: a bit crazy and a bit fast and slightly manic." The melody Eddie devised could reasonably be described in those terms. Unfortunately, the guitarist's knack for a riff let him down on this occasion: 'Biff Bang Pow's insistent, charging refrain was lifted from The Who's 'My Generation'.

In an age where a premium was put upon individuality – something that tied in with the compositional self-dependence The Beatles had started in pop – this is the sort of thing that didn't go down too well. It also provided yet another justification for the media's Who-Creation comparisons that were the bane of Kenny's life. Eddie acknowledges the similarity between the two songs' riffs: "There was that kind of drive and the way the chords were played so it was probably right that it ended up as a B-side." Bob, surprisingly, says he never spotted the resemblance: "I can't remember ever thinking about that before. You've brought that to my attention. I didn't realise it was anything similar."

A couple of people in the studio that day had worked on the 'My Generation' session: producer Talmy and pianist Nicky Hopkins. Hopkins was Talmy's first choice of keyboardist for his sessions. A staggeringly gifted and prolific studio musician, he had already inspired the Kinks song 'Session Man', which would be released on their (Talmy-produced) 'Face To Face' album that October. Hopkins played harpsichord on that track.

He would later briefly be a band member in The Jeff Beck Group and Quicksilver Messenger Service and even released a couple of solo albums but it was as a sideman that he did his best work.

He wasn't merely prolific: he seemed to have an extraordinary knack for being in the right place when landmark records were being made. Not many musicians could boast of having played on records by the Beatles *and* the Rolling Stones *and* The Who *and* The Kinks. There again, it was logical that someone of Hopkins' talent should be in demand by the most important artists of the era.

By the time of his premature death in 1994, Hopkins had graced some of the finest rock recordings of all time with some of its most memorable keyboard riffs and/or solos. Among them were the doomy, coiling piano lick of the Rolling Stones' 'We Love You', the background honky tonk-isms on The Beatles' 'Revolution', the elegant piano work throughout The Who's imperishable 1971 'Who's Next' album (most notably 'Getting In Tune'), the show-stealing accompaniment on John Lennon's 'Jealous Guy' and the beautiful solo in the Rolling Stones' 'Angie'.

Hopkins' work on The Creation's songs would not be quite so ornate as his contributions to the aforementioned tracks. Though he would be present on most or maybe even all of the Eddie Phillips-era sessions, Talmy used the pianist on The Creation's tracks for a similar reason he had him on Who sessions: to fill out what would otherwise be the thin studio sound of a three-piece band. Explains Eddie, "In the studio you haven't got the volume you would use on a live performance to sort of bridge the gap."

However, though Hopkins is clearly audible throughout The Who's 'My Generation' album (except on the title track, although Talmy remembers him playing on the song), on most Creation recordings he would almost always be just-discernible background. "It's subdued a little bit and the piano worked really well," says Eddie. "Kind of a nice musical pad... You couldn't really hear him on a lot of (tracks) 'cos I dare say when they was mixing it, if they didn't think it suited the song they probably were mixing it down.

"What was good about it was when you were actually playing in the studio, he'd just be there sort of rattling along with the swings and filling the whole thing out. That was the only session musician ever used on Creation stuff." Talmy describes Hopkins as "absolutely brilliant...he would adjust himself to whatever the track was and would do whatever I asked him to. If I needed him to be more prominent and give me some solo-type stuff, he'd do it, like he did on The Who." Eddie: "He would come in and listen to what we was doing and make notes and strip it all down and he'd just sit down and play it. Fantastic player. Nice guy as well, Nicky."

Bob recalls "a very quiet sort of bloke who would sit and listen to the song once through; they were maybe three or four-chord songs, so he didn't have a problem with that. I think he probably found himself in a position where (he thought), 'This is good. I've been to classical school of music for the last 20-odd years and there I am just jingle-jangling, everybody likes it'. When you listen to some of (it), it's almost little country jingles really. Nothing outstanding because Shel didn't want it to be. He just wanted the right notes filling in little gaps."

In contrast to the multiple attempts at 'Painter Man', the band only had two bashes at 'Biff Bang Pow'. Both were complete and take two was chosen for the master. It's possible that by the time they'd gone through so many attempts at 'Painter Man', the band were so in the groove that they knocked off 'Biff Bang Pow' with ease. More likely is the possibility that, because it had already been decided that 'Painter Man' was the A-side and 'Biff Bang Pow' the flip, it was felt that wasn't worth agonising too much over the latter track.

And yet, the annotation on the tape box's ledger reveals something rather strange. It seems barely believable but it may be the case that, after recording, it was decided that 'Painter Man' wasn't single material. On the ledger, next to 'Painter Man's title is a big 'X'. Above it, someone – not Pantry, whose handwriting is discernibly different – has written 'Not using'. This seems to be referring to the actual song, not merely a specific take number. Beneath 'Biff Bang Pow's title, however, there is an arrow pointing down to where someone has appended to the ledger 'With Instrumental Two'. Also written just beneath 'Biff Bang Pow's title is 'Original For Records and Tapes'. The logical conclusion here seems to be that 'Biff Bang Pow' was originally selected for the A-side of the second Creation single and the subsequently recorded 'Instrumental 2' aka 'Sylvette' was chosen to be its B-side.

The mind boggles at the possibilities such a course of action might have brought about. In the short term, choosing 'Biff Bang Pow' as the A-side of the second Creation single might have meant that the huge success the band enjoyed in Germany – where 'Painter Man' made them stars – did not happen, which in turn may have led the band to split up sooner than they did, for German money was what kept the group going at various junctures. In the long term, the windfall 'Painter Man's composers (and Shel Talmy as publisher) received in the late Seventies when it became a most unlikely hit single for another act would never have occurred. On the other hand, it may have been the case that 'Biff Bang Pow' – despite its 'My Generation' derivation – might have been the hit UK (and/or US) single the group was in need of.

Rather bizarrely, a hit cover of 'Painter Man' was released in Australasia the following year when Larry's Rebels had the song recommended to them by an Australian music publisher. Released in New Zealand, it climbed as high as Number 6 before it was taken off the airwaves when a housewife rang an radio station to complain that she had heard the line 'labels all around shit cans'. (The phrase 'dirty postcards' – which actually is in the song – would also have been risqué in what was a very conservative country in the mid-Sixties.) The same band re-recorded the song with a raunchier guitar track for Australian release but this one failed to chart. The Creation and their producer had absolutely no knowledge of these versions.

The last day of August 1966 saw The Creation and Talmy visit IBC for another recording session. Lyon-Shaw was acting as engineer, probably because by this point Glyn Johns was no longer a welcome presence at Portland Place. Always a tempestuous character, with an ego as large as his undoubted talent, he had finally gone too far. Lyon-Shaw: "He had a fall-out with the manager who I think he actually decked!"

Not that the two tracks Lyon-Shaw supervised on this day particularly required an engineer of genius. The tape box for the sessions describe them as 'Instrumental 1' and 'Instrumental 2'. These titles are typed. After 'Instrumental 2' somebody has appended in hand: 'Title "Sylvette". 'Sylvette' is clearly not an instrumental at all but the backing instrumentation to the Holland-Dozier-Holland song 'Leaving Here', although that didn't stop Kenny and Eddie nabbing the composers' credit when it appeared on a French Vogue EP in 1966 under the 'Sylvette' title. Similarly, 'Instrumental 1' sounds like a backing track: the dynamics are not of an instrumental but of the instrumentation to a number intended to have a vocal. None of The Creation can remember whether it was intended as an instrumental or whether it had a title.

It's quite possible that everybody who took part in the session had completely forgotten of it existence by the time in 1998 Ed Strait of

Retroactive Records, planning the first ever American Creation compilation, looked down the list of recordings supplied by Talmy's offices and noticed this hitherto unreleased Creation recording and, presumably with some sense of excitement, decided to give it its very first release (for which he tweaked its title to 'Instrumental #1').

It is not possible to detail the number of takes the band recorded of each number because the only tape box for these two tracks has a typed ledger that merely details the three-track stereo master rather than the takes that produced said master. Two other tracks, for which original tape boxes no longer exist and for which therefore it is not possible to confirm the recording dates, were possibly recorded around this period. The tracks are covers of Larry Williams' 'Bony Moronie' and 'Mercy Mercy Mercy' (which the Buckinghams would take to the US Top 5 in 1967).

Because these two recordings were paired for the very last Sixties Creation single (a German-only one), it has previously been assumed that this was a product of the very last line-up of the band (containing Kenny, Jack, Kim Gardner and Ronnie Wood). Yet one listen to the caterwauling guitarwork on 'Bony Moronie' is enough to confirm that it is unlikely that Wood – a rhythmist supreme but no lead player – is responsible. In addition, the drumming doesn't actually sound like Jack but instead bears all the pattering hallmarks of a session drummer. As for the bassist, Kenny suggested he was also a sessioneer but seemed uncertain as to exactly who. He told *Record Collector* in 1995, "'Bony Moronie' and 'Mercy Mercy Mercy', featured just me, Eddie and Jack and a session bassist – Herbie Flowers, I think'."

Yet John Iles – another recording engineer who worked with The Creation – opines of the tracks "I worked with Herbie many, many times. Didn't sound like Herbie to me." Jacks says, "Nothing to do with me. 'Bony Moronie' might go back to the Mark Four. I really can't remember that. I didn't know it was released in Germany. I seem to think we recorded a few of the old rock'n'roll stuff in the Mark Four and 'Bony Moronie' I'm pretty sure was one of them. I've got a feeling that somebody got hold of the tracks and just pushed them out." He adds, "I never worked with Herbie Flowers."

Talmy: "I never hired session guys with Kenny. That's a definite." And Kenny's assertion about using Herbie Flowers? "He may have done on one particular session if the other guys weren't around. That's possible. I certainly used Herbie a lot for various sessions but I have no memory of Herbie being on any of The Creation sessions. As far as I can remember it was them. I can't tell you who was playing bass. I don't think it was Herbie."

Kenny's later comments to Rod Siebke go some way to unravelling the mystery but sill leave unanswered questions. "That would have been late '66, same time as 'Sylvette' was recorded," says Siebke. "This was Kenny (said this). Herbie Flowers is supposed to have been on bass. That's what he told me. Definitely said that to me. Ken also said that Ed was playing a Vox guitar." Flowers failed to respond to an interview request for this book so it's not possible to verify Kenny's recollection on that point. As to the issue of who provided the drumming, Siebke recalls, "From the way that Kenny was talking, it was definitely the latter part of '66, so it's quite possible that Jack was out of the band at the time. It could have been during that period."

This is just about plausible but if was recorded during the period when Jack was not in the group (Dave Preston, incidentally, says he took part in no recording of any kind during his tenure), then Kenny's mental landmark of the recording of 'Sylvette' is wrong, for Jack was back in the band by then. Siebke concludes, "It was more of a rehearsal session than anything else. I would say it's probably a rehearsal that was taped. When you think about it, in '68, there would have been no need to have done a 'Bony Moronie' and 'Mercy Mercy Mercy' (because they were writing their own material)."

There is one other fact that possibly pinpoints the recording period: in 1966, Larry Williams toured Britain "which," says Siebke, "would add some credence to the fact that the songs would have been picked up on. Maybe." Maybe. Kenny told *Blitz* something completely different. Speaking of 'Midway Down', he said , "We recorded that at the same time as 'Mercy Mercy Mercy', which was on the B-side of Bony Moronie' in Germany. The Germans didn't like 'Midway Down'. They wanted another A-side. So I said, 'Well, let's do a Larry Williams song'. So we did 'Bony Moronie'. That was the last one we ever did." A master session ledger does exist for 'Midway Down' – dated 26 February 1968 – but there is no mention on it of 'Mercy Mercy Mercy'.

Whenever they were recorded and whatever the personnel involved, these two tracks are – along with the three cover versions included on their continental album 'We Are Paintermen' – among the least significant of all The Creation's recordings, even if 'Mercy Mercy Mercy' is rather pretty.

n September '66, The Creation embarked on a two weeks tour of Germany, Holland and Sweden. On 29 September they appeared on the German TV show *Beat-Beat-Beat* (not to be confused with *Beat Club*, the well known German pop programme from the same period). Another Stratton-Smith act, The Koobas, also appeared and performed four numbers. The Creation played 'Making Time', 'That's How Strong My Love Is' and 'I'm A Man'. These are the recordings on the 1998 Retroactive album 'Making Time'. 'That's How Strong My Love Is' is particularly powerful, with Kenny turning in a smoky, moving vocal performance and Eddie peeling off a solo that spurned his normal chord work/violin bow stuff for the sort of fluid, conventional lead guitar lines he rarely used in those days, at least on record.

It was around this time that June Clark took over the running of The Creation fan club. Though still a schoolgirl, Clark already had quite a lot of experience, having helped run The Who's at the tender age of 16. "I got to know them when they were The High Numbers," recalls Clark. "I came to know their fan-club secretary at the time, Deirdre Meehan, because I used to phone up the office to find out what gigs they were doing if I hadn't seen them for a while. Deirdre was working as secretary to Kit and Chris. Deirdre took over running the club (and) asked me to go in and help her... So in my school holidays I used to go up to Kit and Chris's office and work out of their office.

"Then, to help Deirdre out, I used to have mail coming to my home address where I lived with my parents. And then Pete Townshend, he had a friend called Chris Thomas, who later became a well-known producer. Chris had started a band called The Cats and Pete asked me if I would run the fan club for Chris's band, so I did that from my mum's home as well. They only existed for about a year and they went nowhere, sad to say. So I got an inside look at how to run a fan club from working with Deirdre."

It seemed logical for The Creation to ask Clark to run their own club. "The fan club was being run by the secretary at Arthur Howes' office," says Clark. "She really wasn't doing a good job and the band were a bit disappointed with the way things were being ignored and there wasn't a lot of marketing going on. So Bob suggested to Eddie and the rest of the band that maybe I could take over and work out of Shel's office. They all agreed to it and I did the best I could. I was really on top of what was going on and put the word out." Clark did this work for love: "No-one paid me anything. I did it because I wanted to help promote them."

While she was perfectly happy not to receive money herself, she was quickly disillusioned by the fact that very little was made available for the fan club: "I think a lot of it comes from Shel's area of responsibility. Not enough money coming from there to back the band and push it. Whereas with The Who, Kit and Chris put every penny they had into them. I saw that nobody was willing to put money into my ideas to promote them and fan clubs were really one of the best marketing tools a band had. Can you believe they weren't even willing to reprint a flyer with my name and address on the back and I had to cross out 'Arthur Howes'? That's pretty sad."

Clark would work in the luxurious surroundings of Talmy's apartment when taking care of fan club business. "He had a really nice flat in Knightsbridge," Clark recalls. "Shirley Bassey lived in the building. I remember (The Creation) used to say, 'Unh, but she walks around in curlers and she only wears wigs so her real hair is really scruffy and she doesn't look very pretty'." Clark continues: "Although I'd get a lot of fan mail at home – and that was the address to write to – a lot of people would still write to Shel's office. A lot of publicity material would be at Shel's office. There was a room where I used to work from with a large dining table, not a normal square thing like my mum had in her house! I used to spend quite a lot of time up there."

Clark estimates that when she took over the club, it had a grand total of about 12 members. Though this membership level did rise over the following few months, it never topped more than approximately 50. "That's sad," she says. "And some of them were in foreign countries, like Poland, Belgium and Germany. I would have thought I would have had more from Germany, they were so huge there. I would get letters from there but not as many as I thought. They were really scattered. Very strange."

For their five shillings membership fee, The Creation's fans would receive a membership card ("The Creation Create You No __"), a group photo and all the available previous issues of the fan club newsletter. They would also receive 12 copies of the newsletter, published monthly. It was a simple photocopied affair but brimmed over with Clark's enthusiasm and a certain amount of expertise: "It would only be maybe two or three pages and I would list the gigs and I'd try and fill it up with information about what they were doing as a band and then some personal stuff. I based this on The Who's newsletter. The format. I used the same idea because I felt that it worked, it was informative."

In addition, Clark sent out a promotional flyer: "It was a card which is about six by eight (inches) and on the front was a photo of The Creation with the name 'The Creation' and on the back it's got 'The Creation', then it's got 'fan club', the address, 'agents', then 'Arthur Howes', recordings: 'Making' Time and 'Painter Man'. Then it says, 'On Planet Records'." The fact that the flyer was not updated but had to be amended manually illustrated, for Clark, the complete lack of investment in the band: "I crossed out the name of Pam c/o Arthur Howes Agency with their address and hand-wrote my name and Shel's address in Knightsbridge because they wouldn't pay for another one to be printed."

Things got farcical on this score when The Creation's third single was released. Clark: "For that release I've added '"If I Stay Too Long" c/w "Nightmares" on Polydor Records'." The fact that neither Stratton-Smith or Talmy would even agree to the modest investment of updating the fan-club flyer made the dreams Clark harboured for the club preposterous: "I wanted to have little items that the fans could buy like a pen, a keyring, something with The Creation name on." The contrast with the diligence with which The Who's fan club had been run was distressing: "Everything – everything – that could be done was done. It was amazing.

"When we used to send out the newsletters, we used to send out all kinds of printed material of The Who and stuff it in those envelopes. And ideas. And pushing them to go to gigs. Deirdre and I would go to gigs: 'If you go to a gig come up and see hello'. It was like cheerleading, pushing the band on, to get the public out there to see the band and to push the name. It was very, very difficult to do that with The Creation because I didn't have any money – I was a schoolkid – and my parents didn't have any money so I had to get the money from Shel."

For Clark, The Creation's name was always barely on the pop world radar: "It had to be due to the management not releasing publicity. Band activity had to be covered in the music papers that were read. They didn't get coverage of their gigs. Reviews. The Who would play a gig or the Small Faces would play a gig and you'd read about it." One member of the Creation fan club was Pete Townshend. "This was something that was worked out with me and Deirdre (Meehan of the Who fan club)," says Clark. "I said, 'I'm running The Creation fan club now, do you think that Pete and the guys' – I knew Pete in particular – 'would like to know what they're doing and receive the newsletter?' and Deirdre agreed. And The Creation were honorary members of their fan club."

(The November/December 1966 issue of The Who's fan club

newsletter announced that Eddie Phillips had become an honorary member. The same issue carried the line, 'Eddie Phillips of The Creation was knocked out with Pete's revue on their record in the *Melody Maker* (Painter Man)'. The personal listing was dropped for the January/February 1967 issue, with 'The Creation' taking Eddie's place.)

Townshend was most certainly a genuine admirer of The Creation. His name is now inextricably linked to the band's story. It was in September 1966 that the first mention was made in the music papers of another staple of The Creation's legend, namely that Eddie had been asked to join The Who. The story reported was that Pete Townshend had been so impressed by his counterpart in The Creation that the invitation was extended to become the second guitarist in his own band but that he was rebuffed by Eddie.

For many, the story seems unlikely. Townshend was a profoundly gifted musician, possessor of both a remarkable rhythm-lead powerchord guitar style and a brilliant songwriting ability (melodies and lyrics). Such was the span of sound created by his guitar playing that nobody had ever suggested that The Who lacked sonic impact despite being a set-up with only three instrumental sounds. (Indeed, the complaint for many years was that – the 'My Generation' single excepted – the Who never sounded as powerful on record as they did in the flesh despite having the studio option of beefing their sound up with overdubs.) Why would Townshend, then, want a second guitarist in the group – particularly when, as Lyon-Shaw claims, Townshend at that time in his life was a rather insecure young man?

"Pete hated guitarists," says Lyon-Shaw. "He walked out of the studio because Jimi Hendrix walked in. He went home because it was a threat and so I can't understand that he would have had another guitarist of that nature in the band." Furthermore, if this approach had been made, one would expect Eddie's colleagues to remember it: it's not every day that an already established band – and one which would subsequently become one of the most important in rock history – attempts to poach one's lead guitarist and co-songwriter. Yet none of Eddie's bandmates recall hearing of such an approach.

"Load of bollocks," says Jack. "I think it was a publicity thing at the time thought up by someone...a good story created by Stratton-Smith." " I don't know whether Townshend actually went to Eddie and said that," says Bob. "Because Pete was number one, the honorary member of our fan club. I think there was some sort of publicity angle. He probably asked through other people more than anything. Whether it was to join the band I do not know. If you look at The Who then, to have two guitarists like that on the same stage, I don't think that was the image. I think Kit Lambert would have probably said no."

June Clark – as in the loop as anyone around the band at the time – also has no recollection. "I never heard it," she says. "I only read this later. I read this 20 years later. I knew that they admired each other, and you can see why. Their style is so similar." Chris Stamp – co-manager of The Who – says, "I have no recollection of Pete asking the guitarist Eddie to join the Who. Pete may have asked him to perhaps play with the group or something, over a drink at the Speakeasy or The Scotch of St James. It was never something that involved The Who, Kit or myself."

And Eddie himself? "I don't remember anything about that at all," he says. "I honestly don't remember that. If it happened, I didn't know about it." The final nail in the coffin for the rumour, one would conclude. And yet. At the risk of sounding patronising to Eddie, he definitely has the weakest memory of the surviving Creation members, sometimes shockingly so. Yes, shocking enough that it's possible he fails to recall that one of the most famous groups of all time requested his services on a permanent basis.

Which would mean nothing were it not for the emphatic assertion of Shel Talmy that the rumour is true. Talmy insists that he was told of the approach by Eddie himself. "My only memory about it is that Eddie mentioned it in passing and that he wasn't going to take the offer," says Talmy. "He wanted Eddie to join to become I think probably a rhythm guitarist – which would have been really a ridiculous thing for him to do." Eddie is a modest individual and it's inconceivable that he would have pretended such an occurrence had taken place if it hadn't. To which the cynic might reply that, as Talmy had ceased working with The Who in acrimonious circumstances, and as Eddie could plausibly be posited as the pet guitarist with which Talmy had replaced Townshend (ditto The Creation for The Who as a group), it might have been Talmy concocting the story as a form of one-upmanship.

So the obvious answer to this decades-old mystery is to approach Townshend himself. Initially, the response from the Who man was puzzlement. "I can't remember who Eddie Phillips is," Townshend responded. "Can you refresh my memory? What period is Shel speaking about? There was a short period Roger was sacked from the band and all kinds of strange things were going on. I can vaguely remember a warm feeling of replacing Roger with someone I liked. Maybe Eddie was the man?"

However, upon being supplied with music-paper articles about and pictures of The Creation, a lightbulb seemed to click on in Townshend's head. "I remember now," he says. "It is true, though I may well have been expecting a rebuff and had no power to invite him anyway. I can see that happening, but I can also see that it was a bit of a pipedream. They were one of the bands I liked best at the time.

"The Creation played the Marquee at the same time as us, supporting us perhaps once or twice then getting their own very successful engagement there on some other night of the week, I think. The Creation was one of the only bands other than The Vagabonds that I would get there early enough to watch. In fact, once The Creation did do a set after we'd finished. Can't remember what happened. Keith got ill or something, we only played 15 minutes and they came on again."

But Pete's response raises as many questions as it answers. How can one forget having asked a second guitarist to join the band of which you are the creative fulcrum? This would surely be the only time that anyone was ever formally asked to join The Who once the personnel of Townshend-Daltrey-Entwistle-Moon had been established. Surely, this would be something easy to remember even after the passage of nearly four decades? Additionally, he appears to be incorrect about his (uncertain) statement that The Creation had a residency at the Marquee (though Bob remembers they did appear at the nearby 100 club after the Who had been there).

In any event, he is almost certainly referring to late 1965/early 1966, when The Who were regulars at The Marquee and The Creation didn't exist, in which case he is confusing The Creation with the Mark Four. That doesn't rule out what he is saying – after all, the personnel was three-quarters the same and remembering the Mark Four as The Creation because the guitarist used feedback and a violin bow in both doesn't mean he is wrong about later asking that guitarist to join The Who – but it might be that Townshend's long-dormant memories of the situation may understandably have become conflated with the story that appeared in the music papers at the time, ie that he is not actually remembering but thinks he is remembering.

However, Townshend insists, "I don't have a clear memory of it but I have enough of a memory of it to know that it's true. I can't remember what was going on at the time – because of course a lot of the time I would have been doing amphetamines and so would he and we probably went and hung out together a few times. We loved the band. They were the best support band that we had at The Marquee. The Creation had a much purer audience contact than even we had at the time, because they brought their audience with them."

Townshend says Lyon-Shaw's assessment of him as a man who hated other guitarists and was threatened by Hendrix is unfair: "I may have had a bit of low self-esteem in that department but I knew what I was good at. No, when Jimi came to meet The Who at IBC, I didn't walk out – I spent an hour with him telling him what amplifiers to buy. I remember he was the one who seemed in awe of me at the time – a situation that was going to change within a couple of weeks. I was always a big fan of other guitar players that were kind of more in my area as well. I loved Dave Davies from The Kinks."

Townshend adds one other point that sheds a whole new light on the issue. The possibility is that he approached Eddie not to join The Who but the band he intended to create from The Who's ashes. "You can see if you look at Who chronology that it's quite possible that The Who were in disarray around the time this happened," says Townshend. "You remember that story about Keith and John wanting to leave The Who to form a band with Jimmy Page and call it Led Zeppelin? That may have been happening at the same time, so I may have been cooking up a new band."

The events Townshend is referring to occurred in May/June 1966. It's impossible to pinpoint the exact time of Townshend's approach to Eddie other than to say we know it was in or before September '66, when it was first reported in the music press. That would certainly make the scenario Townshend suggests feasible. He recalls a mind busy working over possible permutations of musicians at the time of Moon's and Entwistle's disgruntlement. Townshend: "There were a couple of players that I really liked from Pete Meaden's band called (Jimmy James and) The Vagabonds: Phil Chen on bass, I probably would have imagined, and so it goes. So I may have been trying to make an alternative band, seeing trouble ahead."

While some may be sceptical about whether the approach by Townshend happened, most everybody seems unanimous that it would have been a bad thing if Eddie had taken up any such offer. Shel Talmy speaks for many when he opines that Eddie would have been relegated to a secondary rhythm guitarist role in The Who: "What else would he have had him as? After all, he was the leader of The Who. I can't imagine him saying, 'Oh by the way, from now on we have a new lead guitarist. I'll take second fiddle.' I can't see that happening." Jack: "Eddie was a star in his own right wherever he went...why would he want to play second fiddle to Pete Townshend?"

Townshend does not share the belief that there would have been no meaningful role for Eddie within The Who. "I think he would have fitted in very well," he says, "because if you go back to that period and listen to live recordings, I couldn't play and he could. I really wanted to concentrate on my role as a writer and a powerchord man and I thought that the way that he played would fit in really, really beautifully with my powerchords. I often did play with other musicians and when I played with Eric or Stephen Stills or Leslie West (the person I always wanted to play with was Jimi Hendrix) just to think if they had me playing rhythm behind them – fucking hell, how extraordinary that would be. I think that's where it came from."

Talmy does recognise that, being human, there may have been a monetary temptation on Eddie's part to take up the offer, if it did happen. "I'm sure it was extremely tempting," the producer says, "but I never really thought that the money was as important to Eddie as it was to other people in the rock business. So if he turned it down it was because he thought he could do other things, wanted to do other things, not because he was going to go grab the bread." "I wouldn't have done it anyway," confirms Eddie. "At the time, we had our own thing. I know it's wrong, but I used to think of The Creation as my thing. It wasn't, it was everybody's thing – but I used to think of it like that and I would have known that once I left that and done something else, it wouldn't be my thing. It would have been their thing. And that was important to me."

There would also have been practical considerations. "We're talking hypothetical, but I could never imagine how it would work," he says. Nonetheless, the idea of teaming up with the guitarist with whom he has always had more in common than any other naturally intrigues Eddie. "What would have been fun was playing powerchords along with Pete and having these two powerchords going on each side of the stage," he says. "As you'd sit out the front you'd hear this whacking great thing coming at you in stereo. That could have been good."

Whether or not Townshend asked Eddie to join The Who or an intended post-Who band, one suspects that the reason the story found its way into the papers – and subsequently into rock mythology – was because of Stratton-Smith's acute ability for what we would now call spinning. As we have seen with the mini controversy over the Creation's name and with the *Monitor* story, he had a Fleet Street journalist's ability to take something with a grain of truth and shape it into something with an angle that the papers would find intriguing enough to devote space to.

If Talmy did have reservations about the aesthetic or commercial qualities of 'Painter Man', he clearly got over them – for in October 1966 it became the A-side of the second Creation single in both the UK and US, with 'Biff Bang Pow' as the flip. The UK press release for the single was outlandish indeed and made prominent use of the phrase Eddie had coined to describe his band's music. Interestingly, it reversed the order from its first appearance in the 'Making Time' press release, lending credence to Bob's suggestion that it was indeed originally "purple with red flashes" . The release read, in full:

"'We see our music in colours – it's purple with red flashes...'– CREATION 1 v ii

THE CREATION PAINTER MAN a veritable hit!

Electronic music, feedback, imaginative identification with colours and art and unique sounds is their art-form. We feel we are contributing to the 'total sound culture'. This culture will take its place in the world just as the Renaissance and Picasso's Blue Period has.

For further information contact – HUGH MURPHY"

The press release featured two photographs, one of the band smilingly standing and lounging on grass and wearing casual mod clothes, the other a shot of the group lined up against a picket fence dressed in their quasi-military outfits.

That press release seemed positively conventional in contrast to a music-paper advert for the record, whose wording is presented here in full, with idiosyncratic grammar retained:

"dark from the Catacombs of Mind and Memory. Sinuously emergent – traumas rampant! The New Word, Sam, Etched indelibly – PSYCHEDELIC! So suffer a psychosis, Sam. Airwaves a' trembling – it's PAINTER MAN. A new neurosis. Melting minds from Waxworks spherical (Planet, etc.) Hysterical. The psychedelic sensation. Remember! THE CREATION! PAINTER MAN by "THE CREATION" . PLF 119. creep in and buy, Sam. Pow, like NOW!"

The analysis of the disc by *Record Mirror* was more sober in tone. "We tipped the boys' last one and it just missed," the pop weekly said in its 8 October issue. "This could be a sizeable hit. Story of a student's laments and most distinctive on the instrumental side. Flip goes like a bomb, very urgent and fast. The 'monotonous' riff comes off."

The record got some valuable publicity on 30 October 1966, when the Atticus column for which they had given an interview appeared in the *Sunday Times* under the heading 'Psychedelic'. The column was written by Hunter Davies, whose piece on Paul McCartney and The Beatles' 'Eleanor Rigby' in the same column the previous month was one of the reasons he would become the first person to write a full-length Beatles biography. Davies had decided (or maybe been persuaded by Stratton-Smith) that The Creation fitted the new psychedelic genre he had elected to write about. It was arranged that the group would be interviewed for the piece at 10 o'clock in the morning. A hungover Jack arrived at 10:15 and remembers the journalist (presumably Davies himself) because he was the first person from whom he had heard the term 'psychedelic'.

Davies' published piece began, "The American pop world has had a bit of an inferiority complex these last few years, ever since the Liverpool lads got going. Recent reports show that they've got on to something new, all by themselves. It's called, as you may have guessed, psychedelic. A writer in the British pop newspaper *Melody Maker*, in trying to explain what it was all about last week, started off by apologising for the title. 'I know it's a hard word but make a note of it.' A psychedelic experience is the sort of thing you undergo when you take drugs like LSD."

Davies then pointed out that the music of the psychedelic groups – of which he estimated there were over 50 in the United States – attempted to convey the experiences on such drugs, though acknowledged that not all the groups were drug users. After a paragraph on the Mothers of Invention, he went on, "Some British groups have already been affected. Last Wednesday, at the Flamingo Club in Wardour Street, a pop group called the Creation performed a song called 'Painter Man'. It's now Number 31 in the charts. As they played, a series of paint bombs exploded onto a screen behind them. When the painting was complete, the lead guitar (sic) rolled it up, used it as a violin bow for a few bars, and then threw it to the fans.

"The Creation say they're not on drugs and there's nothing really psychedelic about them. 'It's just different and it amuses the kids'. They teamed up about six months ago and chose the name The Creation from a list of a hundred. 'It's been a very good name', they say. 'We get a good plug in that Adam And Eve film'."

The piece then went on to talk about Pink Floyd. Though the Creation material formed only a quarter or so of the article, it was they who were pictured: a quite striking performance photo of Eddie bowing his guitar while Kenny in the background painted a canvas. The caption read: 'Painting to pop'.

There was further publicity in the *NME* dated 4 November 1966 under the heading 'Creation paint as they play'. Written by Norrie Drummond, the piece read: "A most exciting group enters the *NME* chart for the first time this week: the Creation at Number 22 with their own composition, 'Painter Man'. Many people have compared them to The Who. But The Who – as well as the Walker Brothers – really admire The Creation. A recent newspaper article described The Creation as 'psychedelic', a description which they detest. 'We just want our act to be visual as well as musical,' they say. 'We want to give the public real value for money' . For those who have yet to see The Creation work, they use violin bows on their guitars – and on stage, they paint pictures while they play!

"This week, I met their energetic young manager, Tony Stratton-Smith, who explained: 'They paint because they feel like it, not simply because it's gimmicky. They just paint when they feel moved to. They experiment with their movement, too. At the moment they're working something out using a violin bow and a potato. But I'm not quite sure what it is.' The group – Kenny Pickett (singer), Eddie Phillips (lead guitar), Bob Garner (bass) and Jack Jones (drums) comes from the London area, and has been playing together since the beginning of this year. 'We see our music as colours,' they say. 'It's purple with red flashes'."

The 19 November issue of *Record Mirror* also provided some publicity – though this was the very week 'Painter Man' dropped out of that paper's chart. A large panel with a picture (the band wearing non-matching mod-type jackets and trousers, not purple uniforms) read, "Is the visual thing taking priority over sound? Psychedelic music and 'freakings-out' depend heavily on visual tricks to get their full effect. *RSG* announce a Spring policy of 'using groups who have really got an act'. The Creation with their current hit, 'Painter Man', is one group prospering on the change in taste.

"'Our show is a premeditated moving picture,' says lead guitar (sic) Eddie Phillips, 'non-stop movement – not action for its own sake but action which deepens the whole feel. That's one reason why we like The Koobas – we think the same and try not to stand there like a sack of potatoes.' The Creation. shrug off that 'psychedelic' label as being unimportant. Titles coming up on their next session are 'Private Hell', 'If I Stopped Moving I'd Fall Out Of The Sky' and 'Closer Than Close'."

These latter tracks have become something of a holy grail for Creation fans, for no songs with those titles were ever released, raising the tantalising possibility of material buried in the vaults ripe for bonus track-dom. However, none of the band recall recording these numbers and the list of Creation tracks in Talmy's vaults reveal no titles other than the ones previously released. Furthermore, it's doubtful that these songs were ever even written. "That one about 'If I Stopped Moving I'd Fall Out Of The Sky', I vaguely remember Kenny talking about that as being a good title for a song," says Eddie. "I don't think we ever actually did anything with it. Pretty sure we didn't. It normally didn't work like that. I would kind of get a structure of a song and I might get a bit of a chorus. I'd play it to Kenny and then he'd go off and do a lyric for it." (In the latter part of 2003, Eddie decided to pick up the reins of Kenny's thought processes and began writing a song with that title.)

Jack, too, remembers the 'If I Stopped Moving…' title but, like Eddie, thinks it never progressed beyond the title. "He had a few titles," Jack says. "Kenny never wrote anything unless he had to. If he was going in the studio that day, he'd start writing songs the night before. That's how he worked. But he had a couple of these titles and thought they might produce some good songs but I don't think he ever really got into working on them. But yeah, he would have had it in his mind to expand on (them) later."

And yet Joe Foster offers an anecdote about 'If I Stopped Moving…' from the 'Power Surge' period that suggests that when the titles were mentioned to a journalist, it might not have been merely Kenny taking the mick: "Kenny sang a song when we were on a train of that title. Quite impressive too. But whether he just made it up on the spot I don't know. Tony Barber felt that he'd just made it up to wind us up, but if he could make up songs like that, there should have been more publishers after him. It sounded pretty rockin' to me." Meanwhile, inveterate Creation fan Paul Weller evidently decided to write the song 'Private Hell' for Kenny. A superb song of that title appeared on The Jam's 1979 album 'Setting Sons'. Its first line? 'Closer than close.'

'Painter Man' did considerably better than its predecessor. The *Record Retailer/Record Mirror* chart registered it as scoring a peak of 36 while in the *NME* chart, it climbed as high as 22. This was despite less media exposure than 'Making Time' had received, though the band did get another *Ready Steady Go!* slot. In his April '67 *News Of The World* article, Stratton-Smith claimed that he had hyped 'Painter Man' too. "Last September, a group of mine called The Creation had a 'single' released called 'Painter Man'," he wrote. "By judicious fixing – and quite without the group's knowledge – I got it to the very brink of the Top 20. In consequence The Creation were re-booked for the *Ready Steady Go!* ITV programme which at that time was still a power in the pop world. Pirate radios began plugging the record heavily. I had given the 'kiss of life' to a record which in fact had been flagging. Sales picked up.

"Why did I stop? Why not go all the way into the Top 20, aiming for the rich pickings to be had there? There were several reasons. Pushing the record had already cost £600 in addition to more legitimate promotion and I felt that if the disc did not 'take off' naturally after all that effort, then it was a loser anyway. Secondly, I have a genuine respect for the Top 20. I feel it should honestly reflect what is currently most popular. My chart rigging has always been in the lower regions. I have never tampered with the Top 20, though I have every reason to think others have."

It's difficult to judge how much truth there is in Stratton-Smith's recounting. As has already been indicated, he had an ex-newspaperman's knack for putting the right spin on a story to give it maximum publicity. On the other hand, he did indeed have the sort of olde-worlde ethical code that might have made him think nothing of rigging the Top 50 but consider the Top 20 too sacred for such seediness.

Both Gail Colson and June Clark preferred 'Making Time' to 'Painter Man'. "When you look at 'Painter Man', I think that's a bit poppy," opines Clark. "'Making Time' certainly isn't – that's got the raw sound that's typical of them. 'Painter Man', that's got more of a middle-of-the-road sound to it. The guitarwork on it is great but when it comes into the hook and that repeated chorus, it kind of slows down and that's when you can tap your foot." Clark certainly doesn't remember any despondency in The Creation camp at this point over the fact that their obvious talent and innovation had not yet translated into cracking the Top 20. "I thought they were all ecstatic," she says of their reaction to the chart progress of 'Painter Man'. "I think everybody thought that it was gonna go up there and that this was just paving the way for their success. We really all thought that they were going to be successful. I don't think that there was ever any doubt. It's just a matter of time before it clicks. And it takes years: there's some turning point and then somehow it takes off.

"We all thought there was gonna be a turning point. I just couldn't see that there wouldn't be. They were so good. They were unique. They had everything going. It was just a case of pushing it there somehow. I wasn't disappointed. Obviously, you wanted it to go higher but I always had hopes that then the next one will do better. I don't think they were particularly disappointed. I don't ever really remember them being down in the dumps about things until towards the end when they were breaking up. When after two years, then they were becoming a little bit discouraged."

By this time, Clark was beginning to get a handle on The Creation as personalities and had come to the conclusion that the two she liked were Eddie and Bob and the two she wasn't keen on were Kenny and Jack. "Eddie was great fun," she says. "He was very outgoing. He was (a) very warm, nice guy, very sincere. Easy to get to know, very friendly. Just a great, great person. Very sensitive. Eddie was just adorable. You just wanted to hug him and kiss him. Well that's how a woman felt, anyway."

She is emphatic that Eddie was the leader of the band who "knew what he wanted. Musically, I think Eddie was a strong person." She was as fond of Bob as Eddie, although found him an almost diametrically opposite character to the gregarious guitarist: "Bob's a very funny guy: he's very emotional but he never shows it. Keeps his feelings to himself. Bob is not very expressive. To get something out of him you have to ask and you have to drag it. He's not quite as bad now but he's still a bit like that. But he's a very shy person. Even though he can get up on that stage – all his life that's all he's ever done is be on a stage – he really is a shy person and very, very private. Bob I thought was really good-looking but shy, so he wasn't outgoing or did anything wild or didn't behave differently on stage because of his personality.

"I couldn't believe once when he wore this really beautiful sequinned coat – absolutely gorgeous. When he put that on it was like the Queen wearing a T-shirt. He looked good in it but it wasn't Bob. It just wasn't his personality because he never really wanted to stand out." Jack the drummer was "an absolute drip," Clark says. "Jack I looked upon as this old person that didn't fit in. He was very quiet and I always looked upon him as old-fashioned. I was really amazed he was in the band but they seemed to like him as a drummer. Never as far as I knew caused any trouble. Jack was like the mature, sensible one. Didn't goof off after a gig. He'd sit in the dressing room, very quiet. The others weren't like that. They were all still hyped up."

Though Clark's disdain for Jack was to do with what she perceived as a lack of personal charisma, her objections to Kenny Pickett were based on something more significant. "He had an ego so big you couldn't get into the same room with him, and I don't like people like that," she says of the vocalist. "I like quiet, sincere people. It's the opposite of me I suppose. Kenny was gregarious in that he loved himself so much and he thought he was God's gift to women. And he assumed that I therefore had the hots for him. Even though I was going out with (someone else) he still would make a play for you and I hated it. Kenny was very pushy, very self-opinionated. What he said, he thought should rule. You could see he was more academic. You could see that it gave him more self confidence. He was better read. A bit more worldly. He was more educated, more intelligent. The others were very much blue collar, work environment. Bob was from Warrington. His father worked at a steel factory."

Eddie concurs with Clark about his colleague's cerebral nature: "He had a pretty good education, Ken. We was all secondary (modern) school boys and he went to a grammar school, it was a bit posher."

Tony Stratton-Smith was a figure Clark was very fond of, not least because his homosexuality meant he was at least one male she could be assured would not be leching over her. "He was a gentleman," she says. "I know he was a heavy drinker but I remember him as a gentleman. You've got to remember, I was young. I don't have an ego, but I was attractive. I had long blonde hair, a nice figure. And men were constantly all over you. Strat never made a pass at me. He never put his arms around me, as men did back then. Strat was never like that. So respectful."

His gentlemanly mien was not restricted to mere chivalry: "Always in a suit, shirt and tie, pinstripe suit, three-piece. Always looked so smart, very professional, not a slob. Extremely well spoken. Obviously very intelligent. I'm sure he went to university, which in those days was something. Lovely guy. I was so fond of him. I would have done anything for Strat." As for Shel Talmy, Clark says "Very influential. Highly regarded. Shel was a very, very strong factor in The Creation. Almost more than Strat. He was greatly respected, and quite rightly so, by the band members."

At some point in 1966, each member of The Creation started to get their own vocal showcase on stage. A cover of the recent Shirley Ellis hit 'The Clapping Song' – which Bob had sung with Lee Curtis – became the bassist's showpiece. "That was my thing from Hamburg," explains Bob. "I used to do the song 'Just A Little Bit', 'The Clapping Song' and something else." Jack, too, had a share of the spotlight in the shape of Percy Sledge's

'When A Man Loves A Woman', which he would sing while still attending to his drumming duties. Meanwhile, Eddie opted to tackle 'Hey Joe', recently introduced to the British public by Jimi Hendrix. Bob: "People say we were doing it before Hendrix. We weren't." Jack: "It was just Eddie wanting to do a vocal onstage: Jimi Hendrix had had a big hit with it so he said, 'How about I do my version of that?' It came out great."

Jack was not so pleased about 'The Clapping Song', a singsong number with many of the qualities of nursery rhymes, becoming part of the act. Jack: "Guy comes into the band, you want to make him welcome so he offers these numbers which he used to do in the Hamburg club so you feel you got to accommodate him a bit. But I wasn't happy with that. I didn't think it was anything to do with the band."

Though they had a busy December, things were looking grim for The Creation at the end of 1966. Shel Talmy decided that Planet Records – after 22 singles and two albums (one of which did not obtain a UK release) – was no longer a sustainable concern.

As with the commercial failure of The Creation's two Planet singles, Talmy pins the blame squarely on distributors Philips. "As it happens, with all their best efforts, I still made some money out of Philips," he says. "But nothing like I should have made. With the ludicrous contract I had, they refused to amend. I said, 'You know, fuck you, I'm out of here'." Bob, however, has always had misgivings about the fact that The Creation's first couple of records were not on a major label. "To be an independent label in 1966 was a bit of a brave step," he says, "and in my opinion the reason that the records didn't stand a chance – a proper chance – (is) because they never got to the shelf."

An era for The Creation was coming to an end in more ways than one. Not only would the group now be looking for a new label but they would shortly require a replacement manager: the new year would see an irreparable rupture in their relationship with the man who had essentially fashioned The Creation, Tony Stratton-Smith.

CHAPTER 3

CAN I JOIN YOUR BAND?

December 1966 had been an unusually good month for The Creation. Despite their continued failure to obtain that coveted top ten (or even Top 20) hit single, they had managed to secure a healthy number of gigs. Yet the new year saw the band scratching their heads as they realised that the correspondingly healthy amount of money they'd earned was not feeding through.

Jack: "We'd worked every night through December all over the country and I used to keep the books with the money in and I worked it out that we'd earnt 11 quid a week each. So we said, 'Well where the hell's the money going?' So we went up to Arthur Howes and said, 'Look, can you get these cheques in because we're not getting the money through' and he said, 'Well you've had the cheques – we've passed them all over to Tony'." When the band asked Stratton-Smith about the matter, their manager explained that he viewed the money as something with which to finance his other acts. "He was using the whole stable's money to keep The Koobas going," recalls Jack. "We (said), 'You can't do that man'... And he said, 'Yeah but when we all make it we're all gonna get rich'. He was giving us this chat. We were saying, 'Oh come off it. You're a bit out of order'."

The notion of using money The Creation had earned in order to support his stable was yet another indication that Stratton-Smith's finances were both perilous and chaotic. "I think he wasn't in such a good state of repair himself at that time," says Bob. "He was drinking a bit and he had money problems. I remember going up to his office once and there was some people coming down with an Alsatian dog. Somebody chasing some money or something. So things wasn't that rosy for him. I think he was beginning to wonder why he'd ever got into this thing in the first place. I think he'd spent his savings."

"In the end we couldn't really carry on with him," says Jack. "That was a pity because we really sorted of regretted that." The 14 January 1967 issue of *Record Mirror* carried this simple statement in its Pop Talk column: "Arthur Howes is now both agent and manager for The Creation."

"I don't think there was an actual break," says Bob. "It just faded out more than anything… In actual fact, I can't remember the end of Tony Stratton-Smith. I certainly didn't put me hand up and say, 'Let's leave Stratton-Smith'. I was unaware of it happening and I think Tony Stratton-Smith really threw the towel in round about the same time as that happening. I never went to Stratton-Smith and said 'We don't want you as a manager'. I don't know who did but at the same time I think Stratton-Smith was probably saying, 'I don't want to manage you either'." Jack has a contrasting recollection: "It was quick. I think Tony agreed to tear up his contract and we were then managed by Arthur Howes and Shel Talmy."

Despite the split – and subsequent dubious and semi-spiteful activities like the *News Of The World* chart-rigging exposé – no-one in The Creation camp has a truly bad word to say about Tony Stratton-Smith and all attribute the dispute over the missing money to anything but dishonesty. Bob says, "In the first early days, he was paying us a few quid here and a few quid there when we wasn't doing anything. Especially with Eddie, 'cos Eddie was married then with a couple of kids. The other thing was, that era, that time, it was like money wasn't everything." "As far as I know Strat was completely 100 per cent honest with them on money," says Clark. "Bob has said he has not been aware at all of Strat doing anything underhanded with the band, which is pretty unique. He seemed to be such a gentleman and handled business so straightforward."

"It was a shame because Stratters did a great job and he was a lovely bloke," says Jack of the split. "It wasn't a question of anything really naughty going on. It was just he had one vision and we had another: 'It's our money, man, you can't really use it'."

The fact that The Creation did not consider Arthur Howes to be a suitable long-term replacement for Stratton-Smith is illustrated by the fact that they approached Ashley Kozak, then manager of Donovan, with a view to him stepping into Stratton-Smith's shoes. "We had a talk with him," Jack recalls. "He said, 'I'd like to see what publicity you've had'." Jack handed over his scrapbook of Creation press clippings. He was not to clap eyes on that or its recipient from that day on. "We found out that he'd gone bankrupt and some guys were looking for him," he says. "We'd never see him again. That was the Sixties, man."

Bob remembers this period as being difficult for the band, with money being tight due to a dwindling number of gigs. Bob blames Arthur Howes who, despite the undoubted benefits he'd given The Creation – including quite possibly saving their career after the uncovering of the rigging of 'Making Time's chart position – was not sufficiently down with the rock'n'roll crowd. "He wasn't getting us much work because the type of work he dealt with was mainly theatres," Bob says. "He was too upmarket for the pop thing, really. For those London club things, Harold Davison, they were more into that kind of thing. I think that was Stratton-Smith's choice. I think that was misguided really…

"We were running out of work. I remember Arthur Howes or somebody got us a job in Newcastle. Those days, we had a little J4 van and it was the old A1. It was like a ten hour bloody journey, to go all the way up to Newcastle. It didn't mean a thing to go up there and play at a club there. It was like: 'I've got you a job'. There was very little work. It was like a breath of fresh air when Germany popped up. It saved the band a little bit earlier than what it would have finished, 18 months earlier if Germany hadn't have happened. Money-wise, it was just like, 'Well where we going?' We weren't even getting the little gigs that semi-pro bands were getting."

Kenny shared Bob's feelings and made his admiration evident for Kinks managers Robert Wace and Grenville Collins. Kenny would later cite his colleagues' refusal to switch to Wace and Collins as a factor in his quitting The Creation. According to singer David Garrick (another Wace/Collins act), it was the latter two who were responsible for booking the dates on the tour of West Germany on which he, The Kinks and The Creation embarked in January 1967. Garrick also insists that he got the impression that, during this period, Wace and Collins were the managers of the Creation.

"They did manage them, very briefly," Garrick says. "I think it was about a month. Arthur (Howes) never did Europe. He went to Robert Wace. Robert Wace sorted out the German side of it." Bob: "I think there was rumours that they were considering taking us on. That's the only thing I can remember. There was some sort of rumour that they might be interested in taking the band on. They may well have booked us on that tour for whatever reason." Jack can't recall any more than Bob about Wace and Collins being putative Creation managers but said he would probably have been in favour if it were the case. "They got The Kinks out to the United States and kept them going in the limelight for a long time," Jack reasons.

"I remember Kenny trying to get with him," says Bob, probably referring to Wace, who was the most visible of the two partners. "'Cos the gigs the Kinks were doing were more what we would have fitted in with." Jack doesn't recall the approach or any discussion about switching managers and/or agent but says, "With Kenny, anybody who didn't get us a Number 1 hit and a world tour within two weeks, he wanted to change 'em. He's not known for his patience. He was always plotting and everything. I don't remember that one. I used to sort of say, 'Oh shut up, man, get on with it. Just come over and write some good songs. We'll get our Number 1 that way'. He used to go scowling at me but he'd come round next day. That was Kenny. He was in a hurry to be a big-name star."

The tour of Germany lasted from approximately 16-21 January (there may have been a couple of dates immediately prior to this on which The Kinks did not appear). John Dalton at this point wasn't a member of The Kinks, his first stint in an on-off membership having lasted from June-October 1966. Garrick was a balladeer with a smooth blonde image (and an incongruous rasping Liverpool accent) who had recently had a couple of minor hits in the UK. Like the Creation, he would find greater favour in West Germany, where 'Dear Mrs. Applebee' would become one of the biggest-selling singles of all time.

Bob and Garrick (who actually resembled each other physically) went back to 1964. Bob: "When I was with the so-called Midnighters, we was in a record studio just off Dial Street in Liverpool and while we were doing a couple of sessions – we were doing some jingles for Radio Caroline – the guy in there said, 'I've got a singer'. He wanted us to back him. And we did four songs with him in the studio – one was 'Distant Drums' – and then he wanted to do a couple of operatic things. I think he did 'Ave Maria'. And then we did a few gigs on the road with him. The next time I saw him, he was in the dressing room at the Marquee, all suaved-up with his mink coat or whatever."

There were 12 gigs at which The Creation supported the Kinks. A package tour under the title Beat In Carneval, it usually involved two shows per night in different towns three hours apart. A band called The Impact also played all these dates and there were appearances on various days from talso played all these dates and there were appearances on various days from The Monks, The Icens, Phantoms, The Generals, The Dressman-Guys, The Red Rooster Group, The Mods, The Beat-Garde, The Beatstones, The Others, The Knights, The Souls United and The New Alliance. The tour took in Offenbach, Frankfurt, Krefeld, Dusseldorf,

Ingolstadt, Augsburg, Stuttgart, Pforzheim, Bonn, Cologne, Munich and Nuremburg.

Bob remembers Kinks supremo Ray Davies as a strange bird. "He sat down at breakfast, wouldn't speak, then he'd write something down on a serviette," he says. "He was really strange." Garrick recalls, "We had a problem with Ray Davies. He called me an old poof or something like that and so we never spoke for like five days." Part of the reason for Davies' disdain for Garrick may have been because, after a certain point, the promoter decided that, in order to reflect who the German crowds most wanted to see, Garrick was installed over The Kinks as headliner.

Ray could seem a positive angel, though, compared to his brother Dave, The Kinks' lead guitarist and as extroverted as his brother was sullen. On one occasion, Dave's behaviour was so obnoxious that the gentle and good-natured Eddie Phillips felt compelled to take drastic action. "Eddie actually threw a full litre of beer over him in a nightclub," reveals Bob. "He was larking about doing something, he pushed Eddie too far and Eddie just threw the drink. I remember he stopped him in his tracks."

Bob and Garrick, meanwhile, got along famously. "He was a great guy," says Garrick. Garrick had only recently taken up live work and suffered from bad stage fright. "He helped me because I wouldn't sing live on stage because I hated it," says Garrick of The Creation's bassist. "I was frightened. He went, 'Get on there'. He used to model his hair on mine. He used to do my hair with curling tongs. I'd do his hair and he'd do mine."

The best legacy of the tour was the fact that The Creation finally secured their first *bona fide* hit in any territory and as a consequence became huge stars in Germany. Ironically, the hit came about because The Creation on this tour acquired the sort of bad-boy reputation that was so natural to the Rolling Stones but did not come easily to such a quiet and sedate bunch. Or, indeed, any other group at the time. As June Clark points out of the 'Sixties, "You had to be pleasant and nice. You couldn't get away with Johnny Lydon's antics. You'd got to be clean cut. You've no *idea* what everybody thought about the Stones. You didn't want to have a bad image. You didn't want to be rebellious. In fact, you'd defend yourself if it came across that way. Even John Lennon defending himself about the Jesus Christ issue."

The Creation's bad-boy reputation began when their fire-starting got out of hand upon the occasion of the tour party playing the Circus Krone in Munich on 22 January. Jack: "We played more or less in the ring and we were surrounded by kids. And of course that went up and I think they were unhappy 'cos they hadn't been warned about it." Bob: "That is quite a high building, so to set the place on fire you would really have to go some. They didn't know we were going to do a fire and they responded as firemen do. As soon as they saw the fire, they came in and extinguished it. They burst in and doused it before the thing got off the ground."

Jack: "We had the police threatening to throw us out of the country and everything." Clark recalls Bob sending her a postcard and promising to 'tell you more when I come home'. "I know Bob wasn't happy about it. Bob doesn't like things where it makes a band look bad. Bob gets upset by that sort of thing. He'd keep it to himself but he used to tell me. He didn't think that was funny. Bob was very sour about it."

Although the group were allowed to remain in the country they were – with considerable publicity – banned from Munich for life. No particular measures were taken to ensure this prohibition was upheld. As Bob points out, "Afterwards, I've got photographs of me with The Creation in the Big Apple Club in Leopold Strasse in Munich." Nonetheless, The Creation were in the news and, in an anti-authoritarian era where any perceived rebelliousness was ultra-chic, their stock in Germany shot through the roof.

As discussed before, Bob considered Arthur Howes too much of an old-school impresario to be able to operate in the areas that The Creation needed to in order to make a good living from live work. Jack also had misgivings. "He was more of a theatrical agent I think," says Jack. "Arthur Howes was a nice guy, but you need a manager that's going to concentrate on the band like conventional managers do. They get out and about. Arthur Howes had an agency and he had, I dunno, maybe 10, 20 acts altogether and he oversaw that. That's totally different to being a manager. He wouldn't have the time to devote to us. Arthur was a nice man and he did a fair job for us, he got us a lot of the German (work) but really we needed a manager who would devote more or less all his time in pushing the band on and no way Arthur Howes could do that 'cos he had people like Helen Shapiro, the Walker Brothers – who were very big at the time."

It seems logical that – even if Garrick is mistaken about Collins and Wace having briefly assumed The Creation's management duties – this was the period when Kenny approached the managers of The Kinks: not only were the band suddenly in need of a manager in the first few months of 1967, but Kenny cited the failure of the band to employ the aforementioned duo as one of the reasons for his departure, which occurred in late February or early March of that year. Kenny recounted the attempted ditching of Howes to *Blitz* in '82. (In the interview, he bizarrely confused Collins and Wace with Howard and Blaikley, managers of – and songwriters for – lightweight pop acts like Dave Dee, Dozy, Beaky, Mick and Tich and The Herd. Just in case, the author contacted both Howard and Blaikley and both confirmed they recalled no approach from The Creation).

"Because we weren't breaking here in Britain but were successful in Germany," Kenny said, "we were blaming our management, our record company and our agency in this country. So the band got together and said, 'Okay, let's leave Arthur Howes and put our management with someone else.' At the time Howard and Blaikely (*sic*), the managers of the Kinks, wanted to take us over. I said that I would be spokesman and inform everybody that we were going to leave, which I duly did. But when it came to the crunch and there were conferences going around, nobody in the band would back me up! 'What? No! we don't want to change our managers'. Etcetera. So I thought if it was going to be like that, and I wasn't seeing eye to eye with Bob Garner or Eddie Phillips at that time, I told them I was off."

Another name that crops up in the Creation's search for a manager is Robert Stigwood. Some of the Creation's personnel had known Stigwood for a few years: he had booked live work for both The Mark Four and The Creation. Recalls Jack, "A guy named David Oddie was our booker with Starlight Artists as the Mark Four. When we become The Creation and we got put with Stigwood with agency work, David Oddie was our booker again, so that was a little coincidence."

Stigwood was moving on from agency work. Now a manager, he had on his hands two acts who would shortly be very big indeed: Cream and the Bee Gees. Both of these acts were, like The Creation, Polydor artists (albeit, in Cream's case, merely distributed by them). "Shel was sort of talking to Stigwood those days," Bob recalls, but "I think the Bee Gees took up most of his time really. I never met him or anything like that." Jack adds: "The thing about Robert Stigwood, is, you'd get to talk to the band and then you wouldn't be able to find him for three months. He'd be in America or somewhere, raving around. The Bee Gees were his number one band."

Not only did Stigwood not become The Creation's manager but the band never acquired a full-time manager again. When asked why, Jack can only offer: "I don't know really. I mean, we had Arthur Howes, we had Shel, we were making records, we were earning good money and we were doing good gigs." The inertia hinted at on the band's part by Jack's comments seems incredibly short-sighted. The absence of a manager with sufficient vision to see the immediate rewards of small-scale gigs as merely subsistence-garnering stepping stones to global stardom rather than an end in itself may have been crucial in the ultimate lack of success of The Creation.

Despite their unsettled management – and record label – situation, The Creation were still able to make great art. Their first recording session of 1967 took place on 15 February and saw them lay down two superb new, self-composed tracks: 'Can I Join Your Band' and 'Nightmares'. As before, IBC, studio A was the setting. Talmy produced, John Pantry engineered and Damon Lyon-Shaw tape op'd. It's possible that Polydor – which would be The Creation's new record label – had agreed to release their product by the time this session took place, and it's equally possible they hadn't: funding recording sessions whose results he would lease to labels was something Talmy was used to, so he wouldn't necessarily have waited to commit some more Creation material to tape.

'Can I Join Your Band' was a milestone for Eddie Phillips on all fronts. Though the publishing attributes the song to Pickett/Phillips, it was the first 100% Phillips composition. Furthermore, not only did he write both melody and lyric, but he sang the vocal too. The melody and arrangement were both excellent – giddying key changes aplenty and galvanising switching of tempos, culminating in a heart-stoppingly exciting move into a double-time climax – but the lyric , for a first effort, was astounding. The picaresque tale of a frustrated pop band member, it saw Eddie reeling off not only instantly memorable slogans but verses into which were packed the plots of entire novels.

Eddie himself is mystified as to his inspiration for the track. While the origins of the couplet 'Can I join your band, I'm a hippie guy/Always stoned and eight miles high' are clearly a nod to the Byrds' classic 'Eight Miles High' single – released in Britain the previous April – lines like 'My daddy was a soldier, he played the fife and drums/Left mummy and the children starving in the slums' are so apparently drenched in raw experience that they inevitably lead one to assume they stem from Eddie's own life. Yet he insists they are not autobiographical. "I don't know!" Eddie says when asked from whence he dug such material. "Don't ask me.

What's all that? I don't honestly know where that come from. Sometimes, you pick things out of fantasy."

The middle section of the song was a respite that saw Eddie – bowing his guitar – and Nicky Hopkins engaged in call and response patterns. "I remember Nicky getting really involved with that one in the solo especially," says Bob. "The piano, for The Creation, is quite upfront." Bob has reservations about the repetition of the title phrase towards the close: "The vocals get a little bit messed up towards the end. We were just going round and round and we just thought, 'They'll fade this out' but they didn't... After the repeat – 'Can I join your band?, Can I join your band?' – and there's another line underneath – 'Ca-a-n I jo-oin your band' – one stops too soon and one goes on."

As with his lyric-writing entrée, Eddie's debut recorded vocal was highly impressive. "I can't remember, really," says Eddie of why he decided to take the mic. "I just sung it. There was no big reason why I did. Probably seemed a good idea at the time." Bob, though, remembers a certain sense of mission about the decision, one probably tied in with the issue of his colleague's first lyric-writing outing: "He had to get off his chest. Wanted it on tape and out of the way... It was one of those things Eddie sang himself and it was his own little thing."

It was an impressive performance, as confident and expressive as any Creation vocal track laid down by Kenny or, later, Bob. "I think he was a very good, commercial singer without having a great voice," says Talmy. "In the same way that I suppose Ray Davies does not have a great voice but he's got a very commercial voice." If the band had decided, when Kenny left, that Eddie should have been the vocalist, would Talmy have been in favour? "Yeah, absolutely. He was extremely good. I (later)did some (solo) singles with Eddie, so obviously 1 must have thought he sang okay."

From what Bob recalls, the song itself originated the previous year or very early in '67, because his memory has Stratton-Smith still being on the scene when the composition was being used to try to acquire the band's songs a new publisher. Bob: "Stratton-Smith took us to some publishing company and they said, 'Yeah, but you'll have to change 'Always stoned and eight miles high'. I remember thinking, 'Goodness me'."

Jack was thoroughly impressed by the song. "'Can I Join Your Band' I thought was a great little number for the time," he says. "The guy running along behind the bandstand or whatever it was carrying a guitar and he wants to join. It was one of his better lyrics... I thought it was the best thing Eddie ever wrote. He never wrote a lot of stuff." For Jack, it was yet another confirmation of the way that a caterpillar had blossomed into a beautiful butterfly: "When Eddie first joined the band he was a guitarist who played nice little solos but you could see the progression all the way through. When we got The Creation he started using feedback and all this stuff. He just got better and better and better. I thought 'Can I Join Your Band' would have made a great single."

There were eight attempts at the basic track of 'Can I Join Your Band'. Takes 1, 2 and 7 were breakdowns and track 4 a false start. All the rest were completes and it was take 8 chosen for the master.

At the 1993 Creation reunion at the Mean Fiddler, Kenny explained of the other, more tormented song recorded this day, that it was written following a bad drug trip: "I was lying in bed. It was about four o'clock in the morning and I was having these awful, awful nightmares." The musical part of 'Nightmares' was another rich, highly melodic effort from Eddie, with a rousing chorus. Eddie's guitarwork on the track was highly innovative. So innovative, and tricky, in fact, that ever since he has had severe problems in replicating it on stage. "If you want to do it exactly like the record it really is difficult," he says. "It starts off tapping on harmonics and that's always a bit hit-and-miss live."

The technique Eddie refers to involves a guitarist knocking the guitar's strings with his fingertips twelve frets (one octave) above the chord he is forming to produce an intriguing bell-like effect. Eddie: "And the riff actually is played on harmonics by tapping on the harmonics. Again, that's okay if you're in the studio environment, where you're sitting down where you can just tap the harmonic and get the sound, but when you're in the live situation, it's not gonna come through enough – so nine times out of 10 I'm just playing it."

As it that weren't enough, the four-to-four stage of the process saw yet more cutting edge experimentation in the form of an attempt to overdub a backward guitar part. This process – which may have taken place at another studio – does not seem to have resulted in a part that was considered usable: nothing on the completed track has the slurred, gulping qualities of the backwards technique, the most prominent example of which thus far had been George Harrison's break in The Beatles' 'I'm Only Sleeping' in August '66. Bob: "They definitely tried it because there was the Harrison thing. I think they even tried putting it through a Leslie speaker and all that kind of thing but it didn't work."

Lyon-Shaw can't remember trying the technique with The Creation specifically but says of the process: "We used to play the tape backwards and record the guitar forwards and then when you play it back the right way the guitar sounds very spooky. Very difficult to do, I have to say." Talmy: "I probably decided it wasn't good enough or something. We tried all sorts of stuff on a regular basis. It was that time in the music business where everything was fair game and I kept trying new things with every band I produced. Some worked. In fact, most of 'em worked, I'm glad to say."

The possibility that the two songs may have had more work done to them outside of IBC arises for two reasons. Firstly, though Talmy, Pantry and Lyon-Shaw definitely began the four-four process at IBC that same day, the name of Glyn Johns – *persona non grata* at IBC – has been added to the engineers' credits on the ledger in a different hand, presumably his own. It is this same hand which details the specifics of the four-four process.

It was take 2 of the four-to-four that was chosen for 'Can I Join Your Band', with the additional tracks comprised of 'rthm', 'guitars' and two vocal tracks, one of which would have been the lead vocal (unless, in a highly unlikely move, Eddie had opted to sing live on the basic track). The same handwriting explains the overdub stage of 'Nightmares' thus: 'A rthm C 1st vocals D rthm'. (B was left blank.) Only one take was deemed necessary for 'Nightmares" four-four. "The four-four's we did but to what extent I don't know," says Lyon-Shaw. "He might have just mixed it down from four-track. I don't know why Shel would have gone back to him (Johns) but it might have been that case. It might have been a long time afterwards. I suspect that he actually did something with our final four-track."

The other reason for believing that the tracks were added to outside IBC is that Bob is almost certain that his vocal for 'Nightmares' was done at Pye studios. It's conceivable that Kenny had laid down a vocal track for 'Nightmares' at IBC. However, when the track eventually saw commercial release, it was Bob Garner's voice that would be singing the words Kenny had written, for by then Kenny was no longer a member of the Creation.

Kenny Pickett's departure from The Creation seems to have been brewing for several months and to have had three main causes. The first was a relationship with his songwriting partner in The Creation that was always uneasy. "He and Eddie were feuding," says Talmy. "I never really understood what they were feuding about. I was friendly with both of 'em. I continued to be friendly with both of 'em individually." Bob saw things in slightly less dramatic terms: "I never saw them arguing. Maybe just a little: 'This should have three in' and 'This should have four in'. That kind of thing." However, he does add, "Both very strong-headed people. Both probably realised their worth to each other."

The respective modus operandi of Eddie and Kenny in attempting to get their way in a dispute were very different but, from the sound of it, equally bad. Kenny would boil over and rant and rave if things were not to his liking. Clark remembers of Kenny, "Had a terrible temper. Terrible. He was the one that would cause arguments in the band. Eddie would just have an opinion but not cause arguments. Kenny was nasty about it. Very aggressive person. He to me was the troublemaker in that band."

However, Eddie's attitude could be characterised by a certain sulkiness. "Eddie's far too emotional to this day," says Clark. "Very, very emotional, and is led by his emotions. Whereas Kenny was a bit more strong-headed and a bit more business-like about it. He's a bit of a softie – he's an absolute sweetheart – but business-wise, your emotions can't get in the way in a business. You've just got be very factual about it and Eddie would get hurt by things, Eddie would carry grudges. So he wasn't strong in that way. Intuitive, yes, very sensitive, very creative. Not always good at enforcing his ideas in an appropriate way... His heated emotion would prevent him from calmly discussing a subject."

The other reason for Kenny's disgruntlement would seem to be a conviction that his territory was gradually being eroded. The position within a rock ensemble of a singer who does not play a musical instrument is always one that leaves him vulnerable to scrutiny and even paranoia. He is theoretically the one who is most expendable: unless tone deaf, any one of the other band members could do his job with a certain amount of competence, yet he can't do any of their jobs. This doesn't matter so much if the singer has such a great voice that it is integral to the artistic or commercial worth of the group. Eric Burdon's position in The Creation's contemporaries The Animals, for instance, was unassailable – and that despite the fact that he had only a smidgen of Pickett's lyric-writing ability. Kenny's vocal abilities were good but Burdon had one of the most distinctive and exciting voices of his generation.

Kenny's insecure position must have been brought home to him every time he ceded the microphone to Jack, Eddie or Bob on stage and had to stand there doing nothing except singing backing harmonies, knocking a tambourine or shaking maracas for the duration of their respective showcase number. When that situation was brought into the studio by Eddie's decision that he was going to sing 'Can I Join Your Band', it can only have worsened Kenny's paranoia on the issue. However, it would seem Kenny was far more concerned at the threat he felt Bob Garner posed to his position.

From what Jack recalls, it seems not even the knowledge of the fact that he had a well above average lyric-writing talent could quell the insecurities nagging at Kenny. "He was sure we were trying to row him out of the band and (felt) it really wasn't on," says Jack. "I think Eddie wanted to do a few more vocals and Bob wanted to do a few more vocals and Kenny saw that as a way of himself being pushed out. He was just being over-sensitive... Ego, really. Bob had been in a band where he'd been the bass player and singing all the songs so just standing there playing the bass, I think after a while he started thinking, 'I'm a bit fed up with this, I want do a vocal'. And then Eddie suddenly...started going down the Hendrix path a bit. It was like everybody was on an ego trip and I couldn't really hold them all together. I was quite happy just playing drums."

A final reason for Kenny's increasing discomfort in The Creation is his impatience for stardom, one that would seem entwined with his desire to recruit Wace and Collins and to which Jack has previously referred. Jack: "I didn't mind Kenny. I thought his singing was okay, he wrote good lyrics, he was a decent sort of bloke. But he was a bit of a headcase at times 'cos he was so impatient. He wanted to do everything yesterday."

All of these frustrations on Kenny's part came to a head in either very late February or early March 1967. As late as the 25th of the short month of February Kenny was performing 'Painter Man' with The Creation on German TV programme *Beat Club* and the band played a gig in Bremen (where *Beat Club* was recorded) the following day. That TV performance – The Creation apparently plugged in and in front of a live audience but miming – certainly gives a clue that not all was well among the band's personnel. Towards the close of the song, Eddie repeatedly mock-whips Kenny with the broken catguts hanging off his violin bow. Something other than playfulness is suggested when Kenny, unsmiling and almost grimacing, flaps his hand at the insistent bow. This peculiar picture of what may be innocent fun but may also be a snapshot of shortly-to-explode tension bubbling just below the surface is commercially available on the DVD *Beat Club – The Best of '67*.

Back in Britain, it was Jack whom Kenny approached to speak of his unhappiness. Recalls Jack: "He came round my house once and he said, 'Look, I hear there's rumours you're going to throw me out of the band'. I said, 'What you talking about? No, not true'. He said, 'Well that's what I've heard and nobody throws me out of the band. I'm quitting'." Mindful of the involvement Kenny had had in Jack being jettisoned from the group six months previously, Jack wasn't inclined to beg his colleague to reconsider: "So I thought, 'Well sod you, please yourself pal'. And I said, 'Well look, Ken, that's up to you, that's your decision'."

Jack suspects there may have been another factor in Kenny's resignation decision: "I think one of the things was he'd just wrote a book and Shel was going to publish it for him. I think he saw himself as a big, successful writer". Gail Colson's memories tally with Jack's on this point: "I knew Kenny was going to leave because he told me but he was always moaning and talking about it a lot. He wanted to do other things – be a writer."

Not that, once Jack had informed the rest of The Creation of developments, the band necessarily took Kenny's gesture seriously. "You had to know Kenny," says Jack. "Don't get me wrong, I like Kenny, he was a good bloke, but he was volatile and he would go off half-cock on these various avenues. The thing was, we knew him. We said, 'Oh leave him alone, he'll come round' and once you left him alone..." However, it quickly became apparent that Kenny was serious. Laments Jack: "We knew how to handle him but he'd heard this rumour and Bob did an awful lot of stirring."

Indeed, it is Bob Garner that Kenny himself specified as his main reason for departing the band in his '82 interview with *Blitz*. "Basically, it was a personality clash," Kenny said. "I didn't like Bob Garner. Never did. He was one of those people I loathed. In fact, I still do." In '97, Kenny told *Ugly Things*, "I'd always thought he was a nasty piece of work, the one who originally started the whole business of splitting the band up and getting his mates in there." Gail Colson, who was close to Kenny at the time, offers: "I have never heard of Kenny thinking Bob wanted his job – but on the other hand Kenny was a bit of a moaner, God bless him."

June Clark was astonished at the vitriol aimed in Bob's direction. "I had no idea, just as Bob didn't, Kenny hated him that much," she says. "When that came out in *Ugly Things*, Bob phoned me. He was hurt. We were both stunned. Bob said to me, 'Did you know that?' I said, 'No I didn't'. I had no idea Kenny hated Bob that much or resented him that much. Bob said to me, 'I didn't think I ever caused any trouble did I?' I said, 'No you didn't'. And he didn't."

Shel Talmy also aimed some vitriol in *Ugly Things*, where he said, "People from up north, like Warrington, have a fucking attitude! I mean they're born with like three chips on their shoulder. That was Bob. That was what pissed me off. He was a disruptive influence." Says Bob, "That's what inspired Kim to phone me. He rang me and said, 'Have you heard these things...?' I said, 'Yeah'. He said, 'Well I spoke to him and I told him none of this is true'. He said to me that he'd spoke to Shel to say he didn't agree with the comments of me. He was talking to me and saying, 'That wasn't how it was, was it?' and I said, 'Not that I (recall). What trouble did I cause?'... I thought, 'This guy is from Los Angeles in America and he's qualified to tell the difference between somebody who lives in Manchester or Birmingham or London?' And if there is any difference apart from the accent, there's good and bad in all counties."

Clark finds the notion of Bob scheming completely unbelievable: "(Bob is) very, very easy-going so it really, really is untrue that he caused problems in the band. If he did it, it was without himself knowing about it and it was all down to his personality. People misreading him. I do assure you of that because he's a very gentle person. Just like when they came over last year (2001), played in Brooklyn, Bob didn't care who Eddie brought (to play). He said, 'Whoever Eddie's got with him is fine with me'." June remembers Bob as a neutral element of The Creation's chemistry in the Sixties: "Bob went along with just about anything. He doesn't like ever rocking the boat. He might put an opinion forth and then see how it goes but in the end he'd sooner just go along with the others to keep the peace."

Bob pleads innocent to the charge of plotting to wrest Kenny's frontman job from him and suggests another reason for what had occurred: "I think it was the frustration of we were coming up with the goods but the management and everybody else wasn't and it was almost like Jack may have had revenge on Kenny... What I mean was because Kenny really forced the issue of getting Dave Preston in, that when the twist came that Kenny should go because he was getting perhaps a little bit unruly that Jack was probably thinking...'Now it's your turn'. If Jack had've been asked, 'Should Kenny go?' I think Jack would have said 'Yeah'." Bob says that Jack's indignation at the way he was treated manifested itself in an enduring resentment toward Kenny: "(When) I met (Jack) in later years, he was still stinging."

Yet, from Jack's point of view, it was predictable that Bob was handed Kenny's job after the latter's exit. "Suddenly I found that Bob had become the singer of the band and I thought, 'Hang on, this is what he's been angling for for a long time'," Jack says. Bob counters: "I didn't know he was going. I think it was, 'Will you be alright doing the vocals?' and I can't remember who said it to me or anything like that. It was just another of those things, I was just picking up the pieces again, and said 'Okay'."

When doing interviews about The Creation upon their Nineties reunion, Bob found journalists asking him questions about his alleged plotting against Kenny thirty years before: "There was a lot of things pointed at me, saying I split the band, I did this... I said, 'Hang on – I can't see where you've got that from. I not only can't remember, I certainly wouldn't do what's been suggested'." He has a theory about why the image of him as a schemer might be plausible: "At the end, I picked up that many pieces: all three of them had left the band. I'd been in the band continuously from first day of the name Creation 'til the end and all of them had left. It's me through the middle just picking up the pieces – yet it's down as I've got rid of him, sacked him, done that..."

Talmy has no difficulty accepting Kenny's perception of Bob as a schemer. "Bob Garner was always awkward," he says. "He's an awkward son of a bitch. I can't help that. Disruptive sometimes, other times no. He always seemed to have a chip on his shoulder. Some people have an attitude. That's the way he was. I think he rubbed pretty much everybody the wrong way at one point." When prompted, Talmy is unable to provide an anecdote that illustrates this awkwardness.

He bristles slightly when then asked if this means his perception of Bob comes second-hand from Kenny, with whom he continued to be friendly after the latter left The Creation: "No, I make my own decisions, thank you. I don't need people to tell me about how I feel about people. There are some people who had an attitude. He had one. It was basically a chip-on-the-shoulder attitude. Roger Daltrey had it. Lots of people have it. You try to minimise it and work through it. He was good for what he did. I would not have been unhappy to see him leave the band, which he eventually did at some point, because I don't like disruption."

Jack is able to provide an example of Bob's 'stirring': "One time he came up to me at a gig in Stoke and said, 'Oh I'm fed up with all this feedback row. I know a really good guitarist in Liverpool'. And I said, 'Why don't you piss off Bob?' It was all I could think to say and he went away. How could you chuck Eddie out the band, for Christ's sake? The bloody band was built round Eddie."

With Kenny now gone, a new singer was required. Bob Garner was the obvious choice in that he had an impressive, smoky voice he was already used to utilising on several stage numbers. The fact that he also possessed the kind of good looks normally associated with pop frontmen can't have gone unnoticed by his colleagues either. Instead of Bob singing while continuing to play bass, it was decided to draft in a new bass player. The one chosen was Kim Gardner, who just happened to be on the books of Arthur Howes, then acting as both The Creation's manager and agent.

The similarity of Gardner's surname to that of Bob Garner has caused confusion down the years. One fanzine in the Seventies even stated as supposed fact that Bob had changed his name during his time in The Creation for legal reasons. It is because of this potential for confusion that The Creation members are referred to by their Christian names in this narrative.

"We got Kim Gardner in because we had an awful lot of work in the books and it was immediate and we had to put a band together and do this work," says Jack. "We said, 'Well Bob can do the singing' – 'cos that's what he'd always been angling for anyway – and we told Arthur Howes we needed a bass player and Bill Fowler rang me up and said, 'We've got a guy here named Kim Gardner, used to be bass player with the English Birds, and he seems a nice guy and he's a good player'. So we met up with Kim and it was great."

Kim told *Ugly Things* in 1997 of his recruitment, "The music was fun and the money was nice. I'd never been in another band except the Birds, so it was kind of a transition and it was very exciting. It was something I could sink my teeth into."

Couldn't Bob have played bass and sang? Jack: "He could have done but it would have changed the image of the group. Like, one singer surrounded by three things. It did seem better." Asked if he feels he could have continued to handle bass duties while taking over the singer's role, Bob says, "Well I do but that decision I didn't know anything about." Of course, Eddie's impressive performance on 'Can I Join Your Band' theoretically made him a candidate for the singer's job but, asked if he thought of himself in that role, Eddie says "No, not at all. I do a lot singing now but in those days I was quite happy just to be a guitar player."

And what of the possibility of continuing as a three-piece, with Bob both singing and playing bass? Eddie: "No, never fancied that one, although we could have earnt more money (each)... When Kenny left somebody just told us Kim Gardner was on the scene, looking for a band and we thought, 'Well, maybe Bob could do that and Kim could do that." Jack offers a further reason why Eddie taking over the singer's role would have been unwise: "I think really what Eddie was doing on stage with his bow and all the feedback and the sounds, he had more than enough really to cope with . It did seem a natural thing to put Bob up front and we were very lucky we found a bass player in Kim. I thought the band sounded great, actually."

Bob also says, "I think it was just the image of three instruments and then somebody at the front and also if you're doing the painting and everything, you need somebody hands-free. It's like when we did the American thing (Cavestomp in 2001), Eddie and myself could have done it just with a drummer but we said, 'No, we'll do the whole thing, the screen and everything, and that's why we did it as a four-piece'. That left me free to do whatever I wanted to do on stage."

The recollections of Jack and Bob of how Kim Gardner came to join the group are almost identical. Bob: "To be perfectly honest with you, I went up to Arthur Howes' office and Kim Gardner was there and I went, 'Oh look' and that was that. I really didn't know that Kenny was going. Nobody said to me. I don't know how they got hold of Kim Gardner, don't know where he came from." Asked the same question, Eddie says, "No idea. I can just remember him being there." Not that it matters whether the band were delivered a *fait accompli* by an agent who had a spare client on his hands or whether it was their own idea: The Creation's surviving members are unanimous in their praise of Gardner as both a musician and a person.

Kim's previous band The Birds were an ensemble who never made the big time despite being an aggregate that oozed talent. As well as having one of the country's finest bassists in Kim, they could also boast no less a guitarist than Ron Wood. Unfortunately, any hope this group had of making the big time was probably destroyed when an American group had a UK Number 1 in the summer of 1965 with their electrified cover of Bob Dylan's 'Mr Tambourine Man': The Byrds. Though the lawsuit they served on the Americans during their August '65 UK tour gave the Birds a turn in the spotlight – probably the main reason for the action, as no court was going to believe the US group had tried to cash in on the name of an unknown band – it also marked the death knell of their hopes of stardom. From hereon, they were destined to be remembered only as the group of also-rans whose name was similar to an band who would become legends.

The Birds had not quite split at the time that Kim was recruited to The Creation. Birds member Ali MacKenzie explained the situation thus to *Ugly Things*, "Basically we hit a lull like any business where work was slack... Kim and Pete (McDaniels, drums) were at loggerheads...It was agreed that we should have a couple of months rest from each other...and we never got back together again."

Jack Jones was delighted at having as his rhythm-section partner a man who was not only technically proficient but who carried on The Creation tradition of being at the cutting edge of rock'n'roll. "Kim was superb," enthuses Jack. "I thought he was one of the finest bass players around at the time. He had a great sound as well. He was a joy to play with... At the time, bass guitar strings were of a type and then somebody invented wire-wound strings and Kim was one of the first guys to take them up. It gave you a twangy sound, almost like a string on a grand piano. Kim took that up and got a tremendous sound. Absolutely beautiful."

Eddie, too, was galvanised by the new element in the sound: "He was a really good musician," says the guitarist. "He was a really good, inventive bass player and he would sometimes play along with me, kind of lead lines on the bass as well. We played a lot of unison riffs together and that was probably the first time I'd done that with a bass player."

June Clark knew something about bass virtuosity from her friendship with John Entwistle and found the playing styles of the two very similar. "Kim really was a dedicated bass player," she says. "He loved bass. He was so good on it. I think he improved (the Creation's sound). He brought something to it. It was a little bit more creative when Kim joined." Personality-wise, however, Kim could not have been more different from the one known among Who fans as The Quiet One. "Kim also had such a good personality and you picked up on it on stage," says Clark. "He was always smiling where Bob was always looking down and serious and the shy one. Kim brought a lot to the band. A lot of goofiness. I think they had more fun than ever before because of him but Kim was a good talent, a really serious talent. And they knew that."

"Kim was a great fella," says Bob, who also thinks that he was the closest the Creation had to that Lennon-esque figure he always felt the band missed: "He had a little bit of outrageousness about him. I think if he'd have been given his leash, he would have perhaps made a little bit of noise, publicity-wise. He had that ability to go in and wind people up. I don't mean aggressively – he was quite a funny lad, actually – but we were just laid-back, really." Eddie: "His personality...was tip-top. You just thought, 'We've got to have this man'."

"Kim Gardner was funny," says Clark. "Antics? Oh, he'd wear you out, absolutely wear you out. Keith (Moon) and Kim Gardner – very similar, although Keith was a bit more extreme. Kim was so wild. Kim was always joking about everything. Sometimes it was almost hard to have a quiet conversation with him. But a real sweetheart."

Though Kim undoubtedly had considerable qualities as a human being, perhaps one should be suspicious of the party line his friends take about him having no real malice in his character. Certain of his pranks were completely distasteful, such as an incident about which he told *Ugly Things* in which he locked the Bee Gees in a toilet overnight. His supposedly mitigating observation about an ordeal that must have been distressing in the extreme to the victims – that he meant to release them after a short while but forgot about them – was somewhat undermined by his complete lack of visible remorse. Nonetheless, the enjoyment Eddie, Bob and Jack took in Kim's company seems genuine enough. As Clark observes, "I think (they were) more settled. They really liked having Kim there."

Bob says he didn't miss playing the bass. "I remember showing Kim what I'd done on a couple of tracks just to make it the same as, and that was it." In any case, he had a new job to grow into. It was a job in which Bob feels he found his own style: "When I've listened to things, I was singing the songs different than Kenny anyway. I wouldn't try to mimic Kenny." As a frontman, however, he did take some cues from people behind whom he'd previously stood on stage. "I'd never stood as a frontman before, singing without an instrument," he says. "The only thing I can draw on there was that I had enough experience of watching some of the good entertainers, I'd stood behind Freddie Starr watching him as a solo performer, watching Lee Curtis as a solo performer. Worked with your Sheridans and that. I had a good idea of what I was supposed to do, so I just went into it naturally."

An indication of what would probably have lain in store for The Creation had Kenny not departed was provided by a bizarre incident that took place at the very first rehearsal attended by Kim. By this point in time, Creation band practice was taking place at a house in Harrow, north-west London rented by Bob, Creation roadie Alan Smith and two girls (neither of whom were romantically involved with Bob or Smith). "I think one was Australian," says Bob of his female housemates. "I honestly can't remember how they cropped up but it worked out okay. We just shared the place. We was hardly ever there when they were there and so on."

Clark says of the residence and its arrangements, "He used to share a room with Alan…they were very close friends. I don't know who owned it. There were two girls that lived there. I think it was their house and they rented out rooms. It was detached. It was like a posher area. Long way away, 'cos I was living in Plumstead Common. It was like the other end of the earth for me to go all the way up there." The fact that the house was detached and the way its interior was arranged made it ideal for a pop group's rehearsals: "It had space," says Clark. "They had a big living room that flowed through."

Jack: "The place in Epping was far out the way whereas (Bob's place) was very convenient for everybody. A nice central point. It was a nice big house and we took over the living room, the front room if you like, and there was plenty of room. We didn't rehearse at Harrow very long, probably about a month or something." Bob agrees that they only rehearsed at this venue for a short while, adding, "There wasn't a lot of rehearsing went on." But why were they rehearsing here instead of a conventional rehearsal space?

Clark: "They didn't have any money. Nobody seemed to want to give them any money to do anything."

The way Kenny recounted the circumstances of his exit from The Creation to *Record Collector*'s John Reed in 1995 revolved around the rehearsal at Harrow at which Kim first played with his new bandmates. "I heard they were rehearsing up in Harrow, where Bob lived," Kenny said. "I drove over, took my stuff and drove off." His comments failed to mention the fact that he had already left the band by the time of Kim's musical baptism. His actions on the day in question similarly seemed to suggest amnesia about his previous resignation.

Jack's recollection of the incident runs thus: "We were having a mini rehearsal over Harrow and Kenny turned up. I think I was in one room. He come to the front door and shot off again so I didn't get to talk to him, but it was like two weeks after me and him had had this conversation in my place about (how he'd) decided to quit."

"Kenny did turn up," says Bob, "and I'm almost certain that Ronnie Wood was there as well. He wasn't rehearsing with the band but I'm almost certain that he was there that day." Ronnie Wood later confirmed this. In Terry Rawlings' book *Rock On Wood*, he was quoted as saying, "I'd always thought Eddie Phillips was cool and I'd heard about how great a guitar-player he was. I'd heard he played with a violin bow and fucking hacksaws, which was way ahead of Jimmy Page, so I went along with Kim to watch."

Bob: "Kenny didn't really say anything to me. Because I'd been living at Kenny's house and I'd only just moved away. I never remember any sort of backlash towards myself. Again, between the three of them, this previous thing kept on cropping up."

In *Rock On Wood*, Kim recalled of Kenny's behaviour that day, "He was storming about calling everyone cunts and I didn't actually know who he was because The Creation mostly played on the continent. So I'm standing there and Ronnie's sitting on the amps watching all this. I turn to Jack and said, 'Who's that bloke?' and he goes, 'Oh that's the singer' and I'm like, 'I thought Bob's the singer', and Jack says, 'Well he is but he was the bass player', and then I look over to John (Dalton) and say, 'Well, who's he?' and Jack goes, 'He's the bass player too'... and I said, 'What the fuck! How many fucking bass players does this band need!' and Ronnie just cracked up."

Yet John Dalton – who one would imagine would remember witnessing such bizarre goings-on – denies being at this rehearsal. "I wouldn't be round anybody's house," he says. "I would go and see them at a gig if they were local but that's about it." Yet he does append: "It sounds like Ken, though."

"When Kenny came round, it was too late," says Jack. "We'd given Kim the job. What were we supposed to do? Say, 'Oh, Kenny's changed his mind, sod off Kim, Bob go back on bass'. You just can't do that."

"He probably tried his bluff really," says Bob.

June Clark, who heard of the incident second-hand, says, "Everybody was in shock". She attributes Kenny's apparent memory lapse about his previous resignation to, "Second thoughts. Regretting your anger, regretting your temper."

While Jack may be unsympathetic to Kenny's second thoughts, he feels the misunderstanding over his position that led to Kenny quitting in the first place was avoidable. "I feel the whole thing about The Creation was stupid 'cos if we had sat down in a room together – with, say, Stratton-Smith (or) Shel Talmy in the room – and sat there until we got all our problems sorted out, there wouldn't have been any of this crap," says Jack. "A lot of it was based on just nonsense. There you go. That's guys, innit?"

The first Creation gigs with the Eddie-Bob-Kim-Jack line-up took place in Scotland in March '67. "Basically Kim learnt most of the act in the van going up to Scotland," says Jack. Gigs in Dundee, Dunfermline and Dunbar saw them supported by the Dream Police. An unhelpful but accurate Creation mention appeared in the Pop Talk column of the 18

March *Record Mirror*: "Despite having two singles in the charts last year, it is over six months (actually five) since The Creation's last record and there seems no sign of a new one being produced in the near future." In fact, it would be a further three months before the new Creation single – cumulatively, a very long hiatus for the period – and one wonders whether the Creation's commercial fate was partly sealed by this loss of momentum.

It would be a while before their supporters and friends in England got to see the new Creation line-up live. When they did, the opinion of most seems to have been that Bob was not as strong a frontman as Kenny.

Jack: "If you want my opinion, Bob's a fair singer but he was based in a Georgie Fame style and I don't think really The Creation would have suited what he did. He was a little bit more jazzy. Myself, Eddie and Kenny were the embryo of The Creation from five years back. We'd come through the Bluejacks and the Mark Four and all that and basically grown up as guys and musicians until we got to The Creation – that was us, and then we added Bob to it. But what Bob wanted to do was then say, 'You've added me to it but now I want to be the frontman and I'm going to change the whole style of the band and everything to suit me'. It just weren't on… I always preferred Kenny because he had more of an aggressive approach to rock."

"Very powerful image on stage, Kenny had," says Clark. "So self-assured. Whereas Bob had this very soft image. That comes with his personality. So very different images with two different singers. Very different voices too, very different pitches. Bob spoke less. Kenny's much more interactive, lots of fun, very positive, he would grab the audience. Really a good frontman because of this ego he had. It worked for him. It's what you need as a frontman. In that way, Bob wasn't as good, although I preferred Bob's voice. I think Bob's got a very unusual voice and I prefer that. Bob I think is better-looking than Kenny but Kenny had a better personality."

"I think Kenny was better," says Talmy. "I like Kenny's stuff better. I'm not denigrating Bob. He did fine. I preferred Kenny." He admits of the new line-up, though, "It made some good records. I don't know what I felt about it except could I make good records and I guess the answer was yes. Some of the records are as good as the old line-up… It already was not The Creation as I had started recording The Creation. But they actually kept their end up. They seemed to have a knack. They went through various permutations, obviously, and I managed to always get (the best) out of them regardless of who was there. Obviously the spirit really being Eddie Phillips because it's really his band, his sound, and everybody else was somewhat interchangeable… I really just wanted to try and preserve the group and if that was the way it was gonna be, that's the way it was gonna be. I tried to make do with what was happening until such time when it became impossible."

Meanwhile, Kenny Pickett had other fish to fry. The book he had presented to Shel Talmy, possibly even before quitting The Creation, was called *The Herberts*, a semi-autobiographical novel. Talmy recalls it as being in the kitchen-sink drama mould of Alan Sillitoe's *Saturday Night And Sunday Morning*: "With that Cockney influence. It was an excellent book. It was well written and was absolutely of the time – somebody should have snatched it up."

Talmy had branched out into literary agent work with *All Night Stand*, a novel by Thom Keyes depicting the world of the Beat Group. Published in 1966, the book sold well but is now forgotten. At around this time, Talmy took on Jenny Fabian and Johnny Byrne, whose novel *Groupie* not only sold well on its 1969 publication but is now considered something of a pop-culture classic. "I think I had always thought I'd like to move on from just purely record stuff to other things," says Talmy. This was despite the fact that there was far more money for Talmy in record production: "I still wanted to expand what I was doing into other fields and publishing was certainly one of the things that interested me greatly so eventually I got into it."

Talmy rejects the suggestion that Kenny's literary ambitions were the reason he took the plunge and left The Creation: "I think that was an adjunct to stuff he did. And he was a damn good writer. I don't think it had any influence whatsoever." Bob suggests, "I think it was just a way of saying, 'All is not lost, I'll try and do something else'. I will give him that he was always writing things down." Bob, however, says he never considered Kenny the intellectual of the band. "It never sort of came across to me that he was. I've met people for years who write things, even keep a diary, that kind of thing. It's never been my cup of tea. Some people like running, some people like writing. I never thought he was any more intelligent or studied or learned."

On August 27th 1967, the Atticus column in the *Sunday Times* carried a piece about Shel Talmy's stable of writers. Though the column was at this stage edited by Philip Oakes, the interviews for the piece were done by Michael Bateman (who may even have written it). Under the title

'Groupthink', the item began, "Shel Talmy, a 26-year old American recording manager, has made quite a good thing of packaging pop stars in this country. One wall of his sitting room in London is dotted with gold and silver discs from record companies marking big sales. Now he thinks he can do the same thing with writers."

It went on, "'I sign up a writer, exclusive, pay his salary while he works for me, then sell him as a property to the film world...' He has contracted four writers and one of them has just made £30,000 by selling his book to Twentieth Century Fox. This is Thom Keyes, 25, with glasses and a Lennon moustache, who wrote *All Night Stand*. Other members of Talmy's stable so far; Johnny Byrne, 31, a poet; Roger Jones, 27, a teacher, and Kenny Pickett, 21 (*sic*), former lead singer of The Creation. Talmy is subsidising them all."

A paragraph each followed on Keyes, Byrne (whose *Stopcock* was revealed to be a black comedy about a man who strangled dogs) Jones and Kenny. Atticus revealed, "Kenny lives in Hertford with his family and feels a bit out of it. 'I wrote *The 'Erberts* first but it was a bit like Thom's book, all about the scrubbers chasing the pop groups round. Like it happened to me, yeah. Six quid a week with a group, and all the perks. Then I did *Only Just Married* about a girl in a working-class family. The sort of book my family would read. Shel's given me the encouragement. I saw *The Family Way* and said 'I can do that'. Now other people say to me, disbelievingly, "How can *you* write?" It even bothers the others. I get up their noses a bit, I write so fast'."

The item concluded, "Talmy, who draws a percentage of all his writers' earnings, is hugely confident. He knows all about packaging, only a little about literature. But just enough to sign up his stable on seven-year contracts instead of the five-year contracts customary in the pop business. 'I figure that writers work more slowly than pop singers,' he says." The piece carried a photograph, with Kenny seated in the foreground and the other three writers, Talmy and 'Shel's PA' (presumably Gail Colson) standing behind him.

Talmy tried in vain to land a deal for *Only Just Married* but, despite his conviction that it was a worthy book, failed to get a publisher to bite. The same fate befell Kenny's next literary project. "The second (*sic*) book was a humorous dictionary of rock entitled *A to Z Of Rock*, to which Kenny, another guy and I contributed," reveals Talmy. "And it's been so long that I don't remember what happened to it." Asked how disappointed Kenny was by the rejections, Talmy responds, "Most everybody I know who is an author is not despondent by rejections because that's the order of the day. Unless you get awfully lucky, most everybody has been rejected. It's just part of the deal."

It's unfortunate for Kenny that at the time Talmy had not yet branched out into publishing. In the early Seventies, he set up Talmy Franklin publishing. This house published material like the phenomenally successful *The Dice Man* by Luke Rhinehart, Xaviera Hollander's *The Happy Hooker* and *Lennon Remembers*, the full transcript of the infamous myth-debunking interview given to Rolling Stone by the titular ex-Beatle. Talmy Franklin were clearly a house who deserved the epithet 'rock'n'roll publisher' and it would have been the perfect opportunity for Talmy to show the faith in *The Herberts* and/or *Only Just Married* that he had always had and print one or both himself.

"I honestly don't remember what happened with why we didn't or how and why it didn't happen," says Talmy. It also seems surprising that in 1967, Talmy didn't use his position to produce Kenny as a solo artist. In mitigation, Talmy says, "I tried to get everybody either jointly or severally to do stuff. Kenny, who was an extremely ballsy guy, fell under the influence of a very nasty female and sort of lost his ballsiness. Something I never understood and don't to this day."

Meanwhile, back in March 1967, The Creation drove down from their last Scottish gig to England. Jack: "We played the Mojo Club at Sheffield and had to leave from there immediately after the gig to get down to Heathrow to go out to Germany and join the Stones tour." The tour Jack refers to was probably the most prestigious of their career, supporting the Rolling Stones on a trek through West Germany and Austria. Lasting from 29 March to 2 April 1967, the tour saw The Creation and Australian band The Easybeats (also produced by Talmy) support the band ranked only behind the Beatles in popularity in venues of up to 100,000 capacity. In West Germany, the tour stopped off at Bremen, Cologne, Dortmund and Hamburg, playing two shows per day.

"That was a great tour 'cos they still had Jonesey in the band," Jack says. Not that The Creation got too much opportunity to socialise with Brian Jones or any of his colleagues in the Stones. Jack: "It was very difficult. It was a question of: on stage, back in the coach, back to the hotel." Bob: "But we obviously got on the planes together, got on the coaches together. It was okay, no big deal. Their time was taken up with press and everything. You did the short burst tours then – five days, six. You never really got the chance to get to know anybody really."

The only time Jack remembers The Creation getting the opportunity to chew the fat with the headliners was not a happy occasion. "It was a big track stadium where the Great Britain team were competing in a tournament and the rock venue was on the side of it," says Jack. "I think it might have been like a cycle track with a built-in stadium. But everybody was in the same hotel...We sat around and had a drink a little while with a few of them. That was that time when Mick Jagger upset one of the British team... I think he'd had a drink. He didn't mean to be offensive I don't think but a few swearwords went off and Lynn Davies, who was one of our great long-jumpers, said, 'Watch your mouth'. Of course it wasn't Mick who really got involved so much as his minders. The bouncer got involved and it was all a bit silly. There you go. Boys will be boys."

It was on the Stones tour that Eddie discovered through an employee of the Stones that Jimmy Page of the Yardbirds was now using his violin-bow trick. At the end of the previous year, Page had become the sole guitarist in the Yardbirds following Jeff Beck's departure. Eddie was initially understandably upset by what he viewed as a blatant theft of his innovation. "Without a doubt," Eddie states when asked if he is convinced Page got the idea off him. "You know when it's your idea, 'cos you knew how you started doing it, and I didn't see anybody else do it."

His distress must have only intensified when, during the Seventies, the bowing grew to be a Page trademark as he became a superstar with Led Zeppelin during a period in which Eddie was reduced to driving a bus to make a living. Time and Eddie's good nature have dissipated any lingering resentment and he failed to tackle Page over the appropriation of his innovation when they finally crossed paths. "I met him about five years ago at somebody's birthday party," says Eddie. "Jimmy was there with a few of the other Yardbirds. Just said, 'Hello'. Never mentioned the violin bow. Shook hands, grinned, that sort of thing."

At least Page brought something new to the method rather than merely copying Eddie's moves. "He used it in a different way," says Eddie. "I sort of raved with it, played it really hard. I think he tried to be a bit more musical with it. I was into making sound and noises. Making a guitar do everything that it wasn't supposed to do. Jimmy was like the other end of it. He was trying to be musical and creative with it in his own way." Kenny Pickett – the only person ever to see the contrasting techniques of Eddie and Page close up due to his subsequent employment by Led Zeppelin as a road manager – said much the same thing to *Ugly Things*: "Jimmy had a different way of doing it... He had a much more casual touch, an easy touch to it. Eddie used it more as a saw. He'd really dig into it."

Kim has recollected that on the first or second night of the Stones tour, The Creation's and the Stones' drinks were spiked with acid and they played high as a kite. "We couldn't find out who did it and we were real angry," he told *Ugly Things*. "During the show I was tripping my mind out... I mean, thousands and thousand of people and I hardly even knew the songs, y'know?" Kim seems to have taken the trip on his own. "No, can't remember that one," says Eddie when asked if the drinks were spiked in the way suggested. "Not mine anyway." Bob says that the only time he ever took LSD was not this occasion and it resulted in a song: 'Through My Eyes'. Jack simply says, "Bollocks. Somebody just telling fantasies. We might have been pissed and we might have had a joint but there was no acid around."

There was certainly grass around when the touring party reached Vienna, Austria for their 2 April shows. A grand welcoming party had been arranged for the headliners. Bob: "When we got to Vienna, we all got off the plane and there was a coach waiting for us and there was a few thousand kids at the airport all waiting for the Stones and a brass band and everything and they took us out of the airfield on a side entrance. We never even went to where all this was going on. It was like, 'Oops'.

"We were escorted to the hotel and the passport controllers were on the coach and they did all that on the coach. We were sat there and one by one this piece of marijuana almost the size of a brick was passed down the bus. The first time we saw it was when it was our turn to hold it while they checked the one in front, then we (passed) it to the people behind. This thing went up and down the bus in case anybody was caught with it."

With Kenny out of the group, the aerosol graffiti work was now the province of Bob. " I'd seen what Kenny had done and I just picked up little pieces," Bob recalls. "I had no idea. Just sort of blasted away and that was it. When you look at it later, it looks a mess. But cut up into little pieces, it's okay. Alan Smith used to set it on fire."

Fire, of course, has made the Creation's name on their previous visit to West Germany and it was on this tour that the band capitalised on the gains they had made through the exposure generated by the Circus Krone incident. As the result, it would seem, of a combination of the controversy caused by their last call and the publicity granted by playing to the Stones' huge audiences, the Creation's current West German single 'Painter Man' (probably released in early 1967, although ascertaining exact release dates for German releases of that era is rather difficult) became a smash.

It entered the chart on 1 April and ultimately climbed to Number 8, spending 18 weeks in the charts, four of which were in the Top 10. These figures relate to the official charts. As in Britain, various papers carried their own charts and, in fact, these alternative charts would seem to have possibly more credibility than the official one for it was the clear perception of more than one member of The Creation that 'Painter Man' was not a mere Number 8 but a German chart-topper.

"That was by far their most lucrative country," says Talmy of The Creation's success in Germany, "although they did well especially in Holland and in Spain. Some of the tours they did earned them big money in those other countries as well." So why did the Germans take them to their hearts? Talmy: "I have no idea whatsoever. It didn't sound like oompah music to me."

"I really don't know why that happened," says Eddie. "It's a bit of a mystery to me but they did and it was great." Bob is convinced that their initial success with 'Painter Man' was based on the song's anthemic and rhythmic nature. "In Germany, you needed, those days, that thumping, because they didn't really know what they were singing," Bob opines. "It was repetition and they grabbed hold of the 'Bomp! Bomp! Bomp!'" Jack feels there was something deeper at work: "I think they liked the band that was different. So many bands were just going over there and standing up singing their songs. We were actually trying to create music on stage every night we went on. We were trying to create new sounds and music. Sounds a bit pretentious, but loosely that was a lot of it. We gave Eddie free space to create whatever he wanted to on the violin bow and stuff like that. Okay, everybody had a guitarist who played a nice solo but, instead of just the solo, extend it to the sound."

Whether or not Bob's analysis is the more accurate one, the type of process he refers to is part of the reason for the 'Big In Japan' syndrome: the contempt many critics feel when an act achieves success in a non-English-speaking territory while success in the US or the UK eludes them. Such success is devalued, the suspicion being that the audience in the relevant country is so enthusiastic because they don't really understand the music or are generally naïve about music. This feeling inevitably also resides in the act themselves. At least, it does in many of them. For The Creation – though they became increasingly frustrated and/or sad about their lack of success in Britain and though bemusement seems to have been part of their psychological reaction to their German success – they also seem to have been genuinely grateful for and pleased by making it in Germany.

Eddie: "You could leave this country being *there* and then when you'd get to the other end you'd come out and you were *there* in popularity rating and people would come up and give you flowers off the aeroplane. It was weird." Gail Colson: "I am sure they were over the moon about having success anywhere and Germany kept them going for a while. I don't understand the 'Big in Japan' syndrome. I should think any band would be very happy to be successful in Japan."

"They were huge over there," says Clark. "And I think that that probably also gave them hope for England. Like, 'Well, we're doing it there, it's a case of it clicking over here'. That's what I felt too... They were thrilled that they were so successful, they never snubbed it in any way. Not at all. It was like, 'Oh we're going to Germany' and 'Oh it's great, we always do well ever there, we always have crowds'. Always looked forward to it, always loved going." Bob, though, does add, "When you have a hit in this country you can almost appreciate it, you can see it. In another country, it's almost like, 'Well, yeah but it's not where you want to be doing it'."

Of course, practicality also came into the equation. Bob: "It was like, if that's where your fortune is. And then that took us away from the British scene. It also gave us a little bit of cash to get by, because we wasn't doing that many gigs in the UK." Was he frustrated at not having success in his home country? "It wasn't a big problem, to me anyway, I knew we hadn't had any big hits in this country so we didn't miss it..."

In one way, there was even a glamour attached to continental success that couldn't be found in Britain, namely the colour picture sleeves in which singles were packaged on mainland Europe. In Britain, sleeves were then still "plain old boring patterns in the paper covers," recalls Clark. "In Germany they always had the photos, which I thought was great. Bob used to bring them back and show me. I used to think, 'Wow! They're doing so good'."

I n losing Kenny Pickett, The Creation had not only lost a singer and an above-average frontman, they had also lost a significant lyric-writing talent. Eddie, of course, had recently developed a skill that was – quite astonishingly – on Kenny's level with 'Can I Join Your Band', so could conceivably have assumed Kenny's mantle. In the event, however, Eddie would forge a songwriting partnership with Bob Garner, who would adopt Kenny's previous role of word provider, although was also able when necessary to provide chords behind those words. This new role alleviated a frustration of Bob's. "I was trying to put an input on the early songs as well and in fact I did have certain things which are laid down in stone now but never got credited for," he says. "But I found myself talking to (them): I said, 'Why don't we do this instead of this?' It was almost like, 'This is our department'.

"I didn't realise that you could make money out of this. They knew about that before I did. Obviously I knew you could make money out of writing songs, but I didn't realise the sort of value…I suppose Jack can say the same thing." Jack concurs. The drummer had written songs as far back as the age of 18 but none was ever in contention for recording in the original incarnation of The Creation. Says Jack, "My stuff was more in a Bob Dylan folk-rock sort of thing and the guys really wouldn't want to listen to me. Eddie and Ken seemed to think they had the rights and they weren't letting anybody else in. In those days, the 'Sixties, wearing kaftans and all the rest of the crap, I wasn't going to get hung up about money. I was quite happy just to make music. I wrote my songs and it didn't really worry me if people liked 'em or didn't like 'em. I was just happy to write a song."

The material Eddie and Bob would jointly compose was arguably even better than the previous Pickett/Phillips collaborations and unarguably produced some of the most well-loved Creation numbers. Even Talmy – no great fan of Bob as a person or a singer – has to concede, "Garner stepped in and actually did a damn good job. In fact better than I could have really hoped for because his lyrics actually were very good."

As it happens, the Garner/Phillips songwriting partnership got off to a singularly shaky start. "As we was playing together in dressing rooms and things, I said, 'I've got this idea'," Bob recalls. "I don't think he was that impressed." The idea in question was for a song called 'Life Is Just Beginning,' a mid-tempo recounting of the wonders of evolving from adolescent to adult and the privileges the latter state gives one access to. Although it was the first collaboration between the two, it would actually be the last Creation original recorded while both Eddie and Bob were in the group. Bob: "It was my idea, but he made a musical contribution after."

The song was a clear break from The Creation's past. Bob: "I was conscious of…taking it away from the big powerchord-type thing, more melodic." He says of Eddie's initially underwhelmed reaction, "I don't think Eddie saw it as a Creation song. It was only afterwards, when the influence of 'Sgt Pepper..' and that type of thing was coming along that we could see we hadn't made it one way we might be able to influence people in a more musical way."

"I thought that the chorus was a bit ambitious for us to get the best out of it, as far as the harmonies needed to have been there," says Eddie of his first, negative, impressions of 'Life Is Just Beginning'. "I've always thought, looking back at it, I'd have loved to have had a band where we played The Creation songs but then the other side of the stage they had something like a 15-piece choir doing the necessary bits. All those intricate harmonies we worked out.

"Probably the idea was great but I don't know if we had the vocal ability to actually do it. I said to Tony Barber who was doing the American tour last year, 'It'd be great if all we had to do was just play this music and have the choir there just doing all the bits in, like, 'Tom Tom' and 'Life Is Just Beginning'. 'Cos that chorus in 'Life Is Just Beginning' really would suit a bunch of good singers. You could do something with that. That would really be quite unique to get some kind of sound balance where you have The Creation music – which could be sometimes sort of hard and rough – and yet with that really nice polished vocal there…

"There was never any suggestion that we could get help on backing vocals. I think the Ivy League sung on early Who records. If someone had said to me, 'Do you want the Ivy League to come in and do some harmonies?', (I would have said), 'Yeah!' Probably would have done a better job than us."

On 9 April 1967, The Creation made one of their rare appearances in a national newspaper. This was no matter for celebration, however, for the occasion was Tony Stratton-Smith's confessional *News Of The World* article about chart-rigging. Stratton-Smith's piece may have been prompted by a front page story in the same paper the previous week headlined 'FIXER CONFESSES HOW WE RIGGED THE POP CHARTS'. The source of this story and the beneficiaries of the fixing were anonymous, leading to a rather bloodless read. Stratton-Smith's piece was a little more juicy.

In an article that dominated one of the *News Of The World*'s then-broadsheet-sized pages, Stratton-Smith started, "I have been chart-fixing – that is, making sure certain records appear in certain hit parade charts – for more than a year. In the trade, we call it hyping." He elaborated, "In the beginning I did my hyping through paid contacts… then, dissatisfied with their results, I worked out my own system and cut out the 'middle men'." This led into the former Creation manager's confession about his hyping 'Painter Man' into the chart. Following several paragraphs explaining how crucial chart placings now were to pop acts, he returned to the subject of his ex-charges.

"Take the case of The Creation. I firmly believed they could make it, provided they were given a good start. They have since proved me right. In Germany, one the world's three biggest record markets, their disc 'Painter Man' is currently Number 3 – and no fiddle! Yet here in Britain, had I not paid to fix a chart, I doubt if the record would have made the Top 50." A plug then followed for The Koobas, who he claimed "..have consistently refused to let me hype their records high into the charts" Stratton-Smith then went on to say, "Even without fixing, the whole hit parade business is a farce. There are four main charts in Britain – that of the *New Musical Express, Melody Maker, Disc* and the *Record Retailer.*"

Pointing out the sales discrepancies revealed in that particular week's charts, he said, "Four charts, three different records at Number 1 – take your pick!" Then in a statement of breath-taking *chutzpah*, hypocrisy or both, he suggested a solution to the problem: "Just as Hollywood set up the Hays Commission to give the industry its moral guidelines, a similar unit – with teeth – should be set up in Britain, paid for by the record companies. All it would require is an office to correlate and audit weekly sales figures from each company. It would then become wildly uneconomic for *anybody* to attempt chart fixing." After mentioning his first dabbling with chart rigging for Beryl Marsden (who he also said was unaware of the hyping), he concluded with his anecdote about how he had had to pay in a vain attempt to merely restore 'Painter Man' to its genuine position in the charts.

"Didn't do us any good at all," Jack says of the article. Though Stratton-Smith was at pains throughout to stress that The Creation knew nothing about his shenanigans, more than one member of the band feels his decision to sell the story was motivated by spite over their still recent parting of the ways.

On 22 April 1967, The Creation played at London's Roundhouse along with Soft Machine and the Sam Gopal Indian Group. "Tony Stratton-Smith (*sic*) got us a couple of girl dancers – probably strippers or something," says Bob. "But they didn't strip. They were in a body stocking and we painted those and we painted the girls. That had not been done before." Bob recalls the incident as creating a minor scandal in one of the newspapers.

Though Kenny had split with his colleagues in The Creation in acrimonious circumstances, he still knew which side his bread was buttered on. Consequently, when The Creation contacted him with the excruciatingly embarrassing task of asking him how the lyric to 'Nightmares' went in order to enable Bob to overdub a vocal on the backing track already recorded, he opted not to exult in their discomfiture or to slam the phone down but to recite it as requested. "He was probably thinking of the royalties," says Bob. "You don't cut your nose off, I suppose."

And who had the difficult task of making the call? Bob: "It might have been myself. Or it might have been Shel in the first place, but I remember writing them down." Bob has a feeling that there might even be a version of the song with a Pickett vocal track, ("If Kenny had done a vocal on it, I perhaps couldn't understand some of the words – it was something like that"), which would be an intriguing bonus track on any Creation box-set.

Because the band – or more likely Talmy – chose to use the basic track recorded before Kenny's departure, 'Nightmares' is the only Creation recording with Bob both playing bass and singing. "If we did the track at IBC I don't know, but I remember singing it at Pye," says Bob. The date for this overdubbing is unknown as it wasn't annotated but it doesn't seem to have been on the same day that The Creation recorded two brand new songs at Pye Studios on 26 April: the tape box for 'If I Stay Too Long' and 'Tom Tom' doesn't bear the name of Glyn Johns who, because of the annotations to the tape box for 'Can I Join Your Band' and 'Nightmares' mentioned previously, would appear to have had some hand in the four-four/overdubbing process of those tracks. Instead, it was engineer Alan MacKenzie (known to his Pye colleagues as 'Mac') and tape op Alan O'Duffy (aka, at least to Talmy, 'Irish') who joined Shel Talmy in the control booth to help with the production of the first Garner/Phillips songs committed to tape.

Pye, located in London's West End, was affiliated to the record label of the same name, although it also hosted clients recording for other labels. "Pye studios was in the basement of ATV House which is behind the Odeon in Marble Arch," explains O'Duffy. "Nowadays it's a casino. It remained a studio up 'til maybe '89. it was owned by Pye Records and therefore bands associated with Pye made their records in that studio. The studio itself was designed by a man called Keith Grant in conjunction with his dad. His dad was an architect and between Keith Grant and his father, they designed Pye 1 and 2, which was a wonderful bit of work in its own style. I imagine Pye was equivalent to Abbey Road at the time. They had a string of hits coming out of the place."

The most famous artist on Pye's roster was probably The Kinks, which was why Talmy was very familiar with the studio. Asked whether there was a particular reason why he decided to move over to Pye from IBC, Talmy says, "None that I can think of. I just probably felt like going to Pye. I used three or four different studios on a regular basis. I used various engineers. I probably had a good feeling about Pye at the time." IBC's Damon Lyon-Shaw suggests, "One of the good reasons was availability, because if we started doing albums no-one got a look in. You just couldn't get the time in the studio. That might have been the reason, I don't know, but it was one of the busiest studios in London at the time. I certainly worked with Shel a long time after that so it wasn't a political thing that he stopped using IBC."

As with IBC, Pye was divided into two studios. The Creation – as with many pop acts – would use Pye's second studio. Explains, O'Duffy: "Studio 2 was small and studio 1 was huge. Looking back on it, it was such a pokey little room. Studio 2 would not be more than 25 by 25 feet, which is very small really if you start bringing in amps, screens, dividers and all the rest. And it had a Lockwood speaker above the door so that if you wanted to play back an overdub you'd hear back the backing track or whatever it was through the foldback speaker – because even then the idea of headphones was fairly new and they didn't always work."

Nonetheless, Eddie says, "I always found Pye at Marble Arch a good studio to work. That was always a good room" . Jack: "That was quite a nice studio, I remember. That was okay. I never had any problems with IBC, really, but the thing is what you get is – these record producers don't tell you these things – but sometimes they can do a deal, they get a studio a lot cheaper. So they would change studio. But I can't think of one studio really wherever we worked where the sound wasn't good. I think Shel knew the ones where we'd be suited." Bob adds, "It was a lot more intimate because it was small, it was cosier. I thought we got on better there. It did change the sound a bit, or it seemed to do on the tape."

However small studio 2 was, great ingenuity had gone into its design by Keith Grant (who would also design the even more well-thought-of Olympic Studios and is no relation to the Keith Grant who was responsible for the painting *The Creation*) and his father. O'Duffy says of Pye, "The studio was a wooden studio and had a wooden wall which was a very strange shape which was a flat wall to look at but the wall had slots in it which were the length of the bit of wood. So the wood was quite thick with this slot in it that had a channel running behind it so the channel maybe looks like a ball with a spike on it. So the sound supposedly would go into the hole and get nowhere and die. Both rooms were like that." There was certainly no argument about studio 2's capacity to turn out commercial products. As O'Duffy points out, "The small studio is the one where we churned out all The Kinks records. Really, 2 was the hit room."

Indeed, O'Duffy's recollection is that the success Talmy had enjoyed with The Kinks' records on which he had worked with MacKenzie and O'Duffy was partly behind them teaming together for The Creation's material. "Alan MacKenzie was responsible for 'Dedicated Follower Of Fashion', 'Autumn Almanac', 'Waterloo Sunset'," says O'Duffy. "A whole phenomenal list. I think there's five hit singles that he was responsible for apart from an album called 'Kink Kontroversy'. He did that with Shel Talmy. (That's why) we were chosen to do The Creation, I suppose. I was just a junior. I was only seventeen or eighteen at the time. I was a tape op, Alan was the mixer. There was a feeling that this record was going to be (made) with the same team that had done The Kinks."

To some extent, MacKenzie sounds like an off-the-wall genius. "He was a Scottish television engineer who came down to London and was not liked by the rest of the staff at Pye," says O'Duffy. "He wasn't in the in-crowd but he kept coming up with wonderful records. For example, 'Dedicated Follower Of Fashion' had a sort of funny vocal sound. What we think that it was, looking back, is that it was the jack for the vocal somehow came into the control room and went into a patch field and came out of something but it wasn't pressed fully home so that it had a 'half a voice' sound…very sort of telephon-y." MacKenzie would probably have brought know-how from television that the ordinary pop engineer wouldn't have possessed. O'Duffy: "He was an innovator and interested in sound. He left television because he felt they were too restrictive about what you can do. He was a very go-ahead fellow."

Asked whether any part of the reason for moving The Creation work from IBC to Pye was the opportunity it afforded him to work with the Kinks' production team, Talmy says: "No, nothing to do with that at all. They were certainly good engineers, as was Glyn, as was Damon and various other people I used. What I was looking for was an engineer who was good enough so that I wouldn't have to tell him a whole lot. He could get 90 per cent of what I needed before I opened my mouth. That saved me a lot of hassle. I did not depend on an engineer for hits, which is I suppose what has been implied or maybe what you're implying. That was never the case." Of the respective merits of the studios, Talmy says, "Close. Considering what was available in terms of equipment, they were equal that way and both of them were very good acoustically. So I was quite happy going between both of them (and occasionally Olympic)."

The two Garner/Phillips compositions recorded at the session on April 26 were a mixture of atypical and typical Creation songs. 'If I Stay Too Long' was unlike any other self-composed Sixties Creation number, being both a love song and a conventional soul-tinged ballad. It featured a languid, humming, uncoiling guitar part running throughout. "That song started off with that guitar solo riff thing," says Eddie. "Just playing with that idea of sixth, fifth and fourth string with an open fifth and running up and down the fingerboard. You get different harmonies by doing that. That's how the song came about: we almost wrote it around that idea."

This guitar part actually sounds complicated but, Eddie points out, "In actual fact, it's not that difficult. I didn't play finger-style on it, it was done with a plectrum. You're kind of playing a fourth and a sixth string all the time, but leaving the fifth open, and you're playing it on the octave. I suppose it was a bit unusual in its time but it worked." Bob: "I think the little riff around the title was a little idea of Eddie's. If you listen to the open-stringed chords on that, that's one of those things where you get hold of the guitar and you think 'How the hell has he done that?' I've showed other people and said, 'It's easy when you know'. I just came up with a lyric."

That lyric concerns the nervousness of a man approaching the home of a lover with whom he is having a stormy relationship. Bob: "It's the only time in any of the songs where 'I love you' is in it. We didn't write lovey-dovey stuff. That was one of the things we stayed away from. I don't think that was intentional. I don't think we were like Lennon and McCartney: love was this and love was everything. I think we were the opposite. Even as people, I don't think we were lovey-dovey people. I don't mean nasty people, but nobody was in love with anybody."

Though Bob provided the words, as with many collaborations between him and Eddie, the title came from the guitarist: "It was Eddie's last line. I think it was 'if You've Gotta Go, Go Now', the Bob Dylan thing. [He said] 'If I Stay Too Long'. I said, 'Yeah, okay'. And then I wrote all the verses and Eddie just then filled in the chords and things for that. And it wasn't like I didn't know any chords."

'Tom Tom', in contrast to 'If I Stay Too Long', was much more in the group's anthemic and unusual lyrical traditions. Eddie once again provided the music and lick and gave Bob a fragment of lyric upon which to extrapolate. Bob: "He'd say, 'I've got 'Tom-tom, nah-nah-nah-nah-nah'. He had that nice riff and everything and I went, 'Tom Tom the piper's son'.

"Every verse, if you listen to it, is about old British nursery rhymes. Tom-Tom (was the) mad hatter. Playing games with British nursery rhymes." Some have suggested – probably partly due to the fact that it was the follow-up to 'Painter Man' in West Germany – that 'Tom-Tom' was written to resemble 'Painter Man'. "Not really," says Eddie. "Tom Tom's always a hard song to play live because you have to play this riff thing and then play chords over the top of it, *with* it almost. Bit of a hard one to do that. 'Painter Man's a pretty easy song to play live. 'Tom-Tom's a bit of a weird one."

"I didn't like Tom-Tom," says Jack. "I thought it was a load of nothing, really. I know Bob's idea was good – he was trying to put together a load of nursery rhymes – but I don't think it was a Creation thing at all. I thought the record was...a soppy little pop song. There's no message there or trying to get a point of view over or anything. It was like a skipping rope or something."

It has to be said that the ledgers for the tapes of the two songs indicate that 'Tom Tom' had far more work done on it than 'If I Stay Too Long', a sure sign that the former track was initially considered A-side material and the latter fit only for a flipside.

The basic track of 'Tom Tom' was attempted first. Track 1 was a complete, 2 a false start, 3 another complete, 4 a breakdown, 5 and 6 completes, 7 a false start and 8 a breakdown. From here things seemed to get complicated, with a bewildering succession of annotations indicating the use of edit (meaning the tape has been spliced together from different takes), intercut (possibly meaning the take of an edit section), at least one change of mind about the finished master and torturous reference to segments of tape between 'leaders', leaders being the dead, coloured tape used to enable recording staff to easily locate a particular take.

Much layering was done at the four-four stage, with the reduction overdub process taking in lead guitar (on two separate tracks), bass drum, vocals, third vocals and tambourine. Track 5 of the four-four stage ended up as the song's master, following tracks 1 and 4 being completes and 2 and 3 false starts.

Only four passes were made at the basic track of 'If I Stay Too Long'. All takes were completes bar 3, a false start. Just rhythm and lead guitar were added at the four-four stage and two attempts at the reduction master – both completes – were made, of which the second was chosen.

The pleasing results of the first two Garner/Phillips compositions to be recorded would have done much to quell any unease about the way Kenny's departure had broken up a good songwriting team. Bob, however, points out, "there was no proof that they were a good writing team because there was no success in what they were doing. I don't think anybody thought, 'We're losing a good songwriting team'. I didn't, anyway." Not that Bob's sole yardstick for success was chart positions: "My ambition was to be able to stay alive in the music business, entertainment business. It wasn't compulsory that you had to make it for me."

Of composition, Bob says, "I'd learned how to put a song together because I'd watched it all the time – watched the lads do it – and made contributions myself." Just as he was in favour of The Creation's songs taking on a more conventional melodic bent, Bob's aim with his lyrics was to come up with simpler material: "My thing was, try and make it a little bit commercial. 'If I Stay Too Long', 'Life Is Just Beginning', 'How Does It Feel (To Feel)', – they're quite understandable. They're mainstream."

"It was good and it worked the same as Kenny and myself," says Eddie of their co-writing. "Bob had a slightly different approach to it but he came up with some decent lyrics. I probably sat down with Bob more to get these things together, whereas with Kenny I would just say, 'Here's an idea, what can you do with that?' He'd go and do it and then he'd bring back a sheet with the lyrics done and then we'd sit down and work it out. With Bob, I probably worked it through a lot more to get the right result." Bob adds, "Because I can play myself, if I had a (lyric) I would have the chords to go with it so that was already established but Eddie has the ability to make my chords, use them and play them better. Because he's more confident on the guitar than I ever was or will be. That was the thing.

"Kenny used to write just words. He didn't play then. (He did when I met him later.) When I was doing words, I'd sit down with a guitar, so I already had the chord sequence and played like that and Eddie would sort of improve on my chord sequence... Even to this day, if I give him a chord sequence, he'll put another note in – but usually to the better. He can pick little melodies out of a chord sequence. If I give him a chord sequence to sing the song, he's always added. It becomes more an Eddie Phillips arrangement than mine. Even the country stuff we've done recently: it's the same chords but Eddie will play another note or miss one out."

"I think that just happened because Eddie had more reason to interact with him because he was singing the songs," says June Clark of the new Creation songwriting axis. "They do seem to have something and it's because they're opposite characters. Eddie is the true, sensitive, emotional, moody, reactive one and Bob is the deep thinker, he's very caring, he's very, very dedicated, he's reliable and I think this is why it works with both of them. Because he'll fall into whatever Eddie's schedule is, whatever Eddie wants him to do with writing, anything. That's really quite a talent and that certainly works for Eddie because he's the more unpredictable one, he's the one that says, 'Let's do this tomorrow instead'. Bob likes to plod along, Bob doesn't like change, he's the consistent one."

It's possible that a couple of other Creation recordings – both sung by Eddie – whose date can't be pin-pointed due to missing original tape boxes were first committed to tape at around this juncture. One is 'Ostrich Man', a denunciation of a 'straight' the kind of which was very common in the Sixties (for example, The Kinks' 'Mr Pleasant', The Beatles' 'Nowhere Man'). The fact it has an Eddie vocal dates it as post-'Can I Join Your Band', as everybody remembers the latter number as being the first studio Phillips vocal – and, of course, it would pre-date Eddie's departure from the band in October. "Probably early '67, I suppose," says Eddie. "I think we would have done that at Olympic Sound in Barnes."

This track would actually not see the light of day until 1982. "I remember 'Ostrich Man'," says June Clark. "They used to do that. Kenny used to sing that. I never really liked it. It never did much for me." Jack seems to concur with that appraisal. Jack: "'Ostrich Man' was one of the numbers you put down and thought maybe was an album number in the future. It never featured big in any of our thoughts." Both the content and delivery of the song's opening line – 'Living your life with half-closed eyes' – is uncannily similar to the famous line in the Beatles 'Strawberry Fields Forever' 'Living is easy with eyes closed' .

'I Am The Walker', meanwhile, was not released until the 1973 Charisma album '66-67'. As touched on previously, the fact that a song is credited to Pickett/Phillips does not guarantee an input from Kenny but on this occasion Jack recalls it as having a Pickett origin, even though Eddie sang the recorded version: "I remember Kenny talking about writing that song; he'd gone out walking and afterward he'd been walking along the river and saw this man with a bald headed dog or something. The whole thing came together in his mind and he wrote the song." Like 'Ostrich Man', which is augmented by harpsichord, it features promient keyboards so conceivably could have been recorded at the same session.

Strangely, Bob has no recollection of recording either. Bob: "They were done after I left." (This must be incorrect, as Eddie left the group before him). Bob: "That's when Ronnie Wood came in. 'I Am The Walker': the words are stranger and stranger there. Something like, 'I see a man with a dog in a plastic bag'. Nobody knows what that's about. There's some sort of mind-bending substance there I think. I never played on 'I Am The Walker'." Of course, as Eddie sang both tracks and Kim was now the bassist, there would theoretically have been no need for Bob to be in the studio while they were being recorded, so both tracks could have been laid down while Bob was still in The Creation – maybe without his knowledge.

One Creation song Bob certainly does have a recollection of recording is 'How Does It Feel To Feel', an epic, magnum opus. The song actually first experienced life at the house in Harrow when the group were learning Bob Dylan's 'Like A Rolling Stone' in the front room. That Dylan song's unforgettable refrain – apparently directed at a former lover – is "How does it *feel*" , sung with a hair-raising vengefulness. Bob: "I'd been and seen Jimi Hendrix and he was doing it." The refrain was sung with something of a wistfulness when rendered by Hendrix and it was the mellow Hendrix version (preserved for posterity on the recordings from the June 1967 Monterey Pop Festival) to which The Creation's version owed a greater debt.

They initially had trouble deciding how the number would finish on stage. Bob: "It's one of those songs it's not easy to end. So we was going through the ending bit: 'Like a rolling stone.' We was going, 'Well just stay on that chord. Keep going round and round until we come to something that becomes obvious'. And as we were doing 'How does it feel?' I just sort of (said), 'How does it feel to feel?' and we both looked at each other and went, 'Hang on'. Because we've gone into a grove trying to end it and we liked it. We said, 'Hang on – "How does it feel to feel?" That's a bit clever, innit?' We was sobered into thinking, 'This sounds like a clever play on words'. In other words, for the first time you felt this and you felt that. 'Okay, we've got a song here'."

Of his melody, Eddie says – presumably referring to a later date – "I got the idea of crashing out these chords. We wrote that in…Harrow. I remember going over there on Sunday afternoon. I was living at home then but I did go over there in the middle of a sunny afternoon, draw all the curtains and put all these psychedelic lights – flashing all over the place. It was all a bit weird, just make a bit of a racket over there with a little amplifier in the room and that's how that song came about."

The melody Eddie devised was graced with a quite stupendous lyric from Bob. "The other words were, I suppose, experience from the previous two years," says Bob. Many have assumed that dazzling imagery like "How does it feel to slide down a sunbeam/Bursting clouds on your way" was the consequence of ingesting LSD, but Bob says this is an incorrect assumption. However, he does say of that unforgettable pair of lines: "That's the high and the low of being on a trip, I suppose. You can go up the moonbeam and down the moonbeam. Doesn't mean anything, really."

Eddie admits that 'How Does It Feel To Feel' is the only collaboration with Bob where his partner truly surprised him with the lyric he devised. "The lyrics are brilliant," enthuses Clark. "They're brilliant. And he finds it so easy to write. He has no problem at all. He doesn't push himself. He's just one of those people. I swear to God, he could be far more successful than he is already. He still writes but he doesn't do anything with it. He writes on his own as well. He's more talent than he realises. He's very versatile because he's so easy-going and he could be far more successful as a songwriter than he wants to acknowledge."

With a great lyric and fine melody under their belts, as well as no doubt some idea of the instrumentation, The Creation would take this idea into the studio that June and add the *coup de grace* in the form of a pulverising performance, an – for the time – intricate production and some of the most extraordinary lead-guitarwork in rock history.

Following Talmy's dissolution of Planet, the band had needed a new home for their recordings. The label on which they ended up was Polydor. Their producer recollects that it was he who brokered the deal, as opposed to Stratton-Smith before the latter parted company with the band. Talmy: "I think it was me. In fact I'm *sure* it was... It's the only time actually I can think of where Polydor was a decent company. Roland Rennie was running it, who was a very nice man, and it's about the only time I ever had a good time with Polydor. After that, they became the rat finks of all time."

Bob: "I can honestly not remember signing a record contract with any label whatsoever. Probably signed to Shel Talmy." He adds of 'If I Stay Too Long', "It was strange, that one: we weren't even told it was coming out on Polydor. It wasn't like, 'Oh we've done a deal with Polydor'. It was just, 'Oh look, it's on a different label'." Would The Creation's music have been so radical if they had been directly signed to a label? Bob: "Probably not, those days."

Similar closure did not attend Talmy's negotiations with Atlantic in America. Talmy claims he was on the verge of signing The Creation to a five-album deal with the US giant (although in *Rock On Wood* he said the label was United Artists) but Atlantic got cold feet when Kenny left the group. "The whole thing blew up," Talmy laments. "They didn't want to know. I still think they would have had hits but it didn't happen."

The six-month lapse between Creation releases mentioned by *Record Mirror* in March had turned into eight months by the time The Creation's third single finally emerged in June 1967. Talmy says this is not because it took him a long time to get a label to agree to sign the group: "At that point, it was scheduling. Polydor, which was a relatively new company in England, had a much longer lead time than the other ones because they were still getting their act together."

Friday 26 May 1967 saw The Creation occupying a spot on the Six Hour Non-Stop Bank Holiday Rave at the Hotel Metropole, Brighton. An 8.00pm to 2.00am extravaganza, the headliners were Dave Dee, Dozy, Beaky, Mick & Tich with The Springbeats, The Beat Girls, DJ Dave (The Vicar) Turnbull, The Herd and The Kult constituting the other support acts. "People didn't know what we were doing but it was okay," says Bob of The Creation's reception.

The headline act with the mouthful of a name were purveyors of lightweight – and at the same time strangely surreal – pop records. Bob: "I remember meeting Dave, Mick and Tich and all that on the promenade after. We stopped and had a burger or something. Probably they struggled more than we did because although they were a Top 10 group, they didn't have a lot of respect. They were all gimmicky records. We was probably more on the ball and on the button than they were. They were like a show group, almost like a Barron Knights type of thing: leaning on each other's backs and spinning each other round. Like Freddie and the Dreamers – that kind of thing."

In probably late May '67, The Creation took advantage of their new star status in Germany to embark on their first visit to that country as tour headliners. They took along with them their roadie Alan Smith and a friend of Smith's named Kenny White, who was a guitarist himself, having played in Jimmy Powell and the Five Dimensions and a band called The Score. White was at a loose end and came along in return for bed and board. "I think suddenly there was a gig came up in Germany which was something to do with this TV programme and that was in Frankfurt," recalls White. "There was also some gigs. I think the thing lasted for about two and a half weeks, that was all. Nothing big.

"We were in Frankfurt a lot of the time. I do remember that 'cos we stayed in a hotel on the top floor and I think the lower floor was full of whores. Typical Germany, of course. I'm pretty certain that on the show we did, which would have been *RockPalast* or one of those, there was The Move and Hendrix was playing on it." White is almost certainly referring not to *RockPalast* – which started in the Seventies – but to *Beat Beat Beat*, which broadcast an edition on which The Creation appeared at the end of June.

For Bob, the gigs the band were now capable of getting in Germany were something of a lifeline in a period during which they had no new product on the market and hadn't had for some time. "Germany filled that gap with work," he says. "And I think that's why we didn't go into the studio so much. It was almost taken away from us. It was like, 'Let's get to Germany and make some money'. And we're talking about wages. Not just make some money. Let's get some wages out of this."

Though Bob doesn't consider the money to be particularly high, he does admit that one gig's work in that country would probably be the equivalent for each band member of a working man's weekly wage. However, Kim, speaking to *Ugly Things*, was in no doubt about how financially privileged The Creation were when visiting Germany. "I used to have to come to England to spend money," he marvelled. "I used to have a suitcase full of it. I couldn't spend it all. I used to have bridal suites and I still couldn't spend money. I made £13,000, which is about $30,000, just in gig money... We didn't have a manager to pay or anything."

Jack, too, considers the German money to have been good, so much so that returning to play venues in Britain was a let-down. "We were travelling abroad a lot, working in France, Germany, places like this, earning good money. We'd had a couple of Number 1 hits in Germany and had a tremendous scene over there. And, of course, coming back to England and going up to Nottingham and working the Boat Club... Good club but lousy money." Of course, Kim and Jack could conceivably be talking about a point in time after Bob had left the group, but this seems unlikely as the point of The Creation's greatest commercial value in Germany was during Bob's tenure. For his part, Jack says he wasn't particularly worried by the long gap between second and third singles. "We was just looking forward to the next release," he says. "In the meantime, you'd got so much work."

"They were very popular," recalls White of the tour. "Not like Beatlemania but they were liked a lot." However, not even the enthusiasm of screaming girls and fawning interviewers could inure them to some of the tedium involved in the business of show, as illustrated by an incident when the band were hanging around waiting to do their TV appearance. "*RockPalast* (*sic*) is a thing where there's loads of people on it, one after another," says White. "At one point in the studio, because we were so bored and it was day or a two-day thing, we found a little tricycle, a metric motorbike, which Bob and I drove around the studio until we were chased off by the security guards."

In The Creation's *Beat Beat Beat* set, Bob's manner does seem to confirm June Clark's assertion that he was a rather uncomfortable frontman. He is not so much self-conscious as over-keen, exulting in his new job as lead singer of a rock'n'roll band and doing too much instead of being just natural: in the instrumental breaks, he steps back and claps his hands but it is unconvincing. Among the four songs the band played on the programme was 'Painter Man' but in truth it's a fairly lacklustre version of the band's signature song – Bob is a little unfaithful to the original melody line and the chorus is a thumped, rigid affair. But things change dramatically in the instrumental break. When Eddie spins toward his speaker stack, grabs his bow and spins back to start playing the solo in one seamless movement, it is an utterly breathtaking spectacle.

By June '67, the third UK Creation single had a release date. Before its appearance, though, Talmy funded another visit to the recording studio. June 7 1967 saw the group returning to Pye's Studio 2 – the two Alans once again assisting Talmy – for the purpose of providing material for the one market that was actually hungry for Creation product, West Germany. Now that they had achieved a *bona fide* hit in that country's singles chart, an album was justified. However, the album would not be the kind of organic entity then just becoming the norm in the long-playing field but a throwback to a year or two before when most pop acts merely cobbled together the A- and B-sides of their singles thus far, a new self-composed track or two and a clutch of unimaginative cover versions. 'We Are Paintermen' – as the group's Continental album would be ludicrously titled – would contain eight of the tracks the band had recorded hitherto plus three songs recorded on 7 June, plus another track that was laid down on 27 June.

Though one can understand Talmy opting not to include the two instrumentals on the album, the fact that he funded a recording session rather than place on the disc several tracks already recorded – the two cover versions 'Bony Moronie' and 'Mercy Mercy Mercy' and the two originals 'I Am The Walker' and 'Ostrich Man' – actually calls into question the assumption in this text that those numbers were in existence by this point, not least because Talmy stood to gain some income from his share of the publishing by including the latter two numbers.

Only the fact that Eddie sings on 'Ostrich Man' and 'I Am The Walker' prevents one from concluding that Bob's lack of any memory of playing on 'Bony Moronie', 'Mercy Mercy Mercy', 'I Am The Walker' and 'Ostrich Man' means that they were all recorded after he left the band: Eddie departed The Creation before Bob did. (Although there is a theory on the part of Jack, addressed later, that might explain the last point.) "Everybody was doing that," reasons Talmy of the inclusion of covers. "The Who, The Beatles, The Stones. This was the thing because at that point in time, it was the accepted thing to do covers on an album because nobody until the Beatles started doing it wanted to hear just an album of songs by the people that were writing them. So everybody did covers. It's part of their set. That was the other reason why it goes on an album, because they did it in their live set."

However, considering scams of Talmy's in this area – such as getting both The Kinks and The Who to record public domain number 'Bald Headed Woman' and then ensuring the arrangement credit, and thus royalties, went to himself – it seems unlikely he would choose to include covers for any other reason than there weren't sufficient numbers of band originals available.

Of the 7 June session, Jack recalls, "Shel did say that he'd like to put about four tracks together because they want an album on the continent and we needed about another four tracks. Could we just come in – he'd book a four-hour session – and we'd just put 'em down. So that's why we ended up doing some of the stuff we did." The four tracks in question were not all filler material: as well as Dylan's 'Like A Rolling Stone' (filtered through Jimi Hendrix's consciousness), Billy Roberts' 'Hey Joe' (ditto) and The Capitols' 'Cool Jerk', they also started recording work on the sublime original 'How Does It Feel To Feel'. The latter track would not be included on the 'We Are Paintermen' album, presumably because said album needed to be ready before the additional work that was done on this track at a later date.

Jack wasn't happy about doing cover versions: "I'm saying to them, 'Well, look, these numbers have all been recorded by other people, probably better than we've done 'em and there's nothing original there. Why don't we just do our own songs?" Of covers in general, Bob says, "There was just little ideas we would kick about in the studio and Glyn Johns, he'd just say, 'Okay, we'll bang that down and see how it comes out'. Sometimes in-between, while they were doing something, we'd kick about something we was learning. If you listen to '…Rolling Stone', I don't know where I got the words from but they're not the same as what Dylan's singing. The same with 'Cool Jerk'." Of 'Like A Rolling Stone', Bob recalls, "We cut it short. There's only like two verses on our version. I think on the original there's about five."

"'Cool Jerk' was a Tamla (*sic*) thing which we used to play in our stage act because that was popular music of the time," says Eddie. " You needed to play that kind of stuff in your stage show'." 'Cool Jerk' seemed to present The Creation with quite a few problems. At least ten attempts were made to get the basic track. There may even have been more but the tape box's ledger has been torn off where the annotation would reveal whether that is the case. The problems with 'Cool Jerk' continued into the reduction process, when the vocals would have been overlaid. "There's a little bit of harmony stuff there and when we did it live we didn't bother with it," explains Bob. "I used to just sing it but it needed (harmonies) on the record. I can remember going over that a few times."

Eddie got to commit his stage vocal showcase, 'Hey Joe', to tape. Not that The Creation's version was what we would now call a tribute. "In those days you didn't do tributes", says Eddie. "You just did it 'cos you liked the song. You only do tributes when the person's died or something. (Hendrix) was just another performer on the scene at the time whose work was being recognised. Yeah, it was good – let's do this song." Eddie had seen Jimi perform, probably at the Saville Theatre, but definitely not at the places where he'd really made his reputation in his first few months in London such as the Bag O' Nails and the Speakeasy: "I didn't go down those joints. As soon as the gig was finished, most of the time I was getting back home."

The lyric was discernibly amended, with Eddie appending a spoken word, possibly ad-libbed part. "We wasn't a copycat band," explains Bob. "If we did it, we did it our way. We'd pick up the song and after a few times it'd change anyway." He does add, though, "We didn't do it that many times on stage." Eddie is somewhat lukewarm in his feelings about The

Creation's version of the song. "The Hendrix thing, I don't know why I did that really," he now says. "I loved Hendrix when he came over and he started playing, I liked 'Hey Joe' as a song but the version that we did – I didn't really like it much."

For Bob, however, the recording was significant, not because he thought it particularly noteworthy aesthetically but because of the strangest feeling he experienced when he heard Eddie enunciate the line, 'Goodbye everybody'. "I think that was Eddie's leaving swansong and it was almost slap-dashy, really," he says. Bob is mistaken in his belief that this was the last track Eddie recorded for the Creation but his impressionistic memory is strong that Eddie was communicating his intention to leave the group that he had helped build: "I picked up on it at the time. He almost talks it: 'Goodbye everybody' – and it was in his mind then to leave....I'm not on it at all because Kim Gardner's playing bass (but) I was there, I remember him doing it."

That torn ledger prevents one knowing exactly how many takes were attempted of the basic track of 'Hey Joe' but, judging by the gap between that and the annotation for the next recorded track, it can only have been one or two. Additionally, it would seem that no reduction work was done on the track at all, implying that Eddie sang it live. The first three takes of 'Like A Rolling Stone' were all breakdowns. Take 4 – the first complete – was used as the master.

The rest of the session – and in fact the first song recorded at it – was taken up by 'How Does It Feel To Feel'. This number would be a huge production by Creation standards, with much overdubbing and studio trickery. Or *productions:* there were two released versions, one – the more raucous rendition – referred to as the American version because it was chosen for US release. There were three basic track takes attempted, all of which were completes. The ledger is annotated: "Master: take 2 or take 3."

The track starts with a huge, booming drum part. Explains Jack, "We did that to create that sort of cave sound. Something echoey. We wanted something really big and heavy."

It was decided that this called for the use of a special type of microphone, namely a German mic called a c-12a. Pye engineer Ray Prickett was brought into studio 2 to arrange this. "Ray had a phenomenal record of wonderful records that he had made and he used to make the Tony Hatch sessions, which included 'Downtown'," remembers O'Duffy. "Ex-RAF I think. He wasn't a great mate of mine. Fabulous at his job but a bit regimental in his way of working. People thought he was a bit straight."

No doubt those who considered Prickett not sufficiently with-it for the age rolled their eyes in familiar contempt when Prickett objected to The Creation's plan of action. O'Duffy: "Ray was appalled that we were going to use this mic on a bass drum. We did anyway." Prickett's counsel turned out to be the wiser one. "The drummer did a Hawaii-Five-O on the kit," says O'Duffy, "concluding with a bass drum kick and in one bash we blew up the microphone. That mic was at the time really expensive and is now priceless."

"Yeah, well," shrugs Jack of the occurrence. "How can you move on into space if you don't explore the frontiers?" Evidently, some other way of capturing the colossal percussion the band wanted was discovered, for the finished record(s) did have a highly impressive bottom-end in the intro. "With the bass drum, they got such a good sound because they added some echo or reverb or something and it just made it so full and gave that real sense of power," Jack says. "The studio guys can take a lot of credit for that." Jack remembers some of the drumming being re-recorded at an additional session. Jack: "It was really only doubling up... It's just that really heavy bass drum coming into it so we spent some time trying to create what we created. We got it how we wanted it. We had a big blast at the beginning."

'How Does It Feel To Feel' featured much call-and-response vocal work and en masse chorus chanting. Explains Bob, "What happens is, we all sing, 'How Does It Feel'. On the first verse, (Eddie does) the response, on the second verse, (I do) the response. On the third verse – which is like a verse and a half – we both do it, do a harmony on it." The laying down of the harmony vocals occasioned a small mishap: an ashtray fell to the studio floor with an audible "Clung!" "On the beginning," says Bob. "There was an ashtray on the stand. Somebody dropped it. It's there on the recording. Voices (going) 'Ssh!' (and) giggling."

The recruitment of Prickett to help with the drum part, incidentally, would judging by Bob's recollection of Talmy's secretiveness at Pye, have led to some skulduggery. "I do remember there was a crossover of people dashing from one studio to the other," he says. "And I always remember that when somebody came in from the other studio, everything was switched off. It was almost like, 'You'll not get a chance to listen to any melodies or what was going on'. Everything was switched off. 'Yes, come in. What do you want? Right, okay'. And then the person went out, roll the takes again. Nothing was ever played when anybody outside that session came into the room."

Work on 'How Does It Feel To Feel' may have spilled over to the following day or another day. Although there is no annotation on the tape-box ledger confirming this, the ledger records a "Retake" of the song which is numbered "1" after 'Like A Rolling Stone': the previous 'How Does it Feel To Feel', 'Hey Joe' 'Cool Jerk' and 'Like A Rolling Stone' were numbered 1- 4 respectively. Had the retake occurred on the 7th, it would seem logical that it would have been numbered "5" . This retake is presumably the alternate version – either the US or UK version. As with the first version, there were three takes, all completes.

No less than two entire tracks were devoted to guitar, with that guitarwork on both tracks itself augmented by "new guitar" (O'Duffy: "I am going to guess that it's perhaps a new solo guitar/alternative rhythm guitar or a particular Creation effect guitar".) All this guitarwork indicates that it is this recording of the song that is the so-called American version. Take 3 was chosen for the reduction stage where, continuing the strange symmetry that seems to have surrounded this song, there were three takes, all completes. More 'rhythm' (additional bass and drums, or perhaps just drums), two sets of backing vocals, tambourine and lead vocals were added at this stage. Take 3 of the four-fours was designated 'master'.

Whereas the UK version would appear to feature no violin bow work, merely cranked up guitar and a picked solo, Eddie's violin-bow work featured throughout the US version. This was spectacular, helping make the US version a blaring, feedbacking, exquisite *blitzkrieg* of a recording. Bob recalls "really long, drawn out swipes with the bow." The American version's solo also featured delicate, spidery figures. Eddie has no idea how he conjured them but Bob suggests a methodology: "He also uses the stick of the bow as well. Not just the horsehair. He tended to scratch as well as the hair sort of sound." Whatever the method, Bob is simply overwhelmed by his colleague's technique in that area: "He is a master. Other people have a go at it and I will say this now, nobody can do what he does with that on the guitar."

In the second half of June, The Creation's third single finally hit the shops, a full eight months after 'Painter Man'. In the Sixties, when an absence of even a few months from the release schedules was considered to be a matter for some concern, a return to action like this required a re-entry that packed a punch. Of the songs in the can, the one that best fitted that description – excluding 'How Does It Feel To Feel', only just recorded and in any case probably not quite finished – was 'Can I Join Your Band'.

Fascinating lyrically and almost unbearably exciting musically, the release of this record as The Creation's third – indeed, comeback – single would surely have secured the group a significant chart placing. Though 'Making Time' and 'Painter Man' had been strong records, there were unusual circumstances surrounding their release and distribution which explained why they didn't climb to the positions in the charts their artistic worth merited. It seems inconceivable that a record of the brilliance of 'Can I Join Your Band' would not, if released and with Polydor's distribution muscle behind it, have made the various charts and that therefore history – Creation history – would have been very different.

Yet the record chosen for release was not the explosive and characteristic 'Can I Join Your Band' but 'If I Stay Too Long', that nice-enough but hardly awe-inspiring ballad. Furthermore, it was a track, that went against the grain of one of the Creation's virtues, namely not sounding like any other band.

Jack remembers feeling bewildered and not a little frustrated by the choice of 'If I Stay Too Long'. "It was basically a nice little ballad", he says. "It was okay but the one myself and Arthur Howes and the Arthur Howes agency presumed was going to be released was 'Come And Join My Band' (*sic*). That was more in line with the band but Polydor insisted on turning this one out because they thought it was more commercial. Bob was quite happy because he liked it and it was a nice ballad. He said, 'It'll be a change for the band, it'll be something different'. I said, 'Yeah but we're going down the wrong image and the wrong style. Anybody can do this'. But Polydor insisted and we didn't get a say in it. I don't know what Shel's version of that is; whether he had a say in it I don't know. But the thing was released and I just thought, 'Well, they've just changed the style of the band'."

Talmy's version of events is this: "As I recall, that seemed to be the best side for a single at that time because in those days we were putting out singles regularly. I liked it a lot and I thought, 'Let's put it out'." He says he can't recall the decision stemming from a desire on his part to move away from the semi-psychedelic sound that had to some extent resulted in commercial failure with the first two singles: "Nobody to my knowledge sat down and analysed: that doesn't fit exactly the mould of the other one. We just went by what we liked."

He adds, "Everything we did, I recorded as a potential single. That's the way in fact I tried to do every track with everybody I recorded. Some obviously were not, some never would be, but the mindset was that everything I was going to record could be a potential single. They thought that was great. Definitely they went along with, 'Yeah, everything we do is a potential single'."

It certainly seems to have been assumed by The Creation camp that 'Can I Join Your Band' would be an appropriate release in the 45rpm format if this snippet from the Pop Shorts column in the 18 February 1967 issue of *Record Mirror* is anything to go by: "The Creation record their new self-penned single 'Can I Join Your Band' on 15 Feb and are currently undertaking several television appearances in Holland. The group are now managed by their agent, Arthur Howes."

June Clark does suspect that some parties felt it was time to put the radical music on the back burner in order to get a hit. "I think that they thought maybe their sound was a bit too hard," she says. "'Cos it really was harsh. If you think about what else was coming out at the time, it was very harsh. And I really thought it was going to work but it didn't. 'If I Stay Too Long' I think might have been just a little bit too… moaning."

Eddie: "We just had at the time this mentality that you'd go in, you'd write a song, you'd go and record it and then you left it to the management, thinking, 'Oh, they know best'. I can't remember what actually our attitude was towards that particular song ['Can I Join Your Band']. I don't think we actually ever went in and recorded an 'album track'. All the songs we did, we thought they might be some kind of single, an A- or a B-side. With 'Can I Join Your Band', I suppose we went for it as a single."

For her part, Clark says of the decision to put out 'If I Stay Too Long', "I was thrilled because it was a ballad. People do like ballads. Ballads sell very, very well. I actually preferred it. It's still actually my favourite song they do. The words are beautiful to me, and the way its sung and the way it's arranged, I just love it. But I'm not in the majority. It's weaker and it doesn't have their sound. You would not think it's the same band." Of 'Can I Join Your Band', Clark says, "It was much punchier and it's got a hook to it whereas 'If I Stay Too Long', it's a really pretty song but of course doesn't have the same impact. I think you can put out a ballad if you've already made it."

Bob points out that Eddie's vocal may have been a consideration: "I would have probably have had to re-do the vocals if it had been a single."

However, a half-hour studio session would have taken care of that problem. Jack continues to suspect that Polydor were behind the decision, one which he insists he was not alone in being appalled and amazed by: "At the end of the day, record companies had the final say, or they did then. Our booking agent at Arthur Howes at the time, Mr Fowler, agreed entirely with me: he said, 'I just can't figure out what's going on'."

Though Jack recalls Bob being pleased by the decision to make 'If I Stay Too Long' a single, Bob was also surprised by the decision and doesn't think the track was suitable single material: "Not for that period. If you listen to it now, if somebody like Boyzone was to put their interpretation on it, with more vocal and a boy-band type thing, you can hear a song there. But not The Creation. It's a ballad with changing, haunting guitar on. There's no middle eight to it – I think that doesn't help it either. It was just a song. Didn't think, 'Oh this is gonna be an A-side'. It was their choice."

In fact, 'Can I Join Your Band' was actually released as a Creation single in Belgium. 'If I Stay Too Long' was also passed over in West Germany, where 'Tom Tom' was chosen for release in July. The latter entered the official West German charts on July 8 1967 and would ultimately peak at Number 14, spending a total of 11 weeks on the charts.

When 'If I Stay Too Long' backed with 'Nightmares' was released in Britain in late June 1967, it was actually to quite a promotional fanfare. In an era when the *New Musical Express* – then the pop paper with the world's largest circulation – carried advertisements on its front page, The Creation's new record label took out the cover of the *NME* dated 1 July 1967 to announce the arrival of 'If I Stay Too Long'. "It was about three hundred quid, I think – which was a lot of money in those days," says Jack. The ad used a picture of the band from the same session as has produced one of the more enduring images of the group.

In the ad, Kim and Eddie are standing, Jack is perched on a chair and Bob is sat on the ground. Eddie is holding an open umbrella. The paisley shirts and neckerchiefs sported by Eddie, Kim and Jack – Bob is the odd-man-out in a checked jacket – are reflected by the general psychedelic nature of the ad's design: the ostentatiously fake background The Creation are placed against is an X-Ray effect wood with a tree to the foreground within the trunk of which some fashionably distorted lettering spells out the group name, record title and producer credit. It was a very striking image but gave a completely misleading impression of the record it sought to promote. Anybody buying 'If I Stay Too Long' on the strength of the ad would almost have a case under the trades description act: the advertisement absolutely captured a psychedelic *zeitgeist* that the record itself bore no relation to.

Bob and June had other misgivings about the *NME* ad. Bob: "The psychedelic tree...that title's written in there, it's like looking at a paisley pattern – you don't really see it. It's very clever, very nice, very hippie and all the rest of it but if it had been block capitals it would have had more impact. It just looks like a frilly pattern round the photograph."

Asked if she was impressed that Polydor paid for a front-page ad, Clark says, "Yes I am, but I don't think it was enough. It's better than nothing but how consistently did they do that? That does say that they believed in it, not embarrassed to be associated with it but it was as though nobody seemed to have the belief in them. That they had to try and do it on their own. That they felt that they were doing enough for them and if attention wasn't being grabbed by then, then it just wasn't going to happen." Jack's recollection about Polydor's promotion of the band chimes with Clark's: "What we found was that they would do nothing and then make a big splash, and then do nothing and make a big splash." Bob offers, "I can't remember anything exciting coming from Polydor. I never spoke to anybody from Polydor."

The issue of *Record Mirror* cover-dated 8 July 1967 gave the single a reasonably good review, opining, "A slow-burning, powerful effort here, a Shel Talmy production with nice restrained but powerful vocal. Could well be a big hit with enough exposure." Whether or not that assessment was correct, the exposure deemed a prerequisite for chart success was not forthcoming. Unlike 'Making Time' and 'Painter Man', there were no television slots. Jack: "It didn't get many plays on the radio either." Bob offers, "We didn't get the TV...I think they'd exhausted that on the other singles: 'Well, we've give you the chance'. I don't know exactly but maybe that had something to do with it."

'If I Stay Too Long' did not register on any of the various charts of the time. "I suppose we were getting used to it," says Bob of the record's failure, while Clark was "very disappointed that that didn't do anything and I think *they* were. I don't really think that it went up uphill from there. I think it was difficult from there. As we're talking, it really does seem that Kenny not being the singer has made the difference. That doesn't surprise me."

The latter is another point that Clark and Jack – completely independently – concluded. "It was getting pretty frustrating," says Jack, "because I felt that the only way we could get back on track was to get back Kenny on vocals. Get back the original image of the band. Get Kenny back on vocals and stop pissing about. We could be okay. We had a good band. We kept cutting our own throats, messing ourselves about. If we just stuck to a line we could be okay." Someone at least appreciated the song. Bizarrely, a Dutch band called Big Wheel hit Number 22 in Holland in 1969 with a cover of 'If I Stay Too Long', a record of which, like the Australasian 'Painter Man' cover, the band were oblivious.

On 27 June 1967, the same period, as they were promoting 'If I Stay Too Long', The Creation went into IBC studios to work on a new song. 'Through My Eyes' was a number whose lyric was the consequence of the one and only occasion of Bob ingesting lysergic acid diethylamide, or LSD, the pop-star drug of the season. The resultant psychological delusions – or so-called acid-trip – were not sufficiently interesting for Bob to want to ever repeat the experience but they did lead to a great song.

Bob: "That was the first and only time and I came up with, 'If you can see through my eyes/You would get a big surprise/Things you haven't seen before/Things you haven't seen I'm sure.'" Clark confirms The Creation were "not huge on drugs. They were doing the average kind. Not really heavy. And most of it was pills back then and smoking marijuana. They weren't heavy drinkers. I don't remember any of them being drunk. The Who are a different story. Heavy, heavy drinkers from when I first knew them."

Eddie's melody was as effortlessly superb as ever, a surreal, slightly spooky affair whose chorus was unusually for pop (although quite common in tripped-out 1967) slower than the verses. Collective reverberating band voices echoed the last word of each and every verse line to assist in the general air of otherworldliness, while Eddie's guitar was as huge, distorted and exquisite as one was now getting used to it being.

Despite the band's low standing, at least in their homeland, Jack remembers this period as being a happy one. "It seemed to be summer all year long, that's all I can remember," he recalls. "Just a good warm feeling. It was just a good time for making music." The summer of that year was, of course, the Summer Of Love, the apotheosis of the ideals of those (recently dubbed the counter culture) with an alternative outlook on life whose anti-authoritarian, anti-class structure and anti-bigotry outlook had been building not just throughout that year but since the advent of The Beatles and arguably as far back as when Elvis Presley first became famous.

In 1967, the progressive young seemed to be the dominant cultural force, underlined by the Monterey Pop Festival in June which saw 200,000 outlandishly-dressed teens and twenty-somethings congregated in California to watch the likes of The Who, The Jimi Hendrix Experience, The Grateful Dead, Otis Redding, Ravi Shankar, Simon and Garfunkel and Eric Burdon & The Animals perform at rock music's first such mass, extended gathering. June had also seen the release of two stunning albums, 'Are You Experienced' by the Jimi Hendrix Experience and 'Sgt Pepper's Lonely Hearts Club Band' by The Beatles, records which were doing much to change a prevailing view of rock music as junk for undiscriminating adolescents to a recognition that it was a valid art form.

"We were walking about in Indian smocks and the like," Eddie recalled in *Blitz* in 1982. "I wouldn't have dared to do that any time, before or since. But it was an absolutely wonderful time. It wasn't something manufactured. It slowly grew out of itself. Everyone became a little more liberated then."

Ken White's contemporaneous home movie footage certainly shows an apparently cheerful band. "Came back to England, they were recording," White says. "I don't know why we did it but we went into Hyde Park and I took a load of footage. I think the idea was that we would splice it all together and show it on the backdrop at the next gig. Which is exactly what we did. Every time we went anywhere, I filmed it. That was in and around England." The footage is at times of an almost Marx Brothers quality (helped by its lack of a soundtrack). It's also striking because Bob – usually seen as sexily moody – never seems to be without a smile on his face. White: "If you see the footage I took in Hyde Park of them, they're very jolly, they're having a great time, they're getting on well. It's a lot of fun and it struck me it was like that."

Despite the fact that ostensibly the band and its individual members were not in a good position – classic records repeatedly flopping and Eddie's marriage on the rocks – Bob too remembers it as being a happy time. He attributes much of the reason for this to Kim Gardner, and credits Kim in helping him come out of his newcomer's shell in The Creation. "Kim is a good-time person and I think you either join in with Kim or you'll be the object of his fun," he says. "Kim came in as like a breath of fresh air really. It took me back to happier days in Hamburg. It wasn't me being moody. I was probably suppressed really a little bit from what was all ready established. I couldn't make my mark. We had some good fun with Kim and I thank him for it."

Everyone in that Summer of Love was overwhelmed by the baroque brilliance of the Beatles' new masterpiece. "I bought it on the day that it came out," Bob says of 'Sgt Pepper'. "I managed to get a copy of it. There was a music shop in Piccadilly Circus selling it at twelve o'clock that evening. I more or less wore it out. It's one of those things you listen to and every time you listen to it there's something there you didn't hear before. To me, it's probably about the best album that was. It was almost a musical. I loved the way the songs are all joined together and different ideas and not just playing rock'n'roll."

"Bob was crazy about the 'Sgt Pepper' album," says Clark. "I can only assume Eddie was. How could that album not have influenced musicians at that time anyway? Everyone was flipping out over that album. I remember Joey Molland, who later joined Badfinger, he couldn't believe 'Sgt Pepper'. It was phenomenal. I went to this really old-fashioned Victorian grammar school and I'll never forget that my music teacher brought that album in and she said, 'We are going to listen to this because this is one of the most brilliant pieces of music I have ever heard'. And she deciphered the whole album, the construction of the chords."

O n 19 July 1967, The Creation recorded 'Life Is Just Beginning' and put the finishing touches to 'How Does It Feel To Feel' at Pye Studio 2 with the assistance of Talmy and Alans O'Duffy and MacKenzie.

The tape box's annotation relating to 'How Does It Feel To Feel' refers to 'Retake', indicating that this involved yet more work on that guitar-heavy version recorded some time after the 7 June session.

Nobody in The Creation camp seems sure why it is that the additional guitarwork was deemed necessary on this track, especially as the unadorned version was deemed fit for release in the UK. "I really don't know," is Talmy's simple answer to the question. Bob, at least, has a theory: "The original recordings would be mono and I think they tried to do a stereo thing with them. I've heard 'em both and it's not true stereo." (Ed Strait of Retroactive Records remembers both versions being mono, however, when he re-released them in 1998.)

Everybody is in concurrence about the quality of the final outcome of both versions. Asked if he concurs with the general feeling that the song is The Creation's masterpiece, Bob says, "I would agree with that. It's got everything in there. Slow, sluggish and it's got a minor chord in there as well which helps it out. The solo's good and the words – they're not complicated but it makes you think. I have people saying about that song, like I've thought about 'I Am The Walrus'. That pleases me."

Eddie demurs from the view that the track is quintessential Creation ("It's not early Creation – I think 'Making Time' summed up the early Creation – but it is definitely late Creation") but he too is extremely proud of the track(s). "It's a bit off the wall and it's a bit wacky, it's a bit weird," he says. "It's a little bit out of tune here and there but it don't matter. Those haunting sort of lyrics." Talmy: "It's one of my favourites. It's really a good song and I like how it turned out in the studio." Jack: "I think it's a great number and it's a great feel about it. I think it's the best song Bob ever wrote. Good stuff."

It is almost certainly 'Sgt Pepper's influence that can be heard on the classical string parts on 'Life Is Just Beginning'. Talmy, though, denies everything: "It's been suggested it had something to do with the way The Beatles were doing stuff," he says. "It had nothing to do with that at all. It just sounded like a fun thing to do. I thought it fit the song so I overdubbed it." Bob's recollection is completely the reverse. "I was just trying to stretch the music a little bit more, that was all," he says. "I do think looking back 'Life Is Just Beginning' was a little bit more 'Sgt Pepper'. I don't mean the same tune or anything but there was more incorporated to make it a little bit more interesting and stretch the four-line verses of rock'n'roll."

Not that the strings that made many think of 'Sgt Pepper' were laid down at this session. Indeed, that is from Bob's point of view, a bit of a problem: "The orchestra was put on afterwards. I was going to Shel and going, 'Listen, put a few strings on it, this I how is imagine it'... That was another way of stretching the sounds and things... And Shel got a little quartet and banged them on, but they weren't done at the same time and the timing on it is all over the place. The conductor was trying to keep the lads playing in time with what we'd done. The track that we did, the tempo changes unintentionally. Jack's speeding up and slowing down – or we all are – so when the orchestra come to play along with this, they were finding it difficult. Those lads were probably strict-tempo musicians. If it had been done in the first instance together, we could have done something different."

Jack, though, considers the strings to be a mistake per se, something brought home to him when he heard the band's version on the 'Lay The Ghost' live album. "The strings, for me, detracted from it," Jack says. "We did that, it was recorded live on stage – we never played it live before at all, we'd just recorded it. When I heard it recorded when we did it on stage I thought it sounded great. It was much better than the record. It was just the band paying without the strings."

However, Eddie – whose misgivings about the song had helped prevent it from being recorded for several months – says of the quartet's work, "That was kind of neat." As can be seen from the above quotes, there is some confusion over who thought of adding the strings, confusion that Eddie only adds to when he says, "I might have played it on the piano to Shel and he might have thought, 'We'll get the strings in to do that'."

There is also confusion over whether the song was played live. Like Jack, Bob recollects that the band never played this track on stage in the Sixties but Eddie has recalled the group playing along onstage to a backing track containing the quartet's contribution. Ken White's recollection chimes with Eddie's. "I've got the reel-to-reel tape that the string quartet was put on," White says. "We used to use the string quartet (tape) on stage and they played along with it. We had it dubbed down onto a quarter-inch tape from the master. That's why I've got the quarter-inch tape. I don't even know how successful it ever was. It was well in advance of playing along with this sort of thing so one didn't think much about timing and really you need headphones for the drummer. It was one of the little jobs I did on the second tour we did."

The direction of 'Life Is Just Beginning' is something – all things being equal – Eddie would like to have pursued. "It might have been nice to experiment with something a bit more orchestral linked to rock at that time," he says. "I had a bit of a vision of that: a heavy rock thing with some classical undertones to it. 'Specially with cellos, the deeper strings, the violas. That could have been really good if we'd had the opportunity to do it but you couldn't really do it in those days. They were spending huge amount of money. The Beatles were able to do it on 'Sgt Pepper' because they had the budget."

On 29 July 1967, The Creation appeared on the bill of the Love In Festival at the Alexandra Palace, London. A star-studded event, it also featured Julie Driscoll, Arthur Brown and Pink Floyd. Also appearing were Tomorrow, who included some of the personnel of Four Plus One, the band who had so impressed the Mark Four a few years before. It was at this gig that that the band heard Julie Driscoll performing Donovan's 'Season Of The Witch' and subsequently incorporated the song into their own act.

This gig, incidentally, seems to have been confused in Creation chronology – including by the band themselves – with another gig at the Ally Pally the previous April, the famous 14 Hour Technicolor Dream benefit for the underground/hippie paper *International Times* which had recently been raided by the police. Though they may have been billed, The Creation almost certainly didn't play at the 14-Hour Technicolor Dream: nobody at that event seems to be able to remember seeing them there and the band themselves strangely don't recall the fact that two bands played at either end of the hall simultaneously.

Additionally, the Creation remember their Alexandra Palace set starting at sunrise but at the Technicolor Dream everybody recalls Pink Floyd having that notable spot. Because the line-up and the hippie ambience at both events at the venue were very similar, an understandable conflation in people's memories seems to have occurred and, when asked by journalists about playing the 14-Hour Technicolor Dream event, the band members have responded as though they had.

In some senses, playing the Love-In Festival seems to have been the capstone to what had been – despite underlying frustrations about lack of success – a blissful and creative summer for The Creation. Memories of the gig, surely the closest the band ever came to the privilege enjoyed by many of their contemporaries in playing festivals like Monterey, Woodstock and the Isle of Wight, might be confused as to its date and cause but they are uniformly rapturous.

Jack: "I don't know how we got onto it. It would be through Arthur Howes. Arthur would get us booked into anywhere. That was a great gig. We went on about four o' clock in the morning and just as we struck up, the sun come out. And of course, with Alexandra Palace, it was a glass roof and so you had all these people out there and they're all sitting there sleeping in their sleeping bags and all the rest of it and as we struck up, everything just came up. The light came up, the sun came up and all the people started waking up. It was a bit surreal, actually. We did about 35 minutes, 40 minutes."

"Probably about an hour I would have thought," Eddie demurs. "I know it was about four o'clock in the morning. I think it had a glass roof then, the Alexandra Palace. The sun was just coming through some of the skylights. We would have got there about ten o'clock that evening and stayed right through the night."

Bob recalls an occurrence which only underlined the dazzling, exotic feel of the event: "There was a West Indian drum band and they started off in the dressing room and they just walked round the whole place. They walked round and round and round and just played all the way, got back into the dressing room – I don't know how many there were of them, maybe 12 – and they all stopped at the same time. It was amazing. Who told 'em to stop? How did they know all to stop then? It was one of those sort of: boomp! Deadly silence." He adds, "That was the first sort of hippie experience that I saw full on where people were sitting down painting each other." Bob also recalls a less savoury fashion spectacle: "I remember this girl, she had sort of strips of bacon as a necklace. They were wearing food as accessories. Awful. Another day, that'll be going off, like. It was quite weird, that one."

In such a blissed-out environment, how the Creation went down was almost an irrelevance. "I think everybody was too out of it to care at four o'clock in the morning," says Eddie. "Most of the audience was lying on the ground, completely exhausted, but some people were still flying around, probably out of their nuts. But I think it was okay." Bob rates The Creation's reception as "okay, but that was probably under the influence, so you'd be fooling yourself. It probably wasn't quite as good as you thought it was."

September marked the start of another Creation sortie to West Germany to fill their boots. Their three-week visit probably coincided with the release of their one and only album, 'We Are Paintermen'. Not that the group considered it to be an album as the term is understood. "We never made an album" says Bob. "We didn't go in the studio and record an album. They're the songs which have been put together and there's enough to put an album out. We never went into the studio and said, 'We're going to make an album' and were never asked to make an album. The first album as far as I'm concerned that The Creation have made with intentions of releasing an album was the live gig at the Mean Fiddler ('Lay The Ghost')."

The tracklisting of 'We Are Paintermen' was 'Cool Jerk', 'Making Time', 'Through My Eyes', 'Like A Rolling Stone', 'Can I Join Your Band', 'Tom Tom', 'Try And Stop Me', 'If I Stay Too Long', 'Biff, Bang, Pow', 'Nightmares', 'Hey Joe' and 'Painter Man'.

Though the cover versions are by no means disgraceful, the very way a hoary old chestnut like 'Cool Jerk' gives way to the cutting-edge sounds and raw aggression of 'Making Time' sums up the pointlessness of including covers on a Creation record. Additionally, the fact that the Creation were, in 1967, a band with an almost indescribably modern sound is undermined by the cheap option of knocking off covers of other artists' records, a fact not alleviated by Bob Dylan's original of 'Like A Rolling Stone' and Jimi Hendrix's definitive version of 'Hey Joe' being magnificent records. "From start to finish, it's as disjointed as the experience of the band was," says Bob of 'We Are Paintermen'. "There's no continuity. That's typical of the band." He adds, "I don't know who thought of the title. It's a bit corny."

Talmy was more concerned about other deficiencies. The German edition of the album had poor sound quality and re-channelled stereo mixes, the latter a decision that resulted in a 'diluted' feel. (The Scandinavian edition was apparently better.) "Because I didn't master it for them," is Talmy's explanation of the unsatisfactory sound quality of the German disc. "They were sent parts and did their own mastering. Later on, after all that happened, I had stuck in my contract that I did all the mastering from that point on, because the quality varied too greatly. The last time that ever happened was when I allowed whoever the hell it was to master The Easybeats – and it sucked."

'We Are Paintermen' would never gain a release in Britain. "It should have had a UK release and I honestly don't remember why Polydor didn't do it," says Talmy. "My guess is they didn't think there was enough sales there." June Clark was actually oblivious to fact that the disc existed: "I never ever had that. I was actually surprised when I read that there had been an album at the time." Jack: "I bought one out in Germany and I've still got it. Went into a German record shop and just bought one. The record company never thought to give us any."

Though Bob's splendid lyric to 'Life Is Just Beginning' had detailed a man's ecstatic realisation that his existence is blossoming into complete fulfilment, life was certainly not just beginning for The Creation. When they completed that track and 'How Does It Feel To Feel' at the same session – two of their greatest recordings and tracks which would have instantly been universally recognised as classics had they been committed to tape by The Beatles or The Rolling Stones – the group were weeks away from disintegrating. This was to be the last Sixties Creation recording session for both Bob and Eddie.

Talmy says he had no intimation at the session that it would be Eddie's last, even though he was friendlier with The Creation than any other band he worked with. Talmy says, "I generally speaking kept a semi-arm's length relationship with all the bands because we were all fairly close in age. I chose that path because somebody had to steer the ship and as I decided it was going to be me then I had to retain some authority. I couldn't be one of the boys, which in many ways I regret, but that was a fact of life. So I did not get involved with the reasons for what was going on with them outside the studio."

If Bob's interpretation of his singing the 'Goodbye everybody' line in The Creation's recorded version of 'Hey Joe' is correct, Eddie Phillips had made up his mind to leave The Creation as far back as June. This seems rather early to have reached that decision, not least because he stuck around for two more sessions and a further three or four months. However, it can be said with certainty that The Creation's guitarist had resolved to leave by September 1967 because the tour of Germany and Switzerland on which the group embarked on the 10th of that month was known beforehand by both group and management to be Eddie's farewell.

Eddie's marriage had been under strain for some time, a strain exacerbated by the sole bit of real success the band had enjoyed. With the only lucrative market for the band in West Germany, Eddie was spending more and more time away from home. The normal pressures that puts on a marriage were only worsened by his wife's conviction that he was unable to resist the temptation of the women he met on the road. But Eddie did admit to *Ugly Things* in '97, he had also been ground down by the Creation's commercial failure. "I figured we'd done our bit and if it wasn't going to happen, it wasn't going to happen," he said. "I think even if I hadn't have had problems with my marriage, I probably would have left it anyway. It's a shame when you get close but not close enough."

In his '82 *Blitz* interview, Eddie mentioned a further motive for his departure, one that doesn't seem to have been mentioned anywhere else. "Another reason for leaving was the last tour of Germany in 1967, where everything went wrong," he said, "Cars broke down and there was a guy who met us at the airport and drove us around and said he was from the agency. He was taking ten per cent every night, then he disappeared. The playing was good on that tour, but that's when I decided it had to come to an end."

"It was a bad time in the band," recalls Jack. "Eddie was short of money and his wife was talking about divorce and I think it was breaking him up. He just went into a shell, really. He wouldn't talk. You could see it coming. He just withdrew." Jack did try to persuade his friend and colleague to reconsider: "I did everything to stop him. I said, 'Listen man, you're gonna leave the band but what you gonna do?' And he said, 'Oh, I'll get a job down at Ford in Dagenham'. I said, 'For Christ's sake, you can't work on an assembly line. You wouldn't last two weeks, man. You're an artist. You're a bloody good guitarist, now don't bloody throw it away'.

"He said, 'I can't take it. I've got to make some money and I've got to get a steady job. My solicitor tells me if I do that, I might have a chance of saving my marriage'. Well what can you say to the bloke? So it's very sad and I was disappointed but I could see Eddie's point of view."

Jack sees Eddie's decision to leave the group as something akin to a tragedy: "Very sad 'cos when that happened I thought Eddie was on the threshold of moving up into the big time and [becoming] his own man. You could see Eddie's potential. If you look at the band from the start, you listen to his guitar: as we go on, you hear him growing all the time and it was getting to a stage where he was a top man, I tell you. Live, he was great."

Eddie admits that he did agonise before making his final decision. "Looking back, my marriage was falling apart...I never really made any money through The Creation and I think that really didn't help matters," he says. "Now and again in your life you feel like the world comes down on you and it just happened to me then and I had to walk away from it. Looking back, it's sad. Shame I didn't just persevere and carry on. Might have gone on to better things – but who knows? When the ground shakes, you just go."

Eddie's agonising is confirmed by the recollections of Ken White, who recalls something of a protracted nature to his departure: "At some point he was never too sure that he was actually going. I think there was that impression that maybe he wouldn't go ever – but he did. I always got that impression." Remembers Clark, "It was really bad for Eddie. He was really, really upset. It was sad. Because he's such a sensitive guy, you can imagine the impact that had on him."

Talmy too tried to dissuade Eddie from quitting: "Yeah of course I did. It didn't happen." The producer adds, "I have no solution for what constitutes band dynamics. They seem to develop a life of their own. Sometimes it works out and most times it doesn't. That's the reason why most bands break up. I suppose a psychologist could make a complete study of this kind of thing and probably do extremely well. We just tried to get on and do stuff. People in bands basically I think are out of their minds anyway, as are the people who produce them." Asked if he too tried to persuade Eddie to stay, Bob says, "No I don't think I did. I think I was probably seeing the end of the road myself. I only stayed a couple of months, if that, longer than Eddie."

Were the others shocked at his ultimate decision? Eddie: "I can't remember really. I suppose they must have been a bit upset that this little thing that we had together was going to fall apart a bit."

Talmy says, "That was, as far as I was concerned, the end of the band. He was having personal problems with his marriage, he was frustrated with what was going on or not going on. He was not happy with some of the personnel. I think a bunch of reasons." The producer could be forgiven for feeling resentment at the session he had just funded for 'Life Is Just Beginning' and 'How Does It Feel To Feel' going to waste but he insists, "Well they weren't going to waste. They were created, weren't they?" However, he then says, "Did I feel any resentment that the band was breaking up yet again and that as far as I was concerned the soul of the band was going? Yeah. Eddie was the soul of the band. Without him, it wasn't the same band."

Despite the earth-shaking fact of Eddie's decision to leave The Creation, life to some extent went on as normal for the group, its employees and agents. They had already been booked to play shows in Germany and Switzerland and the decision was made to fulfil these dates. Meanwhile, Polydor had scheduled 'Life Is Just Beginning' b/w 'Through My Eyes' for release in October as the next British Creation single. Eddie agreed to play some of the German dates at the start of the tour and it was decided a replacement would be brought in to perform the remainder of the gigs and learn a few tricks from Eddie during the handover period. The first name thought of by The Creation was that of Ronnie Wood.

Wood, of course, was and is a gifted guitarist but it was in a way a lazy move based as much on convenience as anything else. "Ron was Kim's mate and often Ron would come to gigs with us if he had nothing to do, just hanging out," recalls Eddie. "If The Creation had a run of gigs, Ronnie'd come along, just get in the van and go. That's the kind of relationship we had." At first, Wood seemed amenable but – not for the first time in his dealings with The Creation – he had his head turned by the offer of work with the Jeff Beck Group. Bob: "We asked him to come with us on that Switzerland thing. He came to one rehearsal and we did rehearse with him and what happened was – I think it was the same day or the same week – Jeff Beck asked him to go with him, play bass, and he chose to go down that road."

With the eve of the tour approaching, a replacement guitarist was needed with some urgency. It was Ken White – accompanying The Creation on tour this time on a formal, paid basis – who came to the rescue. White suggested Tony Ollard, a journeyman guitarist (Ollard's own words) who had played with Lulu, Cat Stevens and Dave Clark. "The dates were booked," says White. "I don't think there was any way they could get out of it. Maybe they needed the money but I think if they hadn't have been booked and he'd left, they might have gone looking for a guitar player and spent time. There was no auditioning or anything. A guitar player was needed and I said, 'What about Tony? He's a good player'."

"All the halls had been booked and everything so we had an obligation to go there and do something," says Jack. "I knew Tony from years back. He'd been in a band round Enfield at the time called Norman Jago and the Jaguars." Bob: "We said, 'Well we'll get Tony in just do this tour in Switzerland and then perhaps we can do something with Eddie later', 'cos that was in the bag. We had this tour in Switzerland in so we thought, 'We might as well go and take the money'. It was almost like, 'Will they know the difference over there?'"

"Up to that moment I'd played with a good few bands most styles of music," Ollard recalls. "Earlier on I was with a group named Rob Storm and the Whispers who were a few years older than myself and actually very good musicians playing a wide variety of styles and covers from the Beach Boys to Otis Redding and the Four Tops, etcetera. In fact I'd already recorded a few records with them on the Pye label. They worked with the Harold Davidson Agency so apart from well-paying gigs at Universities/Young Farmers Associations Balls throughout the UK, they also backed Paul & Barry Ryan on their very first tour of England, Scotland and Ireland. This was before Barry's small hit of 'Eloise'. We also made an appearance at *Sunday Night At The London Palladium* and backed Lorne Greene on a Midlands TV show, amongst others. You can see I probably didn't really have a personalised style as such, having to play such a wide range of different music. The Whispers even had a version of 'Maria' from *West Side Story* with plenty of awkward flattened fifths."

Nonetheless, the general consensus seems to be that, when Ollard was offered the job it was intended to be a permanent arrangement or, at the very least, a sort of long-term audition. Clark offers, "I felt that Tony was there, part of The Creation". She does add, though, "but I really didn't think that the band was going to keep it together. Just seemed very, very unstable: everything about it seemed to be, 'Well now we're trying this'. We'll try this and see if it works.' I never felt that anybody really had any faith that it was going to go anywhere and I felt that Shel's interest had dwindled."

Of Ollard, she recalls, "He sort of had a face shaped like Stevie Marriott: round, pansy-like face. Very pleasant fella. He didn't have a big ego. I thought he was just a pleasant guy." On that face, incidentally, drooped a Zapata moustache, virtually taboo for a pop star until that June, when the Beatles had instantly made facial hair fashionable by all sporting 'taches on the sleeve of 'Sgt. Pepper'.

Tony Ollard had not actually heard of The Creation before White got him the gig ("This was at least the second time Kenny found a nice gig for me"). Asked how he would describe his playing style in 1967, he says, "A mish-mash. That's what comes of being a journeyman. It sounded like a good gig." Ollard has only vague recollections of the man whose shoes he was to step into: "As far as I can remember I wasn't even introduced to him – 'Hi Eddie, this is Tony', etcetera. Even today I'm not sure of the situation about his leaving the band, whether it was by happy mutual agreement or otherwise." He adds, "We had just a couple of practice sessions before leaving for Germany. I think they respected me as a guitarist although that didn't help the band much, their entire style being based on Eddie's playing."

"Once I said I was going, they needed a replacement and they (got) Tony," says Eddie. "I dare say they thought that would have been permanent but they probably didn't know how it would work out." When asked how he felt about The Creation signifying their intention to carry on without him, one can feel Eddie caught between wishing to express an incredulity and not wanting to seem egotistical by doing so. "I sort of felt that it was my band and, once I had walked away from it, I knew in myself the band wouldn't be the same... The Creation to me finished at that point," he says.

"I know they carried on for a bit but from how I saw the band, when I stopped working with it, that's when to me the band finished as The Creation." Was he surprised that they didn't just split up upon his departure? Eddie: "Never crossed my mind. At the time I might have thought that that would have been the best thing to do, I can't remember, but then I think, 'Well if the guys want to carry on, it's a free country, innit? Carry on if you want to'. But I knew it couldn't last for long. Somehow I knew that. 'Cos I knew what I used to put into the band and I thought, 'If I'm not there doing that, what will happen?'"

The tour manager for this jaunt was Johnny Byrne, a man with no experience in that role whatsoever. A writer by trade, he got to know Shel Talmy though his friend Thom Keyes, author of the beat-group novel *All*

Night Stand that Talmy was representing as an agent. Talmy encouraged Byrne to finish his own novel, *Stopcock*. Having done so, Byrne was waiting for Talmy to place it with a publisher. "He was like a godfather," recalls Byrne of Talmy. "He used to dole out bits of money. We were the first writers that he'd taken on. Since the stuff that we were thinking of doing was going to be rock-oriented anyway, it seemed interesting and innovative for Shel to do this.

"Thom's book had been picked up at auction in America and he was earning an awful lot of money and because of it, he moved into this very large flat in a beautiful old mansion block. That was the time when everything seemed to be really happening around London. The underground. Rock'n'roll becoming a part of everybody's life and jazz becoming a part of everybody's life. A wonderful feeling abroad at the time." Byrne himself was a musician of sorts, having played harmonium in what he describes as "a mad little alternative crazy group that did magic and stuff called the Poison Bellows". The latter group had actually played the 14 Hour Technicolor Dream gig at which The Creation are erroneously thought to have performed.

"Shel at that time asked me to go to Germany," recalls Byrne. "I think it was really to give me something to do while he tried to sort something out with the book. So I was really pitched into it in a fairly fast way. I'd met Kenny Pickett around Shel's place quite a bit but I didn't know him very well. I wasn't heavy into rock'n'roll and I wasn't more into rock'n'roll until later when I started doing *Groupie* when I got involved with Family, the Floyd and people like that." He adds, "Another reason why Shel wanted me to do this or thought I'd be good at it was that I'd spent years teaching English to foreigners so I had a good knowledge of dealing with people, especially from Germany. And so it wasn't totally off the wall sending me…

"I remember being given this huge itinerary. Every day there was a different place, all over Germany. It was meant to culminate at some gigs in Switzerland. I can't remember how much I got paid. I think it was not per gig but per week or per month or whatever. Certainly all my expenses were paid and there would have been something on top. I was meant to take Shel's commission of 10% or something. Maybe I was getting money from that side of it. They used to carry it all in cash because the money used to be got in cash at the place, wherever it happened to be."

Mixed-race group the Equals were also on the bill on some dates. The Equals, like The Creation, had achieved significant success in Germany:

their single 'Baby Come Back' had skimmed the West German Top 10 the previous July. Unlike The Creation, their German success would eventually be replicated in their native country, the same record scaling the UK charts in '68. (Frontman Eddy Grant would go on to even greater success as a solo artist.) "The funny thing we noticed, they never had a bass player," recalls Jack. "They had about three rhythm guitars… They were a happy little band and they jogged along, a nice little pop group."

The first gig of the tour was a small open-air event. Ollard was impressed by his first proper exposure to The Creation. "I was very surprised to hear all that sound produced by a trio," he says, "although they did have eight Marshall cabinets on stage. I believe the drums were not miked and the PA must have been just a few hundred watts. Those in the public who didn't have their mouths open – agog – were very receptive too."

White: "Eddie played and Tony looked on to try and get some idea of what and how it should be." Eddie says he can't remember giving the newcomer any tuition. "Tony was probably just watching what we did on stage to get the feel of things and try to carry on from where I left off," he says. "I wouldn't like to go into a band under those circumstances and try and be somebody else. I'd like to go into a band and be myself. I think that's asking a lot of somebody."

That The Creation had been smitten by 'Sgt Pepper' was made evident by the fact that they were now opening their set with its title track. "It was fun", says White. "It was a great song and they did a stonking guitar version of it. Eddie played a wonderful guitar opening."

Byrne quickly found himself enamoured of The Creation and its personnel. "It was my own stupidity that I didn't first of all realise how good the group was," he says. "Secondly, I didn't realise how interesting their background was. If it had been any other group around that I had some idea of I would have known but I knew nothing. Shel didn't brief me about these guys at all. To me, they appeared to be four session guys who'd sort of been cobbled together because there'd been an accidental Number 1 or almost Number 1 in Germany. I wasn't into the minutiae of the pop world. I knew the large picture, not the smaller picture, the individuals."

Byrne found it interesting mixing with people whose cultural references were very different to his own. "My impressions of the guys were that they were very tight with each other and they were real musos," he says. "They thought I was a bit of an oddity because I was more literary.

They respected me but I don't think they really understood me. And the life, what it was like being a musician on the road, it's a whole thing in itself and the conflicts and the feuds that come from it, it's almost the same sort of thing that happens in a family and I was aware that there were difficulties."

However, he found none of the ignorant hostility some groups are apt to display to outsiders: "They always treated me well. There was no reason for them to do otherwise. I was an artist but I was a street person and my background was Irish farms in Dublin. I wasn't a snooty upper-crust guy mingling with the working class rock'n'roll musicians." Byrne provides an observation that may have something to do with the fact that for three members of The Creation this tour was a way of trying to prevent their source of future income being cut off, while for the fourth – Eddie – it was one final payday.

Byrne: "They were fairly cynical about it, they were not in it for love, they were in it for money in terms of being on tour, which is I suppose a necessary implication of what they were doing and the facts of their life." Nonetheless, this tinge of cynicism, for Byrne, detracted in no way from how impressive he found them creatively. "They were very good," he recalls. "They were professional musicians and I quickly realised that, yes, while they had all the skills that you might expect from session men – because I knew quite a few jazz session people: you're in, you're out, you get paid and that's it – when I started watching them playing, I realised that they were an absolutely amazing group.

"It was really quite classically exciting to hear, especially when Phillips was playing. He was a very charismatic guy. You could see that he stood out as someone very special. He had that look, an even more impressive look and feel almost than Pete Townshend. And there was a similarity in their build. They were sort of lean, quite athletic and virtuoso, riffy movements of that time and in command in the sense that there wasn't much that Phillips couldn't do with this machine. I loved watching him."

Byrne found the group to be comprised of a disparate set of personalities. "My initial reaction to Jack was that he was grumbly, a bit cynical, a bit discontented," he says. "I think he was a bit bolshy. He was the one who would grumble most... But he also had a very wry, laid-back sense of humour and I warmed to him a lot by the end of the tour. He was just always warm. He does have that sort of grumbly disposition and I hope I'm not doing him a disservice." Byrne took more quickly to the bassist. "I got to know Kim best of all," he says. "He was very warm, very interesting, very crazy and very funny. Kim was the one who was most interested in *me*. He was interested in my life, what I was doing and things like that so if I knocked around with anyone it was Kim.

"My feeling about Bob is that he was a very complicated guy," he continues. "He could be very pleasant and agreeable but I sensed that he was perhaps one of the most ambitious of them in purely earthly terms. I sensed more of a commitment to Bob than I did Bob to the group. That there might be another agenda. I didn't experience anything unpleasant from Bob and I didn't ever hear him do or say anything unpleasant in my capacity, because I was in a position (to hear complaints about) who did what and who might not get what.

"Bob I saw as being the sort of spoilt baby. He looked younger than the others. He was I think more self-indulgent, more narcissistic than any of the others. He fitted the picture of the sulky vocalist who's a bit spoiled. But in private he was very nice. He was very agreeable and reasonably good humoured. That was an image that he played and played up. His microphone technique suggested that. There were lots of people like that, Rod Stewart and that. I think people know that there's a hierarchy in a group and that most superficial attention usually goes to the singer."

As with so many people, Byrne felt that the truly special quality of the band was the guitarist. Byrne: "Anybody who saw Eddie Phillips perform in pubic realised I think that they were in the presence of a potential superstar," he asserts. "You just had that feeling about him. There are those people you see. When you saw Jimi Hendrix, you realised it was an amazing talent and it just so happened that he got the breaks that gave him position commensurate with that talent. Eddie Phillips was one of the best I have seen in my experience, and that includes Andy Summers and lots of people. He had that instant thing.

"By this time, of course, UFO had been going and we knew the Floyd and Syd Barrett had this thing. There are those touched individuals who have that special magic and Eddie Philips definitely had it. No question about it. Fascinating to watch, wonderful to listen to and incredible to see his live performance." Eddie's magnetic stage appearance was a contrast to his ordinary-bloke offstage persona. "He was not a complicated person," says Byrne. "He was one of these people who are transformed. It's like a little lurcher dog I got. Spindly little thing, it had mange and I cured it. Then I took this trembling little thing out for its first walk and a rabbit jumped up nearby; suddenly it realised what its entire existence was about and you saw that instant, amazing transformation. Eddie Phillips was like that."

In terms of internal band relations, Byrne says, "I think Bob tended to be more of a loner than the others. Kim and Eddie Philips were quite close, and the drummer. I always seemed to be (around) when Eddie was there, but that was because whoever Kim was with I would be with." He has a vague recollection of a certain amount of friction between Jack and Bob: "I think there was a certain amount of jealousy. If my memory serves me right, Jack was the kind of guy who would probably have resented anyone doing well or getting special attention. And since Bob was the one who was doing the vocals, an awful lot of the attention would have been on him."

Eddie's swansong tour, of course, was always going to be a psychologically strange and sad affair. "I remember there was a tremendous sort of down feeling and sadness at the fact that he was leaving," says Byrne. "But I could never understand why he was leaving because they were very loyal to each other. They might try to give each other fucking hell but they never really took it outside. I would try to understand. Here were guys who went onstage and thousands of people went apeshit. It seemed to me that they were doing what it was they'd set out to do and they had every reason to be happy and I couldn't understand all the things that made them unhappy about their situation. I detected a sadness.

"They had everything and more for the making of a world-class megagroup and it was frustrating for them I think, whether through actions of their own or (others) that they were not where they deserved to be. They were people who believed that they deserved better and over in Germany they were going through the motions." Not that this frustration manifested itself in decadence: "They were *never* less than professional. That's what struck me about them. There wasn't the kind of bad behaviour of trashing hotels and things like that. They might get a bit pissed here and there but that was nothing, really. I think they were too intelligent and they were too professional."

The amount of money the group were making – which he always had the job of collecting off the promoter – only added to Byrne's puzzlement about the sadness he detected: "I wasn't surprised, because pop groups are meant to make a lot of dosh, but it seemed an awful lot of money for that time."

Jack found Eddie's attitude to his impending departure to be a mixture: "Very withdrawn...he wouldn't really talk about it. In fact, he was quite aggressive in a way. He seemed to blame everything on the band." Bob remembers more of a melancholy attitude from his colleague: "He was just like, 'Let's get it over with'. Not in a bad way but just like, 'It's gonna come to an end, it'll be better when it's over'."

Memories have now blurred as to the exact itinerary of the tour but strong recollections still exist in the minds of its participants of different aspects of it.

Thanks to Kenny White, The Creation's stage show was becoming ever more interesting. "We used to use a bit of *Batman* footage when we did the Swiss and German tour," he says. "When we sort of showed things on the little backdrop. I spliced it all together with odds and sods of...I don't know. I can't even remember now. There was *Batman* I know, probably going backwards or something. It was just to try to make something out of nothing really. You're talking original *Batman*. We had black and white old-fashioned *Batman*, what we used to see at Saturday morning pictures, kids' serials, that sort of thing."

This wasn't the only innovation The Creation were using in their stage act. They were by now employing what we would these days call strobe lighting, courtesy of an investment Talmy had made in that nascent technology. They may have been the very first group to do so. So unused were the audiences of the time to the Nosferatu-type shadows and menace created by the effect that Kim actually recalled some members fainting at the sight, although this may have been exaggeration.

Although he "loved" the work he was doing, Byrne was finding his first taste of dealing with rock'n'roll promoters to be rather vexing. "There was a certain point when I had to keep the promoter in my sights because they would rip you off like anything," he says. "It was quite an important job for me. I was quite young, I was mid-twenties, coming up to 30, but inexperienced. I wasn't used to dealing with money. I was a poet. I think I got everything that was due them. There were one or two incredibly gangsterish exploits because a lot of the guys who would set these things up in Germany were gangsters. I would always try and get a handle on the money. The very first thing I did when we arrived a venue. By the end I had to vacate the stage and I had to be around wherever the money was and sometimes you had to be taken to places.

"Obviously it would have been professional suicide for anybody to be overtly dishonest because then they would be struck off and people wouldn't play (their venues again), but working for me was the fact that Creation was the number one group in Germany. It saved them a lot of hassle". He does admit though, "Once we had to lock some fucking guy in the place to get the money from him." Of The Creation's attitude to wealth, Byrne says, "They used the money in the way that people who are not really interested in money use it. Kim might have a suitcase full of money but he'd just toss it around – easy come, easy go" .

Byrne continues, "The other big problem was always getting them to the places on time. One of the things that really surprised me about Germany was that the fucking trains didn't run on time. They had to travel by train here and there. The trains just did not run on time – I thought Hitler had sorted that one out. I'd been in Italy the year before and I found the trains did run on time. We sometimes went by car. Germany's a huge country."

As the tour progressed, Byrne was ever more impressed by The Creation's mix of mainstream and radical music. "They were a revelation to me because if anything I spent more of my time by choice with jazz musicians," he says. "But this was the time where the distinctions between jazz and rock'n'roll were sort of beginning to blur round the edges. They weren't avant garde to me, because I was avant garde and I had spent the early Sixties doing action paintings in clubs around Soho with poetry with Graham Bond, the saxophonist, and people like that. So everything that they were doing was about three or four years down the line from what I'd been doing.

"But what surprised and intrigued me was to see it coming into a much more popular cultural thing as opposed to the kind of esoteric fringe activities and happenings. For people to see this happening up on stage was new. They were straddling two camps. They weren't quite in one thing or the other. Had they been authentic underground, if they'd taken a bit more acid, maybe they might have been completely dug out of sight. As it was, they were still playing around the edges of it. They weren't truly avant garde. They were using it as part of a performance but they were opportunistic and adventurous. That's how I would describe them."

The Creation were a band he observed as practising continuously: "When we were sitting around for hours and hours at a time, they would always, always be practising chords on an un-amped guitar. Always. Especially Kim. And Eddie did that. And sometimes you'd see them – you could hardly hear these plinkings going on – but one of them would look up and catch something and you could see something flash between the two where they would sort of rattle off these chords. They were doing little things like that and… this riff that they'd pick up would somehow surface in some of the gigs. They didn't always play the same thing the same way. That's what made them enjoyable to watch. Otherwise I would have gone crazy."

Not that most of the crowds who attended the gigs seemed inclined toward such sophisticated musical critiques. Byrne: "It was a bit Beatlemania. The scene in the some of the clubs, especially at the Star Club, was professional, cruel appraisal but out in the sticks – we went everywhere – it was still a kind of last hurrah for Beatlemania. It would be lots of yelling, lots of screaming, lots of really full-on type of response. It wasn't just sitting there appreciating. If you listen to 'Painter Man', it's one of those Beatlemania tunes with one of those sort of rocking choruses. The thing about it, it's just so well made as a tune, it's just so well produced and well played and performed and they did it almost perfect. To listen to them play it on stage was like listening to a first-class studio performance. I don't know how they did it, I don't know who was miking up the band, but listening to them you got that sense of being surrounded by stereo sound."

There was always plenty of female company available. "Chicks would usually go for Bob, then they would try to get to Eddie," Byrne recalls. "There were different chicks for different type of guys, I know that from *Groupie*. I have one picture somewhere. It shows The Creation with some of the key members of Procol Harum and myself and a group of morning-after girls, just standing outside, thinking about getting on the road or something."

Not that overtures from the fairer sex didn't sometimes bring problems, Byrne recalls. "One night where the guys came offstage and we had to go straight to the bus to the next venue. They had to walk the gauntlet because all the girls had gone crazy about them. We were coming out that night and there must have been thousands of kind of young pro-Hitler youth outside, hating everything about the English, spitting and trying to get at them. It was really nasty to see and it all became potentially violent. It wasn't that they were just jealous that the boys had the attention of the girls. They were expressing this in a way that was very anti-English and very Nazi-like. After all, it was only 20 years since the end of the war. I thought it was quite frightening... I remember thinking, 'We're not going to get to the end of this very long walk'. All it would have taken is for one of (The Creation) to say something."

Jack estimates there were about 20 troublemakers, adding, "Difficult to tell 'cos there was other, ordinary people around. These guys were coming out with a load of shit. We were in the van ready to go and Alan was out the front and a couple of them pushed him a bit and they was spouting off. So I got out the van. I thought I better back him up. Alan said, 'Get back in that fucking van!' And then he got back into the van and just drove off. But it was a nasty little incident. Nobody got hurt and it only lasted about five minutes." Byrne, for his part, was "happy to see them out of there."

The band also found themselves under attack from the opposite end of the political spectrum on this tour. While in Berlin, in order to kill some spare hours, the party decided to visit the eastern half of the divided city, which in those days necessitated going through the famous Checkpoint Charlie. "It was Iron Curtain territory," recalls Byrne. "We all got in this car. We'd been told to be careful because they looked like decadent western pop musicians and they wouldn't find too much favour in East Berlin. So we went through Checkpoint Charlie and we were into a completely different world.

"East Germany had not really moved on from the Thirties and Forties. It was all full of tea-rooms with string quartets and waitresses with little pinnies and black circlets around their necks and a kind of genteel communism: everything was very run down. We walked around the streets and we were followed everywhere. We were stopped by the police two or three times. The Germans in the east at that time either abused them or stopped and asked them what the fuck they were doing there and why didn't they piss off back. Others would just ask who they were and what they were doing and showed extraordinary hostility… It was in those situations that I think I was helpful. I could deal with these people."

"Bloody awful," is Jack's recollection of what they saw on the wrong side of the Wall. Like Byrne, he recalls an arbitrary aggression from the older inhabitants of East Berlin: "One or two made a few remarks. I don't know what they meant because they were speaking in German but of course we all had long hair and sort of hippie-ish clothes if you like and to them poor buggers everything was so grey. There was just no joy there at all. Young people were on our side. The older people, they'd been ground down and you could see from the arrogance of the way the police marched up the pavement and all that that you were in a police state. You could smell it."

Byrne was impressed at The Creation's reaction to what they saw: "That was a very eerie experience and I think it made them very thoughtful, being in that situation. I was fascinated by it. I'm a historian by inclination and I know quite a lot about the wartime history of Germany, the Balkans and Yugoslavia, so it gave me a chance to air my knowledge a bit about the things that had been happening. It was interesting. They had a life beyond music... We used to talk about politics and stuff like that in the odd moments."

Ollard meanwhile, was preparing for the formidable task of taking over the reins from Eddie. "After a couple of gigs they took me into a music shop in Germany to buy a couple of bows," he says. "I didn't get on very well with (the bows). I was never flamboyant like Eddie either, which left the whole musical thing suspended really. I must say again, I don't think any guitarist could have replaced him, Jimmy Page included, unless the band changed their entire style. Perhaps Pete Townshend could have been the nearest...

"Not only was Eddie's style of playing original," Ollard adds, "his entire stage appearance drew your eye to him rather than the lead singer. The couple of times I saw him he wore a black shiny orchestral conductor's jacket/suit with large lapels and a detachable-type white high-collar shirt with folded-up ends. Very impressive when he was using the bow."

Flying from Frankfurt to Hamburg, The Creation noticed the Bee Gees at the end of the airport hall. "I think they really took exception to that," recalls Byrne. "They felt that the Bee Gees were something that had no bearing to them at all. They wanted to be big famous and rich (but) what they feared being seen as a manufactured item and saw the Bee Gees as a manufactured item – a little bit unjustly, in a way. The Bee Gees helped in that perception themselves by the way in which they packaged their talent. I think there was some kind of confrontation. I was probably dealing with tickets or bags or God knows what and I did get a report that a.) the Bee Gees were around and b.) that maybe Jack might have got into something. It was only second-hand."

While in Hamburg, on 15 September, The Creation played at the famous Star Club. "It had a big stage, big hall," It was good to play the Star Club," says Jack. "I wanted to have a look at it, get on the stage and play something. The Star Club is legendary..." Bob was also pleased to play the venue, though, of course, for him it wasn't the first time. "What was nice to me", he recalls of returning to such old German haunts, "a lot of the venues we went to – the big clubs like the Star Club and the K52 club in Frankfurt – I'd played residencies. Because I'd been doing eight-hour nights there and I was there now just doing one-hour sets and the management was still the same, it was almost a pat on the back: 'It's come good for you'."

Eddie was less happy. Because the band's gear had gone missing (it would turn up in a day or two), they were forced to borrow others' equipment and Eddie found himself using the guitar he had long admired visually, the Fender Stratocaster. He wasn't impressed. "It didn't compare at all (to the Gibson) really," he recalls. "I use a Fender now and I quite like it but it was very thin-sounding. I couldn't get to grips with it at all."

At the Star Club, Byrne saw something which got his writer's brain working in overdrive. "This was 1967," he says. "The Beatles had been over there in about 1962, I think, so it was only about four years, maybe five. They were known at the Star Club, Bob was known, and we immediately fell in with this line of abut four or five of these incredibly attractive young German girls who had been there during the time of the Beatles. Obviously been bed partners. They were what you would call groupies later on. And they were still in their early twenties and they were talking wistfully, like old broken war heroes, of how terrible the scene was now.

"That really struck me as bizarre, rather touching and interesting and something that got my mind spinning on doing something on people like that, writing about girls of that type. We spent two or three days around Berlin (sic). It was a rather extraordinary thing because the Beatles had been there but it was now a more knowing, cynical audience. This line-up of girls especially were rather looking down their noses at these late arrivals, these johnny-come-lateleys... These 22, 23 year-old 'has-beens'...were like the hub of a huge wheel and their life had spun out through the lives of all these rock stars that had criss-crossed through their lives.

"They'd never gone to England. they'd always waited for England to come to them. They were still sitting there waiting. It was coming in succeeding waves and for this lot each wave was less interesting than the last and I wondered when they'd finally reach rock bottom." To some extent, the band whom Byrne was with escaped this withering scrutiny: "The Creation had a certain amount of cred because they knew Bob Garner; he obviously (was) one of the lesser people there but at least he'd been there."

Byrne was so intrigued that he was thinking of a piece of writing, possibly a book, about such girls, who would provide the crucial dramatic foreground story elements against which would be a background comprised of The Creation, or, rather, a group very like them. "I think I kept a diary, but I lost it," says Byrne of the tour. "I kept a record of what happened at the places we went to, the money we got and my observations because I thought Shel might want a report. It was meant to be an aide memoire for me that would enable me to provide a list of everything that had been going on. When I was into it and I got to know the guys a bit better, I was really challenged and my thinking completely became centred around what I was doing and it would have been a fascinating book.

"I wasn't interested in writing a documentary. Rock reportage. I'd been asked to do that by *Rolling Stone* on a number of occasions and it just wasn't for me. I like to transmute the experience I go through into something else and I saw this as a fantastic way of providing the background and the insight I needed to tell the story." The Creation's bassist took an interest in Byrne's vague plans. "I spoke to Kim about this quite a bit," Byrne says. "We spoke about either helping him visualise some of the ideas that he had in terms of a book or a movie. We had a lot of young man's dreams on the way in the moments we had together."

After around a week of gigs, Eddie prepared to return to England. His last gig was not a happy occasion for a reason other than the obvious one. Reporting to Jack – filling his usual role of dividing up the money – he was expecting to receive a bonus which apparently had been guaranteed him by Talmy back in London. Jack was surprised to be told this. Jack: "(He said) 'Oh, Shel promised me so and so and so and so'. So I said, 'Well sorry Ed, you'll get equal shares. If Shel offered you any more money, you'd better see him when you get back'. 'Cos that was the way the band always was: everything four ways." Because of this, Eddie and Jack parted on bad terms.

After this no doubt distressing end to the ultimately – good times and great art notwithstanding – lamentable series of circumstances that had been his experience in The Creation, Eddie flew back home in the company of just his guitar and two 8x10 Marshall cabinets to start the rest of his life.

I t seemed to go okay," is Tony Ollard's verdict on his first gig with The Creation, which took place somewhere in Germany. He adds, "You have to remember audiences of the time were not so demanding." The first gig was a matter of, "Just the right chords." Of the material he found himself playing, Ollard notes, "I don't think any of The Creation's songs were particularly difficult to play in any way. With no offence, many seemed to be simple singalong melodies. The difficulty would have been re-creating Eddie's sound and style on the guitar... I'll tell you the truth, in my opinion all three were pretty good musicians considering the era. Not mind-blowing as such. They were nice blokes too." Ollard used the violin bow onstage but only temporarily: "I tried a few times, then gave up."

As for his official status in the band, Ollard says, "There was no formal contact or agreement at all. I'm sure that was pretty usual for the time, though". Strangely, his financial conduit was Bob: "We didn't even talk about money for gigs at all. I took it as normal that whatever sum it was would be split equally between us. He was the fellow that paid me. I never met any manager of The Creation except a woman record executive in Germany who was there mainly to show us around and look after us in general. I truly and honestly can't remember the exact amounts. I was paid per gig as the other members were, not a fixed weekly sum...I do remember it varied quite a lot depending on the type of place we were working: stadium, large club, small club, etcetera.

"All I can say is that it seemed sufficient to live on quite well but it was nothing spectacular. You have to bear in mind they were one-off single gigs with sometimes perhaps as much as several days between each. They paid for travelling expenses but not hotels and food. Having previously worked in clubs in Germany six nights a week with various bands it compared fairly well over a period of time. I think I managed to save a few quid."

"I remember he did whatever he was supposed to do very competently," says Byrne of Ollard. "You wouldn't have noticed any difference in syncopation and in terms of what the group was pumping out. But he wasn't Eddie Phillips and you didn't realise that you'd miss not having Eddie there until Eddie wasn't there. One of the reasons why I don't remember Tony so well is I didn't watch it after the ninth thousandth time. I would watch it because I loved to see what Eddie would be doing that night: if he played the fiddle or if he'd do something different. With Tony, the songs were there, the beat was there and the crowds still hung out but it was a very different thing."

"It sounded okay," says Bob. "It wasn't the same though. It wasn't as good. Eddie looks good with a guitar. From my point of view I was saying to myself, 'If this is not as good, I'm going as well'. I probably grabbed the money and ran."

Of Bob as a person, Ollard says, "He was quite respectful towards me and that was mutual of course – we chatted often enough, though I can't say I remember we had any great laughs. Perhaps they were all worried about the future. From what I remember he seemed a very nice bloke. Kim seemed to be more happy-go-lucky than Bob or Jack, perhaps because he wasn't a founding member of the band. He was always good for a laugh and I'll never forget the fixed grin on his face. Jack never said much to me. He seemed to me a little retiring. I remember I did visit his parents' house once in Cheshunt."

While in Munich, The Creation gave an interview to Radio America, a station which broadcast to the eastern bloc countries. "They did a lot of interviews and stuff," says Byrne. "Everywhere we went we were asked the same banal questions. The guys would handle them very well. They didn't treat them with contempt, which they deserved. But then these questions were put by naïve people who think they have a handle on things and haven't a fucking clue. Kim was always full of barbs. He had a very elliptical, surreal sense of humour. He was always very nice. He would never insult people and he was a very generous man. But you didn't always understand what he was saying.

"I was struck when I met him again in 1999 that that whole aspect of his personality had become more complex. You would only catch one in ten things of what Kim was saying. And it wasn't stoned consciousness. He was a naturally surreal-minded person." Another interview sticks in Ollard's mind: "We were interviewed by François Hardy's sister!"

Ollard also remembers miming on a TV show recorded in Berlin: "I remember they paid for first-class five-star hotel rooms we had to move out of after a few days." He recalls the group being treated well by the record company and remembers a German record executive "who often accompanied us and paid for hotels and food." Asked if he recalls at any time himself or the band being confronted by anyone over the fact that the personnel had changed , he says, " Nobody, as far as I can remember." It's possible The Creation also appeared on a TV show recorded in Hamburg. Though Byrne has no recollection of where any of the TV appearances were recorded, he is certain about one thing: the track they would have played. "They would have done 'Painter Man' without a doubt, because that's the only thing the Germans wanted to hear."

When the tour moved on to Switzerland, Ollard found the crowds just as receptive. This was not particularly surprising as "we only played in the German Canton". He also recalls "signing autographs on the records in a chain store and being mobbed. We had to leave under a police escort and out the back way." For some – possibly all – of the Swiss leg of the tour,

The Creation were the support act to Procol Harum, a band basking in having produced one of the anthems of the Summer of Love in 'A Whiter Shade Of Pale'. Kenny White was delighted to find out that Procol would be appearing. As he explains, "I went to school with BJ Wilson, the drummer, and I was involved with the Paramounts who became Procol Harum. I actually played on the demo of 'A Whiter Shade Of Pale'."

Of The Creation's relationship with Procol, Byrne recollects "no aggravation between them. They partied a lot together. It sounds almost unreal, that you have all these groups and all these egos and they got on well, and yet they did." The Equals, however, had a slightly more edgy relationship with The Creation: "They did a lot of leaping around and things and were a little bit jealous. They'd been over in Germany quite a while. We did a lot of gigs with those guys and kept meeting up with them at other gigs. There was a kind of friendly rivalry between them. They weren't as friendly with each other as they were with Procol. The Equals had been there before. They had a kind of prior right (to be) there."

For Byrne, though Procol Harum were the headliners, it was The Creation who were the superior act: "Procol struck me as less interesting by far than Creation, both as individual musicians and potentially as a group. They didn't seem to have much room for any kind of expansion, they just got very good at what they did."

In Germany, The Creation had given interviews to the teen magazine *Bravo*, and pin-up pictures were duly taken. As with the interviews, Ollard was given equal space with the other members when the article was printed. In his section, he said that he had never really been happy in a band until now. This apparently harmonious state of affairs was actually nowhere near the truth. Far from beginning to gel with his new colleagues as they played more gigs, Ollard came to the realisation that he was out of his depth.

"It never did work," he says. "The gigs went okay, sort of – nobody complained that I know of – but there was certainly no musical chemistry. It didn't take long for them to realise Eddie couldn't be replaced. That doesn't change the fact they were all very nice towards me – and certainly respected me as a musician. I'm sure they all knew I was trying to step into the shoes of someone else and appreciated the fact that it was practically impossible to do. I clearly remember sitting around in a hotel room and strumming the bossa nova-type rhythm to Ben E King's version of 'I Could Have Danced All Night'. Musically that seemed to impress Kim!"

Perhaps it was this dawning realisation that this was not going to be another easy stop on his journeyman's career that caused Ollard to indulge in behaviour that made Jack conclude, "I don't think his heart was in it." By the time they got to Switzerland, Jack continues, he was messing around a bit. We could see he wasn't really interested. He had something else on his mind. He'd disappear in a hotel in a week with a bird and we'd never see him again, we're trying to get hold of him. It's not really worth going into, honestly."

Jack could, however, understand Ollard being daunted by the task before him: "I think he knew that he wasn't getting right into the band. Shame. These things happen. Replacing Eddie was impossible. Where the hell do you get a guitarist to replace Eddie back in 1967? Ring up Pete Townshend, yeah, but who else? You hear about Jeff Beck using a bit of feedback, but that was five years later."

The comments of Ollard's good friend Kenny White are almost identical to Jack's. "Tony was a good guitar player, there's no doubt about that, but his style didn't match The Creation," he says. "You're a four-piece band – a three-piece band in reality – so you've got to be that type of guitar player. There's not lots of guitar players like that. You've got to be able to play lead and rhythm at the same time without letting things drop out and I don't think Tony was the ideal choice, but he did his best and it was fine. Which is not taking away anything from his guitar playing abilities. He wasn't Eddie Phillips."

Ollard readily agrees: "To me it was clear that things wouldn't – couldn't – go on lacking the mainstay in the band. Of course there was no way I could replace him in either style or stage presence. He was at least 80 per cent of the band."

As if to underline just how much Eddie was missed, when The Creation flew into Britain on 1 November or thereabouts to promote 'Life Is Just Beginning' – released on October 27 – on BBC Radio's *Saturday Club,* they left Ollard behind and reunited temporarily with Phillips. There was some skulduggery involved in this episode: for some reason, the band didn't want Ollard to know Eddie was returning to the fold, if briefly.

"Before they left Switzerland I was told it was simply an interview," Ollard recalls. "There was no way I could have copied Eddie's sound so I suppose it was quite understandable. They still had what was thought to be an important record coming out after all. I had no personal rancour about it after I found out some time later." He adds another reason why it was reasonable for him not to fly over with them: "I suppose it may have caused even more difficulties, with questions being lobbed at me regarding Eddie that I couldn't possibly reply to. Not only that, it was a saving on air tickets before the days of cheap charter flights."

Saturday Club, hosted by Brian Matthew, was a crucially important piece of promotion for any band, possibly more important than a television slot. Its audience was a quite astonishing nine million, around a sixth of the entire population of Britain. Jack recalls the Creation doing three numbers on the programme. Of Eddie, he says, "We met him there. He was sort of friendly enough but distant. Me and Eddie went right back to the beginning almost and we'd been pretty close." In some respects, the episode seems to have been one final throw of the dice to secure The Creation a hit single and a future. That is, a future as a band with Eddie Phillips as its guitarist.

His return to the fold for the radio programme could plausibly be dismissed as one last favour by and/or payday for Phillips, but it seems rather significant that the publicity in the music papers and the press release for 'Life Is Just Beginning' was extremely devious regarding the current line-up of the group. No mention was made of Ollard or personnel upheavals and a pretence maintained that Eddie was still the guitar player. Jack: "I think we wanted to play it down a bit because Eddie was in such a mental toil…we thought that maybe if he was to calm down we might be able to get the band back to the original thing: 'Give him some time, let him try and get his head together, maybe sort out his family and he just might come back to the band,' But it didn't work out."

"They didn't fly back straight away and a couple of days passed before I saw them again," says Ollard. "They turned up again after a few days and we played a gig or two or gave a few interviews, not sure which." Ollard had found some amenable female company and opted not to return to his home country immediately once the tour was over.

Asked if the end of the tour prompted any discussion among the band as to what to do about Ollard, Jack replies, "No not really. I think it was accepted by the end of the tour that he'd be going his own way and we'd be going ours." There was no formal message that his services would not be required in the future. As Ollard puts it, "I never left – nobody called me anymore! Although nothing was said, I wasn't 100 per cent sure they would contact me so it came as no great surprise." Nor was Ollard unduly bothered by his rejection. He says, "What many people don't realise is at the time, and providing you weren't fussy, it was easy to find another regular job. While you were doing that, you looked round – in the *Melody Maker* usually – for a pro band."

Sure enough, Ollard got other work soon after his Creation stint ended: "Firstly, I was with a band called George Bean and the Runners and later, amongst other bands, I worked with an R&B group named Warren Davis' Monday Band from Leyton. I came to Italy for the first time with this second group and met a previous acquaintance who enquired if I was interesting in joining a band in Rome." Ollard has been domiciled in Italy ever since. "Since those days I've worked professionally in a good few other bands in Italy and elsewhere and I'm still working semi-pro over weekends."

Ollard's main income is now from a very different line of work: "I'm responsible for the export division of a middle-sized Italian multinational in the telecoms field." The Creation seems. for him, to have been merely one of many gigs in his journeyman career. Their current semi-legendary status bemuses him: "I find it a little strange that their popularity as a band is being recognised nowadays whereas at the time they were pretty much unknown except in Germany" .

Though Johnny Byrne had got along famously with The Creation – particularly Kim – during the tour, he did not socialise with them back in Blighty. "Our lives were completely different," he explains. "I was leading this underground life and they were in the world of rock'n'roll. I think I saw Kim a few times down the Speakeasy. We had many friends in common because I knew Twink very well, and Phil May from the Pretty Things. I knew that they were staggering on. Shel never mentioned anything. He'd sometimes mention what they were doing but I couldn't understand why someone wasn't getting them by the throat and giving them the equivalent of talks. Building up their belief in themselves as a group. They had amazing belief in themselves as individuals and musicians. They lacked that commitment to what they were doing as a group and I think that's the difference between them and The Cream. The Cream didn't give a fuck. They just loved what they were doing and it turned mega."

Byrne's idea of a book in which The Creation – or their fictional counterparts – would appear never materialised. "When I got back I was asked to start writing scripts on the side," he says, "doing script doctoring and things like that, and I put book writing on hold for a year" . When he did return to prose, it was to collaborate with one Jenny Fabian on *Groupie*, her novel based on her experiences associating with the group Family for which Shel Talmy acted as agent and which was a phenomenal success.

Nothing about Byrne's experiences with The Creation ended up in *Groupie*. "But there *was* something else," says Byrne. "Around this time and before this – during the period of writing *Groupie* and being with Creation – Harry Saltzman wanted me to write a film script for a group called Toomorrow. They were meant to be the movie Monkees. The man who made the Monkees, Don Kirshner, had fallen out (with them) eventually, and now he was going to do the same thing in a series of movies. Harry Saltzman was the man who did Bond and he was rolling in money and he wanted to make other things. They brought these four people over – I think they were still casting for the girl and Olivia Newton-John and Susan George were the two people involved ; I think it might have gone to Olivia Newton-John.

"I was in at the very early part of this and it was going to be about a group: how they came together, what they thought it was going to be. It was going to involve an awful lot of stuff on the road and travelling and that's where I was going to use all my background knowledge. I got involved with the auditions. This was a manufactured group, but they were fine musicians. One had played with Gladys Knight and the Pips. There was a period in London, about four or five weeks, getting to know them, being with Kirshner, speaking with Harry Saltzman and then I started to put a story together. Harry Saltzman, you need the patience of a saint to deal with him and he started disputing the thing I wanted to write. I had Shel there with me and when he insulted Shel I walked out. I wouldn't have it. So it never came to be. I hadn't done the whole script. I'd done the story."

During the Seventies, Byrne became one of the most successful scriptwriters in British television, contributing many episodes of the gentle TV vet drama *All Creatures Great And Small* and the Gerry Anderson science-fiction series *Space: 1999*.

There was another Creation-related film project that nearly happened. Thom Keyes' novel *All Night Stand* was optioned by a film studio and Bob Garner found himself in the frame for a role as a band member in early 1967. "I was interviewed by a couple of people, I think (from) 20th Century Fox," says Bob, "and the key members that were gonna be in there was gonna be Gibson Kemp and Mick Jagger's brother. They was talking to me. I can't remember who the other one was. In actual fact, in the book I think it starts off in a club in Warrington, where I'm from, the Heaven And Hell club I think it was...

It was like an indoor screen test. They took photographs but they didn't ask me to read anything out. They was quite happy with the accent. [In American voice:] 'This guy sounds as if he comes (from there)'. Yeah, of course I do." To Bob's disappointment, the film never happened. He was also disappointed by Jack's attitude towards the prospective role. Bob: "I do remember Jack finding out and he was quite annoyed about it, saying, 'Why would you want to do that?' I was *asked*." In the discussions for the film, there had been no talk of The Creation writing its soundtrack. Bob: "In fact, Ray Davies wrote the song. It's released on Planet I think." Bob is referring to 'All Night Stand', recorded by The Thoughts.

According to the press release for 'Life Is Just Beginning' prepared by Project Publicity Limited, The Creation returned to Britain on 8 November, four days after the broadcast of their *Saturday Club* performance. The previous week's *NME* – cover-dated 4 November – ran a short news story on the record alongside an ad for 'Life Is Just Beginning'. The story displays the deliberate deception then going on as to Eddie Phillips' status in the group. Under a headline that ran 'WHY AREN'T THE CREATION HERE – IN BRITAIN?', the story read:

"The Creation are being kept in Germany – the German audiences just won't let them come home. After having two records in the German top ten and with their current continental release, 'How Does It Feel To Feel', zooming up the charts, The Creation have become the third top touring group, and the fifth top recording group in Germany in a matter of seven months. And now The Creation are out to make the British Top 10 with their latest release here, 'Life Is Just Beginning' on Polydor. (Released Oct 27th.)

"'We hope the title is an appropriate one. We're keeping our fingers crossed that the record marks the beginning of a successful life for the group here in Britain,' says Eddie Phillips, lead guitarist. The record does sound like a hit, it has that unmistakable ambience about it that marks out a big hit in a whole pile of new releases. The group's manager and record producer is Shel Talmy, a man who know what hits are all about. His productions have sold many millions of records. He says "The group is a hit group and this song is a hit song. So I'm not worried at all. I've got a feeling that the success they've been having on the continent is going to spread. The group deserves it."

This deception over Eddie' status was carried over into the promotional material issued at the time. The Project Publicity press info – headed 'Near-Classical Creation Disc – Another Hit For Shel Talmy' – made no mention of the fact that the most vital member of the group had departed as it gushed about the new record and boasted of their exciting stage act and success in Germany. (There was even a somewhat bizarre panel headed 'Boutique Owners' that read: "The Creation are willing to paint abstract pictures with dye-sprays on to your plain mini-skirts! Whenever The Creation are appearing, they'll oblige local boutique owners.") Further press info for 'Life Is Just Beginning' featured biographies of the group and started "They are four, consisting of lead-rhythm, master mind, experience expanding guitar player called Eddie Phillips..."

The author of the press release made up in style what he lacked in honesty. Of Bob Garner, he/she poetically noted, "Out in front of this thick line of sound is a boy who is sexi (sic), soft, hazy springtime looking..." (a pretty accurate description of Bob's sleepy good looks) "...with a summer of tomorrows and a winter of yesterdays in his voice." Almost as eye-catching as that section is a passage in which Jack – without knowing it – made a remarkably accurate forecast about the way The Creation would become far more successful after their split than when extant: "We can wait. Van Gogh made a fortune. Years after he was dead, that is."

As they had with 'If It Stay Too Long', Polydor seemed to pull out all the stops in promoting The Creation's new single. As Ollard recalls, "A while after returning to the UK, I noticed a full page ad in the back of the 'Melody Maker' for 'Life Is Just Beginning'. That must have cost an awful lot of money even in those days" . He adds, "It was a face of a very old woman with deep age lines everywhere and I believe it caused a bit of a scandal. They say that because of this adverse publicity the record never sold and that put a dead stop to the band too."

The old woman in the ad to which Ollard refers was clearly a vagrant. She was sticking two fingers up at the photographer taking her picture. It was outrageous imagery on more than one level. Pictures of the unfortunate and the dirty were simply not usually seen in the context of an advertisement selling a commercial product in the Sixties. Furthermore, though the two-fingered sign – the British equivalent of the American middle-finger gesture – is less remarkable now than it used to be, it was definitely shocking in 1967. Even worse, the deliberate contrast between the bleak future of the depicted woman and the title of the song being promoted implied a certain contempt for the photographic subject. This was punk imagery ten years before punk occurred. At the very least, it was several years ahead of its time. Much of the general public – and in many cases for far more admirable reasons than priggishness – would have been offended, even repulsed by the ad.

June Clark, who was provided with a promotional flyer to send out to fan club members by Talmy with the same picture says, "Very strange. That was a radical, very unusual thing to do. Not with a picture of the band, not with anything related to the band. That was quite an artistic decision. I always thought it was an amazing picture. I loved the connection with 'Life Is Just Beginning' with this old lady. Might have been a bit too artistic. I have no idea where they got the picture. That was a shock to me when I saw what they had chosen or what had been chosen. I don't know who chose it.

"I went to Shel's office and sent it out to all the people in the fan club and did mailings. I do remember that everybody was really excited when this particular record came out and I thought that that flyer – the woman who was so old associated with life just beginning – was very avant garde and really a cool image... (So did) everybody I showed it to. It was really like standing out in the left wing, doing something like that, because it was so different. But again, it did nothing. It got little attention at all and even less on the radio that I remember."

None of the band members share Clark's enthusiasm for the ad. Jack says, "I remember that because my old mum – who would have been about 50 at the time – she said, 'Why on earth did you have somebody like that? It's horrible'. And I said, 'We don't get much say in it'. It suddenly appeared. It was the record company's idea. They said, 'Here, we're going to do a big advert on your record this week, check out the *NME*' or whatever it was in. I think it was a French woman. I think the idea was just to shock because you get so much stuff goes through and if you can actually make people stop and actually notice something, it's half the battle. It was pretty horrible for the time and I don't think it helped us much."

"People in those days weren't probably ready for it," says Eddie. "We might have been just in front of public opinion. These days it would be considered no big deal. We were shown it and I think we was asked , 'What do you think of this?' and we must have gone, 'Yeah! Why not?' A bit off the wall again."

"I can't remember whose idea that was," says Bob. "On the same page, there's a photograph of two young children – they're Shel's twins, boy and a girl about four or five years of age – just puckerng up to kiss. So you've got the opposite end of the thing: the old lady and the two young children kissing and life is just beginning. It was a twist on that but I think the children got unnoticed because the other was a bit too.. you dropped it like a hot poker, that one." (The picture of the children kissing was used as the picture in the ad that accompanied the story on the record in the 4 November *NME*.)

A review of the single in an unknown paper declared, "Another one of those discs with strong classical overtones. It opens like a Haydn string quartet, then suddenly breaks into a thumping mid tempo beat opus."

Theoretically, of curse, all the publicity surrounding 'Life Is Just Beginning' – as well as the record's brilliance – could have garnered them a hit. Its baroque nature definitely made it a record in tune with the times. "Good job it didn't go to Number 1," says Eddie. "I'd have been in a right dilemma." Would he have gone back to the band if it had? Eddie: "I don't think I would have done, quite honestly. I felt so right about what I was doing in leaving it, I don't think I'd have gone back. I don't know. I might. Let's face it, if someone says, in those days, 'Here's ten grand', I might have thought, 'Oh hang on a minute'. Maybe that would have helped me to sort the other side of my life out, I don't know."

This was all academic, in any case. 'Life Is Just Beginning' became the second Creation single not to register on the UK charts at all. In West Germany, it was passed over in favour of 'How Does It Feel To Feel' ('If I Stay Too Long' was the flip). "The record company in Germany wanted that one," says Talmy. "They figured they knew their market better than I did so I let 'em do it." Eddie: "That was pretty much a company decision. We wouldn't have had control over that." Jack: "The band didn't have any say. I think the German people took what they wanted to take and they thought would sell in Germany and on the British side they were just looking for quick hits." Bob's feeling about the delayed UK release of 'How Does If Feel To Feel' is "Probably frightened of it.".

Though it was the tamer version of 'How Does It Feel To Feel' that was released in West Germany, it was still a fine recording so it is surprising that it failed to register on the official charts. The more ferocious version of 'How Does It Feel To Feel' did make it onto an A-side in America, where it appeared on Decca backed with 'Life Is Just Beginning' – a double whammy if ever there was one – that November.

Eddie doesn't know why or how a different version came to be used in the States. "I was only the artist," he says wryly. Eddie, in fact, points out that he probably wasn't even aware at the time of the difference, or even, possibly, that there had been a US release. Eddie: "Things weren't the same then. We tend to judge everything by today's standards where everybody knows what's going on but in those days you didn't."

The US release of 'How Does It Feel To Feel' even garnered a review – albeit a semi-illiterate one – in the US industry mag *Cash Box*, who opined, "Squawking electronics overwhelm the ear and grab attention to his (*sic*) hard-hitting rock side in a low-down version of a psychidelic (*sic*) session. Could turn up on discotheque turntables and pop programming lists." The review went on to erroneously credit the writing of the B-side to 'Stuart, Jackson'. The review's prediction about exposure was, sadly, incorrect and the record – one of the finest released in the States in what was one of the finest ever years for popular music – sank without trace.

For Bob, it was time to call it a day, a decision he'd made while still in Switzerland. "I felt any one of the band dropping out really was a problem," he says. "When Kenny went, it was a problem…Eddie leaving, something was missing. And I suppose it would have been the same me leaving. It was one of those things (where) I thought, 'Well hang on, this is not getting anywhere'."

"Eddie really was his partner," says Clark of Bob's decision. "I think he felt that if Eddie wasn't going to be there, *he* wasn't going to be there… Everything seemed to be a mess and Bob had just given up. He said 'I'm leaving the band'. I said, 'Well what are you gonna do?' He said, 'I'm going back to Warrington. I'm going to work in a bakery'. As soon as Bob left, I thought 'It's all gonna crumble'. Now it's so far removed from the original line-up that whatever they did from there I couldn't imagine it making it. I almost felt like saying, 'Well I'm not gonna do anything for you anymore because there's no point'."

Byrne says he was not surprised when he heard through his loose, post-tour connection with the band that Bob had departed. "Maybe some of the things that you picked up from Bob had to do with unresolved things in himself about where the group was going and all of that – but I did feel that he had something else slated in his life," he says. "There was something else Bob was aiming towards. I don't know what it was and I didn't want to ask probing questions. I didn't want to get involved in the personal dynamics. That would have been difficult because I had to stay above it. I took things pretty much on face value, but it did not surprise me that Bob would have left.

"I think all of them, to a certain extent, were waiting for the other to show either total commitment or total abandonment. They were not sure and that's where the leadership of the group really let them down. Maybe a belief in themselves as a group was not fostered strong enough. Maybe that's Shel's fault, maybe it's their own fault, but they seemed to be a group of all soldiers and no generals. Nobody was thinking the big thing of what it would need. They seemed to be waiting for it to happen. Marking time, I suppose.

"It surprised me that Eddie left because I thought that he could make anything that he was a part of into something special. When Bob left, it half occurred to me that maybe he might have had a better offer or something like that and it wouldn't have surprised me if he had."

With both the singer and guitarist – who jointly also happened to be the band's songwriting axis – gone, it seemed that the game was up for The Creation.

CHAPTER 4

DETERMINATION AND BELIEF

im Gardner certainly seems to have thought the game was up. The final couple of months of 1967 – or perhaps early 1968 – saw him recording with Ronnie Wood, future Deep Purple keyboardist Jon Lord and Twink, drummer with Tomorrow. This supergroup-in-reverse (all the members would go on to significant success after this aggregation) recorded three instrumental tracks under the supervision of Gus Dudgeon, who also co-wrote them all with Lord: 'Porcupine Juice', 'Albert' and 'Rubber Monkey'. The project foundered when the tracks failed to secure the group a recording contract and the songs – credited to 'Santa Barbara Machine Head' – eventually dribbled out on an Immediate Records compilation.

The Terry Rawlings book *Rock On Wood* suggests this session occurred before Kim even joined The Creation but Mike Stax, editor of *Ugly Things*, doubts this because he saw Kim's diary for sessions and gigs from the Birds era and it was not mentioned in that. Another reason is that when talking to Twink for his magazine, the drummer said the session happened during his time with Tomorrow, which would have placed it between 1967 and 1968.

Twink recalled the session for *Ugly Things*: "At the time I was sharing a flat with Jon Lord in Chelsea. He was in The Artwoods at the time but they weren't doing very much. I think his idea was to put a band together with me and Ron Wood and Kim Gardner. Ron and Kim were real good buddies of Jon's from way back, and I'd been hanging out with The Artwoods and The Birds and stuff so we were almost sort of buddies (too), right? So Jon organised a session up at Decca Studios with Gus Dudgeon producing, and that's how the Santa Barbara thing happened. We went up there just for fun."

"Kim was still in the band as far as I was concerned," says Jack. "If he was doing other things I didn't know about them." In the midst of this period of uncertainty in The Creation's story – late '67-early '68 – Hit-Ton released a new Creation single. With no active band in existence, let alone new material, they bizarrely opted to issue the cover 'Cool Jerk' as the A-side with the sublime 'Life Is Just Beginning' as its flip. It was an appropriately uncertain release for a band in disarray. "Everything was falling apart really," says Jack.

Just as 1967 had started with upheavals related to Tony Stratton-Smith's position, so the year closed with the band in a parlous state as Jack Jones and Kim Gardner wondered what the future held. Jack saw only one way forward. "I made my feelings known to Shel Talmy through Gail Colson," he says, "and said, 'Kenny should be back in the band.' She looked at me and didn't say anything but about two weeks later I got a phone call from Gail and she said, 'How would you feel if Kenny was back in the band? Would you still take him back?' 'Yes I would,' I said, 'I want to put the original band back together'.

"I wasn't leader of the band but I had my pennyworth... Kenny's face was the image of The Creation and Eddie's sound was the sound of the band and if we put them back together then we'd be back on track. Bob didn't like that. He decided to go back to Warrington. We kept on with Kim and went back and toured Germany with Kenny, Eddie, myself and Kim on bass and it was the best band ever. It only lasted about six months and then Eddie finally packed it in because of his marital troubles."

Never before has it been suggested that Eddie returned to the fold during the group's Sixties incarnation, though Jack seems to have a vivid memory of this line-up. "There's no doubt about it: the best band we had, was me, Kim Gardner, Kenny Pickett and Eddie Phillips. That was a shit-hot band. We went out to Germany and we did a few gigs around but after a little while, Eddie moved on. When Bob moved on, Kenny came in... That band didn't last long – for a few months I think – but it was really a good band."

Intrigued by this previously undocumented twist in The Creation's tale, the author asked Jack, at a subsequent interview, for more information. However, when pressed for specific information that would put this line-up at its correct place in the chronology, he seemed a little confused and then appeared to completely backtrack, saying that Eddie would not have agreed to work with Kenny Pickett again after the first split. Eddie himself insists he didn't return.

So, a mere kink that the human mind can throw up when trying to dig up images and sequences from decades past? One would think so – except for a couple of things. First of all, this quote from Kenny in *Blitz*: "We got The Creation back together because we had a tour of Germany offered. I said, 'Okay, I'll do it but I won't do it with Bob Garner in the band.' Then Eddie Phillips said he wouldn't do it if Bob Garner wasn't in the band." (Bob's reaction to this quote is, "I just left. Nothing to do with Kenny. I wasn't aware Kenny would want to come back.")

The other thing that serves to give Jack's recollection a smidgen of credibility – apart from his initial passion in describing the quality of the line-up – is that, when others involved in The Creation are questioned about the possibility, it seems to ring a bell (if a distant one) with most of them.

"I think that's right," says Talmy, "but I don't remember when it was or for how long it was. They (Kenny and Eddie) put their differences aside long enough to write one song maybe. It sounds right, yeah. It didn't last long." Alan Smith, Creation roadie, says through an intermediary that he thinks this scenario did actually happen. If correct, one could theorise that this was when the band recorded 'Ostrich Man' (as well as 'Bony Moronie, 'Mercy Mercy Mercy' and 'I Am The Walker') and that this explains why Bob has no recollection of playing on those tracks.

Theorising aside, it can be stated with certainty that Kenny Pickett did return to the Creation by early 1968 and that Eddie did not make a long-term return to the band.

Since the last time he had been in the Creation, Pickett's dreams of a career as a novelist had started to dissipate. That and possibly declining income is what presumably led to Kenny being prepared to countenance a return to the group he had quit in such acrimony. "I don't think his book ever even entered into the conversation," says Talmy when asked whether this factor played a part in Kenny's return. "I think he was (dissatisfied) with all kind of stuff he was doing or not doing and he kept getting ragged on greatly by the lady in question. He had personal problems."

With Kenny back in the fold, The Creation now needed a guitarist – and Kim Gardner knew just the man. "We had to find a guitarist and we had to find one quick," says Jack, "and of course Kim knew Ronnie Wood. Kim said, 'Ronnie's not doing anything. He's talking about going to America with Jeff Beck but that's not going to be for a year – and if it works out, he could stay with the band. Why don't we try Ronnie?' Well we knew Ronnie was okay because we knew The Birds – the English Birds. Good band. So Ronnie came down, we got it together and it was fine. We had a nice little band again".

The Creation Mark I on stage:
L-R: Eddie, Jack, Kenny and Bob.

PLANET

45 r.p.m MONO

(1F.116)
PLF.116
Time: 2:51

THE
CREATION
A

MAKING TIME
(Pickett/Phillips)
Orbit/Stratton Smith
A Shel Talmy Production

The original UK disc
of the band's
remarkable debut.

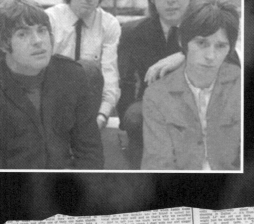

The original Creation.
L-R: Kenny Pickett, Jack Jones,
Bob Garner and Eddie Phillips.

THE CREATION

'OUR MUSIC IS RED
... WITH PURPLE
FLASHES'
EDDIE PHILLIPS
LEAD GUITAR

'CREATION'
BY
KEITH GRANT

DAVID GRIFFITHS

MAKING TIME
c/w
TRY AND STOP ME
PLF 116

A
SHEL TALMY
PRODUCTION
PLANET

Music paper advertisement for the Creation's first single. Note the
use of painting 'Creation' by Keith Grant and the employment of
Eddie Phillips' immortal descriptive quote.

*The Creation on stage in 1967 in
Britain (Courtesy of June Clark)*

THE CREATION

Proof of tight finances:
Creation fan club material
with amendments hand-
written by June Clark

FAN CLUB:

June Clark,
10 Albert Gate Court
124 Knightsbridge
London, S.W.1.

Pam,
c/o Arthur Howes Agency,
Eros House,
29-31 Regent Street,
London, S.W.1.

AGENTS:

Arthur Howes Agency
Eros House,
29-31 Regent Street,
London, S.W.1.   Tel: REGent 5202.

RECORDINGS:

MAKING TIME
c/w
Try And Stop Me.

PAINTER MAN
c/w
Biff Bang Pow.

on
PLANET RECORDS.

IF I STAY TOO LONG
c/w
Nightmares

on Polydor records.

German TV again, but this time the
original, Pickett-fronted line-up
(Courtesy of Jim McElwane)

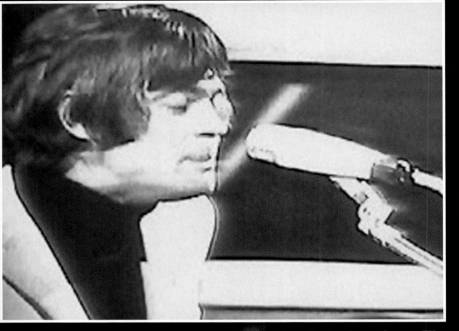

Above: Kenny Pickett performing with The Creation on German TV shortly before his acrimonious departure.

Below: The Creation on German TV, 1967. Now Garner is the frontman (Courtesy of Jim McElwane)

*Jack Jones (top)
and Bob Garner
(bottom)
performing on
German TV.
(Courtesy of
Jim McElwane)*

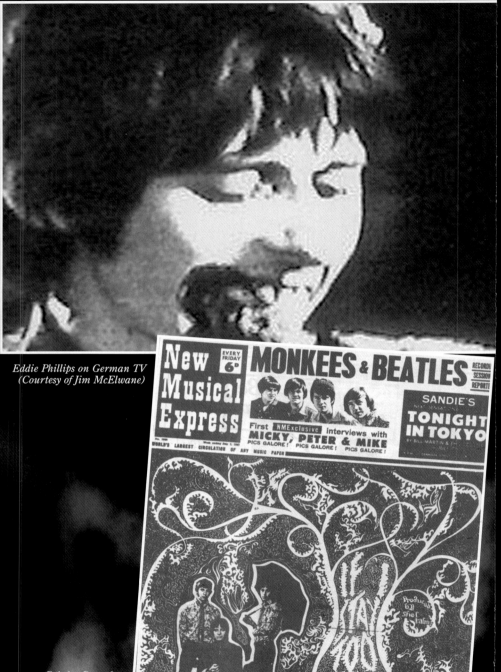

*Eddie Phillips on German TV
(Courtesy of Jim McElwane)*

*Polydor Records
clearly harboured
high hopes for
The Creation. They
took out the front
cover of the NME to
promote the band's
debut for the label,
'If I Stay Too Long'.*

The only Creation album issued in the group's (original) lifetime.

The Creation, 1967. Clockwise from top left: Kim Gardner, Eddie Phillips, Bob Garner and Jack Jones.

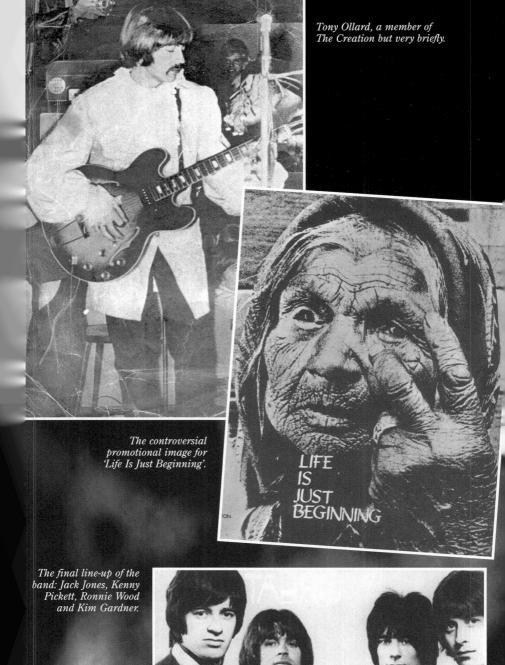

Tony Ollard, a member of
The Creation but very briefly.

The controversial
promotional image for
'Life Is Just Beginning'.

LIFE
IS
JUST
BEGINNING

The final line-up of the
band: Jack Jones, Kenny
Pickett, Ronnie Wood
and Kim Gardner.

n late 1967, Ronnie Wood was at his wits' end with Jeff Beck. Wood – born 1 June 1947 – had been an on-off member of the Jeff Beck Group since February 1967. Though he'd been working with a stellar array of musicians including the gifted titular guitarist, no less a vocalist than Rod Stewart and Nicky Hopkins on piano, Wood was not happy. Partly because he was reduced to playing bass in the band but mostly because Beck had an ego commensurate with his talent, ie considerable.

Many was the instance that Wood had occasion to rue the day in late '67 that he had turned down the chance to replace Eddie Phillips in The Creation because The Jeff Beck Group seemed a better prospect. His salvation came when he found he hadn't completely missed the boat with The Creation: the man who had got the place he was offered on the German/Swiss tour hadn't worked out and he was informed that he was welcome to climb aboard if he still had the inclination.

Wood did – up to a point. Though he started rehearsing with The Creation, it was on the understanding that he was still free to work with Beck. Accordingly, during the first half of that year he actually went back and forth between the bands, doing TV appearances to promote Jeff Beck's solo single 'Love Is Blue' at the same time as he was trying to become assimilated into The Creation. Jack: "And a little bit of session work here and there. Basically he threw his things up in the air to see where they land. He's a good lad Ronnie, I like him, but I think he was waiting to see what would happen. I don't think he was ever one hundred per cent committed. You always get the feeling that if Jeff Beck gave a call, then Ronnie would be gone." (After initially agreeing to do an interview with this book, Ronnie later decided he wouldn't have time.)

Others in the Creation camp say they were never under the impression that Wood was intending to make his a long-term stay. Roadie Roman Salicki, when asked if Ronnie considered The Creation a permanent job, says, "No, I really never got that idea" . Says Talmy, "I always knew Ronnie was going to go off. He was only a temporary stop-gap. That was fine. (They) needed somebody. He was good. As far as I knew, he was always there temporarily." Was Talmy surprised that The Creation were, after yet another set of personnel upheavals, willing to carry on? "No, because there was still money to be made."

Though he continued to fund their recording sessions, which naturally he continued to produce, Talmy admits, "It was definitely missing something. Eddie to me was the band. He was the sound of the band and without him there it was not the same. Not even close. It was a good band because they had all played together long enough and they were all good enough musicians so it sounded okay. But it wasn't Creation."

June Clark, surprisingly, remembers being privately even more scathing than that about the band's continuing artistic potential. "I really thought, 'They're fooling themselves'," she says. "I would have been very shocked if anything had happened." Then again, perhaps the band were not thinking of anything 'happening' as such. A certain pragmatism is implied in Kim's subsequent recollection of the new line-up to *Ugly Things*: "Kenny came back and off we went again – a different Creation again! We had a lot of work so we milked it, really."

When speaking of Ronnie, Jack comes out with essentially the same mantra he applied to Tony Ollard: "To be fair, he was never an Eddie Phillips but Eddie was a one-off. At the time, you think of Eddie, you think of Peter Townshend and you think of Jimi Hendrix and that is about the only three guitarists in the world at the time who were playing in that particular style – and Eddie was catching 'em up fast, believe me." However, Jack also insists, "Ronnie was a really good guy and he got hold of the stuff and he did a good job for us. When Ronnie came in the band I thought it had real potential.

"Ronnie was a bit inhibited. He's inclined to play that style (where) he doesn't play a lot, but if the band had stayed together for six months, a year, touring, working together, Ronnie would have grown into our style. We would have gone to him a bit and I think it would have been really good." Kenny's observations on Ronnie to *Ugly Things* in '97 indicate he gravitated more toward June Clark's prognosis of the '68 Creation than Jack's. "He wasn't a particularly brilliant guitarist," he opined, "but he turned the band into a different direction, leaning more towards BB King, that type of stuff, because that was what Ronnie was into. So we almost got back into doing cover versions again, full circle, which was really weird. The last band was a good band but it wasn't The Creation as people knew The Creation to be."

Things seemed to start well for the new line-up. They began rehearsals in the early part of the year. With both Bob and Alan Smith now no longer part of the scene, these can't have taken place at the house in Harrow, but Jack can't recall where they did occur. Jack: "We might have taken out a recording studio somewhere. He knew the numbers anyway 'cos Kim had been going over them with him. And he was familiar with the band. We all knew each other." The Creation then embarked on another visit to Germany, departing on 5 January . According to Clark's dairy, The

Creation had their own half-hour TV show in Germany on the 14th, something that Jack vaguely recalls.

As with Ollard, Ronnie attempted to adopt Eddie's violin-bow method and was a little more successful than his predecessor. "Ronnie did okay," Jack says. "He was more in the spirit of it. I don't think Tony Ollard ever got in the spirit." For this visit, The Creation had yet another road manager in the shape of Roman Salicki, a Pole who had ended up working for Talmy while trying to make his name as a photographer. "I'd just started and things were really tough," Salicki recalls. "We got together and we got to be friends. He knew what was going on, I wasn't making very much money. He said, 'Come and work for me'."

Asked his exact role in Talmy's working life, Salicki says, "Pretty much everything. He's partially blind – was at that time – so it was a matter of driving him around and taking care of him, taking him to the studios and being with him throughout the sessions. Whatever concerts there were, I was with him there. Administrative assistant, I suppose they would call it today."

Salicki actually hooked up with Talmy at a time when Eddie was still on the scene. Like a couple of other people, he suggests that the reason for Eddie leaving was more complicated than merely the fact of marital difficulties. "Eddie was the volatile one who would consider himself basically the leader of the band and he wanted to do this... There was some misunderstandings between them. I think he was a great musician. No doubt about that. But he had a mind of his own and he wanted to do things his way. Songs, arrangements, what was happening in stage, the presentation of the band. He had his own definite ideas and of course there were frictions there.

"Some of the guys didn't want to do it, some of them went along with it. So it was a typical rock'n'roll band. I don't have any misgivings about Eddie. It's just that Eddie was much more strong-minded than the other three and he just wanted things his way. I think there was a bit of hoo-ha between them when Eddie decided to leave. I think they were pretty pissed (that he was leaving). And he left because basically of the internal politics that were going on within the band. He wanted to go one way and (they) wanted to go another way and they wouldn't meet in the middle so he left.

"This was just before the tour that I was on. I think it was several weeks (before), because the tour had already been set and they had to find a replacement. The band didn't do anything for a period of time because they didn't have the full band together so everything basically stopped. This was at the point where they had a tour booked and everything was put on hold for a little while until they found a new bass (*sic*) player, which was Ronnie."

Salicki's recollection of Eddie still being around only a few weeks before 5 January 1968 seem to support the idea that Eddie returned to the fold after his September '67 departure, although his recollections are of course slightly undermined by confusing Ronnie's instrument in The Creation. Of the new line-up, Salicki notes, "They all wanted the band to go on, the other three. Shel had fairly high expectations of the band and, as a producer, I don't think he saw Eddie's departure as an enormous problem. I can't speak for Shel, but I think he felt that the band could be put back together again. A lot of the members of bands played musical chairs."

Salicki remembers the capacities of the German venues in which the band played this time round as ranging between approximately 600 and 1,500. "Germany was fantastic," he says. "It was like they were The Beatles. The concerts were sold out and I was almost the heavy – like a security guard – because there were fans trying to climb up on stage. I was trying to knock them down, push 'em back. In fact (Kim) at one point – I was down on my hands and knees trying to push somebody away – put his foot in my backside as a joke and shoved me right into the audience."

Salicki's memories of this line-up of The Creation are of an ensemble who were a marked contrast to the emotionally sombre and artistically brilliant group Byrne recalled them being on their last visit to Germany. Asked, for instance, if The Creation were sad or frustrated at the lack of success in their home country, Salicki says, "No. They were just a bunch of crazy young musicians. Just enjoyed doing what they were doing and getting crazy while they were doing it. You were in a band and it was a question of sex, drugs and rock'n'roll. So I don't think they were frustrated."

The Creation secured a lucky break when The Kinks pulled out of a radio show they were due to play in Berlin. As this coincided with three spare days in their schedule, they agreed to fill in for Muswell Hill's finest. "The headline act was The Supremes," says Salicki. "And that was a big deal. There was a huge amount of preparation" Jack: "We had to do about three numbers live on the radio and it was packed. It was a proper show and there was (an) audience, thousands of kids. It was great.

"Then afterwards the guy said, 'Would you like to see the Supremes?'

We said, 'Yeah, sure man'. So he took us around this theatre, which was built into this one great big building, and he sat us up in a box and there was Diana Ross and the Supremes. A whole live show and they were absolutely superb."

As an émigré from behind the Iron Curtain, the situation in a divided Germany could be unnerving for Salicki. "It scared the hell out of me several times," he says, "because we had to go to East Germany to get to Berlin and I was driving a beaten-up old van with a bunch of rock'n'rollers who were stoned most of the time.

"I remember once on the old beaten-up autobahn between East Germany and West Germany, we ran out of gas. All the East German police were around us with their guns and the whole shooting match. So it was a bit of a strange journey." Salicki doesn't remember the group making huge amounts of money at this juncture. "In fact, couple of times I had to get on to Shel and request extra money to be sent out because of problems with hotel owners. They would go into a hotel and destroy it, so one had to pay off hotel owners and various other people. They were all lunatics. I mean, all of them."

Salicki remembers the crux of this line-up of the group as being Kim and Kenny, particularly the latter: "He was a little bit brighter than the other band members. I think he'd had a higher education than the others and Shel considers himself to be a bit of an intellectual, so I think he and Kenny got along very well from that point of view."

It's at around this point that The Creation chronology gets rather murky, partly because press coverage about the band rather dropped off – understandable considering that they were not to release another single in their home country until they'd either dissolved or were just about to – and partly because one half of the personnel of this line-up of the band are now dead, thus making fact-checking difficult. However, even that latter fact does not seem sufficient to account for the bizarre discrepancies of the respective memories of Jack Jones and Roman Salicki, both of whom went on a trip to Madrid with the Creation in late January/early February and only one of whom (Jack) asserts that the band took with them an Australian guitarist in place of Wood – presumably busy with Jeff Beck activity – to fulfil the relevant gigs.

The guitarist's name has been lost in the mists of time, partly because he was patronisingly referred to by the band members as Digger, a UK equivalent of the way Australians refer to Britons as 'Poms' . "That I don't remember at all," says Salicki of Digger. "I just remember Ronnie being there". Kim Gardner, according to *Ugly Things* magazine (1997), also claimed not to remember the Antipodean axe-slinger in question.

However, Jack's story about Digger is corroborated by Clark who, though she admits she doesn't remember what he looked like, confirms he did exist. Indeed, it is only through Clark's diary of the time that we have a clue as to Digger's identity. Part of her entry for 22 January reads, "Creation audition Bob for lead, in Mewley Road." Of course, this may not be a reference to the gent in question, but it seems significant that there is no other reference to auditions in her dairy for that year and that, precisely one week later, The Creation departed for Spain.

Judging by what Jack says, the guitarist – henceforth referred to by this narrative (with apologies if he is reading this!) as Digger – was being tried out by the band during the Madrid gigs with a view to permanent membership. Recalling that he was new in London and had come through Shel Talmy (who has no recollection of him either), Jacks says, "We thought we'd give the guy (a chance). He was playing every night in like a big club. He was a nice guy but I can't remember his name."

The 'big club' Jack refers to was the Piccadilly, a nightspot in which The Creation started a 10-day residency on 1 February. The booking was a rather strange one. "It was a very, very smart night club," recalls Jack, "right in the centre of Madrid. It was almost like you had a gig in Kensington, London. Imagine one of these upper-crust night clubs. It was a very nice place. We were totally wrong for it. Whoever put us in there wanted shooting."

Having said that, Jack does concede, "They were nice, paid the money and we had a nice time." Apparently, Kenny was having rather too nice a time. Salicki recalls it as always being touch-and-go whether The Creation frontman would make the nightly performance due to a fling on which he embarked with a married woman. Salicki: "She was in the modelling world. Spent an awful lot of time with her at her house or apartment. That's when the acid was going down. She was married to a musician. I think he was Spanish. I don't know whether her husband ever found out because we were out of there before he showed up again."

Salicki's impressionistic memories of his two foreign forays with The Creation are one of "craziness". (So crazy, in fact, that he is under the impression that it was one tour.) Salicki doesn't remember this permutation of The Creation agonising overmuch about where they were going and what the future held for them. Salicki: "I think they took the thing one day at a time. I think they were too stoned to think about the future. That's one of the reasons why I left the band. They were stoned pretty much 24 hours a day. It was grass and on occasion it was acid."

He adds, "I was like a babysitter, trying to keep them out of trouble all the time. Getting the clubs to pay for the shows. Getting them to the shows on time when they were stoned out of their minds. Trying to keep it together and get them to the gigs on time and then going through the different cities. Trying to get the hotels organised. All that. It was a nightmare. At the end of the tour, I was so exhausted, wiped out, I passed out on the plane back from Madrid. They had to wake me up after it had landed because I was so out of it."

Back in London – to which they returned on the 14th – the band were left looking for a new guitarist once more. Describing Digger as akin to 'a Bee Gees guitarist', Jack says, "What we were doing was totally wrong for him. I'm sure in his own bag he'd have done a good job but our thing, he had to copy Eddie which was pretty difficult. The guy came over and did a good job but you knew he wasn't right. So when we come back, we said, 'Sorry mate, you're a good guitarist but it's a clash of styles. It's just not going to work.' He understood and off he went, shook hands and never saw him again. But he was okay and I thought the way some people call him Digger (was) almost like they were taking the piss. Little bit out of order."

It was Ronnie Wood who once more stepped into the vacant guitarist's post: he would be The Creation's axe-slinger for the remainder of their existence. Clark remembers this period as being a somewhat barren one. "When Bob left, that was the end of the band," she opines. "That was what the band thought. The re-creation of The Creation that came afterwards was like a thing that dribbled. It didn't have the same motivation, didn't have the same heart. They didn't get gigs. There wasn't a record. There wasn't very much for me to do. I did put newsletters out and tell people that they want to Spain, that they did the John Lewis gig. I did tell them what was going on but there wasn't very much going on.

"I sensed that this was like the last chance at pumping life into the band and pumping some blood into it to try and keep it going. And Kenny really was a great member of the band. He was a great singer. He was right for the band. Even though I didn't like him, he was meant to be there up front. Even with that, and the talent of Ronnie Wood, it didn't work. Somewhere along the line, it just couldn't be saved. Now that was definitely behind the scene and I don't know why it didn't make it.

"I don't know what was going on behind the scenes but there wasn't much enthusiasm coming my way – from Shel and from the guys. I'd call them and they'd say, 'Oh well, we're doing this and we're doing that, we hope we're gonna do this, we're going to Spain..' But I was getting no feedback. It was as though they hadn't enough enthusiasm. Something was drastically missing. I was still there for them but there was something lacking. It was like something died and the life went."

That life, of course, could have been resuscitated – at least creatively – had Eddie Phillips returned to the band. Ironically, by this stage this was something he was in a position to do as his decision to quit had not helped save his marriage. He was now living on his own and there were no ties to prevent him re-adopting the touring life of a rock'n'roller or picking up that remarkable thread of brilliance that he and his Creation colleagues had been working on through 'Can I Join Your Band', 'How Does It Feel To Feel', 'Life Is Just Beginning', etcetera.

Though he did return to music, it was not as a guitarist. Instead, it was as a bassist for TNT, the backing band of pop-soul singer Pat (better known as PP) Arnold. Memories differ as to how soon after his departure from The Creation Eddie took this job. "That was a fair time after I left," says Eddie, (who also suggested January or February 1968 to *Ugly Things*). Jack, however, says, "When he left us he ended up playing bass with PP Arnold within about a month."

The fact Eddie obtained the job with Arnold through Kenny Pickett, who Eddie recalls as driving Arnold at the time, would indicate it was in late '67 – one can't imagine Kenny holding down a regular outside job at the same time as filling the role of The Creation's frontman – or the second half of 1968 when The Creation were finished and Kenny no longer had those obligations.

If Kenny secured the Arnold gig for Eddie before or during his own return to The Creation, it all seems a little bizarre. It would indicate they had patched up their differences – in which case, why did they not choose to work together in The Creation again? Or perhaps – as Jack has speculated – they did and Eddie departed again because, as Kenny told *Ugly Things*, Eddie wouldn't continue in the band unless Bob Garner was retrieved. Whatever the case, it still seems rather strange that it was Kenny who secured Eddie the job with Arnold despite their previous acrimonious parting. But Eddie says, "All through our lives we were like that. We would drift apart for a year, 18 months, and he'd call me up and he'd say, "Ere, I got an idea for this' or whatever. 'All right, come (round) then.' The same thing for me and then we probably might not talk again for another period of time. It wasn't we didn't like each other, it was just the way we were."

Though Eddie played on studio recordings by Arnold, such is the patchiness of his memory that he can't recall whether he appeared on her various hits. However, studying the chronology reveals that it's fairly safe to assume that he can be heard on 'Angel Of The Morning' (a UK Top 30 single in summer '68), as well as part of the album 'Kafunta' (1968). He may also have even appeared on some of the Arnold sessions supervised by Steve Marriott and Ronnie Lane of the Small Faces. This would not seem to include the single '(If You Think) You're Groovy': Small Faces drummer Kenney Jones has a firm recollection of that track featuring the Small Faces as a whole, making another bassist – or even guitar player – unlikely. However, Eddie says, "I remember being at Olympic Studios with her and Steve, but what we did I can't remember." Eddie says he didn't try to get involved in writing songs for Arnold at any point.

"I think it was for a year," Eddie says of his time in TNT. "We was doing one-nighters and little tours and things. I enjoyed that. Ernie Hayes was the guitar player in the band and some nights we'd swap over and he'd play bass and I'd play a bit of guitar." Jack makes no bones about considering this part of Eddie's musical career to be a waste. "I mean, for Christ's sake," he says. "I went along to see 'em and I couldn't believe it. I think he was on a steady wage with PP Arnold and maybe that was the attraction as opposed to with us: one month we'd do very well and another month not so good. At the end of the day it used to work out very good but I think he was happy with a steady wage.

"I don't know why he went with PP Arnold. I never do to this day. Playing bloody bass. The guy's got so much talent and ability and imagination. I've got nothing against PP Arnold, she's very nice, but it's a soul band."

Although it took him longer to realise than did Jack, Eddie seems to have eventually come to much the same conclusion. "What did dawn on me after a while – I did Pat's gig until it finished – it's not the same doing somebody else's gig.

"The Creation was my gig," Eddie says, "and Pat's gig was Pat's gig. I'm playing the music that somebody else wants you to play and, as nice as that is – it's a compliment people asking you to play for them – it's not the same kind of feeling as playing your own music." Apart from some sessions for Shel Talmy – a laborious experience for a musician who couldn't sight-read music – it was to be the last time Eddie ever did anyone else's gig in the strictest sense of the term.

Meanwhile, his former colleagues in The Creation were having their own difficulties. The first recording session of the new line-up of The Creation took place on 26 February 1968. The location was a yet further studio, Chappell Studios in Maddox Street, just off Bond Street in the West End of London. "Probably because I agreed to try it out," says Talmy about the change of location. "They probably gave me a deal."

Chappell was owned by the music publisher of that name but operated as a completely independent studio. It then consisted of a main studio and a remix room. The main studio was about 960 square feet (24x40) and had quite a low ceiling due to the expense of floor area in such a prime location and the fact that the building had been designed more with offices in kind. Even so, the studio could accommodate 40-piece orchestras. Indeed, that was a major type of work that passed through the studio.

Pye, IBC and Olympic – the other venues for The Creation's recordings – are familiar names from histories of top rock acts, but very few rock classics were laid down at Chappell. John Iles, the engineer on the Creation's Chappell recordings, says, "The reputation of Chappell was very strong for strings and brass and that side of it, so (if) it was more of a middle-of-the-road orchestral type thing then Chappell's was probably the studio of choice for pop stuff. It probably wasn't everybody's first choice, although a lot of people liked the vocal qualities and things like that that Chappell's provided. We did a lot of mix-downs of stuff that had been recorded elsewhere as well."

Despite his acknowledgement of Chappell's particular mellow niche, Iles displays the polite boastfulness about his former workplace with which the rock journalist is wearily familiar hearing from Sixties London studio engineers. " It was quite a leader," he says. "Before that I worked at Mayfair Sound. Chappell music publishers burnt down and in the rebuild they decided they'd have a state-of-the-art studio. Because we'd done work for Chappell's in the past they asked John (Timperley) and me to run it. Sandy Brown actually designed the studio. This would have been '67. Trident was actually modelled on Chappells. That's Sandy Brown's design as well – they copied that.

"Chappell was a nice studio," Iles continues, "quite big for its day. Very well equipped. It was the first Neve console with narrow modules, which became standard. In those days, separation was God and both John and I had come from a small studio which had very dead acoustics and which people liked for room sounds for example, keep that sort of very dead, close sound. Chappell's was a little bit of a compromise. We had a live and dead-end room insofar as near the control room the acoustics were fairly dry and at the other end, where there was also a very large separation booth, it was kept quite live. So the top end of the studio we would keep for strings and up by the control room would be the rhythm-section area. From the very early days we found that layout and continued to use it."

Though Kenny had previously written lyrics to songs, he had not established any other Creation member as his new musical foil in Eddie's absence: hence, when they entered Chappell, the band had no new, self-generated material. Or if they did, it was not recorded. Instead, the two tracks laid down that day were numbers provided by outside writers, 'For All That I Am' and 'Midway Down'. "I kept asking them to write songs," says Talmy. "Right from the get-go. Right after Eddie left. I have to assume that I wasn't satisfied with what I heard so I found other songs, at least initially, until they came up with something."

Talmy can't remember how he specifically came up with the two compositions in question but he had contact with several music publishers at the time so would have been receiving demos as a matter of course. In the case of 'For All That I Am', he may even have heard a commercially available version by The Tokens (a Brooklyn male vocal group who had a 1961 Transatlantic smash with 'The Lion Sleeps Tonight') on the album 'It's A Happening World'. He could also have heard another version released the same year by a West Coast group named The Soulful Bowlful, who issued it as a single, complete with modish cello parts.

Both songs were of high quality but of the two only 'Midway Down' fitted in with the Creation's tradition of larger-than-life material. Discounting previous cover versions which were artistically ambitionless and clearly not intended as singles the way the Chappell tracks were, the only previous Creation track that 'For All That I Am' resembles is 'If I Stay Too Long'.

'For All That I Am' was written by Paul Kahan and Stephen Friedland, staff writers with the publishing company of The Tokens. Kahan was the lyricist and Friedland the provider of melodies. "We wrote in every form you could think of," says Kahan. "Sometimes Steve would have a melody I would put a lyric to. Sometimes I would bring in a lyric or a fragment of it, a verse, two verses, half a verse, and we would build it from there. Often we would sit at the piano cold and build the song line-by-line as a complete collaboration. So there was no one way that Steve and I worked together. We were one of those very efficient writing units (which) could write in almost all of the modes equally well."

'For All That I Am' is a song that features a narrator telling a third party that he is grateful to that person for having moulded the personality he is. Like The Kinks' 'Days', this paean of thanks could be interpreted as a tribute to a lover, a friend or a parent. It turns out that in reality the song was inspired by both friends and lovers. "There were things that had gone on in my life and with friends of mine that generated the lyric," explains Kahan. "It wasn't a fantasy." On the lovers side, Kahan says, "If I have to be candid with you, it was really two (previous girlfriends), not just one. When I listen to the lyric now, you wouldn't know that it was more than one person. But I know that when I wrote it there were two people. There was one in particular but certainly there was another." He continues: "There is also an allusion in the lyric to friends I had lost in the Vietnam war. That's woven into the lyric, or at least into some of the imagery."

There is actually one element of the song that is in keeping with The Creation's larger-than-life musical tradition in the way the song's sentiment is written in such a way as to sound like the thoughts of a man as ancient as Methuselah. Kahan: "I think the line is 'As dawn cuts the edge of night/ I look back on the faces I have known/And I see through the curtain of time/It was you who made me a man.' I suppose it was an allusion to some of the events I was referring to in the lyric had not happened at that point in my life. They had occurred two or three years earlier. So the events that were the genesis of the lyric – or at least of the first two verses that I put together and brought to Steve – were things that I was thinking of that had happened in the past."

Kahan took his two verses to his main writing collaborator – although he wrote with others too, he estimates that 95% of his songs were written with Friedland at this stage – to see how it could be taken further. It may have helped Kahan this time round to know that, with this very personal song, there would almost certainly be no embarrassing questions from his partner: "Steve almost never asked me – and we did an awful lot of writing together – 'Gee, what are you talking about here?'" He adds, "He tended to accept a lyric on its face value. He would read a piece, he would look at it, and sometimes the melody would come to him immediately. Sometimes he just took it and a week later, he'd say, 'Oh, by the way, I was looking at this.' and he'd have a melody to it."

Friedland says, "He came into the office one day with this on a sheet of paper. I sat down and I would look at the words and I would just start playing, as I had always done. We had a private office, a piano, a desk: it was great. 1697 Broadway, room 605a, which had become the Ed Sullivan building but then became the Dave Letterman building. We did many songs that way. It was quick to come; we would do it in a day sometimes. That one was rapid. It's a beautiful set of words that he brought in."

Friedland appears to be being modest: Kahan recalls him having a more significant input into the song than merely 'setting' it. "I think I had two verses," Kahan says. "He put melody to that. As I remember, he came up with the release (chorus) on that and then I had to write the third verse in the moment and then that's how we built it. I think Steve came up with 'I thank you for all that I am'. I'm not sure. It might have been that he came up with 'The way I held you makes me a man'. I know Steve came up with the chorus."

With the song wrapped up and the demo finished, it was submitted to The Tokens. Like a few previous collaborations, The Tokens recorded their own version instead of merely publishing it. Friedland: "Every song that we wrote they had first dibs at. If they liked it, they would have done it." It's also quite possible that a demo was being touted around. Certainly, The Soulful Bowlful's version seems to have been issued with an alacrity that makes that more likely than them deciding to cover it after hearing The Tokens' version.

"We had a lot of demos out," Kahan explains, "because The Tokens were very, very generous. So if we had a piece that we liked we would go up to one of the studios upstairs in the same building and would cut either a piano-voice demo or bring a couple of musicians up. At that time, The Happenings were active in the group (organisation) and some of them would come up. So there were a lot of demos floating around that Steve and I had written. I know The Tokens at that point were very aggressive in their attempts to get covers on material that had been written within their organisation."

The pair collaborated on other songs, including 'Will You Care What's Happening To Me Baby', recorded by Bernadette Peters. Friedland subsequently became better known as Brute Force, under which name he released the single 'King Of Fuh' on The Beatles' Apple label in May 1969. Unfortunately, he was able to take only the pride and historical status involved in being one of the select few championed by the Fab Four from that release: the song was deemed too risqué by EMI, who refused to press the record, leading it to gain only a limited release via the 2,000 copies Apple felt obliged to press themselves.

Kahan stopped writing professionally for a 15-year period. "I was very negligent," he reflects. "It came to me too fast. I was too young to appreciate what was in front of me both in terms of opportunity and what I could make of it if I was serious about it and focused on it." Indeed, he considers 'For All That I Am' to possess a commerciality he should have tried to inject into his writing more often. "I think there were a lot of times where I was not as commercial as I should have been. I say that because The Tokens had opened up an awful lot of opportunity for me and, as much as I wanted them to do some new material that I had worked on, there were times when, thinking I was an artist as opposed to a craftsperson, I did not appreciate the opportunity that had been put before me. This was probably one of my better efforts at taking my limited skills and trying to make it commercial." At the time of writing, Friedland and Kahan had recently renewed their songwriting collaboration.

Neither of the writers were aware of The Creation's version of their song until into the 21st Century. Friedland was the first to find out: "It's a surprise but the surprise is a little muted with time when you learn it some 30 years later. That's typical of the music business." He subsequently informed Kahan, who says, "I didn't have a clue. I didn't know until Steve mentioned it to me maybe a month ago. I said, 'You have to be kidding'. He gave me a compilation of material that he's done that has been covered by other people."

Both of them were impressed by the efforts of this British band of whose existence they had previously been completely unaware. Friedland: "I liked it, sure. I liked it mostly because it was done! But it was done beautifully. I can't recall the demo at all. I think it's a good song. It has some very good words and the melody is a very flowing melody, sung nicely by the group." Kahan offers, "The Bowlful's version sounded very Sixties West Coast. The Tokens were always very good at getting into a studio and working on their harmonies. That was their forte... My wife was listening last night and of the three versions she said that she liked The Creation's version much better. The way she put it, she said 'They were more together as a group, it was much more focused'."

He adds of The Creation's take, "It's very good. You're looking back at a piece of work that was done so many years ago and (you can hear) all the influences that maybe weren't so obvious at the time you were doing it – the influences of the Beatles certainly on production values."

In contrast to the conventionality of 'For All That I Am', the other song to which The Creation gave their interpretation at this session was one with more than a tinge of the surreal. 'Midway Down' was the work of John Wonderling, a 22-year-old American songwriter who had been in the business for around a year. Sadly, Wonderling died of a heart attack in September 2003 not long after granting an interview for this book.

"I was actually a songwriter working for a small publishing company and they were giving me 50 dollars a week or something," Wonderling recalled, "so most of whatever came in went back to them because they were giving me advances on my writing." Wonderling had already placed a couple of songs with prestigious acts The Cowsills (whose album 'Captain Sad And His Ship Of Fools' featured his co-write 'Ask The Children') and The Strawberry Alarm Clock (though the latter wasn't released and Wonderling thinks it might even have been the same song).

'Midway Down' is a song with the bobbing feel of a ride at the sort of fairground it describes and has a slightly menacing, spooky undertow. It originated with a summer visit Wonderling made to a fair, the setting of whose carnival sideshows are known in the States as midways. "It was just very depressing to look at," he said. "I was seeing these very sad sort of performers. There were these midgets and these large people and women with bears and all kind of things and they didn't seem like very happy people. I got a whole different perspective in looking at this as opposed to when I was a kid and enjoying it all. I was an adult and really feeling for these people 'cos they had nothing else in life.

"It was: 'Bearded ladies, dancing babies waving hello/ The ten foot titan finds it tough to lift a feather/ And the three-foot midget hopes he won't be small forever.' That's where the lyric was and that's just the whole point of view of it." A friend of Wonderling's named Lew Shapiro received a co-writer's credit on the song. Wonderling: "That was the first song he ever wrote and it might be the last. I was in the middle of writing it and he happened to come over that day and added a few little things. So that's how we wound up being co-writers of the song. He was a promotion man in the music industry. He happened to drop by, saw that I was in the middle of this tune I was trying to finish and contributed a few different things, so I put him down as co-writer."

The title phrase appears nowhere in the song. "As opposed to Halfway Up," Wonderling explained. "I could have gone the other way round: Down Midway. But I had to come up with a title and basically the chorus is a la-la-la thing; I couldn't call it that so that's the best thing I could come up with at the time." As to how the Creation came to record it, Wonderling explained, "I was recording myself at the time and, being a songwriter and always open to having other people record my songs and thinking as a songwriter as opposed to an artist in wanting to save everything for myself, I just had everybody recording the things that I was writing.

"At the time I didn't know who The Creation were. I believe it was through my publishing company, otherwise someone might have gotten hold of the recordings I was actually doing. I was bringing my recordings that I was actually doing for Warner Brothers at the time, giving them back to my publisher. My publisher might have been sending them out. My publisher knew Shel Talmy and I believe that's how that got started. We got a phone call from England or a telex or something saying that they recorded the tune and then I think a couple months later I actually saw the tune on the charts (sic) before I actually even heard a copy of it, I was so involved in recording my own album.

"They did hear mine. Whether it was a demo or the master that I did for Warners I'm not quite sure. They had to have heard my particular version of it for them to do it because I was the only one that had recorded it at the time. It's not like we sent them a lead sheet and they took it from there." Wonderling has mixed feelings about The Creation's version of his song. "Theirs was a little grungier," he said. "They were a lot looser than I was and mine was a little more pop-sounding. They might have taken the lyric literally a lot more so than I did. I was very new at recording at the time so I was thinking about the record as opposed to the real darkness of the lyric. So they had their own interpretation, plus they had their own style and I didn't really have a style at the time because I was still a fledging trying to learn my way around the studio.

"All I did was record the song as a songwriter. That was my mindset as opposed to being an artist. Consequently since then I've heard a lot of other songs recorded by people that are very close to mine, others were quite different from mine, but as a songwriter I'm flattered because people had their own interpretation for whatever lyric, the way they're seeing it. I don't think it was improved. I just think it was a difference of opinion. There were certain things about it that I didn't particularly love at the time – and I haven't heard it for years so my opinion might be totally different today. I don't actually have a copy of it.

"I didn't like the looseness of the way it was recorded. I was a lot more precise in how things should and shouldn't sound and I think that they were very lazy, maybe the enunciation was wrong or maybe they were just a little bit sloppy and I couldn't quite hear the lyric. I can't quite put my finger on it now but I think my initial feeling was that it was not my particular choice of how the song should have been recorded. It was very different from what I was doing but it was also very flattering because somebody happened to pick up on it.

"Yes, I did think it was going to be single material. Whether or not I thought The Creation version was single material was not really my opinion because we had our own limited understanding of what was going on with the English population. There were. bands that were successful over there that we didn't get a chance to hear here."

Wonderling did, however, prefer The Creation's version to his own, which he put on his eponymous 1969 album, having originally recorded the song as a single for Warner Brothers the previous year. His version was considerably gentler than The Creation's. "I was new at songwriting at the time and didn't really get an opportunity to let my hair down, so to speak, until later in life," he said. "Ergo my staid version of the song. Theirs is better because they had a sound of their own, while I was still groping for an identity. But it's still nice that they heard the possibilities in the tune despite my white bread version."

Any pleasure Wonderling obtained from having The Creation cover him was entirely artistic as opposed to financial. "I don't know if I ever physically held on to any royalties in my hand," he said. "I should have been getting statements but the company that I was working with – I think I was only with them for a total of eight or nine months – by the time I left them the company was gone and I don't think I ever got a check from any of that stuff. I had no idea what happened with the publishing company, where the rights went, and again I was doing a lot of other things at the time. Since I hadn't heard anything about the record I figured, 'Well, it didn't really matter much if I made 30 or 40 dollars on it.'"

Wonderling subsequently remained in the music industry, as songwriter, producer and song publisher. "I've produced people like Aaron Neville and Dr John and I do a lot of jingles on TV," he said. "I've had songs on albums. I had two songs on Laura Branigan's 'Gloria' album. But I've basically been concentrating on a lot of jingle things and I've turned into a publisher." He added of The Creation, "I met Woody once very briefly and we didn't actually didn't get a chance to talk about The Creation or any of that stuff. That's the only person I know in the band that went on (to other things), so to speak."

With regard to recording these two tracks, John Iles explains the way a rock group like The Creation would have been placed in Chappell: "The drums were put into a corner with screens around them to try to improve separation a bit and our policy was always to place the musicians as close together as we felt we could get away with separation-wise, so the bass guitarist would be placed alongside the drums for example, and the guitarist would be placed alongside him. And they'd all have cans (headphones), of course, with each other as well but there'd be a close proximity. Also any leakage that there was between the microphones also sounded better because there wasn't any large time intervals between it."

As for Talmy, whom Iles did not work with very often, he says, "I seem to recall him as actually quite an affable, creative, positive person. As an engineer in those days, what you really wanted was someone who knew what *they* wanted. That's all you could ask for, really, and Shel was that type of person. He was quite…not forceful but he knew what he expected to get out of it. He knew what good sound was, bad sound was. He knew what needed to be corrected."

The recording session for 'Midway Down'/'For All That I Am' – which Iles suspects was almost completely finished in a session that would most probably have been an evening one (MOR sessions tended to fill the studio in the daytime) – seems to have been a rather difficult one for The Creation. In contrast to the way the basic tracks of great recordings like 'Making Time' and 'Can I Join Your Band' had been knocked off in around half a dozen takes, the slightly torturous annotation of the tape box suggests that these two numbers were committed to tape with a hesitancy and lack of fluency.

There were numerous false starts. Wood of course was new to the band and the line-up couldn't be expected to gel instantly in the studio. However, even though incorporating a guitarist is more difficult than incorporating a bassist, it still seems a strangely marked contrast to the way 'Making Time' had been captured so well and with so little effort mere weeks – and one gig – after Bob Garner's arrival.

Furthermore, it's possible that the recordings were done in a slightly edgy atmosphere. The tape box shows, rather unusually, that Talmy was instructing the engineer to spool back the tape to record over unusable takes. "Take 4 was the first complete take we got, which wasn't unusual" says Iles of 'For All That I Am', "but then we went through take 5, 6, 7, 8, 9, 10, 11 and 12 – which were all false starts – and then take 13. (It was) then decided that they would run back to the last complete take – which would have taken a little time to find – and to erase all those false starts… Then we continued on, again with false starts, until we got to take 14. From 5 to 13 was wiped and then we continued numbering from 5. So it went from take 4, the last complete take. All the other outtakes were erased."

"I always did that," insists Talmy. "I just rolled back and started over again. We didn't have money to burn at that point." And the time taken to spool back to the last usable take? "It took no time at all. Very easy to do." When it is pointed out to him that none of the other surviving tape boxes for Creation basic tracks show him doing this, Talmy says, "Well that's because they got new ledgers." Talmy is wrong on this: Alan O'Duffy and Damon Lyon-Shaw recognised their own handwriting from other Creation tape boxes. Of the 10 further takes of 'For All that I Am' recorded after the tape had been spooled back, take 6 (i.e. the second new take) was a complete, as were 10, 12 and 14; all the others were false starts.

Take 14 was the take chosen for the reduction stage. 'Midway Down', meanwhile, seems to have had its basic tracks wiped over twice. After the first five attempts had produced five false starts, the tape was spooled back to record over them. Four or possibly five more failed attempts were then made, three or maybe four of which were false starts, and were then in turn recorded over. Then four more takes occurred. The first three were false starts. The fourth was, finally, a complete – and one assumes a certain weariness motivated the fact that this marked the end of the recording process of the basic track of 'Midway Down'. The first complete out of 13 attempts was used for the master.

Iles, incidentally, thinks that though the basic tracks and the four-fours were demonstrably done at Chappell, additional overdubbing work on one or both tracks was done at another studio. "Listening to it, I don't think that I remixed it," he says. "I think the recordings that I made was the original recordings that were laid down, first on a four-track machine, building up tracks, and then it was bounced onto another machine so that we could build up some additional tracks.

"Now, I've got no memory and from listening to the mix it doesn't sound like anything that I would have done. There's handclaps in 'Midway Down'. That's not listed on the box at all. And we wouldn't have recorded claps with the voices. It would definitely have been laid down as a separate track. It may be that they literally just ran out of time and wanted to do some more work elsewhere. I can't remember if there was any friction or problems. I don't think there was. It seemed to be a fairly normal session in terms of creativity. You tend to remember the very good ones and the very bad ones and certainly it didn't fall into either category as far as I was concerned.

"Sometimes people moved from studio to studio for different aspects which they felt was better from one studio to the other. So they may have felt that they wanted to get Glyn Johns involved because they wanted him to remix it or something like that. Difficult to know but listening to the mix, it doesn't really sound like my work. It wasn't quite as driving as I expected it to be." The handclap overdubs were probably done by Glyn Johns at Olympic: certainly a tape box for masters for 'For All That I Am' and a later Creation track, 'Uncle Bert', exists with Johns' credit appended.

Despite all of the above, The Creation emerged from the session with two highly worthwhile performances. That Talmy opted to use the sole completed take of 'Midway Down' for the master indicates that it was initially intended for the B-side of a single for which presumably 'For All That I Am' was the planned A-side. In the end both tracks would be used as A-sides in Germany and it was 'Midway Down' that was released as a UK A-side, although in each case not until the band had split up or were just about to.

There was actually a new Creation single released in the UK that month of the recording of 'Midway Down' and 'For All That I Am', although it wasn't the product of this session. Instead February 1968 finally saw the release of the Creation's masterpiece, 'How Does It Feel To Feel', albeit the slightly less great British version. The flip was 'Tom Tom'.

The Chappell session is the last for which original tape boxes are known to exist at the time of writing, excepting 'Sweet Helen'. Subsequent dates for Creation sessions in this text are therefore based on annotation on master boxes and cataloguing notes written subsequently by employees of Talmy.

On or around 4 March '68, the creation attended Olympic Studios to record a new track. This one was something of a breakthrough: the first post-Eddie Phillips original composition. Furthermore, 'The Girls Are Naked' was in the best Creation tradition. Without Eddie, there was none of the radical instrumentation that had graced previous Creation recordings but there were a couple of other quintessential ingredients in a cutting-edge lyric and a fine melody.

The song was written after a visit by Kenny to London's red-light district. "That was a typical Kenny song," says Jack. "He was wandering through Soho and he was looking at all the ads you get: 'The girls are naked and they dance'. Hookers and all this stuff, so he wrote a song about it and it seemed to work. I thought that was a good song. It went down a light."

The track went some way to easing Talmy's concerns about the lack of songwriting ability of the new permutation. "'Girls Are Naked' actually turned out to be a very good track," says the producer, "and I did one other with them that turned out pretty good. It still wasn't Eddie. It wasn't

The Creation as I knew them but I'm certainly not displeased. That track was good." The writing of the song was credited to Kenny, Kim and Jack.

'The Girls Are Naked' was a session attended by a famous visitor, although one we can probably safely assume had not purchased previous Creation discs: Val Doonican, a crooner whose chosen image was literally a rocking-chaired one. "He was a big star then," says Jack, "had his own TV series. I think he was going to record something and he just came in and sat down in the studio for a while. He's a nice guy."

8 March saw another recording session for a Creation original at yet another studio. It was IBC that Talmy chose for the recording of 'Sweet Helen,' engineered by 'PW' – probably Phil Wade – and tape op'd by John Pantry. This track was an autobiographical piece by Kenny. The titular Helen had actually worked at The Flamingo when The Creation had had their residency there two years previously. "The DJ was this beautiful, big, blonde girl called Helen," Kenny explained to *Record Collector*. "Hair down to her bum. I fell in love, had a fair old time with her and wrote this song."

Says Jack, "Kenny always tried to draw from life. I think they were gonna get married at one time but she wanted him to get a steady job and Kenny wasn't having none of that stuff. He was a musician. In another time they might have got married. She was special to him." The track was rather ornate due to its cello decoration, which may have been played on the mellotron. "They were in the very early stages then and we had a little dabble on it," says Jack.

When 'Sweet Helen' finally achieved a commercial release in 1993, its composition details were listed as 'Unknown'. The writing of the track has since been attributed to Kenny alone, which seems unlikely in light of the fact that, at that stage, he seems to have been purely a lyricist.

There were six takes of 'Sweet Helen' attempted. Take one was a false start, take two a breakdown and the rest were completes. The last was chosen for the reduction stage, details of which have been lost. Not quite as good as 'The Girls Are Naked' but pleasant enough, 'Sweet Helen' meant the band had two new compositions under their belts when they embarked on their last visit to Germany on 15 March. (This trip may also have involved gigs in Holland.)

On or around 2 April 1968, The Creation laid down another new song, 'Uncle Bert', at an unknown studio. The master was prepared by Glyn Johns (on the same day as he prepared a master for 'All That I Am'), and it seems safe to assume he was the engineer on the session for 'Uncle Bert's basic track, judging by Kenny's recollection in *Record Collector*.

"Shel walked out of the 'Uncle Bert' sessions because we were looning around, so Glyn Johns ended up producing it." Talmy, incidentally, denies leaving the studio. "I can only remember one session I walked out of and that wasn't it," he says. "It was not Creation."

He would have had some justification for walking out, at least on artistic grounds. Musically, 'Uncle Bert' was quite galvanising but it carried a grotesque and slightly nasty lyric containing references to a sex offender and derogatory comments about homosexuals. Kim acknowledged he wrote part of the lyric and its buffoonish content hints at the nastier side of his celebrated joviality. Jack wasn't impressed: "'Uncle Bert' was a bit of a piss-take. I didn't have much interest in that song. I did my part in the record but I thought we were capable of doing better stuff than that."

Kenny recalled the origins of 'Uncle Bert' in his *Blitz* interview: "On the way to the studio, we were saying, 'Imagine a flasher with a wooden leg. What would the woman look at – the wooden leg, or...? So we wrote this silly song about a dog running off over Hampstead Heath with the wooden leg between his teeth and the flasher standing there on one leg! It seemed to tickle us at the time. We wrote it when we got to the studio."

The publishing credit for the song reads 'Garwood Pickjohn', an amalgam of the surnames of all four Creation personnel. Says Jack, "Kenny was writing the songs and bringing them in and Ronnie would sort of work the chords out and we'd all chip in a bit. It was a bit more democratic. 'Listen, instead of one or two hogging all the songwriting, let's put them in the name of the band so that everybody's then got a shared interest'. That was the way the music scene was going. So it was becoming a bit less selfish than it had been before. But by then it was too late."

Too late for a couple of reasons. The Creation obtained meagre domestic bookings in 1968. June Clark's diaries reveal only a paltry three gigs in their homeland that year, all in April. The other reason is that, shortly after those promising sessions with the new line-up, the band found themselves yet again in need of a guitarist.

Ronnie Wood may not have liked Jeff Beck very much but in early '68, he came up with an offer Wood couldn't refuse: the chance to tour America. For musicians in the Sixties, this opportunity did not come very often. All except the most successful British bands had problems taking their music to the mythical land of rock'n'roll's birth, a country that seemed much further away in an age before instant global communication.

"If we'd had more time, I think everything would have developed," says Jack. "In The Stones, he's confined to rhythm guitarist but Ronnie could play guitar and I think the band would have developed if we'd stayed together for longer. But then one day he walked in and said, 'I'm sorry lads. I've always wanted to go to America and Jeff's putting a band together. We're going in a couple of months. I'm going to have to leave.' And that was a blow. America…everybody wanted to go there…but there'd been real problems with visas. The American unions wouldn't let the British bands go out there at first until they were forced to. He had this opportunity. Jeff Beck was Jeff Beck."

This semi-bombshell (Jack: "It was never agreed he'd join permanently but we just hoped he might") left Jack and Kim and, to a lesser extent, Kenny in a position with which they were wearily familiar: facing the task of obtaining a guitarist to fill the slot once (and definitively) occupied by Eddie Phillips. Although they'd thus far employed friends, or friends of friends, as opposed to holding auditions, it was one instance of *déjà vu* too far. "Me, Kenny and Kim looked at each other and thought, 'That's about it, man, we've had enough," says Jack. "'It's time to move on'. We got fed up with it because we'd had so many guitarists and we thought we'd found one in Ronnie. We thought, 'We've run our course'. And Kim had also had an offer by then through Shel Talmy's office to join Ashton, Gardner and Dyke so he was thinking of taking that."

Kenny Pickett, in a quote given to *Blitz*, implied that mixed in with this fatigue was almost a guilt at the way the nature of the band had been changed simply so that the personnel could, to use Kim's words, "milk it". "We did that final tour of Germany, pocketed the money and ran," said Kenny. "Nobody wanted to do it any more, because we weren't doing The Creation's sort of music. We were doing all BB King stuff because that's Ronnie Wood. He's like yer natural blues man."

On 19 April 1968, The Creation closed the curtain on their career with a gig in the ballroom that then existed above the famous John Lewis department store in London's Oxford Street. Though the recollection of Gail Colson tallies with that of Jack that the gig was above John Lewis, Clark recalls the gig being being on a temporary stage inside the store itself. "I have to tell you, I was embarrassed. I laughed when I was told they were going to be playing at John Lewis. I thought, 'It's come to this. They're this desperate to get a gig that this is what they're doing'. I didn't think that they should ever have done it. Really too bizarre. I was with Gail and (Rolling Stones employee) Tom Keylock. I couldn't believe they were standing there. That they felt acceptable to do it. I think they just thought of it as like fun. 'Why not?' John Lewis has always been a great store – it was a store young people would go in – (but) it's not playing at Way-In on the King's Road, a boutique. That would have been far more trendy." Did anybody know who they were? "I doubt it," says Clark.

"Up above John Lewis there's a ballroom," says Jack. "You could hire it out and sell tickets, bring people up. It's got a nice stage, everything. Kenny said that we did a gig afterwards up in Nottingham but you never did Nottingham on a Monday and we did that John Lewis gig on a Sunday. I think – I'm sure, in fact – that the John Lewis gig was the last gig The Creation ever did. I think we played pretty good, actually…a farewell performance, if you like."

In actual fact, 19 April 1968 was a Friday but Clark's diary carries no further mention of Creation gigs for that year and she says it is safe therefore to assume this was The Creation's final live performance.

In either April or May, 'Midway Down' b/w 'The Girls Are Naked' was released in the UK – just in time to celebrate the group's demise. One wonders whether Polydor were even aware of the split or whether they were kept as much in the dark about this as they seem to have been about the departure of Eddie. Kenny appears to have been past caring. "I never even knew they put 'Midway Down' out!" he told *Blitz*. This same combination of songs also saw single release in Germany where, as in Britain, they did not register on the charts. Surprisingly for a band who had just about fallen off the public radar, 'Midway Down' garnered a review in a (unknown) music paper: "A fairly good one from The Creation, this – the lyric is a colourful description of a travelling fair with all its intriguing sideshows. The boys present it well, with rich harmonies and background heavenly chanting embellishing the soloist. There's also plenty of those guttural twangs for which the group is renowned, plus a catchy la-la chorus which everyone can join in."

There were two more Creation single releases that year in West Germany, the one country that had given the group the commercial success they deserved. Precise dates are uncertain but the singles in question were 'Bony Moronie' b/w 'Mercy Mercy Mercy' (the A-side was misspelt 'Bonney Moroney') and 'For All That I Am' b/w 'Uncle Bert'. Regarding the first pair of tracks, one postscript – and one last theory about the date of their recording – is raised by a master tape dated 3 July 1968 containing those two songs. Kenny, as mentioned previously, once said that 'Bony Moronie' was the last track The Creation ever recorded.

Could it be the case that Kenny recorded these two tracks after The Creation had split – thus explaining the session bassist he alleges and Jack's lack of recollection of playing on them?

West Germany was also, fittingly, the country that released the Creation's second album. Like 'We Are Paintermen', before it, 'Best Of The Creation' – issued in the summer of '68 on the Pop Schallplatten label, another subsidiary of Deutsche Vogue – featured a mixture of material already released and tracks not heard before.

Making their first ever album appearances were 'Bony Moronie', 'Uncle Bert', 'Life Is Just Beginning', 'How Does It Feel To Feel' (UK version), 'Mercy Mercy Mercy', 'The Girls Are Naked', 'For All That I Am' and 'Midway Down'. However, Pop Schallplatten couldn't resist appending the hits 'Making Time', 'Painter Man' and 'Tom Tom', which had already appeared on the first album, as had 'Cool Jerk', a track added apparently because it had also been a German single.

In contrast to The Creation's fortunes, The Who – the band to whom they had been compared many times and whose leader had once tried (maybe) to poach Eddie – were in 1968 getting ready to conquer the world. Like the Creation, their career had lately stalled. They'd been a hit at the previous year's Monterey Pop Festival and subsequently scored their first Transatlantic top ten in the shape of 'I Can See For Miles' – a brilliant psychedelic freakout classic in the vein of 'How Does It Feel To Feel', but no better than that latter track – but by November '68 were reduced to an appearance on *Crackerjack* – a BBC children's programme no less cheesy and raucous than *Hey Presto! It's Rolf* – in a vain attempt to get the public interested in their less-than-overwhelming 'Magic Bus'. However, just as they had in 1966, they persevered through the hard times and were rewarded by becoming superstars when their 1969 album 'Tommy' contrived to become one of the most famous albums of all time. Their 1971 album 'Who's Next', meanwhile, is widely considered one of the greatest rock albums ever.

"Oh, they would have been as big as The Who, easily," says Shel Talmy when asked the potential of The Creation had they too persevered. "Without question. Townshend would tell you that if you asked him." Did they have the capacity to develop from classic pop singles to album masterpieces like Townshend and company? Talmy: "Of course the one thing is would they have stayed together and I'm not sure they would have. But assuming they stayed together, would they have adapted and changed as they went along? Yes. No question."

Jack agrees. "I always thought – any (version of the) band really – we could have gone all the way," he says. "I thought we could have been someone like The Who, that sort of size. We had a sort of originality about the band. There was a lot of talent in the band when it come to songwriting. And I think we had a sound of our own. So I think tremendous potential there really. It didn't materialise. That's it really. That's showbiz." "Nobody knows the answer to that one," says Bob when asked the same question about potential. "Even if the records had been successful, I think the problems would have stayed in the band. I don't think there would have been anything to stop that. You put a few things in a cake and they don't make a good cake."

"That's a hard question," replies Eddie, the man whose exit began The Creation's unravelling. "Looking back, if we'd have stuck it out I think we could have been at this time in our lives... I was going to say quite happy with it but I'm happy with it as it is. The fact that people all this time afterwards still remember and sing our songs – that's as good as it gets. In a way, that's more than money. I think it would have been nice if we could have stuck it out and got into the Seventies a bit. I think that could have been really interesting because I had this vision of using orchestras with heavy rock, which did happen. Other people did it. But I was thinking about it in '67 and it's a shame I never actually got round to being able to try it out.

"Shel always says maybe if we'd have stuck together for another year (it) could've made a difference and he's probably right. But at that time I couldn't from my end of it keep going with it because I needed to sort my life out, so I had to let it go. It's a bit of shame really but that's what they call life. If Strat had sorted out the thing with those early records, which should have paved the way for the success of the band, then maybe I wouldn't have been in that position." However, in reference to the fact that beautiful losers often have more of a cachet than megastars, he adds, "But there again, if that had happened, we'd have been a Top 10 band, we'd probably be doing chicken-in-a-basket gigs now and not being as well thought-of."

John Dalton, from his perspective as an interested observer, thinks The Creation were just too similar to The Who. "I suppose (I thought) 'They are gonna make it' but I don't know whether people thought they were (too) much like The Who. We've already got one Who, sort of thing. There was always going to be a resemblance 'cos Townshend started doing the feedback and all things like that and Eddie would do the arm-swings exactly the same as Pete Townshend, the old windmill arm. Even Roger Daltrey's and Kenny's voice are not that different. That little twang in there that sounds similar."

However, Johnny Byrne cites a reason for The Creation not making it that hints at a far more fundamental problem. "In talking to you and clarifying thoughts I didn't have – resolutions and conclusions I didn't make at the time – it seems to me The Creation lacked a kind of guiding hand," he says. "They couldn't provide it themselves and it seems those responsible for its fate couldn't provide it either. It wouldn't have taken much for them to be totally committed to this thing. I think it was a lack of commitment that generated all the petty things that might have held them together. What matters if you lose fifty grand here if in three weeks time you're going to make a million?

"It becomes matters of ego, getting a name on the leader or someone being considered the leader of the group. That's why I had a feeling that they were four superbly equipped session men really waiting for that magical transformation into a group… It never quite came about. I think the failing was as much their own as others. They didn't have enough belief in themselves as a group. Just thinking back, the thing that strikes me about (them) is not so much the missed opportunities, it's how very little it would have taken for them to be one of the great rock'n'roll groups."

Byrne's comments are extremely interesting in light of comments by Gail Colson. Colson, after working for Talmy, became involved in Tony Stratton-Smith's Charisma label, of which she was label manager and joint managing director. Having learned about handling rock acts from employers Shel Talmy and Tony Stratton-Smith, she began a career in the late Seventies as an artist manager, carving out an extremely successful career which continues to this day. Her clients have included Peter Gabriel, The Pretenders and Morrissey.

Colson has acquired a huge knowledge about what makes people stars and what makes them also-rans. Asked to explain what she thinks The Creation lacked and which stopped them from achieving the success so many people felt they deserved, she gives a very simple and succinct reply which – unbeknownst to her – echoes Byrne's sentiments exactly: "Determination and belief in themselves."

The return to civvy street after rock'n'roll-star demobilisation is probably an experience whose acuteness only those who have gone through it can appreciate.

For two years, the various members of The Creation had occupied the margins of the big time, and they would not have been human if, in odd moments, they had not assumed that that real big-time belonged to them. How on earth does one face going back to a 'real life', nine-to-five job when one has appeared on television, heard one's records on the radio, seen one's face in pop magazine pin-ups and played on the same bill as Cream, The Kinks and the Rolling Stones?

In Ronnie Wood's case, you join the Stones. He became by far the most successful of any of the ex-personnel of The Creation, apparently gliding seamlessly through a succession of incrementally more celebrated groups, from the Jeff Beck Group (February 1967 to summer 1969, off an on) through the Faces (summer 1969-December 1975) aand onto the biggest (in terms of legend, if not sales) extant rock group of all, the Rolling Stones. Of course, this is a glib summary of a professional trajectory that was no doubt as beset by frustrations, uncertainty, personality clashes and hiccups as many other musicians' careers. Nonetheless, fate has on balance been extremely kind to Ronald David Wood.

The only other ex-member of The Creation to achieve anything like the success he dreamed of while in that band was Kim Gardner. Ashton, Gardner and Dyke – the aggregation referred to previously by Jack – comprised Kim on bass, Tony Ashton on keyboards and vocals and Roy Dyke on drums, the latter both ex-members of the Remo Four. "Ashton, Gardner and Dyke was a whole different approach," Kim told *Ugly Things*. "Playing with a keyboard for one thing and Roy Dyke was an incredible drummer – great musician. So I went through another change. I learned a lot in that band.

"It was a trio in the beginning: organ, bass and drums. We were a big hit in Germany because the Remo Four were big over there – known as a bunch of loonies like The Creation. That worked really good for three or four years. I went through a whole different transition, bass-playing-wise, leaning towards jazz things as well." Ashton, Gardner and Dyke made three studio albums and secured a Top 3 UK hit with 'Resurrection Shuffle' in early 1971. (It also nudged the US Top 40.)

Bob never did take up that job in a bakery and says he can't remember making that remark to Clark. He briefly had a day job before hooking up with a group who styled themselves Smiley. "I took Smiley to Hugh Murphy and Shel to see if he liked the band," recalls Bob. "He said, 'Yes'. We did a few songs for him and he said 'Oh, I've got this song here, "Penelope".' I thought, "Ere we go'. He said, 'Go away and learn this'. Well we thought, 'Jeeesus'. It just wasn't the band Smiley but you do things because if that's the only way in, that's what you do."

'Penelope', a saccharine love song, was released on Philips (about whom Talmy would seem to have temporarily forgotten his disdain) in 1972. Bob was somewhat surprised to learn the identity of the composer: Kenny Pickett. Evidently Talmy was still in touch with the other former Creation frontman. Bob: "When I saw him a few years ago, he said, 'Yeah, I wrote that. I came in one night, I'd had a skinful and I wrote it about somebody on the scene'." Bob wasn't overly impressed by the song: "I think we made a little bit more of it than what was sent to us. The actual demo didn't set the world on fire. We had a bit of input to make it a little bit more group-ey. And then Shel went and put the kids on it." Bob is referring to the fact that the chorus was sung, for no apparent reason, by a children's choir. "That was brought in afterwards," explains Bob. "I never saw 'em. I just thought, "Yeucch. It's another 'Grandad'."

One wonders at the bizarre mixture of joy and displeasure Pickett's reaction would have been had his nemesis secured a smash with his song. As it is, it failed to chart. Bob: "We only did that one. On the B-side (is) 'I Know What I Want', which is mine." The latter would probably have made a better A-side, being a well-crafted attempt to jump on the glam-rock bandwagon complete with glam's unsettling, sinister juxtaposition of minor and major chords.

Smiley continued making a living in working men's clubs on the northern circuit until early 1976. Bob: "I moved house to north Wales and didn't do anything until the Christmas of that year. I went out solo doing a few pubs, just guitar. It was in '77 that I started my first summer season, compering, entertaining, shouting bingo and all that."

Kenny Pickett initially continued to harbour ambitions to be a group frontman following The Creation's dissolution. Accordingly, in mid 1968 he applied for that role in a new band being set up by Jimmy Page, an ex-session musician and old acquaintance from the Neil Christian days. The new group would ultimately find fame – although not with Kenny – as Led Zeppelin. Kenny's application did, however, lead to him securing sufficient employment to keep the wolf from the door for a period. Glen Colson: "He went for the job as the singer for Led Zeppelin and they loved him so much they offered him a job. They said, 'Look, you've got to come and work for us, we really like you'."

Kenny became Led Zeppelin's first tour manager. "I hesitated as I didn't want to hump equipment about," he reasoned to *Blitz* in '82, "but it was a way of getting to the States. So I did it. I went there for about a year." "He worked his arse off," says Glen Colson. "He drove the van, humped all the equipment and mixed the sound. He did everything for them. In those days, you could do it all. Led Zeppelin, as you see them, the first gigs they ever did, he actually took all that equipment in a van, set it up and did the sound, put it all away, and got home about six in the morning. All by himself. Two American tours as well."

Glen Colson also remembers Kenny helping to mould the distinctive Zeppelin sound: "They took his advice early on, I think, with music. I think he gave them a few albums. Because they were session men, they wanted to know what was going on, what kind of music they should be making, and I think he gave them a load of Moby Grape and Doors and The Seeds. He gave 'em a few Spirit." There was already a Creation connection with Zeppelin, of course, Page having adopted Eddie's violin bow-trick and in Zeppelin, Page – as the guitarist of what would transpire to be the biggest rock band in the world during the first half of the Seventies – introduced that trick to millions of people, most of whom assumed it to be his innovation. Glen Colson also reveals of Zeppelin, "They used to rehearse Creation records at soundchecks and things. They used to do 'Making Time' and 'Painter Man' at soundchecks."

Yet Kenny's artistic ambitions remained intact and he continued to attempt to write songs. One collaborator was Herbie Flowers, an expert tuba and bass player and future member of the classical-pop ensemble Sky. In 1970, they composed a number called 'Grandad', mentioned by Bob above. A light-hearted paean to the merits of the paternal grandparent whose verses were sung by actor Clive Dunn – best known for his portrayal of bumbling Lance Corporal Jones in the hugely popular

BBC TV comedy *Dad's Army* – and whose choruses ('Grandad, Grandad/You're lovely') were sung by primary school age children.

Flowers and Dunn had met at a party and Dunn, on learning Flowers was a composer, jocularly demanded he write him a song. (Dunn had just started recording an album at the time.) Kenny explained to *Record Collector* the genesis of his lyric, the verses of which saw the narrator looking back on how the world had changed during his lifetime: "Herbie gave me the tape which sat in my machine for weeks before he called to say he was about to play the song to Clive – did I have the lyrics? So I quickly sat down... A thing on TV about old flying machines gave me my first inspiration: ' I've been sitting here all day, thinking / Same old dreams ten years away, thinking / Now my days are gone, memories linger on/Thoughts of when I was a boy / Aeroplanes tied up with string, flying'. I had a box of Quality Street on the table. The picture round the edge got me further: 'Radios were funny things, sighing / Bowling hoops and spinning tops, penny dreadfuls, lollipops...'"

The record secured the Number 1 spot in January '71, (keeping T Rex's breakthrough 'Ride A White Swan' off the top in the process) and gained Pickett and Flowers an Ivor Novello award for Best Novelty Song of the year. This was clearly music at the very opposite end of the spectrum from The Creation's flash and verve but Kenny was pragmatic about such things. Glen Colson: "I think he just saw it as an exercise. I think he was always very confident about his writing." Creation fan Rod Siebke says of Kenny's attitude toward the song and its success, "As far as he was concerned, 'Grandad' was good. Why not, as a writer? Doesn't matter how you earn your money, does it?"

Unfortunately, though Kenny was happy to be a bespoke songwriter, that first flush of success was not the beginning of a long and illustrious career. Though he scored a further modicum of triumph with Flowers in the shape of 'Our World' – a sort of grander, more global version of his normal socially-conscious lyrics that hit Number 17 in the UK for Flowers' band Blue Mink in autumn 1970 – there were no further Pickett co-written hits until toward the end of the decade and none at any point on the scale of 'Grandad'. Siebke partly attributes this to losing his collaborator Flowers, with whom at some point he ceased being friends ("Kenny was good at falling out with people").

Glen Colson was "amazed he didn't become a full-time writer like those people in the Brill Building. I'm amazed someone didn't guide him that way… He never really struck lucky, Kenny, only touched the fringes a couple of times. I think he could have done something very, very big if he'd have teamed up with the right people or the right person. I think he could have become a hell of a songwriter. If, say, he'd have met Elton John, I think he might have been able to become a Bernie Taupin."

Colson adds of Kenny's feelings on The Creation's failure, "I would say he was always incredibly frustrated that they never amounted to anything 'cos he thought they could have been as big as the Small Faces if they'd have carried on." Kenny explained the course of his professional life following his collaboration with Flowers to *Blitz* magazine: "I got out of the business altogether. I went to live in Kingston-Upon-Thames. I started a discount company, selling things. Then I packed that in and started working as a road manager for a company called International Entertainments as a sound mixer. I did that for about eighteen months. I did most of the festivals here in England, as well as those in Holland and Scandinavia, working with Eric Clapton, Ginger Baker and Delaney and Bonnie. I worked with Canned Heat for quite a while."

After The Creation, Jack, initially, went back to normal life. "I got a job for a while," he explains. "It didn't last very long 'cos I didn't like working – not honest work, anyway. I worked for Tesco's at their head office. I was a departmental head, would you believe. I had a suit and a tie, man, and a haircut and about 50 women that I was telling what to do. You don't get jobs like that very often. But it wasn't me and after about 18 months, I thought, 'I can't do this'. I got hold of some guy who was taking a band out to Dubai and they were just covering the pops. I thought, 'That'll get me back on drums – I'll do that for now'. So I did that and somehow we ended up in Blackpool. After about a year with this band I decided I had to move on because it was pretty boring."

Jack heard that the Charles Barlow Orchestra, who were the resident band at the Tower Ballroom in Blackpool, were looking for a singer. "Well I've always been able to sing so I went along, auditioned and got the job," he says. "So from there I become a vocalist in the Tower Ballroom singing with a big band – 14 guys." As there was already a Jack Jones who was well known as a singer in much the same vein, an identity switch was required: "I changed my name to Jack Hardy. I needed something simple because, being from a drums background, you're not very outgoing so I had to overcome that. I thoroughly enjoyed it. Great guys to work with."

With his foot in the door, Jack could now get other work in the same style. "An old friend of mine had a band at a big cabaret place at Luton," he says, "and he offered me the job as resident singer with his band. I went down there for about a year. That brought me back into London where I carried on doing clubs, some of the better pubs and stuff like this.

"For a while I met up with a girl named Annie Britton and we formed a boy-girl duo. That was lovely as well…lasted about five years." In the small world of showbusiness, Jack's success became known to Bob via a photograph at a venue he was playing. "I was doing the northern club circuit, which I still do, and I looked on the dressing-room wall," says Bob. "I'm looking at the photograph and I thought, 'Hang on, that's Jack Jones'. He was stood behind a drum kit, on his own, (in) a dinner suit."

In the beginning, it was Eddie Phillips – the most talented person to have passed through The Creation's ranks – who was the least successful of the ex-personnel, although he was no longer striving to succeed. Upon leaving TNT, the desire to be a professional musician gradually drained from him. Session work was not an option, even though Talmy loyally tried to put some his way. "I did a few sessions with Shel Talmy but I was never a good reader and that was the problem," Eddie says. "I used to have to get the song a long way in advance and learn it by ear. I could read the chord charts but wasn't an instant reader, whereas some of the guys on the session wouldn't even have heard the song before. They'd come in, (see) the sheet of paper, sit down and play it. I used to have to listen to it and feel my way through it." He says he didn't think about setting up a new band. Would he have contemplated joining an existing band? Eddie: "If somebody had asked me, I would have really thought about it – providing I could have done my thing."

It's interesting that, around the time of the start of Eddie's drifting away from music, a vacancy occurred in a group who would almost certainly have allowed a guitarist of Eddie's ability and credentials to do his 'thing'. In January 1969, Steve Marriott had departed the Small Faces, leaving those brilliant practitioners of soul, pop, rock, psychedelia and music-hall in need of a guitarist and vocalist. Eddie could have certainly filled one of those roles, possibly – remembering his fine singing on 'Can I Join Your Band' – both.

His penchant for fine melody and coruscating guitarwork were in the best Small Faces tradition and the fact that, like two-thirds of the remaining members, he was also an East End boy would have helped him fit in. However, the Small Faces were probably barely aware of Eddie's existence. "I would have liked that but it never happened and I was never asked," he says. "You need to be asked to do things." At that level anyway.

Around this time, Kenny's old employer Neil Christian approached Eddie about joining his band, but he declined.

After fulfilling his commitments with TNT, Eddie decided on a complete change of lifestyle. "When that folded I just thought, 'I've been on the road most of the Sixties. We were coming up to 1969 and things were changing. I thought, 'Am I really happy with all this?" he recalls. "'Well, maybe I'm not…I'll try something completely different. Go off and see what the other side of life is like'. And that's what I did. Just done a couple of day jobs. Nothing fantastic but it was a different way of life, met different kinds of people in the real world. I made lots of good friends and (met) my wife."

Bob theorises on Eddie's retirement: "I got the feeling that he felt that he'd been dealt a bad hand and he didn't want to go down that road again, knowing what the experience is. His first marriage had broken up and he had two children from that. Maybe there was quite a few things. He wanted perhaps to get on the straight and narrow. I think that happens in a lot of those Sixties things: it's like, 'Now hang on, that was wild – let's get back to reality'." A comment Eddie made to *Blitz* seems to bear out some of what Bob suggests. "I really turned my back on music," said the guitarist. "I subconsciously blamed it for messing up my first marriage."

The day jobs Eddie mentions didn't include the Dagenham production line ("Mad idea," he now says) but, for those who were of the opinion that he was one of the greatest guitarists of his generation, they were no more appropriate. Eddie applied for work to London Transport and was rewarded with a job as bus driver, which he maintained for nine years. "I thought I'd do it three or four months," he says. "I was always nuts about vehicles. I always had a thing about buses. I used to like the early buses, like the RTs and that. I was a bit of an anorak really.

The best bus was the Routemaster. That was a nice vehicle. You still see 'em now. The funny thing was, I only went on it for a bit of laugh. But I met some nice people and you just got into it and I found I was able to start playing again." (When Eddie met his present wife in 1969 – they were married in '71 – such was his disillusionment with music that for a while she had no inkling he could play guitar.) "I always had an acoustic guitar at home that I would pick up and have a little plonk," he says, "but because I was doing shift work, I was getting a bit of time on my hands and started (to) make a bit of noise again."

For those wondering whether they might have been a passenger on a bus Eddie was steering during those nine years, he drove the 38. "Goes up to Victoria. Went to Leyton, went up to Victoria, right the way through the West End. I used to have to go round Hyde Park Corner in the rush hour with the bus full of people." Some of his ex-passengers might have unhappy memories of being on one of his buses. "I always had my head full of music when I was driving," he remembers, "and used to have a little dictation tape recorder in the top pocket of my jacket. Often I'd go down the street singing ideas for songs in this little dictation machine.

"I sometimes used to get really carried away and forget what route I was supposed to be on and take the bus on a different route completely! People used to jump off thinking they'd got on the wrong bus, I'm sure. I had to go in all the back streets try and find my way back to where I was supposed to be going. People (who'd) get on my bus used to do a magical mystery tour." Would Eddie say he was happy or unhappy during those nine years? "Most of the time I was pretty happy. Some guys who drive buses – not being unkind – they were bus drivers. I was a guitar player being a bus driver."

Despite his protestations of happiness and his undoubted modesty, it seems rather odd that during the whole of the nine years he was with London Transport Eddie admits he never at any point told any of his colleagues he had once been in a band that appeared on *Ready, Steady, Go!* or had played on the same bill as the Rolling Stones. Jack certainly read something akin to a sadness when the two bumped into each other in the early Seventies. "He had his busman's uniform on and he didn't know where to look," remembers Jack. "It was a real embarrassment. I just went, 'Oh hello, great to see you'. 'Oh hello Jack, blah blah blah'. But I think he was embarrassed. He didn't invite me home. We were only about 200 yards from where he lived but he didn't invite me back."

At that point in time Eddie's options were no better than any of the working-class lads who drove the Routemasters on all the other paths. Without the inclination or heart to assemble another band and without the sight-reading ability necessary to acquire session work, his brilliance on the guitar was almost worthless . Unlike some musicians from the Sixties, Eddie couldn't even trade on a legend, or even nostalgia. As The Creation had never had any bona fide UK hits, the option of the cabaret circuit was not open to him. Of course, that wasn't necessarily the case in West Germany, but Eddie's subconscious would have quickly brushed off any thoughts about trying to exploit that market: foreign travel had already wrecked one of his marriages and, at that point, his happy marriage was probably the only unalloyed joy he had in life.

However, contact from Shel Talmy made Eddie's prospects a little brighter. Eddie: "About '73-74, Shel Talmy called me up and said 'Do you want to come back in the studio and make some more music?'" Initially, this project was going to involve Kenny Pickett. In his 1982 *Blitz* interview – in which he dated Talmy's approach to him as 1975 – Eddie recalled, "He (Talmy) convinced me it was a good idea to run up some songs. Kenny didn't follow it through and I ended up writing them on my own." Talmy liked what he heard and suggested Eddie make a solo album. He also had a suggestion about who should fund its release: none other than Tony Stratton-Smith.

By this point in time, fortunes had swung rather sharply for the once financially embarrassed former Creation manager. Gail Colson – who, after leaving Talmy's employ, went on to work for Strat – recalls him regretting that he'd ever decided to become a manager. "At one point," she says, "he had cash-flow problems and wrote a book for Shel. He was threatening to get out of the business until The Nice and The Bonzo Dog Band came along." It was the success of those two clients that enabled Stratton-Smith to stick with rock management, but it was Genesis who ultimately reaffirmed his choice of career path. This progressive rock outfit – whose name was uncannily similar in meaning to that of The Creation, although as they were named by pop mogul Jonathan King this is clearly coincidence – became one of the biggest acts in the world during the Seventies. In a financial double whammy, their wares were released on his own Charisma label, founded in 1969.

When Eddie and Stratton-Smith met to discuss the idea of a solo project, it was the first time the two had crossed paths since Strat's acrimonious parting from The Creation in early 1967. Clearly, having his album released on Charisma would have been something of a coup for Eddie: it must have felt to him at the time that all the bad times and frustrations experienced though The Creation were to be validated. It was possibly this that prompted Eddie to forget the reason for them jettisoning their former manager, although it's just as likely due to his non-confrontational nature.

The sessions with Talmy produced some good material. None of it was really in the barrier-smashing mould of The Creation's songs – but then, come 1973-74, just about all of rock'n'roll's barriers had already been smashed. The mood was now to make music in a conventional mould to as high a standard as possible. One of Eddie's songs from these sessions, was 'City Woman', a respectable uptempo rock song that was nevertheless so conventional as to approach the generic. 'Change My Ways' was a reflective country song, while 'Duckin' And Weavin'' was a fine working man's lament with brass and string parts and a gritty vocal.

Meanwhile, 'Limbo Jimbo' saw Eddie trying out reggae grooves and a Jamaican accent on a song whose melody sounded somewhat familiar. "That was a bit of down time in the studio and we just started a reggae thing," Eddie recalls. "Then I ended up singing this melody which was very much like 'Painter Man'. A lot of songs actually start off that way, as a bit of a kickaround." Eddie considers 'Limbo Jimbo' to be not much above the level of a joke, "like Chuck Berry's 'My Ding A Ling'. That wasn't a serious attempt at a record."

Unfortunate then that this was the only product of the sessions that saw release on Charisma. "As the sessions were nearing completion they had this big record-company panic 'cos they weren't making the money they thought they were and my project got chopped." It must have been sickening for the guitarist to find another chance at stardom being snatched away from him. Asked if the affair was disappointing, he merely says, "Yeah. But by that time I was used to it."

Having to return to London Transport was a pain that was, perhaps, slightly alleviated by the fact that the Charisma episode did at least lead to some musical exposure. Tony Stratton-Smith decided to facilitate the release of the first ever album of Creation material in the band's home country. The album rather pointedly featured only material from the Eddie Phillips era of The Creation, hence its title '66-67'. Released on Charisma's Perspective label in July 1973, it contained 'Making Time', 'Life Is Just Beginning', 'If I Stay Too Long', 'Through My Eyes', 'Hey Joe', 'Painter Man', 'Cool Jerk', 'How Does It Feel To Feel (UK version)', 'Try And Stop Me', 'Can I Join Your Band' and 'Tom Tom'.

The exclusion of 'Biff Bang Pow' and 'Nightmares' in favour of covers from the 'We Are Paintermen' album is irritating, and it's a pity – if understandable – that the UK version of 'How Does It Feel To Feel' was chosen. However, Charisma redeemed themselves by including 'I Am The Walker', a track that had never previously turned up anywhere. The album had an eye-catching, if meaningless, cover designed by Hipgnosis – then one of the hottest names in LP design – which featured the rear view of a naked female apparently playing bowls.

Bob wasn't even aware of the release of the album, while Jack only learned of it when he saw an advertisement in the *NME*. "Nobody told me or asked me or anything like that," Jack says. "My opinion apparently didn't count. The advert made me smile. From about 1967-68, everything become stereo and Tony had sold this thing as being in glorious mono, which I thought was a bit piss-taking. I was quite amused by it. I thought, 'Oh great. You never know. Might see a few bob royalties one day'." And did he? "I don't think from that album."

Two months later, a single followed on Charisma which coupled the band's two British semi-hits, 'Making Time' and 'Painter Man'. The Phillips solo material, however, did not find itself on Charisma's release schedules until 1976, when 'Limbo Jimbo' b/w 'Change My Ways' was issued under the name 'Eddy Phillips'. In the meantime, Talmy approached Casablanca Records and managed to secure a 1977 release for 'City Woman' b/w 'Duckin' And Weavin'" in both the US and Germany, this time credited to Eddie with the proper spelling.

"I kind of like that," says Eddie of 'City Woman', while Talmy says "I thought (it) was a fabulous song. It made some noise but never got anywhere. I still love that record." Perhaps significantly, no British company in the year of punk found the Americanisms of 'City Woman' deserving of release. However, it was surely the new-wave zeitgeist that led to punk label Raw deciding to licence 'Making Time' and 'Painter Man' and put them on either side of a single in November of that year. (Figureheads of the punk movement the Sex Pistols would play a version of 'Through My Eyes' at rehearsals.)

None of this, of course, affected Eddie's day-to-day life and he was still obliged to carry on driving a bus. This only changed when one day in 1978, Eddie walked into his living room to be told by his wife that, while watching a trailer for a BBC light-entertainment show, she'd seen "Boney M singing one of your songs." "I said, 'Are you sure?' She said, 'Yeah, I think it's that one that goes Painter Man, Painter Man.' I said, 'Yeah that's right, that's one of mine'."

Kenny Pickett had an almost identical experience. "I was sitting downstairs watching *Top Of The Pops*," he recounted to *Blitz*. "Just after it came off, a trailer came up for *Seaside Special*, the Saturday evening variety show. Boney M came on and they were playing this song. I thought to myself, 'It's a pinch from something.' I was trying to think what song it was a pinch from. It didn't occur to me at the time at all. Then suddenly I realised that it was 'Painter Man'! The following day I was making phone calls to everybody to try and find out what was going on."

Boney M were, at that stage, one of the world's most successful recording acts. They started life as a vocal group manufactured by

German record producer Frank Farian to promote a studio concoction called 'Baby Do You Wanna Bump?'.

The Boney M line-up Farian eventually settled on was Marcia Barrett, Liz Mitchell, Maizie Williams and Bobby Farrell. The latter, in fact, didn't actually sing the male vocal parts on Boney M records; these were laid down by Farian himself. Though that first record attributed to the group did not sell, 'Daddy Cool', 'Sunny', 'Ma Baker' and 'Belfast' were all Top 10 UK hits in 1977. In Germany, where Boney M were a phenomenon, all those singles topped the charts. It wasn't to be until '78 that that similar status was attained in Britain. In the first half of that year, they released 'Rivers of Babylon', a cover of a song by the Melodians featured on the soundtrack to the Jimmy Cliff movie *The Harder They Come*.

Having topped the UK charts for five weeks, DJs flipped the disc over and began playing the other face, a nonsense nursery rhyme-style track called 'Brown Girl In The Ring' which promptly climbed to Number 10 under its own steam, making the pairing the biggest-selling UK single that year. The group had two further UK chart smashes in '78 in the form of 'Rasputin' and Christmas Number 1 'Mary's Boy Child – Oh My Lord'.

In many ways, Boney M's massive success was incomprehensible. Not that their records were not well-crafted and fun, in the best bubblegum (or, indeed, disco, with which their records were inflected) tradition. Yet, they were a recording ensemble with no personality. They played no instruments, relied on outsiders for their material and recorded tracks with no linking thread other than their commerciality. They also looked absurd. That millions of individuals were going out and purchasing their product couldn't be disputed, but it was impossible to conceive of Boney M inspiring adoration or loyalty among those purchasers.

Eddie and Kenny, naturally, were not going to agonise over any possible lack of artistic integrity. 'Painter Man' – which made its UK chart debut in March 1979 – was actually the lowest-charting UK Boney M single to date (and wasn't released in Germany at all). In fact, in reaching a 'mere' Number 10 it marked the beginning of a decline in Boney M's fortunes which was only briefly revived by the Top 3 success of the following single 'Hooray Hooray It's A Holi-Holiday'. However, 'Painter Man' had featured on 'Night Flight To Venus', the album that spawned 'Rivers Of Babylon', 'Brown Girl In The Ring', and 'Rasputin'. Inevitably, the album sold by the bucketload (at least seven million worldwide) and, of course, the division of an album's songwriting royalties does not discriminate between the hits and tracks of lesser interest to purchasers that merely happened to reside on it.

Joe Foster, The Creation's comeback producer, later found out why Boney M recorded the song. "Apparently one of the guys who used to be in The Smoke worked with Frank Farian's production company. He had suggested it might be a good idea. Basically Frank Farian, being of the right age to remember these songs being hits in Germany – they (Boney M) did (The Smoke's) 'My Friend Jack' as well – remembered seeing these bands on television and being really excited and thought, 'Well, you know what, they're bloody good songs. I think we should do them'."

The member of The Smoke – contemporaries of The Creation and another brilliant, neglected UK pop band who achieved success mainly in Germany – Foster refers to is bassist Zeke Lund, but he doesn't seem to have particularly strong memories of the decision to record 'Painter Man'. "I recorded most of the Boney M backing tracks at what was once Union Studios in Munich," he says. "Frank then took the tapes up to Frankfurt for the dubs and mixes. I could well have recorded the basics for 'Painter Man' but have no specific memories." (Farian himself didn't respond to an interview request for this book.)

Kenny, of course, was slightly more used than Eddie to the financial windfall that a hit record produces, which is probably why Eddie still marvels of the whole experience, "Little bit of a fairy story." His reaction is understandable: after having gone through two crushing experiences where dreams and achievements swayed so tantalisingly within reach only to be whipped away again, he found that fortune had come his way without him even trying.

"The very fact they'd done that, financially helped me to really seriously get back into music again, that was the over-riding thing for us," he says. "It was unbelievable, 'cos I think the album sold, worldwide, millions. I was able then to start writing again in a serious way and devote a lot of time to it and start playing again and that's what I've been doing ever since. Changed the direction of our lives, which I've got to be grateful for."

"That was good, that was very nice," says Talmy, another financial beneficiary of the record. "From a publishing royalty point of view, it was extremely nice. The lady who handles my stuff called and told me they'd decided to do it. It's a surprise in a way that any of these things were covered although I know a lot of people thought about it and of course things have been covered since. But they were so, I thought, uniquely Creation that they'd be difficult for anybody else to cover. Boney M did a damn good job of it, I thought."

Glen Colson points out that the windfall may not have been as much as people assume: "I don't know how much (Kenny) would have made from it 'cos the deals they did way back in those days with Shel Talmy and publishers and things, they would have been ripped off wholesale. So by the time one publisher collects it, gives it to another publisher, they take their cut then it gets back to England, they wouldn't have been on proper money. I don't recall Kenny ever making absolutely millions on it. I can remember Kenny saying that he didn't make that much...I would say maybe twenty or thirty grand."

Not that it mattered much in comparison to the money earned and the doors it opened, but both Kenny and Eddie were impressed by Boney M's rendition. Though it is slightly passionless in marked contrast to the anguish of the original – how could it not be when sung by a woman with no change of gender? – it is an impressively brisk, hi-hat-heavy and completely dance-orientated rendition. The phrase 'women's books' is dropped from the lyric but – just as on The Creation's single – a strangulated segment of 'Mona Lisa' closes the record, the latter seeming like an affectionate wink from Farian in the direction of the original.

"The way they'd done it, they'd done a good job on it as a disco song of the time and I'd never have dreamed that you could have done it that way," notes Eddie. Presumably referring to the wiggly little lick that preceded each verse, Kenny opined to *Blitz*, "They copied it note for note. The only thing they put in which we didn't have in was the guitar riff."

Bob and Jack were intrigued by the release but, because they were not its composers and stood to make no money from it, were understandably not as excited as Eddie and Kenny. Bob: "I was in Warrington playing with Smiley and we were doing the northern club circuit. I thought, 'Great', but it didn't make me feel any different. I think what happened was, (we were big) in Germany and Boney M started in Germany. The fact that it's not been played in this country much, people didn't know the difference, did they? They got the Boney M version first."

Says Jack, "If you listen to what they did with 'Painter Man', they turned it into a happy little pop song, so I supposed they just made it more commercial. 'cos it had a good catch on it: 'Painter man, painter man, who would be a painter man?' They just lightened it up and turned it into a little pop song and probably appealed to the general public more than our version, which was a bit heavier, or it was handled better commercially. They were doing very well at the time: anything they (put out) would get played on the radio and stuff."

The Boney M cover prompted Kenny to ring Jack to sound him out about the possibility of exploiting the potential new interest and putting The Creation back together. Explains Jack, "Kenny rung me up when I was in Morecambe. Well I seem to have had a bit of a chip on my shoulder at the time 'cos it always seemed that whenever there was any royalties around they seemed to get shared out between Bob (*sic*) and Eddie and I didn't get too much. I didn't think there'd be much in it for me. And I was in the middle of basically building a nice little career for myself on my own. So I said, 'I'm working every night of the week. I'm earning brilliant money. And it's a new thing in a way for me, it's like a new challenge in my music career and I want to see it through'. He said, 'Okay, well I'll get back to you'. I never heard any more." One wonders whether this knockback is what motivated Kenny's subsequent mean-spirited comments in *Blitz* – only four years later – when he described Jack as "the worst drummer in the world."

Jack adds of the proposed '78 reunion, "I don't think it would have come off then, quite honestly. It weren't right. Eddie weren't right for a start. He was still messing around." Not that Jack was insensitive to the commercial potential of such a reunion: it was obvious that an era was dawning in which a new lease of life was possible to those Sixties artists who wanted it. Jack: "I think Kenny realised there might have been something out there for us if we'd have reformed, because a few bands reformed. One of the funny things was of the Sixties, when it got to the end of the Sixties you presumed everybody was going to break up. It was like, 'Yeah, that's it man. it's run it's course'.

"The Beatles broke up. The Stones were in a terrible mess financially and nobody knew what they were gonna do. But then we suddenly found that, in spite of everybody being financially ripped off and skint and all the rest of it, The Kinks kept going, The Who kept going, The Stones kept going. When you're 25, you think 'Yeah, I'm a rock'n'roller'. When you get to 30, you start thinking, 'I'm getting a bit old for this'. And suddenly you realise you're not and you can carry on – people still pay money to come and see you and listen to you. And you can do a good job."

A kind of Creation reunion did indeed happen as a consequence of the Boney M cover. Although Eddie can't remember a full-scale reunion being discussed at this juncture, he and Kenny drifted back into a writing partnership. (Perhaps significantly, Bob seems to be the only member of the original Creation line-up to whom Kenny did not speak or make an overture in the wake of the Boney M cover.) The two secured a publishing deal with the Jet label, with whom they also released a couple of singles under the name Kennedy Express (Ken-Eddie Express).

In a curious twist of fate, the Boney M cover put the kibosh on a cover of 'Painter Man' by punk outfit the Bernie Tormé Band. The titular Irish guitarist had suggested 'Painter Man' – which he had loved as a teenager – after Jet, to whom he was signed, had asked if he was willing to cover something following two self-composed flop singles. Tormé had been unaware that Pickett and Phillips were working for Jet and had happily agreed when the company suggested they produce the cover.

Tormé told journalist Mark A Johnston that, following the unexpected Boney M intervention, "Ken and Eddie suggested 'Making Time', which I did not know. Again a great track, maybe not quite as good as 'Painter Man', but still brilliant. When it came to record it, (Jet) wanted more chorus and more hooks, which was the fashion of the time but which I did not like 'cos it took it away from that cool thing that it originally had. But we did it anyway because we were told to. Our version was not very good, not a patch on theirs, and I don't even have a copy of it. The record company never put it out. Ken and Eddie were both really nice guys. As I remember, Ken was more involved in the production."

Tormé would eventually become perceived more as a heavy metaller than a punk, enjoying a stint in Gillan. Following his departure from that group, he recorded a solo album 'Turn Out The Lights' (1982) and, during its gestation, decided to have another crack at 'Painter Man'. "I wanted to do 'Painter Man', because I felt I had been pushed into doing 'Making Time' under the 'Do a commercial single' circumstances which resulted in something no-one liked," he told Johnston. "So I did 'Painter Man', hoping it would sell loads. It almost charted, but not quite. It wasn't a patch on the original. Less raw, overproduced. I don't really like it. That's how it goes sometimes. You can't beat perfect, and the original was." 'Turn Out The Lights' also featured a track called 'Try And Stop Me', although it wasn't The Creation song of that name.

It was also Jet who in November '78 prepared for release, under the name Men Of Steel, Eddie's solo single 'Hail Superman' b/w 'Keep On Movin' To The Music'. At one point it had been hoped that the A-side might be used in *Superman: The Movie*, released that year. Talmy: "I was very friendly with (director) Dick Donner at the time and got Eddie to write a song as a potential song for the film. It wasn't right for the film but it was a really good song."

Eddie believes "Business got in the way of that one. The song was quite wacky, really, but I don't know what went wrong. The song was good enough. They could easily have slotted it in there. Maybe not use my recording but as a song they could have put it in there somewhere. Maybe they didn't want to pay any outside royalties."

Talmy's analysis seems more likely to be correct. Eddie's song has the smack of a novelty record with its repetition of slogans from *Superman* comic books and the old cinema serials. Such a jokey song would not have fitted the rather stern-browed ambience of *Superman: The Movie*. Because of the absence of the Warner studio's blessing and attendant copyright problems, the Men Of Steel single never achieved commercial release, though Jet promo copies exist.

The first Kennedy Express single was released on Jet in June 1979: 'Little Lolita' b/w 'Stop Stop Stop' actually attracted some significant media interest, becoming Radio One DJ Paul Burnett's Record Of The Week even though it was of no great quality. Another Pickett/Phillips collaboration from this period, 'Teacher, Teacher', ended up a Canadian Top 10 hit for Rockpile in 1980 and even brushed the US Top 50. "Kenny was friends with Billy Bremner, the guitar player and knew Nick (Lowe) as well," explains Eddie.

The other Kennedy Express single came out in 1980 and combined 'Is There Life On Earth' with 'Stop Stop Stop' and 'Little Lolita'. The new track on the A-side was a galloping and melodic number that was not a million miles from the kind of airbrushed, futuristic-but-not-synthy pop that Duran Duran would soon be purveying. Eddie: "It was something I recorded here (at home) and we went to a studio and put live drums on it and I done it on a four-track and that's where I first met Steve Lipson. He was the engineer in the studio at the time. Steve was (a) fantastic engineer, had loads of great ideas. I told him I wanted this (effect). The voice thing on the end of 'Is There Life On Earth', a kind of progressive counterpart harmony, he figured it all out. I just told him what I thought might be good and he was like a wizard, figured it all and did it. It was great."

Also in 1980, a planned Kenny Pickett single co-written by Eddie and Kenny got as far as the promo stage: 'Got A Gun' appeared on F Beat with both sides featuring the same track. An exciting and gritty tale of a desperado with a crackling atmosphere and an impressive vocal attack, it's something of a shame that it never acquired a commercial release. "We enjoyed that time," says Eddie of this period. "The records we had out were songs I put together in my little studio at home and then went in the studio and added live drums because we couldn't quite duplicate that sound. We tried but the demo always sounded better."

He admits the way he was having success by proxy through other artists' interpretations of his songs was making him inclined to settle for being a songwriter. Eddie: "It does colour your thinking. You've got to think, 'There is a way you can make a career out of music without actually being 'The One'. In a way, it's a lot nicer because it's great to write successful songs for people and nobody knows who you are." 1980 also, peculiarly, saw the first album appearance of the Mark Four's 'Hurt Me If You Will' which appeared on a Decca-released Various Artists compilation inaccurately titled 'Mersey Sounds'.

The following year Eddie attempted to take advantage of the Space Invaders arcade-game craze with a single on the US Plantation label: 'Space Invaders' b/w 'Penny Arcade' credited to Eddie and The Players. The same year saw the release (in France only) of a brand new single credited to The Creation. However 'Alpha Beta' b/w 'Man In The Mist', released on the Trema label, was an Eddie Phillips record and one whose sound could not have been at a greater remove from his former band.

The two songs were the only ones ever released from a very ambitious album project of Eddie's called 'The Mitra' (although the back cover of the French single declares 'Extrait de l'album Armageddon' and the proposed album also seems to have been referred to at one point as 'The War Of The Worlds'). "I was working with Steven Lipson on this project," says Eddie. "It was a kind of concept album. I like the Latin language and I had this vision: it was almost like early church music – like 'Evensong' and 'Plainsong' – put to a rock beat and with a mystery about it. I can never really explain the concept to this day but I really felt it strong. It's a weird album. I was singing throughout the tracks on it but then we were tracking up this big Latin chants on it."

'The Mitra' was recorded over the course of what seems to be several years (the booklet made available at the Mark Four reunion gig in '85 made reference to a plan to release it that very year). There were at least 12 tracks completed. It is certainly a strange hybrid with the kind of doomy, massed monk-like chants in which The Yardbirds once specialised sitting cheek-by-jowl with galloping synthesiser music reminiscent of Jean-Michel Jarre's 'Oxygene' and Eighties pop. It's alternately powerful and irritating but always novel.

Eddie elaborated on the project to Mike Griffiths of the World of Eddie Phillips and The Creation website in late 2003: "I did the work with Steve over a couple of years altogether but that included all the writing I did at home in my spare time. We recorded a lot of it in a studio in

Knightsbridge. Think it was around the early to mid Eighties. Just before we got to finish it properly, Steve got asked to record Frankie Goes To Hollywood, which was a huge band in the making, so he had to stop our thing to do that. Unfortunately, it stopped at that point and never got finished. Don't know how those tracks ever got released in France. This is the first I've heard of that and why it was under the Creation name, heaven knows! But it just shows you that nothing is sacred in the music business and people will exploit anything – even a half-finished project!

"At that time, we couldn't do anything with it because the criticism was it was too far outside of pop," says Eddie of the Mitra. "It was left in a state of almost finished, it needed remixing. That's how it is to this day." If this was another deep disappointment for Eddie in his dealings with the music industry, worse was to come. "Jonathan Rowlands was funding that and he sold the publishing to (a) big German publisher. A few years later an act came out of Germany called Enigma and did this kind of thing. He basically nicked my idea of using this influence in singing and style of singing but he put it to a disco beat. That's another one of my ideas that got ripped off. I had a track on that album called 'Enigma' and he called his band Enigma. I look back on things like that and I think, 'What's the point?' You do things and maybe they're a little bit before their time and it gets rejected. Somewhere down the line someone gets an idea for something else – like a spin-off – and makes fortunes out of it."

Eddie could at least console himself to some extent with the fact that in 1984, The Shadows – featuring Hank Marvin, Britain's first guitar God – recorded one of his compositions. "I'd written some music that went underneath a poem," says Eddie. "It was a poem by Elizabeth Browning and it was called 'How Do I Love Thee'. It's a very popular poem. (It was sent) to Bruce Welch as an instrumental, they liked it and they did it on one of the albums which was called 'Guardian Angels'."

September 1982 saw a further indication of the growing reputation of The Creation with the release by UK label Edsel of the compilation 'How Does It Feel To Feel', only the second ever Creation album in the band's home country and one which, coming almost a decade after the first one, helped acquaint a whole new generation with their music.

One such member of the new generation was a 21-year-old Scot and aspiring pop star named Alan McGee. He had first heard of The Creation three years previously. "1979, when I was 18," he explains. "Basically it was a sleeve of 'All Mod Cons' by The Jam. It just said 'The Creation – Biff Bang Pow'. It was on the vinyl and it was like a little seven-inch single and it intrigued me." McGee had to wait until the release of the 'How Does It Feel To Feel' compilation to hear this band whose name and song title had intrigued him.

"It was just punky," says McGee of the music he heard on the album in question. "It was psychedelic punk rock but I hadn't articulated that in my head. I really loved that record. It had all the hits on it – or all the would-be hits – 'How Does It Feel To Feel' and blah blah blah. And that's how I got into them. It's one of these things that you thought you should have known for years. And it was very unfashionable then to be into that kind of music. Now it's incredibly fashionable to like psychedelic garage rock but 1981, man, you either had to be into the Three Johns and the Membranes and pure indie rock (I don't even know in 1981 if there was such a thing as indie rock – there was independent labels, there wasn't even a sound I suppose) or you were in the world of mainstream pop music, Kajagoogoo and rubbish like that." Within 12 years, it would be McGee himself who would be helping bring The Creation's music to yet another generation.

The Edsel compilation appeared just at the dawn of the archival boom that, two decades later, is such a cornerstone of the modern music industry. In a precursor of the kind of deluxe and fact-packed packaging that would be such a part of the archive industry, the Edsel album featured a 12-inch-square four-page insert. Nothing remarkable from today's perspective, but still unusual in a day and age where the staff of record companies were often hangovers from the Sixties with a contempt for the product they were purveying and an attendant disinterest in contextualising and analysing it.

The fact that such people weren't in charge of this project but instead the generation of people who had been consumers in the Sixties was underlined by the fact that the album featured – indeed, opened with – the US version of 'How Does It Feel To Feel'. The compilers of the '73 Planet compilation probably hadn't even known this track existed. Additional kudos go to the compilers for unearthing the never previously released 'Ostrich Man'. The sequencing is good too: purists might quibble at the non-chronological track-listing but a better album-opener (and introduction to The Creation's music) than 'How Does It Feel To Feel' is difficult to imagine, while the double-time climax of 'Can I Join Your Band' makes it an ideal closer.

However, there's still a couple of black marks to be handed out: the exclusion of 'If I Stay Too Long' (an omission the sleeve notes virtually make a virtue of) is illogical – all other A and B-sides of the British singles (except for 'How Does It Feel To Feel', represented in its superior US version) are included and, in light of the inclusion of 'Cool Jerk', knuckle-headed. (The same company at least made up for this by making 'If I Stay Too Long' one of the bonus tracks on their 1990 CD reissue of this collection.)

Around the time the latter CD reissue appeared, Jack became a little happier with the way the royalties were divided. "Kenny went up and did a deal with Shel," he says. "The whole package was that Shel would get 50 per cent and he would do the manufacturing and all the rest of it and the other 50 percent would be split equally between five members of the band. That included Kim. So there was none of this somebody getting a bit more than anybody else, which builds up resentment. (This was in the) late Eighties, maybe 1990."

Bob found the publishing arrangements for the songs a little complicated. "He sold the publishing," he says of Talmy. "Other people have got the titles now. But I think he retains a percentage of them. They're all with different companies. They're all over the place. Shel had 50 per cent to play about with. So if he sold them to EMI or whoever and retained 25 per cent, plus whatever he sold them for, he's still okay, isn't he?"

There were some more interesting archival Creation-related releases in 1983, both on France's Eva Records. A Various Artists compilation 'The Sound Of The Sixties' saw the first appearance of The Creation's live performance of 'That's How Strong My Love Is' from *Beat Beat Beat* in 1966. Even more interesting was the compilation 'The Mark Four/The Creation' which contained a sprinkling of Creation tracks and all eight commercially released tracks from the band out of which they grew. 'Rock Around The Clock', 'Slow Down', 'Try It Baby', 'Crazy Country Hop', 'I'm Leaving', 'Work All Day (Sleep All Night)' and 'Going Down Fast' made their first ever album appearances. Eva tried their best to be comprehensive, to such an extent that – believing a couple of inaccurate magazine articles that said they were connected to The Mark Four – they threw on 'Baby What's Wrong' b/w 'Tango' by the unrelated Mark Five.

John Dalton is amused at the existence of this and other, later albums that collected The Mark Four's records. "People must be mad," he says. "'cos they were so badly made. It seems strange to me that people are putting them on a CD." Consistent, however, with his belief that The Mark Four were "Something to watch, rather than just listen to", Dalton had no problem with people wanting to see The Mark Four live – even 20 years after they'd split up. On 18 January 1985, The Mark Four played a one-off gig for charity at Wolsey Hall, Cheshunt.

Dalton had lost touch with most of his old colleagues in The Mark Four since leaving the group. In 1978, he began arranging musical events in aid of leukaemia charities. "I thought a good (person) to help would be Eddie, see what he's doing," he recalls. "But he wasn't playing. He was driving a bus at the time. I rang Eddie up. We got him over just to play a bit of rock'n'roll. I done a couple of gigs like that. That's when I got Jimmy Virgo back for just another part of it. Just to do the leukaemia stuff. And that's when the old boys started getting back together again. After that, people wanted to book us. We went back to the old days of Jimmy Virgo singing, Eddie playing guitar." The reunion of The Bluejacks merged into a band called Cuckoo's Nest.

The idea for a reunion of The Mark Four came from Rod Siebke. "I was seeing the band quite a bit", says Siebke, "John and Eddie anyway, who was playing with the Cuckoo's Nest, and I put it to them that it might be a nice idea to put the band together for a one-off gig. And they went away and talked about it, come back and said, 'Yes, let's go for it'. I'd met Kenny once during that point. He'd turned up at a gig." It was decided that the line-up would be the longest-running one of Eddie, Jack, Kenny, Dalton and Mick Thompson.

"I'd been playing with Ed for a few years," says Dalton. "That was the good thing: at least two of us had been playing together and could read each other like a book. We both knew exactly what each other was going to do next, or we wouldn't have been able to do The Mark Four. We wouldn't have been able to get together and play after not seeing each other for years but, because two of us had played that often together, it worked." The Wolsey Hall, Cheshunt – scene of so many of The Mark Four's gigs and the band's original hometown venue – was the natural setting for the occasion. "We rehearsed them for about seven nights," recalls Siebke. "That was at the Britannia pub in Waltham Cross. They were going from dire to very good. Kenny hadn't sung on stage for years. Mick Thompson hadn't really had a lot (of practice). In fact, he didn't even have a guitar at the time. He was a roofer. He was playing at home a little bit but not anything special. It was the end of '84 and we rehearsed 'em and got 'em as good as we could and then in early '85 we had the gig."

Dalton noticed a profound change in the character of Kenny, the man who in the Sixties had a propensity to 'jump into something with both feet'.

"I think at the time he was more or less being a house-husband," Dalton says. "Obviously, it's going to change him. Eddie and I used to run a club Friday nights, rock'n'roll club, and Ken used to come down sometimes. First few times down there, we couldn't even get him up on stage. He'd lost that confidence. He was a lot quieter." Though the 300 or so people packed into the Wolsey Hall on the night of 18 January was a far smaller attendance than some of those to which Kenny had played in the Sixties, Dalton reveals that the prospect of walking out in front of them terrified him: "Ken was a nervous wreck," he says.

In fact, Kenny was talking of walking out and going home. Siebke: "Me and him had real words because he wasn't prepared to go on stage. So I sat down and got him drunk enough to go on. He really was concerned about it." Once onstage, however, things went well, partly because the gig had been so well promoted. Siebke: "We really did go to town on asking all the right people and putting the word around. We got mentions in *Sounds*. There was quite a mod sort of group that used to hang around and we got connected with them and word got out with them. It was really well pushed. We had people come from as far as Liverpool and Cornwall."

The Mark Four tore through 'I'm A Man', 'That's How Strong My Love Is', 'Shame Shame Shame', 'Hurt Me If You Will', 'The House Of The Rising Sun', 'Around And Around', 'Mona', 'Hoochie Coochie Man', 'Walking The Dog', 'In The Midnight Hour', 'Painter Man', 'Johnny B Goode' and 'Got My Mojo Working'. Of course, it was the signature extended version of 'Mona', with double drumming, feedback and violin bow, that was performed. "The idea on the night (was) we were going to have two violin bows," explains Dalton of the recital of that song. "I was going to start off with one as well before I got on the drums. So Eddie got two violin bows, one for him, one for me, but he hit his string once with the first one and every catgut went. It all split. So he had to throw that one away and use the one I was going to use."

It's probably the case that many of the people who turned up were more interested in The Creation than The Mark Four and, perhaps inevitably, the group performed 'Painter Man'. Siebke: "Because the crowd wanted it. They'd rehearsed it once but more as a joke then anything but finally the crowd demanded it so they played it. (It went) really well, (though) it was very ragged. I suppose out of the whole gig, there's five songs which really came out very well but it really was more of the feel of the thing – a celebration." Dalton agreed it was a "very, very good night."

"It was good," concludes Eddie. "All these gigs that we've done since have been like turning the clock back. Even the crowd was mods in parkas, turned up on scooters. When we went to New York last November (2002) and we played The Creation album (*sic*), the kids there of 17, 18 – they knew all the songs and they were singing along. It was amazing." Impressively, the gig actually got reviewed by UK music weekly *Sounds*, whose correspondent P St John Nettleton declared in its 23 February 1985 issue, "This unique one-off reunion could have been a disaster, where legends would be buried for all time, but no! Eddie Phillips could still teach Jimmy Page a thing or two, he doesn't look a day older, and when he plucked the bow from the quiver hanging over his back and thrashed his Gibson during 'Mona' the huge vacancy for an exciting acid-blues band became painfully obvious."

There was initially talk of releasing The Mark Four reunion gig as a live album but, as Eddie explained to *Good Times* in an interview published in 1992, "When we listened to the tape, it wasn't that good. We could have changed things because everything was done on its own channel. We could have redone some vocals and some different bits and pieces but we felt that was not strictly right. So we just picked the tracks that were okay to put out." Those tracks – 'Hurt Me If You Will', 'Got My Mojo Working' and 'That's How Strong My Love Is' – appeared on a promotional EP called Live At The Beat Scene Club (Bam Caruso Records) that was limited to 500 copies. The back cover of the sleeve of said EP advertised a Mark Four album that was 'coming soon' called 'Marking Time' (*sic*) "featuring the original records and more live tracks". Unfortunately, owing to the lack of availability of the master tapes for the A and B-sides of the first two Mark Four singles, the project was abandoned.

At the Wolsey Hall gig, an intriguing psychedelically-patterned flyer was handed out declaring, 'The Creation, Lay The Ghost. A New Single Coming Soon On Polydor.' This was the first public announcement of the fact that Jack's two ex-colleagues from the Mark Four were also involved in another project which sought to revive a common band from their past. The project in question was to be a studio album, work for which was already quite advanced. Only three tracks from the project would ever be released but the tapes of the remainder show it to be a truly Great Lost Creation album, with most of the songs (if not the recordings) the equal of anything on which Eddie and Kenny had collaborated in the Sixties.

The plan was always to credit the project to The Creation because, as Eddie explains, "It was because Kenny and I sat down and we tried to write retro. Although it sounded Eighties because it was recorded in the Eighties, we tried to go back a bit and on that session there was songs like 'Lay The Ghost', 'Psychedelic Rose' and 'Radio Beautiful', which are all really Sixties songs. We wish we had done them 20 years previously. I dug the songs out the other day and they sound great."

Judging by a comment in his '82 *Blitz* interview, Kenny had not ceased to toy with the idea in his mind of a Creation reunion in the years since he broached the idea to Jack following the Boney M hit. Discussing the fans who had made The Creation a posthumous cult band, he said, "If a Creation band were put together now and did gigs, what I would like to know is whether these same people who are buying the cult records would actually come to see the band and buy the records they're making now." Accordingly, 'Lay The Ghost' itself was a track that spoke of exorcising the demons of an unfulfilled career, exploring his feelings about The Creation with lines like 'Tryin' to forget what was yesterday/ Tryin' to forget what might have been' and 'Standing on stage in some Deutsche town/I don't understand what they say'. In the chorus, he declares, 'Same old songs are becoming a heavy, heavy load.'

Though Kenny and Eddie clearly hoped The Creation's career could be resuscitated, this didn't extend to calling in their former colleagues in the original line-up. However, one ex-member was mooted. Eddie, who had stayed in touch with Kim, wanted to get the bassist to work on the tracks. Eddie: "I said to the guy at Polydor to get him on the record and they wouldn't fund bringing him over to do it because he'd need an air flight, a hotel for a month or however long it took and they wasn't up for it. But I did mention it to Kim. I was keen to do it."

Jack says he was aware of the ongoing Creation project at the time. "I'd heard things going on but I don't think they were actually contracted to Polydor at the time," he says. "The idea was that Eddie had a home studio and they were putting some stuff down and maybe Polydor would release it if it was good enough. At the time I was doing very well up in the north of England, working the clubs singing and was thoroughly enjoying it, making big money. I knew they were only playing games 'cos I know 'em so I just let them get on with it.

"Kenny was trying to get to write songs again with Eddie and Eddie wasn't that keen but he was going along with it in case there was some money in it but I couldn't really see them pulling it off. I wasn't worried at all. I had my own thing going."

276

The first session for the project was produced by Nick Lowe but was not used. "We tried one of the tracks with Nick," says Eddie. "We sounded really good but Polydor didn't really like it much so we went and did it another way." Rod Siebke heard that "they actually recorded some stuff with him and it was just a disaster. I imagine that would be another version of 'Lay The Ghost'." Ultimately, and despite the tentatively scheduled single and the flyer handed out at the Mark Four gig, Polydor decided to cancel. "It was a period of time when the axe was falling on a lot of projects within the company and ours was one of them," says Eddie. Polydor's axe-swinging didn't merely extend to Sixties musicians without a *bona fide* hit to their name. As Siebke points out, "It was the same time as they got rid of Paul Weller."

Shortly before Polydor bailed out, Mike Fletcher, who worked for the Shapiro Bernstein publishing company to whom Eddie and Kenny were signed as writers, happened to mention 'Lay The Ghost' track to an independent producer and studio owner with whom he was working. This was Tony Atkins, former lead guitarist of Group Five, once one of the stable of artists belonging to Mark Four manager Ian Swan. Atkins had come a long way since the Mark Four and Group Five had sat nursing grievances about Swan's shortcomings. Group Five had mutated into Spectrum, who performed the theme music to the various puppet series of Gerry Anderson (including *Captain Scarlet*).'

Though Spectrum had had three Number 1s in Spain, one in Germany and other healthy chart placings in various territories, by late '69 Atkins had had enough of being a musician and took a job in the A&R department of RCA. He left that post after a year to become an independent producer and set up his own studio, Village Recorders in Dagenham, London. "I was working for Mike on various other projects," recalls Atkins. "He just happened to mention Eddie and Kenny. I said, 'Oh bloody hell, I know them'.

"He said, 'I've got this song' which was 'Lay The Ghost'. And he said, 'I think they've already done a version of it and it wasn't quite right.' I said I'd be really interested in working on that with them. He played me their version and said it needed changing. We met up and they played me that and some other songs they wanted to do." Had his old friends changed since the last time he'd seen them in the Sixties? "Not a great deal. We all got on really well immediately. There were no great problems. We spoke about old times, listened to the songs and gradually knocked them into shape."

Initially, the project was restricted to three tracks, 'Lay The Ghost', 'White Knight' and 'Mumbo Jumbo'. Atkins was doing the financing, although Polydor were still vaguely involved in the project when Atkins started working with the pair. "It was intended to get a deal really," he says. "I paid for it all to start with. I think Polydor were vaguely involved but I don't think there was anything actually signed. They had shown some interest, we sent the stuff up to them after we were doing it and they were still saying 'Let's hear another track', 'Can you change this?' – typical record-company moves. I don't think I believed it was going to be a deal with Polydor, otherwise I wouldn't have been laying out my own money to do the demos; they would have been paying for it."

Eventually via a circuitous route, the project ended up – sort of – with Jet Records. Atkins: "Thinking about this album, I'm not sure that it wasn't the American publishers that said 'Can you get an album together?' I'm not really sure that Jet didn't come in at an even later stage when we'd produced three-quarters of the tracks 'cos we weren't getting anywhere in the States; we were trying different outlets. I think Jet decided they wanted to do an album after hearing all these tracks." The Jet deal occurred through a personal contact at the label: Ron Fowler, brother of former Mark Four roadie Mark.

Atkins was successful enough not to worry much about the project being commercially viable. "Interest, really," he says of his motivation. "You don't have great faith of anything actually happening when you're an independent producer. You have to follow your instincts. You don't think, 'Right, this is the one, I'm gonna crack it with this one'. If you think something's got a chance of turning out to be a good record, you do it.

"I've sold so many masters and done so any deals in the past. Some of them didn't turn out to be overly successful, some of them didn't sell hardly any copies, but the records were good enough to interest the record company and that's the way it worked in those days." Atkins does admit, though, that an Eddie Phillips solo project he recorded and released at around this time was something he did think would make the charts. In 1985, T-Mac – a label owned by Tony Atkins and Dave McAleer – released a 12-inch single credited to Edwin Phillips.

Entitled 'Life On Earth' (though nothing to do with 'Is There Life On Earth'), it was a song motivated by Eddie's disgust when watching television newsreel of a man burning to death in a football-stadium fire while opposing fans jeered at him. It occurred to the guitarist that as animals killed to survive, not for pleasure, then Man must be the planet's lowest life form. While the sentiments might be sound, the record was awful, a clattering assortment of all the kind of special effects that made so many Eighties records so irritating. Atkins: "He'd only just written it. I don't even remember issuing it, to be honest, but I know we did a deal in Germany for it with Intercord. It was a good record, I thought. Pretty unusual. We put sound effects on it – a crowd roaring, like a football chant. The lyrics are very good actually if you listen to it. It's very much a cynical sort of lyric. I thought it was really unusual. Eddie's a very inventive person."

Such seems to have been his *laissez-faire* attitude about the Creation project that Atkins didn't express any misgivings about the plan to attribute whatever results they came out with to The Creation despite believing the name wouldn't mean much to anyone. Atkins: "I didn't think it would. I wasn't even involved at that level. I could have been but I didn't have an opinion about it. I didn't see it as being a negative thing quite honestly because they weren't going to be pop idols. They didn't exactly look young and they didn't have an image that was going to appeal to young people so I suppose doing it that way round was probably the best way. But I didn't give it a great deal of consideration.

" I was more involved in just producing decent sounds and a good atmosphere, so they had some sort of commercial side to it. I was certainly intent on making the records as commercial as I possibly could, rather than being authentic in any other way." Atkins admits that The Creation as a band had almost completely passed him by, although he was familiar with 'Painter Man'. (By coincidence, ex-Group Five drummer Keith Forsey, having become a top session musician in Germany, almost certainly played on Boney M's cover of that song.)

Though Eddie and Kenny had entered the project aiming for a retro feel, this only applied to the songs. The recording would be marked by very modern production methods. "You can't help making them slightly contemporary with samplers and things that were out at that time, little gimmicks," reasons Atkins. "Reverbs and effects were much further developed than they were in the earlier days. I'd moved along as a producer myself. I wasn't stuck in any particular time zone, but the songs and Eddie's style of playing and whatnot pushed them back a bit in time."

Also taking them back in time was Eddie's use of the violin bow on some tracks. Atkins: "He used to always (end) up with about three hairs on the bow at the end of the session. He used to get through the bows like no-one's business." Drummers and bass players were employed on the tracks recorded, although there were also artificial drums on occasion and Eddie would lay down the odd bass part himself. There was no formal booking of session musicians, though. "They were just mates of mine, people round the studio," says Atkins. "All the engineers at the studio were all good musicians. They'd just pick up people rather than anyone that we booked in."

Before the project's completion, Eddie and Kenny asked their former Mark Four colleague John Dalton and Dalton's former Kinks bandmate, Mick Avory, if they would be the new Creation's rhythm section should circumstances require them to promote records and/or play live. (The pair's pictures actually appeared with Kenny and Eddie's on the sleeve of the one single that resulted from the sessions.)

"At that time I was quite friendly with John and Mick," explains Eddie. "We thought maybe we'd get a band together if anything took off from the album." Dalton: "We done the promos and everything for it, all the photograph sessions, but nothing came of that. Eddie was covering himself. If anything did come of it, he had someone there ready to jump in. We weren't doing a lot so we thought, 'We'll have a go at that'. We were just going to wait and see what happened to the record, 'cos I was working with Eddie anyway in another band." Dalton wasn't particularly vexed when nothing subsequently happened. "You learn to think the other way. I've made so many records, I don't think they're all going to be hits." Atkins: "We were going to have some rehearsals. There was lots of little half-fulfilled plans and I think (Dalton) came down a couple of times."

Did Atkins not think it would have been better to have got Dalton and Avory to play on the actual album? "No. I felt we would have achieved more by doing it the way we did; I think it would have been a slower process and wasn't convinced that the end results would be better for it." Eddie may disagree nowadays. Though the strength of the songs holds up from today's perspective, the production (as with so many recordings of that era) has dated badly, particularly the oppressive, cacophonous drum sound. "That was awful," says Eddie. "Those Eighties drums were terrible – it had a whacking great snare drum pounding your head. That was the Eighties way of producing things."

An old-school drummer like Avory could probably have been relied on to produce classic drum patterns that would have been easier on the ear. However, told that Eddie regrets the Eighties drum sounds, Atkins counters, "Yeah, but Eddie has always regretted anything five minutes after he'd done it. He analyses and listens so many times to things and he'll always come to a conclusion. He won't ever leave it alone. I'm not saying he's not right in this case…but I know we tinkered forever, always changing this, simply because it could be changed. I think Eddie will readily admit himself that he tends to carry on with something and try to the ninth degree to get it how he wants to be happy with it. I doubt if Eddie's ever really been happy with anything he's ever done and that's observation, not criticism."

The 'tinkering' informed the way the session progressed. "We did a few tracks and then Eddie's a bit of a re-mix king and we did another overdub on that; then we changed this bit and changed that bit, then we did some more songs and the whole thing moved on in that fashion." Kenny, without a role when instruments were being played, attended the sessions less than Eddie. When he did come in, he would often fall asleep in the corner of the studio, not through boredom but because he had developed narcolepsy, a condition which renders people unconscious in an instant.

"We used to have fun doing it," says Atkins of the album. "It was a good laugh. It was serious, but it was nice to be working together. And we were happy with the end result." His enjoyment of the sessions is hardly surprising, for the set of songs – 10 in total – was strong overall and some compositions were brilliant. 'Radio Beautiful' is a fabulous celebration of rock with a chorus that could be imagined blaring out of ghettoblasters and transistors in parks all over the country. 'Psychedelic Rose' is a highly melodic romantic tribute to a flower child. 'Far From Paradise' is a beautiful lament for a lost love with some exquisite saxophone accompaniment. 'Doing It My Way' is a rousing, fist-pumping paean to self-determination. 'Lay The Ghost' is a powerful expression of regrets for what might have been, although Atkins says, "Whenever I listen to that I always think we did it a bit too slow, which annoys me 'cos I think it's a very hooky sort of song. Good little riff that Eddie's got in the back, very simple riff but nevertheless very effective."

It was also decided the project would include a re-recording of 'Making Time'. "They felt it had been a hit once and they could latch it on to the name of The Creation, gain some interest from the public that way," says Atkins. The original Sixties recording was brought into the studio. "We did listen to it, and it sounded very rough, to be honest. I think it probably had to be. You try and smooth out the edges and you lose the atmosphere."

Though the re-make was impressively beefy and had considerable spirit, Atkins was under no illusion that the re-recording would match the original. "It can't, simply because of the recording techniques, recording equipment, the age of the people when they're doing it, and revisiting something you always think you can do it better... More often than not you don't. We just went for it and as it developed, it developed. It's difficult to change your views on something when you've done it like that. It's hard to do it in a different way."

By this point, of course, the Boney M cover had made 'Painter Man' The Creation's best-known song. Was there any discussion about doing a re-recording of that number? "None whatsoever," says Atkins. "It was never even contemplated. I think it was too poppy in terms of the hit having come from Boney M."

No track got extra attention because it was felt to have single potential. "It was just a matter of doing as many songs as we could that were good enough to be recorded, hoping we'd have more than was required so we'd have a choice." The result was an inspired collection of tracks (even if the riff of 'Doing It My Way' seemed unduly influenced by the theme music to the movie *Ghostbusters*) and, whether or not one likes that booming 'Eighties production style, it can't be denied that it would have fitted in with the times. Had The Creation had the right record company, the album (which neither Atkins or Eddie can remember being given a formal title) would have been a highly commercial proposition. Unfortunately, they alighted on Jet just as that label's death throes were beginning.

The first warning signs came when Jet would initially only commit themselves to one single. Even this might not have mattered if the track chosen had been the right one. Bizarrely, though, airplay anthem 'Radio Beautiful' was overlooked in favour of 'A Spirit Called Love', released in April 1987. This driving, urgent number written by Eddie alone was simply not in the same league in terms of commercial appeal. 'Making Time' was chosen as the B-side, with 'Mumbo Jumbo' – a rockabilly number that was the only track from the sessions sung by Eddie – the additional track on the 12-inch single.

Jet's press release for 'A Spirit Called Love' declared that 'The Creation are back after 20 years, exploding back onto the scene with a dynamic new single "A Spirit Called Love" and an amazing updated version of their Sixties hit "Making Time".' A reasonably well-informed press release made sure to mention the band's innovations with violin bow, feedback and stage paintings, although over-egged the pudding a little when it declared that the setting fire to the latter at the Circus Krone resulted in 'mass arrests and passport confiscation.' It concluded by stating, 'with a single out in April and an album to follow, The Creation have proved that their music overcomes the barriers of time and that they are here to stay in the Eighties.' That album, according to the back cover of the 12-inch version of the single, would have been called 'The Creation'.

Eddie and Kenny set about promoting the single and initially got some good coverage. Jet managed to secure the pair an interview slot on London's Capital Radio. Kenny revealed to the presenter (who, no doubt to his irritation, brought up that old Who-Creation comparison by asking if The Creation had done their 'psychedelic paintings' before The Who has started 'bashing up the guitars and all that') that the two bands who most excited him at the time were The Jesus And Mary Chain and The Alarm, both of whom he said reminded him of The Creation.

Eddie said that, regarding this reunion, "a bit of fun would be very high on the agenda" , to which Kenny appended that they couldn't take things as seriously now as they had in the Sixties, when they were "trying to be stars, we desperately wanted to be rock'n'roll heroes". With valuable coverage like this – and it does seem something of a coup for a band without a real hit to their name to have got a Capital Radio slot – things were looking up for The Creation's (semi) reunion.

Unfortunately, it soon became apparent that, even had there been enough members of the public prepared to purchase 'A Spirit Called Love' to send it to Number 1, they wouldn't have been able to do so. "It picked up quite a bit of radio and it seemed to be well-liked by people," says Eddie, "but nobody could actually buy it! You couldn't actually buy it in a shop. They had a bad distribution problem and the record didn't do anything. You need to be able to buy the record."

Rod Siebke agrees. "At the time I had a record shop," he says. "I couldn't get hold of it. I ended up getting them direct from Jet in the end." Atkins: "I don't think they had the infrastructure to do it. People wouldn't press loads of records until they got some sort of feedback and I don't think the retailers were very pro-Jet Records. Retailers were always against small labels."

Not only was there not the distribution to meet any demand there might have been, but it was becoming apparent that not even a Number 1 single was likely to save Jet. "It was really hard to gee them up 'cos I don't think they had the money to go through with the whole thing," says Atkins. "I don't think much was happening with it. I think they (Jet) were always waiting for some money to come in from somewhere to get the whole thing up and running. I think they was hoping for a better initial reaction. I don't think they got particularly good reaction to most of it and

I don't think Jet had had any success for a while at that stage… The label had been pretty much dormant."

Kenny's interest in pushing 'A Spirit Called Love' began to evaporate. Siebke: "I know he wasn't helping with the promotion of the single. Eddie was doing a lot but Kenny really didn't want to know. I don't know if he knew something that we didn't. (Eddie was) doing radio promos and all the rest of it. (Maybe Kenny) knew something we didn't about Jet's finances."

"The whole episode, I enjoyed it from just working with them and getting some decent tracks together," says Atkins, "but as a commercial exercise it was a bit of a disaster." Jet ultimately declined to release the album and once again Eddie saw all his hard work and musical inspiration come to nought. He could have been forgiven for thinking he was cursed. At the very least, he could be expected to be very, very disappointed. Asked if this was the case, Siebke says, "Yes and no. To be honest, at the time him and Ken weren't on the best of terms again and I think it was a case of 'Ah well, leave it'."

Eddie's comments suggest a deeper hurt. "I was quite happy after that to write and record stuff here and leave the music business well out of it," he says with as much lack of bitterness as he can muster. In fact, Eddie didn't keep the music business completely 'out of it'. in late 1990, he released an interesting album called 'Riffmaster Of The Western World' on the Promised Land label. Explains Eddie, "There's a guy called Mike Ober. He's an American guy. He came to his country about '88-89 and I got this call. He had this mad idea of putting all British Invasion artists together and doing a couple of albums and he said would I be interested in being a guitar player working with Jim McCarty and people like that? I said, 'Yeah', sounded good fun. And then he said, 'Would you fancy doing a solo album?' So I did it. That's something I did at home. I actually did it in the garage…I went mad on it."

'Riffmaster…' saw Eddie revisit favourites written both by others ('Hi Heel Sneakers', 'The Jimi Hendrix Trilogy', 'In The Midnight Hour') and himself ('Teacher, Teacher', 'A Spirit Called Love', 'How Does It Feel To Feel', 'Mumbo Jumbo'). There were two new songs, or, rather, a new song with a reprise: 'Riffmaster' and 'Riffmaster Of The Western World', a co-write between Eddie and Mike Bernard (a pen-name of Ober, who also shared the production of the album). Of that wonderfully-named latter track, Eddie explains, "I came up with a thing called 'Riffmaster' and Mike added the 'Western World'."

The album was generally strong, the new track(s) excellent and the listener got the rare opportunity to hear some conventional lead guitarwork from Eddie on record as opposed to the powerchord work by which his previously released recordings were mostly characterised. On the down side, the album suffered from the same oppressive crashing, synth-heavy production that had afflicted the Jet/Polydor songs. Additionally, the preponderance of cover versions and new versions of previously released songs seems a wasted opportunity: the highlights of the Polydor/Jet album would have been ideal inclusions on an album whose care was finally not in the hands of unreliable record companies but in those of a man like Ober, who was a fan first and foremost and would not have interfered in any way.

The front cover of the album – depicting Eddie playing his guitar with a violin bow against a Union Jack backdrop – credits 'Riffmaster Of The Western World' to "The Creation's Eddie Phillips". This was testament to the fact that The Creation was by now something of a name to drop. That same year saw Edsel re-release the 'How Does It Feel To Feel' compilation on CD, the extra capacity of which enabled them to add four tracks: 'Uncle Bert', 'Like A Rolling Stone', 'If I Stay Too Long' and 'Hey Joe'.

In April 1993 Edsel put out yet another Creation compilation, 'Painter Man', an eight-song mini-album most notable for the first ever appearance of 'Sweet Helen'. Meanwhile – in a development Eddie, Jack and Bob weren't aware of, although Kenny may have been – the band's name was appearing on every piece of product put out by Creation Records, which had been founded in 1983 by Alan McGee, that young Scot who had loved the first Edsel compilation so much.

The label McGee had named after his favourite band was not yet the pop sensation it would become but, having already racked up hits by Ride and Primal Scream, was clearly going places – and it was that very year that they signed Oasis. (The label had also released the first record by The Jesus and Mary Chain, the band who had so impressed Kenny Pickett.) In addition, there had been features on The Creation in magazines like *Blitz, Guitarist, Record Collector* and *Rock Marketplace*, some of which the ex-band members had done interviews for.

Their two German albums had ballooned in price on the collector's market. In possibly the ultimate confirmation that they were a cult, bootleggers considered them to possess a sufficient potential for profit that they were prepared to put out an illegal version of their product: 'If I Stay Too Long' – a bootleg reissue of the Charisma album '66-67' –

appeared in 1980 claiming to be on the Planet Records label but actually on Action Records. The cover featured the 1967 *NME* front-page ad for 'If I Stay Too Long'.

"About three or four years after they broke up, they started being a cult band in America," says Talmy. "But it took probably another ten years before they achieved cult status as the band that should've been but never was. Certainly, they influenced a lot of people. The obvious person is Alan McGee. Jimmy Page picked up on the violin bow and Eddie's kind of rocking style of playing guitar has certainly been emulated by a few guitarists along the way. I suppose that kind of elevates them to the cult status I thought they were in the first place, doesn't it?

"They were a seminal band in many ways and certainly influenced – apparently – lots of people. I guess they're considered as one of the original psychedelic bands, whatever the hell that means. They certainly were one of the great hard-rock bands, or power-pop or whatever the hell you want to call it."

The peculiar way by which a band acquires a legendary status is illustrated by the experiences of Joe Foster, a musician and friend of McGee who went on to become one of Creation Record's in-house producers. "I had that (Charisma) album," says Foster. "I picked it up somewhere unlikely. I picked up another copy (when) I worked in a vacation at school: I did a bit of part-time work at Charisma and picked a copy up again. Meanwhile, there was a single as well that came out in about 1977." Foster is referring to the Raw Records release of 'Making Time' b/w 'Painter Man' "I was quite surprised to see that," he says. "That was, I think, in Beggar's Banquet. I was with Ed Ball and we picked a copy up each."

What was it about the band that appealed to him? Foster: "Hard to put my finger on it. We all thought they were brilliant. They were the perfect band, basically, that we all wanted to be like. This was just pre-punk. I'd had this album which I'd played to death and disappeared. I had also some cassettes. Ed had a couple of bits. We picked up this single: we couldn't believe our luck: 'Wow! Who's put this out?' We could never find anything out about Raw Records except they had a load of shit bands. And they put out this Creation single!"

The scant knowledge of Foster and his friend about Raw was matched by their ignorance regarding The Creation. Foster: "We knew nothing at all about them. We just knew their names off the back of the sleeve and one of them played guitar with a violin bow. That was all we knew. It was just the sound of them – it was magic."

Alan McGee openly accepts that part of the reason for his attraction to the band was that having an unknown ensemble like The Creation as your favourite group was a bit more street-cred than, say, The Beatles. McGee: "I absolutely loved them but I also knew it was incredibly cool." Foster agrees, adding, "It was around the time when – it seems hard to believe now – you could walk about with a Velvet Underground album and there'd only be a few people who'd know who it was. It was that kind of time. People forget. Nowadays, you get reissues of everybody's last burp whereas at the time we're talking about it seemed that every record made before last year that wasn't The Beatles had been deleted as if it never existed.

"I sometimes think the whole bizarre movement of sad, American, no-girlfriend Beatles fans that went on about them all the time was caused by the fact that you couldn't buy any other music pre-about 1973 that wasn't a Beatles record – and of course they loomed a lot more important. When you couldn't buy the first two Who albums and you couldn't buy any Byrds album, 'Revolver' sounded pretty damned impressive. But it doesn't sound that impressive now."

Not that it was merely a pose that made Foster and his musician friends sing the praises of The Creation. "It was the perfect distillation of that kind of music we wanted to be associated with," Foster avers. "Everything about them. They should have been huge and because everything about them is what we wanted to be. It sounds a bit sad but that's actually still true: if we had the choice again, if somebody said, 'Tell you what, boys, you could be in a famous band, get the songs' – they would sound like The Creation."

Foster and McGee, friends since their late teens, jointly discovered Edsel's 'How Does It Feel To Feel' compilation in the early Eighties. "We couldn't believe it because I'd talked with Ed about this (Charisma) album I had and at this point I hadn't got another copy of it yet," says Foster. "And it was like, 'There's no such album'. That was really interesting to find out something about these guys. It was good to realise that they had all these songs and I hadn't imagined it all."

Foster was a founder member of Television Personalities, a group formed in 1977 whose lyrics, song titles and album covers were drenched in references to icons from pop music culture. One of the songs they played live was 'Painter Man'. They were slightly dismayed when Boney M had a hit with it, turning it – in some eyes – from cool to naff overnight.

"People started taking the piss out of us and said we're playing a Boney M song," Foster remembers. "First we were pissed off, and then we thought , 'No, hang on, we'll have a good laugh with it' and we played up to it, did a dance and all that. Knowing that anybody that was a bit cool would know it was a Creation song, not a Boney M song." Asked how surprised he was at the Boney M cover, he says, "From that point of view it's not really a big surprise. When boy bands do a cover of an old song, it's always some sickening load of crap, which makes me think the people behind this were never cool, even when they were youngsters. But Frank Farian, in spite of Boney M, must have had the time of his life."

Alan McGee set up a group called Biff Bang Pow! in the early Eighties of which Ed Ball was a member. It shouldn't be inferred that this was because that song was his favourite Creation track. "I think that was just my sense of humour more than anything else," McGee says. "This is very me. It was like, 'Well we'll call the label Creation because aesthetically that's what the label was: punk rock with psychedelia. That's what all the early records were trying to be. And then if we were going to have a band, it was like, why don't we call the band Biff Bang Pow? It was a reasonably terrible name for a group."

"It's a thing that dawns on you gradually," says Eddie of The Creation's developing legend. "You read this article and you read an article there and you begin to realise that maybe what you did was a little bit significant or it was our contribution to this great pop industry of ours. I'm quite proud of what we did but there wasn't no defining moment when you think, 'Oh yeah, people remember this'. This is something that gradually dawns on you over a period of time."

"I knew that we had a good reputation," says Jack. "You know what showbusiness is like: there's so much hype goes on and people bullshit but I knew we had respect and I knew also that our records were still selling in the States and Germany. I knew we had respect out there which was very important and we had credibility – I was happy with that." It was this developing legend which in the early Nineties effected a change in the status of The Creation in its ex-personnel's minds. Even for Kenny and Eddie – who had tried to resuscitate The Creation, or at least their name and spirit, with their doomed Polydor/Jet album – the band had been a brief interlude in a career which, in the interim, had been considerably dwarfed in length by subsequent developments, even if such developments frequently consisted of disappointments and hiatuses.

This especially applied to Jack and Bob, who had pursued successful musical careers whose markets were so fundamentally different to those of The Creation's as to quite possibly make those days seem like noisy juvenilia. As Jack puts it, "That period was a time of my life which was brilliant, and then you move on." However, what was becoming a distant and irrelevant memory for the ex-members of The Creation couldn't help but turn into something that was relevant to their current lives due to the increasing numbers of people who had a very different perspective to them on the band.

For kids (and grown adults) who had bought the compilations '66-67', 'How Does It Feel To Feel' or 'Painter Man', the members of The Creation were frozen in time as thrusting young practitioners of psychedelic rock-pop. Naturally, such consumers knew that the former band members were older and perhaps had different styles and attitudes by now, but as their only direct perception of them was gained through the images and sounds of them in the Sixties, the psychological effect was inevitably one that overpowered that knowledge. In short, there was a market for The Creation, despite the fact the band had ceased in form and spirit to exist by September 1967 (the date of Eddie's departure) or by the very latest April 1968, the month of their last gig of any kind.

So it was that when Kenny Pickett approached London music venue the Mean Fiddler about booking the band in for a one-off gig in 1993, he found the managers of the venue receptive to the idea. Although Kenny seems to have always had hopes that such activity could lead to something bigger, his sights seem to have been set (understandably) no higher than a German tour which would cash in on the nostalgia felt for the band in that one country. Yet within the space of a year or so, The Creation would be playing the Albert Hall and starting the recording of their first ever proper studio album.

"We thought, 'Let's give it a go – what the hell?'," says Jack. "We could all still play, that was the important thing."

Unbeknown to many, The Mark Four's reunion gig in 1985 was not a one-off. There were two further gigs at which Cheshunt's finest reunited, on 6 and 9 June 1992 at Cheshunt Football Club and a pub in London's Archway respectively. "The guy that was running the gigs at this pub in Archway approached them to do a reunion," says Siebke, "and the annoying thing was he actually put it down as a Creation gig. It was just a one-off thing once again. I saw both of those gigs. They was nowhere near to the standard of the '85 (gig). I'm not saying that because I put the gig on. It was just one of those things. They wasn't together and there wasn't the sense of occasion, really. It was just playing a grotty little back room of a pub and a small hall so it was nothing special."

Insalubrious and under-publicised though those gigs might have been (with Kenny once again imbibing in order to quell his stage fright), they seem to have been the seed that planted in Kenny's mind the idea of a reformation of The Creation. This time, the idea was not – as with the Polydor/Jet album – merely using The Creation name for a tenuously related project but a proper and full reunion involving live work, especially (it was hoped) a German tour.

In 1993, Kenny was at something of a crisis point in his life. For years, his hankering for an involvement in the music business had been complicated by a wife who saw no reason why he should want to be a part of an industry where income was not guaranteed when he was fully trained in another trade which paid very good money. "His wife always said that he should stop messing around trying to be a songwriter and get on with the plumbing and that really broke his heart 'cos he hated plumbing and desperately wanted to be a songwriter," says Glen Colson. "She didn't like anything to do with music. She didn't like any of his friends or anything. I was about the only bloke she tolerated. She thought he should get a proper job."

However, this impediment to his musical ambitions ceased to be an issue as Kenny and his wife became estranged in circumstances which were rather bizarre. Glen Colson: "Although he lived with her, they'd separated and were barely talking for years. He was living in that house under a cloud which must have been incredibly uncomfortable for the both of them, 'cos he would live on one floor and she would live on the other and they would have separate compartments in the fridge. He really wanted to leave and get a houseboat but he didn't have the money, so he was arguing about how much they were going to settle for when she sold the house."

Now that the disapproval of his spouse was not a consideration, Kenny could revive the rock'n'roll dreams that had been stymied for so long. According to Glen Colson, those dreams were not about money – of which he had access to plenty should he so desire – but fulfilment. "He hated plumbing with a vengeance," says Glen. "He'd come in with cut hands, all dirty and grazed, he'd been sweating his arse off all day. He was an incredibly hard worker. He made great money. He could say, 'You want central heating put in – give me a grand' and he'd do it in two or three days. So he was earning good money but he hated it. So he'd do a bit, then stop, spend all his money, then have to go back and do a bit more. It was a vicious circle."

Kenny's rock'n'roll dreams could only revolve around The Creation, for his songwriting career had been too erratic to try to further it, at least in the short term. Kenny first approached Rod Siebke to sound him out about a Creation revival. "He phoned me up and had a long chat about it; he said did I think it was a good idea," says Siebke. "I said, 'Well maybe, if it's not something that's going to go on forever', because I couldn't imagine Eddie getting involved in something that was going to be long-term." Fortunately for Kenny, Siebke possessed contact information for Bob Garner, the only one of The Creation's ex-personnel whose whereabouts Kenny didn't know.

When Bob received the call from Kenny, it had a feeling of eerie coincidence about it. The previous night, he had left his son and friends playing records and gone to bed. When he came down the next morning, he noticed one of the albums they had been playing was still on the turntable: the Edsel 'How Does It Feel To Feel' compilation. Bob was amenable to the idea Kenny put to him in that day's telephone conversation. His mind was also clearly working along the same lines as Kenny's who had opted to contact Bob despite him being a man he had once considered 'a nasty piece of work'.

"When Kenny rang me and said 'Do you fancy doing something?' I said to him, 'On one condition: that it is the original four'," says Bob. "Nothing less than that would do because whatever made people like The Creation songs was those four people."

Bob is of course referring to the inclusion of Jack in the line-up. Unbeknown to Bob, Kenny had contacted Jack and not him in 1978 in the wake of the Boney M cover about reforming The Creation. That time round, Jack had taken a certain pleasure in declining. Now, though, the 'chip on my shoulder' Jack cites as the reason for his previous refusal was no longer a factor, nor were the geographical problems. "Well you've got to remember something like nearly 20 years had gone by and circumstances were different," Jack explains. "When Kenny asked me before, I was living in Morecambe. Now I was back in London and could fit in gigs with The Creation. Before that, it would have been very, very difficult."

Eddie, too, was game – up to a point. "Ken said, 'Do you want to get The Creation back on the road?' And I said, 'I don't know. I don't think so'. I was quite happy to go and do a couple of reunion gigs but Kenny and Jack wanted to start doing German tours, things like that. I told them right from the beginning I wasn't going to get involved in any sort of major comeback tour. I just wasn't into it enough."

The plan to put together the original line-up of The Creation is something some might quibble about on the grounds that original doesn't necessarily mean best. It is perfectly logical that Kenny should not have considered approaching Kim Gardner to take part in the reunion. After all, his role would be brought into question by Gardner's participation: what would there be for Kenny to do if Kim came back and reclaimed the bass role, leaving Bob, logically, with the vocalist's job? And Bob could hardly be easily erased for the equation, not least because it would create a Kenny-Eddie-Kim-Jack line-up that had never (unless you believe Jack) existed previously.

Nonetheless, for many, Kim Gardner's non-participation might be seen as irrational: Creation masterpieces like 'How Does It Feel To Feel' and 'Life Is Just Beginning' were recorded when Kenny was long-gone. Yet many people would agree with the logic articulated by The Creation's former roadie Kenny White: "With Pickett on vocals – that's the real Creation. It's like the real Rolling Stones (has) got Brian Jones in it. The real Creation is probably the original band. That's how it should be. It's like The Nice are The Nice and ELP are ELP and The Nice were better than ELP. Same line-up of organ player, drummer, bass player, but ELP never had the thing The Nice had got going for them, even though ELP had a better bass player."

Though she was far fonder of Kim Gardner as a person than Kenny Pickett, June Clark agrees with that analysis. "The original Creation was with Kenny," she says. "And maybe that's me being old-fashioned and seeing it from a fan's standpoint. To me, authenticity is important; I don't like change and so if a band changes its line-up, it's not quite the same. I personally think that the original line up with Kenny was the right way to go with that line-up." Bob himself offers, "Well there's two periods, wasn't it? 'Making Time' and 'Painter Man' is one section, there's a bit of a blip in the middle and then we finished off with 'Life Is Just Beginning' and 'How Does It Feel To Feel'. Three different periods, but I felt that the main ingredients of what people would remember was still there in the original four." (Bob, of course, is discounting the Ronnie Wood line-up of the band following his own departure, but one gets the point.)

We can only speculate as to what Gardner's reaction would have been if he had been asked to take part, either in the initial gigs or the later recording sessions. However, Ronnie Wood posited in Terry Rawlings' book *Rock On Wood* that he wouldn't even have joined the Rolling Stones if he had been asked. Regretting suggesting Willie Weeks as the replacement for Bill Wyman in the Stones after the latter's retirement from the group in 1993, Ronnie said, "It was only after that I thought, 'Oh fuck! I should have thought of Kim'. But then I thought, 'No, he's got too much loyalty to his pub'."

Kenny approached Glen Colson with his idea of some sort of band reunion. Glen had progressed apace from his early days as press officer for Charisma. He was now running his own management company as well as working on various audio and visual projects such as a Genesis CD-ROM project and had the contacts Kenny needed, including one at London's famous Mean Fiddler venue. Glen: "Kenny said it'd be great to do this or do that and I said, 'Well, do you really want to do it?' 'cos I know the fella up there, I can get you a date'. And he said, 'I'll call the band up'. I figured he called 'em up (and said), 'Do you fancy it? Glen's got a date, we're gonna get seven hundred quid or whatever we get'."

Jack: "Kenny fixed up this gig in the Mean Fiddler. They wanted to put us on 'cos they'd heard we'd reformed. Which wasn't totally true." This belief of an already occurring reunion may have been the result of the inaccurate billing of the 1992 Highgate Mark Four gig, in which case the dishonesty proved fortunate. Glen Colson: "I just said if you want to use me I'll put the gig together, I'll get the money for the (live) album."

The provider of sound equipment for the night was, fittingly, a name from the past: Alan Smith, The Creation's former roadie and Bob's ex-housemate. "Alan Smith has a hire company and he specialised in old Marshall equipment," says Bob. "He had plenty of that going around. Alan provided the 4x12 Marshall amplifiers but the PA was the house PA of the Mean Fiddler." The gig was booked for 6 July 1993. Glen Colson: "And then I said, 'We might as well we record it'. I spoke to a fella called Steve Fearnie and he put up five grand for the album. I hired a mobile and they rehearsed for a couple of days." In addition, it was arranged for the gig to be filmed. "It was gonna be a documentary," says Glen Colson. "They shot loads of footage. It was a great story that 30 years or whatever since the day that they split up they got back together again. It would have been a funny, out-there documentary."

News that the gig would be recorded set alarm bells ringing in Eddie's head. "I didn't really like the fact that our first gig back together for a hundred years or something, they wanted to make a live recording of it," he says. "It's a bit of a tall order. We're not a band to over-rehearse. But we did it, it was all right, but I must admit I wasn't that keen." Siebke: "Initially it was just a gig or two, then the gig was going to be recorded by Manfred Mann's label, Cohesion. To be honest, the first one wasn't the best of gigs to have recorded." Not having played the instrument since 1976, Bob no longer possessed a bass guitar and used a Fender Telecaster bass borrowed from Kenny for the few gigs they did.

Both Bob and Jack have very happy memories of The Creation's first rehearsal for a quarter of a century. Jack: "We got together somewhere down in Acton. We got together and knocked out 'Making Time, I think. Bearing in mind we hadn't played together for 25 years or something silly, we all dropped into a groove and it was like we'd never been away. And we all looked at each other and said, 'Hey! That was pretty good'. We were quite chuffed. We weren't going to make fools of ourselves, which was important, and we took it on from there. We got down to serious rehearsing and got together a bit of a show."

Bob's recollections of the rehearsal (if not the first song they attempted) are virtually identical. "One of the pleasing things was, when we first met in the rehearsal studio after 27 years or whatever it was, Eddie said, 'Well, shall we kick off with "Try And Stop Me"?', he says. "Just counted '1-2-3-4' and the three of us came straight in. You never forget how to ride a bike. We just went, 'Well – that was good'. So we didn't have a problem."

Though the musical chemistry was the same, there were some differences in personality. Bob: "(It was) Eddie that said to me, 'You have changed, haven't you?' and I thought, 'As in what?' 'More grown up'. I don't mean changed, in attitude to music or anything like that, it was just 'You've changed in the way of 'Why make things complicated, just get on with it'. That's the way I understood it. It wasn't 'You've changed personality' or anything. Just being professional, I would have thought. You never see yourself. If I didn't agree with something I might be a bit stubborn that way but not in any aggressive way, verbally or physical."

Glen Colson says of the rehearsals (which shortly moved on to the more affordable Green Dragon pub in Cheshunt), "I think they had to go home for a kip in the afternoon so it was all a bit half-hearted. You know what people are like when they get old: they get a bit fuddy-duddy." However, he adds, "And then they did the gig, which was amazing. It was a great night." Jack: "We went to the Mean Fiddler, did the gig and we couldn't believe it. The place was packed and there were people of all ages. Guys of our age but kids had come along. We couldn't believe it. The response was fantastic and we went down great and went home buzzing: 'Well that was a lift'."

The Creation took to the stage in facsimiles of the purple outfits with epaulettes they'd sported in 1966. Jack: "We thought we'd wear 'em for old time's sake. We still had them. Well, I think one or two of us had to go out and buy a white shirt and dye it purple. We thought we'd do it for the hell of it: 'If we're going to do it, let's go the whole bit'." It has to be said that Kenny's shirt was rather straining at the seams on the night of the 6th. In addition to Kenny's portliness, Eddie's hair was rather longer than was seemly for a man of his age. However, Bob – his blonde mop-top now replaced by grey hair swept and flicked back – looked well-preserved and dignified (Jack was almost invisible behind his kit) and if the original Creation were understandably rusty as a unit, this was all swept aside by the sense of occasion as, after a 26-year gap, they put on show their entire gamut of trademarks, from the purple outfits to the aerosol can painting to the violin bow in a 15-song set that started with 'Batman Theme'/'Biff Bang Pow' and concluded with 'Painter Man'.

A version of 'Life Is Just Beginning' featured a stunning lengthy guitar break from Eddie that was uncannily reminiscent of Jimi Hendrix. Although Kenny handled vocal duties on songs like 'Life Is Just

Beginning' and 'Tom Tom', which he had never sung before, he introduced 'If I Stay Too Long' – the only number sung by Bob – as his all-time favourite Creation song, almost as if to signify that bygones were bygones.

Whatever Eddie's reservations about the viability of The Creation in the modern age, even he was impressed by the Mean Fiddler experience. "We played the classic Creation set, all the stuff people want to hear," he says. "It was a really good night. Really went well, felt good. Bit noisy, but you expect it to be."

The audience was a star-studded one, containing personalities ranging from former Sex Pistol Glen Matlock to ex-pop idol Adam Ant, while Damned drummer Rat Scabies DJ'd. Also in attendance was a posse of people connected to Creation Records, including their MD Alan McGee and Joe Foster. "We all travelled down together, because Harlesden's a Godforsaken place," says Foster. "Myself, Alan and Ed (Ball), Andy Bell and a couple of other people." In light of famously underwhelming reunions of bands who were contemporaries of The Creation such as The Animals, The Byrds and the Small Faces, were these Creation fans not apprehensive that the whole thing might be embarrassing? Foster: "We were apprehensive only in that we thought that, with the best will in the world, they're completely brilliant guys and very talented, but time's gone on, things have changed, they can't possibly be as good as that, but we should give them the respect of showing up, sit through the show and clap at the end and meet them and hang out with them.

"But we knew the minute they came on stage and they'd gone to the trouble of having the shirts just like on their record sleeve, same pants, everything – and the bass drum with 'The Creation' written on it and all that kind of stuff, we thought, 'Well, come on, there's a good chance this is gonna happen'. And it was absolutely brilliant. Best reunion of any band I've ever seen in my life."

McGee agrees: "They were amazing, and more than anything Eddie was amazing. He was the real star of the show. He was as good as it gets. He just got better. We loved it. And we knew loads of people there. It was really weird. That's where I met Glen Matlock. There was a load of people there you wouldn't have thought would be there for The Creation but they'd all showed up. It was nice. It was a nice night. They were really good."

Also in concurrence is Andy Bell who at that time was lead guitarist with Creation act Ride. "It was great," he says. They sounded pretty much how I would have imagined they sounded in the Sixties. I remember being really impressed that Kenny did this spray-can stuff. Obviously they looked like old men – older men – but they were doing the same stuff they did when they first started and it still seemed really modern: the guy was spraypainting stuff on the walls and Eddie had a violin bow out and all that. You had to sort of squint to really imagine you were back there but it was great. The music side of it was really perfect: the singing was great and their playing was great. It's not like some people who could have developed some changes. It was quite a primal sort of thing. It was just there, how it was, preserved..."

Of the rest of the audience at the Mean Fiddler, Foster says, "There were a lot of record collectors. People that owned record shops. All that kind. The usual gang that show up for all these things. A lot of young kids – kind of mod-dy kids. People our age from that kind of mod revival period. A hell of a lot of people were into them. They didn't realise the immense impact they'd had through the Edsel compilation, but a hell of a lot of people were there. It was sold out."

The Creation Records crowd paid the band a visit. Bell: "We went backstage afterwards and they were sitting around really bemused, like: 'Who are you?' It was the first time Alan had spoken to them I think and he introduced himself and said, 'I've got a label called Creation and I've got a band called Biff Bang Pow! It didn't really twig then that this was quite a big label. It was more like, 'Who's this guy in our faces?'

"Kenny was a bit more with-it. The rest of them just didn't care. I think he (McGee) might have gone up to the drummer at first! The drummer guy was just, like, 'Yeah, whatever, gimme a beer and shut up.' Our little gang started to want to get to know The Creation after that because I think we realised they weren't dangerous people. They probably had quite a lot going for them and they sounded great. I think Alan wanted to sign them up straight away. It kind of went from there."

Eddie remembers of McGee, "He told of us then of his connection with our band: he'd always liked it from the early days and just how much we had inspired him in his way he looked at music. We never realised the extent of our effect 'til then."

The Creation's comeback gig was an assembling of people who were somewhat out of the loop of the music industry. By this point Eddie was the only one of them who was a working rock musician. Jack was still singing around London's big clubs but says, "I'd stopped playing drums on a regular basis. I did the odd gig." Meanwhile, Bob's lack of familiarity with the workings of the music industry is underlined by the fact that it was only the reunion that led to him becoming aware of such things as PRS, the device whereby songwriters are paid for the plays their compositions receive in the media. "When I went to the Mean Fiddler, we were in the pub across the road and this guy came in and Kenny said, 'Oh hello so and so. This is Bob'. He said, 'This guy works for a publishing company'. I said, 'Oh yeah? What happens with songs from years ago?' He said, 'Give me the titles tomorrow and I'll chase 'em up'. I rang him, I gave him the titles. He said, 'I've got some good news – I've got a couple of grand here for you.'

"He rang me up a couple of days later and said, 'I've got another thousand pounds here." Naturally, Bob was delighted but the feelings became bitter-sweet when he was informed that his failure to claim other monies owed him over the previous quarter of a century mean they were lost forever. Bob: "He said, 'I can only go back about five years'. So that meant at that time about 20 years had gone missing. I didn't know about Demon Records or anything, so there's money gone down the river. He said, 'I'll look after those royalties for you from now'. They're with some music publishing company and they collect for me and I get a little cheque every now and again. I get a bit off Demon through Shel Talmy. But if you look at the deals then, Eddie and myself are on 25 per cent, Shel Talmy's on 50. That's how the publishing deals were done then: 50-50 – the publisher gets 50, if there's four people writing a song you're all on a quarter of 50.

"There's monies floating around and I think Stratton-Smith just gave us enough to keep us together. I would assume that, if he's giving us hand-outs every week, there must be monies coming from somewhere. He lived on his wits, I know that." Bob was also able to start collecting performance royalties, the remuneration from the copies sold of records he played on. Bob: "When Kenny got in touch with me again, he said, 'Have you not had anything off Shel?' And I said, 'No'. So he said, 'Well here's the address.' And I wrote to an address in London, although he's in Los Angeles. I said, 'Here I am'. I think it was Jonathan Rowlands who I spoke to. He said, 'We'll have to work it out'. Then the first cheque that came said, 'This is what we estimate we have received in the last… Like it or lump it. But as from now you shall receive what you're entitled to.'

"About three or four years ago, I spoke to Kim Gardner in America and I said, 'Are you getting your royalties off Shel?' He said, 'No'. So I gave him the address and then he started to collect. it's something I don't worry about. I just think, 'Well, that's gone'. I wasn't that concerned about making a lot quick. I was concerned about making money for the rest of my working life."

"Sounds like Bob," says Jack when told about his misgivings about the royalties subject. "I know I'm never gonna get 'em so I don't really worry about it. I'm not bitter. All I know is for about 10 years I had a great time and I also know that in the Sixties *everybody* got ripped off. So don't take it personal." Not that Jack necessarily feels the Creation were 'ripped off' by Shel Talmy. "At the time, a lot of bands had bad deals really with record companies. At the time it was a sort of standard deal that you would have had with a record company. When we were with Mercury, I never saw a penny of any royalties when we were the Mark Four. Shel Talmy is about the only person we've ever had any money off, record company-wise. I've worked with a few and I've never had any mention of royalties from them. I've never seen an account sheet saying that no, you didn't sell enough records or whatever. With Shel Talmy, whatever the deal was, at least I saw some money from the guy."

Unlike Bob, Jack says Talmy's payments to him were not belated, estimating the first was in around 1968. "I think it was a cheque for 110 quid or something," he says. "I've never seen accounts or anything. Never really pushed it that much, 'cos I've never really been into money. Me and Kenny in particular, we just loved playing the music and getting all hung up over money seemed a bit, I dunno... Just couldn't be bothered, to be honest with you. Christ, there's other things in the world besides money."

Though Eddie had enjoyed the reunion gig, it didn't alter his scepticism about the idea of a long-term or substantial Creation reunion, something that Kenny was finding increasingly frustrating. Glen Colson: "Kenny would tell me, 'Eddie don't want to do this, or he don't like this or he don't like the other thing and he don't want you to have this'. And I said, 'Why bother then?' That was my attitude. Life's too short to be sitting round arguing with people all day. If someone's difficult, how the hell you going to get on on a tour of Germany? 'cos that really magnifies any differences when you go on the road with someone."

In October 1993, the live recording of the Mean Fiddler gig was released on Cohesion Records as 'Lay The Ghost' with a cover painting by Vivian Stanshall, a former member of another ex-Stratton-Smith group, the Bonzo Dog Doo Dah Band, and a sleevenote from Kenny. Glen Colson: "They were fantastic when they played. I didn't even have to mix the album, I just let it run through. I said, 'Get a good sound on it and we won't even mix it'. 'cos I knew that they'd want to fuck about for years doing overdubs and I couldn't be bothered. I think it sounded absolutely brilliant. It's exactly how it happened. There's not anything been touched at all." The same month, The Creation played a second gig, this one at London's Garage venue. As with the Mean Fiddler performance, they opened with 'Batman Theme'/'Biff Bang Pow' and closed with 'Painter Man'. However, among the usual and expected Creation repertoire, they threw in a couple of pleasant surprises in the shape of the lesser-known 'Ostrich Man' and 'I Am The Walker'.

The timing of The Creation's resurgence was extremely providential. Creation Records were at that point planning their 10th anniversary celebrations, albeit a year late, with a bash at which various Creation label acts would appear as well as bands those behind the label had always admired. Additionally, Creation Records' catalogue numbering was such that the event could be made to coincide with the 200th Creation single. This synchronicity planted a seed in Foster's and McGee's minds that would ultimately lead to consequences even the ever-ambitious Kenny, in his wildest dreams, could not have imagined.

"We were coming up to the tenth anniversary bash and we'd already sorted out the Albert Hall," explains Foster. "I was in charge of getting older artists we admired. Alex Chilton couldn't make it. I got Arthur Lee and a couple of other people. It then came up that what we should do is put out Creation 200, a seven-inch single by The Creation. That was the deal. That's what we were gonna do. If they never do anything else. Because at that time they were like, 'We don't really want to record anything.' But when we suggested that as a project, Kenny and Eddie were very enthusiastic about putting a song together specially. So that project was a go-er and that's what we went in to do."

Memories of the Mean Fiddler gig had dispelled any doubts Foster and McGee might have had that the band could revive the magic after all these years. Foster: "Eddie had his box of tricks, Kenny could still sing and frankly we'd seen them do it in front of us. Basically if we were gonna cut a record in the old-school style, cut it live, in the studio, bang, do some singing on it. They'd done that standing in front of us. How could they not do it in two weeks' time standing in a studio?"

Kenny joined in the conceptual spirit behind the Creation label's thinking. It would be a great idea, he decided, if this proposed 200th Creation single would be a song titled 'Creation'. In other words, 'Creation' by The Creation on Creation. Foster says he wasn't worried such an elaborate gag might result in a product that was rather clever-clever. "It was *supposed* to be," he says. "Kenny was good at thinking of things like that. But the thing is, 90 per cent of you goes, 'No, come on, wait a minute, this is horrible' but every now and again there'd be something and this was basically a promotional device. This is how we're gonna do it. Basically, a promotional device for a bunch of us, Arthur Lee, and The Creation playing at the Royal Albert Hall. I'd have written a song called 'Creation' if (they) hadn't!"

Foster and McGee wanted to get Shel Talmy to produce the record. "We should have done it," says McGee. "I don't know why it never happened. I think Joe just wanted to do it himself. I think they got on well with him." Foster offers, "He wasn't able to be in the country and it was never discussed at any great length with him. I didn't deal with that. It was all dealt with by the admin people and it was like, 'Oh he wouldn't be able to do this and he might do that,' it was going round in circles and I just thought to myself, 'Well maybe they didn't treat the guy with the proper respect or something' and it's like, 'Oh, all that way for a single, I dunno', kind of thing – as one would."

For his part, Talmy denies any knowledge of any approach. "Not true. Never asked me. I don't know who told you that 'cos it's bullshit. He may have been thinking of me but it never went past that. Thank you for holding a thought for me, Alan." Would he have done it if asked? Talmy: "I certainly would have been interested." Eddie, Bob and Jack all say that they would have been in favour of Talmy producing The Creation's comeback.

"I can't remember all the details but he couldn't do it," says Foster, "and I thought, 'You know what, I'm not gonna get some Eighties hack engineer to do this. If I can't get Shel to do it, I'll do it. I'm (not) gonna get some guy whose idea of a good record is The Cure or something'. I wanted someone whose idea of a good record is something that Shel Talmy's made. Now who is there? Hmm. There's me!" Among Foster's previous production credits at this point were Biff Bang Pow, the Jesus and Mary Chain and Primal Scream.

In mid-1994, the Kenny-Eddie-Bob-Jack line-up of The Creation entered a recording studio – the now defunct Greenhouse Studio in Old Street, London – for the first time since 15 February 1967. The tracks recorded at the first session were 'Creation' and 'Shock Horror'. The former was, of course, always going to be the A-side. Of 'Shock Horror' Eddie says, "That was basically one of the songs I first came up with the whole idea (for) and everything. It's a song about crazy headlines in newspapers. It's a little pop song, really. (Turned out) quite well. Was pleased with that."

This was more than could be said for Eddie's feelings about the A-side. "I've never liked the song," he says. "I like the guitar riff in it. in fact, I might take the guitar riff out and use it in something else." His opinions seem strange, for the A-side is the more impressive track, with a dramatic opening – a suitable big bang for a track that addressed the dawn of everything – and a swaggering riff. However, it must be conceded that Kenny's vocal is pitched almost at helium level.

Meanwhile, it's interesting that the epic quality striven for is nothing like as successful as the same feel achieved by the band back in 1967 on 'How Does It Feel To Feel' – this despite massive advances in studio technology. Nonetheless, it was a more respectable return than anyone had a right to expect after three decades' lack of collective practice. Eddie's denunciation of tabloid journalism on the flip was rescued by some wonderful lead guitarwork in the solo and fade, in which Eddie moved seamlessly and mellifluously from conventional guitar sounds to sonics more associated with bagpipes and back again.

Foster was pleased by the results of the first studio sessions of his former heroes for 30 years. "They were great," he says of 'Creation' and 'Shock Horror'. "All their songs are great. Some are better than others but most are better than most band's songs." Of 'Creation', he says, "Pretty good song. Totally mad. Going for it. There was particularly a complicated drum bit they were all very keen on doing in that and Jack had a problem getting it. 'Come on Jack, can't you get this together?' And he says, 'Give me a break, I haven't played the drums for 22 years.' But that worked out very well: the sound and the fury as it were."

Of 'Shock Horror', Foster says, "I thought that was very good. I think that was possibly Eddie's favourite. He spent quite a bit of time getting the overlapping guitar parts. There's a kind of orchestration to that and he spent a lot of time sorting that out." An additional track was needed for the CD, a format that had not existed the last time The Creation had recorded a single. This took the shape of 'Power Surge'. "Can't remember," Eddie responds when asked what the song was about. "Just somebody experiencing some kind of power surge within 'em. Not sure which kind of power." The track certainly had aesthetic power, possessing an urgency, a fine melody, an unforgettable refrain ('I get this terrible urge/Electric power surge!') and a powerful vocal from Kenny that would surely have belatedly made it a candidate for the single's A-side had the impetus behind the choice of the A-side been an aesthetic rather than a conceptual one.

Foster: "We recorded 'Power Surge' separately somewhere else for the CD single, a few weeks later actually. I can't remember the name of the studio. We had to go in at short notice. It was some place Glen found. That's a pretty good song actually. That was Alan's favourite song of the ones we recorded. Alan was saying, 'You know what? If Kenny Pickett was 24, he'd be a fucking star from that song'."

The Creation label's 10th anniversary bash took place on 4 June 1994. Although the Albert Hall remains more known for classical concerts than rock gigs, its name is famous worldwide and it has been the setting of numerous notable rock concerts, including the Deep Purple performance which gave rise to the 1970 'Concerto for Group and Orchestra' album and the Mott The Hoople show in 1971 which led to rock being temporarily banned at the venue after riotous behaviour. However, the fact that its status was indisputably iconic was apparently of little import to Eddie.

Glen Colson: "I think we had to move heaven and earth to get Eddie to agree to that and I just said to Kenny, 'Why bother, if you've got to go through all that grief?' 'cos that was a pretty good break for 'em. But they had to beg and plead him to do it." For Bob, events immediately leading up to the gig did not augur well. "I went to Kenny's house," he recalls. "I was working in Cornwall and had no idea where the Albert Hall was, so he said follow me in his car and I did. A couple of miles from the Albert Hall I got a flat tyre at the back and the traffic was horrendous. He said, 'It's only a mile away', so I said, 'We'll just drive'. I drove there on the flat tyre and parked at the back. Something like £6 an hour. I remember thinking, 'Goodness me, I wouldn't like to stay here all day'."

However, Bob's mood began brightening when the group entered their dressing room. Bob: "The apples, oranges and sandwiches…everything's there. Then we did the soundcheck and all the other acts that were on the bill – like Oasis, Jesus and Mary Chain and all this – appeared to watch these four old farts play. We did it, they all clapped. I didn't know whether it was good or whether it would have been a sympathy vote. But they did, and that was good."

"Fantastically well," is Foster's assessment of how the Albert Hall bash went. (McGee, deep in drug problems, didn't attend.) The Creation performed two or three songs: 'Making Time', 'Painter Man' and (possibly) 'Biff Bang Pow'. "They played semi-acoustically," Foster explains. "Eddie managed to get the roaring violin shit happening on a electro-acoustic guitar. Genius. Absolutely brilliant. It was supposed to be a kind of unplugged type of thing which was really silly. It was a concept that had been put together for the gig. It wasn't me that did it. It worked in most cases, but when you had The Creation and Eddie was really giving it some on the violin bow it wasn't really quite working.

"The other bit that didn't quite work was Arthur Lee. One of his songs has got a big drum solo at the end and he suddenly decided after he'd finished singing, he skipped over to the drums and sat down to play the drum solo and there were no drum sticks and the drums weren't miked up – so he just whacked them with his hands." Bob also had misgivings about the unplugged aspect of the Albert Hall event. Bob: "That really threw Kenny, Eddie and ourselves. How could we do those sort of feedback numbers and all this that and the other with acoustic guitars? I know better now, but Eddie borrowed an acoustic guitar from somewhere – electric, like – and bashed it out on that. I thought, 'Well what's the point of that?' It was a bit weird, that was.

"I think we sort of ignored the unplugged business. We just did the songs as we would have done them. But I'm almost certain Eddie, at least for one number, had a different guitar." "It was strange," Jack says of the semi-acoustic edict. "Eddie had problems (with) feedback." He adds, "But very enjoyable job." Bob concurs on the latter point. "When we did our spot in the evening, for me it was just like, 'I'm going to take all this in'," he says. "And I just looked around and I thought, 'Getting a little bit of a payback here'." However, a reminder that that payback was merely in the form of a gesture rather than a life-changing experience was provided by the necessity for Bob to attend to his incapacitated vehicle. "After beginning the Albert Hall, I'm now out the back door jacking up my van and changing the wheel and I'm thinking to myself, 'I wonder what Rod Stewart's doing now?'," he recalls.

"I went back in and I've got oil or grease all over my hands and everything and then I had to go on and join Ride with 'How Does It Feel To Feel' (covered) with oil and everything. I thought, 'This is my life, this is – I'm on the Albert Hall stage and I'm fixing tyres in the back.' It was a great leveller for me, that was." Andy Bell recalls of The Creation, "They came and did a guest spot with Ride, playing 'How Does It Feel To Feel'." Ride had recorded a version of this song that would be released as a single that very month. "We brought them on as the finale of our set," says Bell. "They were great. They were wandering around backstage loving it. I think it was a happy night for them. They came on and sang two of them on each mic with me and Mark (Gardener, vocalist/guitarist) doing all the harmonies. Musically it was spot-on."

"That was good fun," says Jack of the Albert Hall. "We only did three numbers but it was like the whole Creation package. There was about ten bands on, I think. But we were treated so well. It was beautiful. We really got respect and it was lovely." The Creation's 10th anniversary bash was recorded, meaning that in a vault somewhere lies The Creation's performance, recordings that would make yet more great bonus tracks on a compilation.

Of the shortly released Ride version of 'How Does It Feel To Feel', Bob says, "That was nice. I thought they did a good version of it. I've got a copy of the video as well, which was done in New York. It was tighter, the tempo was tighter." His collaborator in that song's composition was also pleased by the Ride version. Eddie: "I thought it was good. Nice version. I think they tidied it up a little bit. It was more musical, their version. Ours was probably more manic."

Eddie was becoming more and more agitated by the way an initial commitment to play one or two reunion gigs was now becoming a snowball of expectations, including a possible tour of Germany. Glen Colson says of Kenny Pickett, "He wanted to go on the road. He wanted to do tours of Germany and he wanted to go to America and there was quite a bit of interest but I don't think Eddie really wanted to go more than about ten miles away from his home." He adds, "I think Kenny was talking to various people about it. He knew agents here or agents there or I think Bob might have known someone but it wasn't anything I would have wanted to get involved in. I was only interested in doing a one-off sort of thing and a one-off record and seeing how it went.

"I was just helping Kenny fulfil a couple of dreams. Jack and Bob are as sweet as pie. There's no problems with them at all. They're very down-to-earth people. They're happy to get on with it and do it. They'd have been very happy to go out and tour if they had to. Eddie was the only sort of awkward point and Kenny was talking about getting some other guitarist in if he didn't want to do it. I said they shouldn't do that, they should just do the odd gig once every two or three years and make it a bit special. But he was determined to get a band together and go out and tour whether Eddie wanted to or not."

Eddie's disinterest in any long-term Creation plans was turned into hostility by him developing a form of the ringing in the ears known as tinnitus. "I think that happened at the Mean Fiddler," Eddie says. "It was only in one ear, that's the weird thing, but that lasted for ages and, as much as I like music, it shouldn't hurt, should it?" Eddie admits that his nagging problem – which lasted around nine months – made him 'resent' the whole idea of the Creation reunion. He admits, though, that he may not have communicated this resentment – or condition – properly to his colleagues. Jack was unaware of any issue of an ear complaint and is, in any case, unsympathetic. "I've played with Eddie a few times in little local gigs and he played just as loud on them," Jack says. "I think he was trying to do a Pete Townshend or something." Townshend is well-known to have been afflicted by tinnitus. Jack continues of Eddie, "His imagination is getting the better of him, 'cos it wasn't that loud. The Mean Fiddler is not that big, is it?"

There was another problem Eddie had with The Creation reunion, one he is too good-natured to bring up in interviews and which he seems to have been too diplomatic to mention at the time to the other members. The closest he will come is when he observes, "When we rehearsed and played, it all sounded so loose and I couldn't get my head into it. (I was thinking), 'It doesn't sound that good to me,' quite honestly." For some observers, the fact that Eddie was the only working musician (unless we count Bob's use of the ukulele in his cabaret act) was not immaterial. Nor was the fact that The Creation were men in their fifties playing a young man's music.

Siebke recalls of Eddie, "The way he was talking to me was, 'I'm having to carry the lot'. He was carrying the whole band really on stage." Siebke continues: "Jack wasn't the strongest of drummers. Bob didn't even have a bass guitar. Ken was a great R&B singer but wasn't a good rock singer. (Also), he was forgetting a lot of his own lyrics. That was quite general across all the gigs. To be perfectly honest, at the end of the day it was Ed that was having to do all the work, being musical director. Also, on stage, it was his guitar act that was really the focal point. He was dealing with a drummer who on every gig – and I noticed this – would slow up. He'd start a number fast and then would go slower and slower and slower. Bob wasn't rehearsed enough for playing bass. He didn't have a bass guitar at home. So basically the rehearsals were it.

"This was also happening within the studio. It was basically a high-powered guitar band and you need a good drummer and bass player. Really, to be honest, the only way (to make it work), and I did suggest it at the time, was to bring in another drummer to play behind the stage. (At) the Garage gig I found it noticeable that he was slowing up. It needed a good drummer behind it to propel it all. I wasn't being nasty or anything like that. You do slow up and at the time Jack was in his fifties. His drumming was fine (in the Sixties) but as the years go on, you're bound to slow up, especially if you're not drumming all the time."

The ear problem and – one can only assume – his embarrassment at the shortcomings by which he considered himself to be surrounded, made Eddie reluctant to take part in another rather prestigious gig that was acquired for the band that September: supporting Oasis in their triumphant homecoming gig at Manchester's Haçienda. Oasis would rack up five hits that year – including four in the Top 10 – and a chart-topping album in 'Definitely Maybe', then the fastest-selling debut LP in UK chart history.

The band's guitarist and songwriter Noel Gallagher and singer Liam Gallagher were steeped in the lore of rock'n'roll and displayed this in their lyrics, music and attitudes – to such an extent that in some ways Oasis were almost a pastiche of a rock band rather than the real thing. Over the following two years they developed into a phenomenon, culminating in their 'Wonderwall' single becoming the anthem of both 1995 and the Britpop movement of which they were considered the figureheads. The labels and sleeves of the millions of records they sold, of course, all bore the name of the band The Creation.

Oasis were a group Alan McGee had snapped up after catching their bottom-of-the-bill appearance at a gig they had gatecrashed in Glasgow in May 1993. The Creation weren't asked to support pop's hottest young act because the two were labelmates, however. Foster: "Noel rang me up and said, 'Could you get The Creation to come and support us?' He was saying, 'I don't want them to think that I think I'm Mr Superstar and they should support me but basically they said "Who's gonna play with you?" We'll get some fucking shit band, God knows what, and I said to them, "You know what? I'm gonna get The Creation"'." It's difficult to imagine a more potent gig than supporting Oasis at this point in pop history. Had The Creation taken full advantage, it could conceivably have led to them supporting Oasis again at their record-breaking gigs in front of massive crowds at open air concerts at Loch Lomond and Knebworth in summer 1996, with all the benefits that would have conferred.

Foster: "I asked them and it was like, 'Yeah, yeah, that's all fine', then Bob, suddenly, there was something he had to do, some family thing came up, but he said, 'Not to worry, get Ed (Ball) or Tony (Barber) to dep for me'. But then Eddie said, 'Ah, I can't be bothered to go all that fucking way for one gig, you've got to be joking'. He was really down on it." Jack: "The thing about Eddie was, he's a bit screwed up and he had an almost neurotic thing about money. Of course, you know what the rock business is like: we've all been ripped off. He just had this thing that he wasn't doing any gigs now, whatever, unless the cash was in his hand before he started. If it was that everything was a hundred yards down the road from him and he could go down and do it, then he'd be well pleased but the fact he had to make the effort and go up to Manchester... Just too much of an effort for him."

Foster: "So I said, 'What the fuck are we gonna do?' He said, 'Well, if Bob doesn't show up, you just get a dep. Just get one for me'. 'But it won't be the same'. Eventually I thought, 'Who can do this convincingly?' And I thought of Andy Bell. He almost jumped down the phone when I asked him to do it. It was like the biggest deal of his fucking life." Ride's Andy Bell – who ironically would later join Oasis as a permanent member – did not react quite like Foster indicates. Though, as a disciple of Eddie Phillips, he was excited, there was a slight complication that prevented him from accepting the offer on the spot.

Bell: "Kenny phoned me and said, 'We've been offered this gig and we really want to do it, but Eddie doesn't want to.' At the time apparently he (Eddie) had his own thing going doing a solo guitar thing with drum machines and stuff, going off and doing weddings. That's the way Kenny described it. If you are really stuck to the idea of him being a Sixties legend, it's hard to digest. (Laughs) But it's one of those things: it's fair enough, he obviously felt like that was a better option for him at the time. I think he was a bit bemused by it all. But you've got to say 'Respect to Eddie Phillips' because that really marked him out as an eccentric for me."

Bell told Pickett he would be willing provided Eddie didn't object. "So I got Eddie's number off Kenny and rang him almost straight away," says Bell. "I just said 'Do you mind if I do this? Because if you do then I won't do it – I'd rather not offend anyone.' And he was just like, 'Yeah, just do it, it's fine'. He didn't seem bothered either way. So I agreed to do it and then learnt the songs."

The choice of Bell to dep for Eddie was fairly obvious. Not only had Bell participated in Ride's cover of 'How Does It Feel To Feel' but he was become adept at bowing his guitar, something he started as a consequence of witnessing the Mean Fiddler gig. "Immediately I saw them I started using a violin bow because Eddie had done that and I twigged all the history then," Bell says. "He was one of the forgotten pieces in the jigsaw-puzzle of Sixties guitarists. I think he's amazing. He's a one-off because he does something that no-one else does, which I guess is all you really want as a guitar player.

"Pete Townshend can probably play in a really accomplished kind of style now but it's just the way he plays really simple things on a Rickenbacker that really do it. And the same with Eddie. When he plays a violin bow he gets such a good sound out of it. He's more of a sound guitarist. The kind of guitarist I like, anyway, like Townshend, Eddie and in modern terms someone like Kevin Shields, who's just all about the sounds and the chord shapes and that kind of thing rather than anything to do with soloing."

At first, Bell had experienced exactly the kind of problems with the violin bow as had afflicted Eddie in his early experiments. Bell: "You've (got) to put rosin on the bow. That's the only thing that had me stuck for a while. I'd got this violin bow in the classical music shop in Oxford City Centre and I'd gone home with it and tried to make it work and it just wasn't happening. I was thinking, 'This guy Eddie Phillips is a fucking genius because I can't get anything out of this stupid violin bow.' And then someone said – it think it was my mum, 'cos I mentioned it to her at some point and she's a violin player – 'Have you tried rosin on the bow?' As soon as I did that, then it was great, it all happened. At that stage it was just for fun. Then when I got my head round it we started doing cover versions and then for the gig I expanded it a little bit more."

The decision to cover 'How Does It Feel To Feel' rather than any other Creation song was taken for what some might consider a rather bizarre reason. "Because it had a double vocal," says Bell. "Or at least it seemed to lend itself to having two vocals all the time. We had a lot of songs with double vocal harmonies. We tried a few but some of them sound like they could only be done by The Creation. It just felt right." Interestingly enough, the world could have been treated to a version of 'How Does It Feel To Feel' by Oasis were it not for Ride's version, as Bell discovered on the night of the Haçienda gig. Bell: "Liam told me they used to rehearse with a cover of the same song that we released and said, 'If you hadn't done it, we might have ended up doing it ourselves.'"

The Haçienda gig went ahead on 5 September 1994, there having been no opportunity for Bell to rehearse with Kenny, Jack and Buzzcock Tony Barber, who played bass. "They picked me up at McDonalds in Oxford on the roundabout going up to London," remembers Bell. "I jumped in the back of a Transit van and started writing out chords and all that stuff on a little notebook. I knew the songs well enough but you never know what arrangements they were going to play." Bell didn't agonise over replicating Eddie's parts. "I was just playing the chords right and having it as much as I could. If I had been recording with them I'd have made much more of an effort to get it exactly right, but on the night it was kind of a bash... in the right kind of spirit."

Though the Haçienda's capacity was not massive, there was a sense of occasion about the Oasis gig. Bell: "It was packed out because it was the release night of their first album in Manchester, so it was a big night for them." The Oasis crowd, many of whom would not have heard of The Creation, were open-minded about the support act. "I felt like it was going down pretty well at the time," says Bell. "From the stage it seemed to be happening. We did about six songs. It was another great night." Bell was very impressed by Jack: "When I was playing with him, he was looking at me the whole time, which was great, to make sure I kind of felt at home. You could tell he was doing that with Eddie as well. He'd be looking at you to get the times and to get the changes. He knew the parts himself but he was following the guitar player even though I was doing my first gig with him."

Despite the enthusiasm of its participants and the favourable crowd reaction, with half the Creation not present, was there not a danger that the gig could be ultimately meaningless? "Kind of," concedes Bell. "It was good to do it to kind of make Kenny feel good, make the band feel good and get some respect from the next generation of fans. Anything that would have helped The Creation's name go forward is worth doing.

"I don't feel it was an important evening for them to develop as a band. I didn't feel like I was going to join the band or they were going to necessarily go forward and rebirth and get in the charts again. It was like, they wanted to do this. Great, I'll do it. It means I can go up and see Oasis, it means I can be onstage and be Eddie Phillips for a night. Fantastic. I was only 22, 23 years old so it was all exciting."

On the meaningless issue, Joe Foster has this to say: "Jack did point out, 'Look, remember, I was faced with a particular point where everybody had gone and I was the only person left out of The Creation and basically Shel reminded me that there was an obligation... I had to swallow my pride, get hold of Kenny and get Kim Gardner to change his mind and come back and get Ronnie Wood sorted. Basically, it wasn't quite the same but it did work. And this isn't for the remainder of our career. It's for one night.' So I thought, 'You're probably right'. To me, Eddie is certainly the focal guy, the key man, but one does what one has to.

"It started off with them all playing. I don't think (Eddie) was deliberately being awkward by any means. Possibly it was a pretty fucking stupid idea to go all the way to Manchester for one show. So they did it. Tony played bass and Andy played guitar and Evan Dando did backing vocals. It was pretty good, actually. Went down very well." Glen Colson adds of the participation of Bell and Barber, "Kenny was very pleased with all that. He thought it was great. Kenny was excited that young bands were getting involved."

Not so excited – in fact, rather angry – was Kenny's feeling about Eddie not getting involved. In an interview given to Jud Cost just over two months later (although not published until '97, when it appeared in *Ugly Things*), Kenny said, "The current personnel is the original line-up, except for Eddie, who doesn't want to tour unless he gets paid expenses every day, so we decided, 'No thank you'."

The Creation performed one last gig with Eddie. It took place at the Mean Fiddler on 22 August 1995. Though his hair had gone white in the two years since the first Mean Fiddler gig, Kenny was noticeably more svelte than he had been in '93. The group, meanwhile, seemed in reasonably good humour and shape. At one point Bob walked over to Eddie while he was playing a bowed guitar part and whispered in his ear. An obliging Eddie then turned round and applied his catgut to Bob's bass strings. However, this apparent harmony was misleading. Though the group had already started the recording of their new album, the process would very soon break down due to a conflict which caused bitterness that lingers to this day.

Joe Foster seems a bit vague about how the decision by Creation Records to offer the band an album deal emerged. "I don't know," he shrugs. "Once the single – it got a lot of radio – sold a few, Alan just said, 'Don't you think we should do an album?' I said, 'I dunno – well, will they do an album?' And they said, 'Yeah, let's do an album'. So they went and did it."

Jack offers: "When we did the single, we started doing things and this and that and we said, 'What do you wanna do, Joe?' He said, 'Well the hell with it, let's just keep recording and see if we can get an album. See what turns out'." McGee says, not much less vaguely, "We kind of got to know them. Then Joe said, 'Look, give me ten grand (budget) and I'll make a

Creation album' and we gave Joe ten grand and he made the album."

The dream had come true. After splitting in frustration in the Sixties at the way their classic records were falling on stony ground, The Creation had been offered the chance to record a full-length, organic studio album – an opportunity they had never previously been afforded – by a new generation of fans. Despite his misgivings about The Creation as a live unit, even Eddie couldn't find it in him to decline when Creation Records decided that they would extend their single deal into an album contract.

Rod Siebke, however, thinks Eddie only agreed in order to help out the rest of the band. "To be honest, Ed was against the whole thing from the start, really," he says. "The way I saw it was that Ken and Jack really were pushing him into it. It was like a dream to do it for them more than anything but really Jack and Ken were looking at it as more of a career move. Whereas Ed didn't really want that at all. He'd already got his career with his writing and everything else. I don't really think he thought it was a good thing, hence the way it went."

McGee admits that that ten grand budget "was pretty low at the time. Creation had got quite big by that point. We'd already sold fifteen million Oasis albums by that point...we were awash with money." Says Foster, "It would have been the budget for a new band's first album. Not a wild amount, but they certainly weren't held back in any way. There was never any figure mentioned. It was just assumed that they would do what they do and it probably wouldn't cost that much. They were up to book a studio that didn't cost that much and then they could spend as long as they wanted."

Certain fissures began to emerge as soon as the album was proposed. Eddie: "Jack came to the project with a bit of a chip on his shoulder (because) I'd written all the early stuff and he thought I'd made a lot of money out of it. The only decent money we ever made out of it was Boney M, 'Painter Man', but Creation songs never made a fantastic lot of money. That came out in a conversation that I had with him, that he was determined this time to make sure that he got a look-in on the songwriting side. I think that's why him and Kenny ploughed on with that side of it and I just went along with it. They thought that no one person should make a load of money out of this thing. It should all be like a quarter split. I went, 'Alright, fair enough'."

Eddie's unprompted use of the phrase 'a bit of a chip on his shoulder' is interesting in light of Jack's almost identical words about himself when explaining why he had rebuffed Kenny's approach to reform The Creation in the late Seventies.

The majority of the tracks on the album – which would ultimately be titled 'Power Surge' – would be written by Kenny and Jack, with Bob contributing one song and Eddie contributing no more than the three that had appeared on the single and CD single. Jack: "Kenny said to me, 'Well I've got some stuff here and Eddie's got one or two, but you used to write songs – have you got any that will fit?' I said, 'Well yeah, I've got some stuff here that I could adapt to The Creation'. So Kenny come round my place. I play keyboard as well as drums and we sat down and I played him some of the stuff and he thought they were good. I said, 'You're not crapping me now, don't muck me about' and he said, 'No, if I thought they were crap, I wouldn't sing 'em'. I said, 'That's fair enough. We'll go ahead and record 'em'. 'Cos I was a bit concerned whether they'd be suitable for The Creation or not. But I think they work."

Though The Creation would now have far greater recording technology at their disposal, Foster had a vision of recording more in line with 1967 than 1995. "We decided (to) cut it totally punk rock," he recalls. "Just cut it the way they are. If you cut somebody playing the way they do, then that's what you get. We weren't gonna let anybody lay everything down separately and start getting all weird electric piano bits. The thing is, they didn't want to do that anyway. They were going to make a Creation album. They very much figured and planned, 'We're going to do this stuff the way we always did it'."

Of course, there was always the theoretical possibility that The Creation might have decided to record a collection of, say, country songs on their comeback album. After all, the contract was for four people to record an album: there was nothing in the contract that stipulated that the music recorded for the project had to be 'psychedelic punk'. Asked how he would have felt if Eddie had decided not to bow his guitar on any tracks on the album, Foster responds, "It would have been disappointing but I don't think it would have been very likely because that's what this project was going to be. Eddie's got other bits and pieces that he does where he plays in slightly different styles to suit what he's doing and he can do them all very well. This is one of the styles he does and it's the one that suits that music and it's pretty unlikely he'd start playing sort of country (Gene Vincent guitarist) Cliff Gallup kind of thing. He's got a bag of tricks and applies the ones that fit in with the songs."

This, though, raises the issue of whether this reunion was always destined to produce music that was in some respects contrived. When McGee and Foster decided they would like to release a Creation album, they obviously had in mind a record that sounded like the Sixties Creation tracks that they were so in love with. The Creation themselves would have been aware that people picking up a new album would expect certain sounds associated with the band: bowed guitar, surreal lyrics and a musical style that had mixed pop, rock, psychedelia and a pinch of the avant garde. Yet in the Sixties, The Creation had neither played to expectations nor adhered to a musical category. In fact, almost the opposite: they merely made the music they felt like making and gave barely a thought to whether or not there was a market for it.

Of course, its highly unlikely that they would have countenanced 'Cliff Gallup-style' songs back then either – but that would have been on the grounds that it wasn't their scene, not because they were trying to adhere to a formula. They were now attempting to play a style of music none of them had played in the intervening three decades, one which to a certain extent had become an established genre rather than the innovation it was back then. The Creation in 1995 were, in short, effectively trying to pretend to be the musicians (and people) they were in 1966-67, despite the fact that the circumstances and motivations that had generated their music in those years simply didn't exist any more. Perhaps it doesn't matter – after all, the ultimate objective is to produce a listenable record and these circumstances don't necessarily preclude that – but it's a process that smacks of an artificiality that was the antithesis of the music the band made in the Sixties.

There is also another problem about rock-band reunions which has been proved time and again: even with a line-up that had previously made magic, there is always something missing. When bands lay down re-recordings of their classic hits, they never sound as good as the originals, despite the fact that individual members have all improved their technique in the interim. A beat has been skipped and it is never possible to regain that previous rhythm.

As Eddie puts it, "You can never ever turn the clock back and do things like you did. I always say that for every great record you hear, if that record had been recorded three weeks later it would probably have sounded different to what it does." Though he was looking for that classic Creation sound, one thing Foster would have been against was re-recording an old Creation track for the new album like the version of 'Making Time' for the Jet/Polydor album. "I would have advised them against it because we've got Shel's take and that is the classic," he says. "All I could be doing would be to produce a cover version of that, which is one thing if you've got some young band but I'd have felt very funny trying to get some kind of authentic sound together with the same guys. If they'd really wanted to do it, I'd have done it but I just felt, 'Let's leave that for the minute'."

Bob disagrees, saying, "I think it would have been a good idea." Jack sides with Foster: "We felt that they should stand in their own right. People would make comparisons. They were done in that time: in the late, middle Sixties. That's where they belong. But they still sound good now. Not all of 'em but some of them, they really stand the test of time. If somebody wants to do a cover, that's their privilege but the band itself, to try and do a modern version, that would be crap."

The studio chosen was Elephant Studios in Walworth, south-east London "because it had all the equipment: pianos, organs, and you could go in there, rehearse, play live, do whatever you wanted," says Foster. If the band did decide to rehearse, Foster would be present. Asked if they were a bit nervous about recording after such a long gap, Foster says, "No, not at all. They were never daunted by anything. We'd go down the studio and we'd just show up there, we'd have breakfast, we'd start recording, have lunch, record some more. All pretty straightforward and relaxed, really."

Foster – aided by engineer Nick Robbins – had the opportunity as the sessions progressed to get to know the people whose songs he had so admired and had played live so many times. Of Kenny, he says, "Very nice. Straightforward, stand-up guy. An excitable guy in some ways and I can see when he was younger that would have got him in a few scrapes and a bit of hot water, but I think he'd become slightly warier by this stage." Nonetheless, he makes this observation on the aggression of some of Kenny's lyrics:"Kenny was fucking 24. It didn't matter what he looked like. Kenny Pickett was 24 and he was going for it and he was angry and you better not get in his way. He has that in him. He basically managed to sit on it. Certainly in singing or performing it would come out because he had it in him. Kenny wouldn't take any shit off anybody.

"Eddie has his moments," Foster continues. "He's not so much calmer as a bit more thoughtful in some ways, which gives him an air of calm sometimes – but he can hold his own with the best of them. Bob seemed fine. By all accounts years ago he was quite a manipulative fellow but I didn't get any of that from him at all. He seemed to have really made his peace with everybody and (be a) very professional, very co-operative guy. Very good with people. Talented and all the rest of it. No problem to deal with at all. Jack's really nice. Really nice guy. Good drummer. Interesting person."

Asked if he felt Eddie was the leader of the band, Foster says, "Not really. They all seemed very egalitarian and they all had their say. They were all straightforward guys. Everybody had ideas and they discussed them." McGee felt otherwise. "Kenny was the leader of the group, to be honest," he says. "And Eddie was probably the genius. That was the way it broke down."

McGee's perception is supported by Andy Bell, who says of the singer's demeanour, "He always seemed to be the one that was most keen and he'd come and be really polite and nice to everyone and he'd always be trying to meet everyone. If you came with (someone), he wanted to meet them all and find out what he did."

The possibility of old enmities between Bob and Kenny surfacing once the band were in the confines of a studio and facing the possibility of creative differences proved groundless. "They'd taken the initiative themselves to resolve that," says Foster. "You've never seen two guys who've gone from being at each other's throats to being absolutely cool with each other. They were always like that. Bob always spoke abut how he really admired Kenny's singing and his songs and Kenny would always say – against the mainstream of opinion – 'My favourite Creation record is "If I Stay Too Long" , which is nothing to do with me, Bob's thing'. Bob was always quite gobsmacked by that."

The friendliness seemed to go deeper than merely letting bygones be bygones: Kenny and Jack were once genuinely of the opinion that Bob was prone to (to use Jack's phrase) 'stirring' but, from Foster's recollection, were now genuinely of the opinion that he had changed. Foster: "I think it was Jack more than anybody that said, 'Yeah, he did have that about him a bit but he's really got over that. The last few times I've seen him, there's no suggestion of that kind of thing at all'."

Jack and Bob had a lot in common as a legacy of their post-Creation careers on the cabaret circuit. In fact, there had been an interesting division of paths between the two halves of the original Creation: Kenny and Eddie had been required to take day jobs following the split whereas Bob and Jack had become jobbing performers. Foster theorises this had actually changed the latter pair, especially Bob, as personalities: "They'd worked the cabaret circuit and I think they'd both got over the idea of pushing yourself at the expense of others because you can't do that in that kind of scenario. You've got a whole troupe of people – players, comedians and all sorts – and you can't go in there like *Spinal Tap* and say you want the biggest dressing room because everyone will laugh at you.

"I think that's something Bob and Jack had in common that really knocked a bit of silliness out of them. Which is handy. They could laugh about various places they'd played in that incarnation of their life."

Recording, Eddie revealed, "took a long while, 'cos we had to do it in down time when the studio was available and when we could all get together." Foster saw this as no problem. "We'd do a couple of days at a time, and in some ways it worked out better because we had time to think about things and hang out in other contexts. It did end up working out slightly better. They had more time to consider things."

The 'straightforward' process Foster mentions at some point during the making of the album become extremely complicated. "We started off okay," says Jack. "Eddie missed about four songs on it and one of the reasons was he really couldn't find the time. He was very busy. I think he really didn't want to get involved too much because of his other stuff. We were saying to him, 'Come on, Ed, this is just the one chance, a one-off' and he said, 'Well, I've done some stuff for other albums, back in the Seventies, and never got paid.' I said, 'Well this ain't like that, is it?' But his interest was very difficult to keep going.

"When he first came in, he was fine but then he seemed to never spare the time and we had to sort of talk to him, chat him up… The further the album went on the more he drifted off. We got a few guys to finish the album off. So me and Kenny – basically, we sort of ran the thing – said, 'Listen, (if) we want to get this album out, we've got to do the work' so we did all the work. We booked in for three days and Bob'd turn up for one, play his bass and then go. It was really disappointing. Eddie was the same. We were disappointed in the attitude 'cos we thought it was a great opportunity."

Bob says, "I just said, 'Well okay then, we'll see how it goes with what we're doing now'. And sure enough exactly the same thing happened again. Within 18 months it was back to exactly where it was at the end (the first time round) and I purposely made a point of being there on time – a 400-mile round trip for me. I've gone down there and somebody's not turned up and I've had to turn round and come all the way back." Who is he referring to? Bob: "Eddie, probably.

"I turned up at one rehearsal," he adds, "and everybody was there, we just didn't rehearse and I drove 200 miles back." Bob, though he appears to have remained above the fray and generally philosophical, was also puzzled by Eddie's reluctance to fully commit. "I could see Kenny was frustrated with Eddie all the way through," he says. "Kenny was still doing his plumbing. To him, it was his chance of being a professional entertainer or singer again and this guy was saying, 'Nah, I'd rather do me pubs down the road'. And I couldn't understand that either. You know: one minute you're doing the Albert Hall, the next minute doing a wedding down the road. There was a golden opportunity to reinstate – even if it only reached the level we were before – and put The Creation to where it should have been.

"I don't think we would have ever been the top, but we certainly could have put ourselves back on the shelf we were on and really we should have made a fortune." Things came to a head when Eddie informed either the rest of the band or – more likely – Kenny that he would not be attending further sessions unless he was paid for it. Siebke: "Ed was asking for studio fees, session fees. Basically, 'I'll play on it but I want paying upfront first.' Because he couldn't see it going anywhere."

If Eddie had no faith that the modern-day Creation were capable of recording an album that would reap any major financial dividends and the sessions were eating into the time available to perform live work that was, it was logical he would feel entitled to claim remuneration. Its also fairly inconceivable that this gentle character would have done it in anything other than a diplomatic way. Nonetheless, it was a proposal guaranteed not to go down well, especially with someone of such a fiery temperament as Kenny, already utterly frustrated and bewildered by Eddie's ongoing reluctance to take advantage of the offered opportunities. Nor would it have impressed Jack, who had put Creation work over better-paid gigs. Jack: "If I had a gig to do and it interfered with Creation, I would book somebody to cover in my place and I would go down and play with The Creation."

Of Eddie's ultimatum, Bob says, "I don't know but I can hear him saying it." It was decided between Kenny and Jack – Bob, up in Wales, seems to have been out of the loop – to continue recording the album without him. Jack: "When we started off, Eddie was there, Bob was there; then the enthusiasm seemed to die away very quickly and me and Kenny had the job of finishing off the album. So that's what we did. We had an obligation to Creation Records. They'd been great to us. Treating us really good, giving us a decent deal, some money up front, all this stuff. Me and Kenny at least, we felt we had an obligation to get the album finished so that they had something."

The album sessions had, to some extent, been marked by a fluid attitude to who was actually present. "There were one or two sessions which I didn't attend," reveals Bob, "because I couldn't and they said, 'We're going to do this session, we've got Ed Ball or somebody to play bass. Is that okay with you?' and I said 'Fine'... Because at the end I thought, 'As long as I get what everybody's agreed to.' So I just went along with it." However, Bob couldn't accept turning up at one session to find Gary Grainger in Eddie's place because this was occurring without Eddie's knowledge.

Grainger was a guitarist of no little talent, having played in Rod Stewart's star-studded late-Seventies band and co-written several songs with him including 'I Was Only Joking'. However, Grainger's undeniable ability was not the issue to Bob but the way that Eddie was deceived in his deployment. "He was oblivious to the session," says Bob. "I went to the session, met the guitarist, rang up Eddie and I said, 'Eddie, this is happening again'. It was just being honest and telling the truth. I thought, 'What's the point?' It wasn't right. It was almost word for word as it was in the Sixties. I told him (as) soon as I heard it, I said, 'Eddie, somebody else is at the session. I don't like it".

Foster has a different perspective on the gaps in personnel during the making of the album but, as someone who hasn't got a bad word to say about any of The Creation, one wonders whether he is glossing over the real situation when he says, "It would happen on occasion, but they had their B-team there. Ed Ball and Tony Barber would come to the sessions mainly to hang out, but basically they depped for various members, playing stuff for radio sessions, live and stuff like that; nobody had any problem with them playing a bit, laying down a basic track if someone hadn't shown up yet.

"It was material that they'd worked out what they were doing: 'We're doing this song, we know what's going on with it, Tony this is what we want you to do. Keep in mind that Eddie will be overdubbing all his parts on top of this later.' They put down a basic track like that."

Bob rated Grainger a "good guitar player. He was a fan of Eddie's and he copied him." Bob's recollection is that Eddie did not put down the original guitar tracks on 'Someone's Gonna Bleed', 'That's How I Found Love', 'Killing Song', 'City Life', 'English Language' and 'O+N'.

If neither Eddie or Bob were happy about the former being replaced, both were furious over the other decision taken by Kenny and Jack in response to Eddie's supposedly lackadaisical attitude toward the album's sessions. According to Eddie and Bob, it had been agreed at the beginning of the sessions that songwriting royalties would be split equally among the four members, as would the credit. When the conclusion was drawn that Eddie was no longer pulling his weight, the decision was made to tear up that original agreement.

Jack is unapologetic. "We all agreed we were all going to contribute an equal amount of songs and we found that Eddie and Bob just weren't bothering," says Jack. "Bob had stopped writing, I think, because he came up with one song which was quite good but he wrote it in about 1972. I don't know where Eddie was. He was totally screwed up mentally, his attitude. We kept saying, 'Okay, Eddie, we want you to contribute some songs to the album but if you're not going to bring 'em along or whatever, you can't be bothered, then somebody else (will write them)'. He had an attitude. He had a big, big chip on his shoulder about he should have been a millionaire and he wasn't.

"Kenny sorted the dosh out and that was fine with me, bearing in mind that back in the old days I never got any royalties off any of 'em and I wrote four songs on this album. Took my time doing it. They were good songs. They stood up. And Kenny said, 'Hey, listen, I'm not going quarter shares with these guys 'cos they're just not bothering'. So I'm afraid it's same old Creation. Same old shit."

Bob's memory is slightly different: "I had other songs as well but because I was doing a summer season in Newquay in Cornwall, they got the songs together, I'd come over, learn it, play it on the day and that was that. A few times I went along with a little demo tape and a couple of songs and (said) 'Have a listen to these'. It was like, 'Yeah, okay, fine'. I didn't come heavy and say, 'I've got more songs' because the original deal was verbally among us all that we would go equal parts. But when it came to the advance we got, Kenny then said, 'No – I've written eight songs, Jack's written four songs, you've only written one.' They decided to split it up different. So I just shrugged my shoulders and said, 'Well, okay – give me my little bit and that's it'."

Eddie' shares the point of view that Jack and Kenny were hogging the writing. Eddie: "I was coming up with ideas but I would turn up at the sessions and Kenny and Jack had songs ready to do. And I'm not a pushy person. I would never, ever say to anybody, 'Look, I don't want to do those songs, I want you to do one of my songs'. I just go along with it. If that's what you want to do, all right, we'll do that. And they then was really sort of carving up the writing between them so I just let it go that way." He also told *Ugly Things*, "I thought I'd go along with their songs and I'd routine them, knock 'em into shape and do the best I could with them 'cos we're all getting equals out of it anyway."

This latter comment backs up Bob's assertion that it was agreed at the beginning that each member would get equal songwriting royalties regardless of how much he contributed. The decision to make the remuneration for songs accurately reflect each individual's contributions to the album came as a rude shock to the guitarist, one that brought the whole project close to collapse.

As a consequence of this change, of the £10,000 advance the band – or Glen Colson – had managed to secure for their publishing deal, it was decided by Kenny that just under £2,000 would go to Bob and £8,000 would go to Kenny and Jack, leaving Eddie with nothing. When informed of this by Bob, Eddie was understandably unhappy. Joe Foster, standing on the sidelines and trying to complete an album, was merely befuddled.

Foster: "There was something going on between Eddie and Jack where Jack was saying, 'Alright, well look, we can split it four ways or we'll do it this way or do the other' and Eddie wanted some kind of separate side deal going on: 'I think I should get part of this song' and all that kind of thing and Jack said, 'You're quite welcome to part of that song – you give me part of 'Painter Man' and I'll give you part of this song. We'll split 'em all four ways'. It was all a bizarre kind of tiff like that. Something weird was going on that I couldn't quite get my head around but it seemed to be resolved in one way or another."

In actual fact, it was only resolved by a crisis meeting in McGee's office attended – from Eddie's recollection – by himself, Jack, McGee and Foster. What followed Eddie remembers as a somewhat distressing contretemps, the upshot of which was that McGee then secured Eddie a separate publishing deal and advance of £5,000 with Sony. (Jack, by the way, while acknowledging that the original agreement was scrapped, says he doesn't remember this causing ructions. "I didn't know there was any arguments," he says. "Everybody turned up, everybody was nice. We all made an effort to get on with each other and we put the album together.")

Glen Colson adds of the original publishing deal, "I remember having to give back my share for some reason. I was managing them so I was getting 20 per cent of everything that I lined up. If I got them a gig, I'd take 20 per cent of the gig. If I did a record deal, I'd take 20 per cent of the record. We split it five ways. It was the band and me. I can't remember what took place but I got them the publishing deal with my publisher,

Peter Barnes, and then I think he called me one day and said, 'Eddie Phillips or someone's not happy about you having a percentage of these songs' or something. I said, 'Well I don't give a shit, he can have 'em back if he wants.' It didn't bother me."

McGee must have been as befuddled as Foster, not just about the intricacies of the disputed publishing agreement but the fact that a band who were being given a second chance they had never thought they'd have – one that he was financing despite knowing full well that it would never reap great dividends, or possibly any – seemed to be spurning it. However, he denies that at any point he considered pulling the plug on the project. "I just let people get on with it," he says. "Some people would call that non-A&R. I actually call it A&R: let the artist be the artist. That way you get great records or you get absolutely abominable records."

Sessions continued, although Eddie harboured a lingering resentment. "I agreed to finish the album with them and went back in the studio and played over most of the stuff that was already recorded," he says. "I think I played on everything. But I still didn't like it."

There were a couple of tracks that were left off the recorded album. One was 'Out Of My Mind'. A number in then-contemporary synth-pop vein with a lustful lyric, it was fairly unremarkable. From Foster's recollections, it barely qualifies as a Creation track anyway. Foster: "My wife played organ on that. Tony may have played drums, Ed Ball bass. No idea why we didn't use it. Not savage enough, I suppose. My wife (then girlfriend) was credited as Emma Gill. As a former child prodigy concert pianist, she was well capable of playing on many of my productions of that period."

The other outtake was a far more regrettable omission. 'Bald Eagle' was a composition that saw Kenny return to the socio-political seam in his songwriting that went right back to 'Going Down Fast'. A track which tore into the imperialism of the United States, it boasted a brooding atmosphere, partly due to slow tom-tom work by Jack. It would have provided a merciful respite in the indie-band Wall Of Sound atmosphere of the final track-listing.

Foster: "'Bald Eagle' was recorded in an in-between session separate from the main body of the album, along with the basic track to another song. Kenny, Jack, Tony Barber Ed Ball and Gary Grainger played on the basic tracks, and some backing vocals were done by myself, a friend of Kenny's called Ian and his girlfriend. I played tambourine, as is traditional for producers on Creation sessions, slightly more in time than Shel according to a vote among all the band members but otherwise just as badly."

"I thought it was a great song by Kenny," says Jack. "The lyric was superb. He talked about the bald eagle representing America, whereas all the dreams of America have never quite come about. This great land of free power and democracy and all that, somewhere it's not quite come off. I was so disappointed (when they said) they're not going to use it on the album – but then when I heard it I can understand why. We never quite put it together right musically."

Bob: "It's about the American dollar and we did a real sort of 'Apache'-type (version). It was really knocking the American dollar. It's a good song, that. Kenny may have said keep it back or something. I'm disappointed." Foster: "'Bald Eagle' was meant possibly for someone else to record, that's why it wasn't on the album, 'cos it didn't really fit. It was a good idea for a song but once they got it down... It wasn't really The Creation. In the vocal melody, it kind of fitted into that tradition but it didn't really work."

Another disappointing omission from the album – indeed, from the album's sessions – was 'Lay The Ghost'. Versions of this track had been recorded for the previous Creation (semi-)reunion in the Eighties and had been the title track for the live album resulting from the Mean Fiddler gig. Being a song about The Creation, it would also have fitted the project thematically. "For some reason that one didn't come up," says Foster, "I think Ed (Ball) or Tony mentioned at one point that they really liked that song and Kenny was like, 'Aah, fuckin' rubbish'. He would often be like that about his own work. I don't know why."

Jack believes it was "just sort of forgotten. It was a pretty good number but, for some reason, it got overlooked." Eddie: "Maybe we should have done that but maybe that's a sign of how the thinking was within the band that that didn't get a look in. It's a good song and it's a shame to let it go."

The album started with the A-side of the taster single and would-be anthem 'Creation'. Though good enough, it turned out, in fact, to be one of the album's weakest tracks. It was followed by the extra track from the CD version of that single, and album title track 'Power Surge'. This was succeeded by 'Someone's Gonna Bleed', which Jack recalls as a solo Kenny composition. The track's lyric condemns the bloodshed caused by the world's leaders while Jack contributes some excellent drum patterns. Foster commends the backing vocals. "They're mostly done by Jack with Bob and Ed Ball," the producer says. "Eddie sang some of them as well. Either Jack or Bob singing alone is like, 'Bloody hell' but the two of them doing that particular Creation-style backing vocal was like, 'Fuck'. Quite shocking in a way." 'Shock Horror' was followed by 'That's How I Found Love', again written according to Jack by Kenny alone. It's a sweet track very much in the mould of 'That's How Strong My Love Is', the soul cover Kenny had always sung so well. Foster: "That's quite a nice one. I think that's the one Kenny talked about Bob doing part of the vocal on. Bob does sing on that, certainly on the choruses." It's a genuinely affecting number and it is refreshing to see Kenny was capable of coming up with a lyric of unabashed devotion in contrast to the aggressive attitude he'd so often taken to romance in his songs.

'Killing Song' was written by Jack alone "about the way mankind has this habit of killing everything," he explains. "Very simple song. I just like songs that say something rather than 'I love you, you love me, Scooby dooby doo'. Find them a bit boring. I like songs to have a bit of depth to them." The track ends in an impressively chaotic feedback orgy.

'Nobody Wants To Know', Bob's sole songwriting contribution to the album, starts with a slow, booming drum sound that purposely echoes the intro to 'How Does It Feel To Feel'. The song is a wistful examination of the lack of success of Bob's post-Creation band Smiley, pitching a melody of marching ebullience against a lyric of sheer resignation. "I wrote that in about 1969 or '70," explains Bob. "It says, 'We're not stars of stage, screen or radio/Or had three hit singles in a row/You've got to write a song of your own/But nobody wants to know.' I had that song in my back pocket for years."

He's not completely happy with the way the recording ended up. "I tried to steer them into the 'How Does It Feel To Feel' thing but the engineer and everybody else was trying to steer it away," he laments. "If you listen to that, you can imagine if it was done a bit more stricter, it would have turned out okay. Good solo in that Eddie does as well." Bob is being too hard on the track: it's one of the best on the album and would have made a fine bookend to Kenny's ruminations on a similar subject, 'Lay The Ghost'.

It would have been appropriate for Bob to sing 'Nobody Wants To Know'. Questioned as to why he didn't get a vocal track on the album, Bob says, "I asked and it was 'No'. The only way I could get a song in was to let Kenny sing it." Kenny did insist on some input. "He didn't like some of the lyrics on that," says Bob. "It says, 'I've got to make it before I get too old' and he didn't like that line. He's a little bit paranoid about getting old, I think."

'City Life', a Jack Jones song, has a real punky ambience, sounding like a hybrid of The Jam and the Sex Pistols, with Kenny's vocals even resembling Johnny Rotten's in places. "It's a pretty rocking kind of track," declares Foster. "Fairly straightforward, not very adventurous, but there's some nice mad Eddie guitar bits in there." Kenny's 'English Language' is that rare, perhaps unique, beast: a rock song about a dialect. Kenny maintains impressively the conceit of the English language as a persona commenting on its own uses, misuses, achievements and failures. The Chuck Berry guitar licks and old-style rock'n'roll chord changes sound out of place, though, and its only the knowledge that The Creation were always trying to break the musical rules that inhibits the comment that such music has no place on a product bearing The Creation's name.

"I think that's supposed to be of humorous piece," says Foster of 'English Language'. "That's why it's got several different guitar bits played in slightly different styles. It's supposed to be a humorous piece but I think the humour was supposed to be more in the music than the lyric. Good melody, though." The layering of guitars was not all done at the same session. Foster: "Basically (we had) a plan to put different types of guitar more or less doing the same thing at different spots in slightly different styles. We would go back to it whenever anybody fancied doing it. It depended who was about. Gary Grainger was over there one day and did one as well."

'Free Men Live Forever' is a profound-sounding track that is one of the album's highpoints. "Jack originated that one," says Foster. "Before it had a lyric, it wasn't taken all that seriously. Kenny and Bob used to call it 'Three Gays Live Together'. Jack didn't like that because it was his title, he was quite proud of it. Jack's quite deep in his own way." Jack explains, "'Free Men Live Forever' is based on what Abraham Lincoln said at the Gettysburg address. I heard that and I thought, 'Christ, I like that'. And he was killed a little while after that. I wrote a song round it."

Though it may have been Jack's song, this track marked the only time Eddie managed to get the vision of a marriage of rock and medieval chanting that he was pursuing on 'The Mitra' onto a mainstream release (if we discount the French Trema single). "Eddie came up with that odd Gregorian chant-ey kind of vocal, kind of scary Rasputin vocal," says Foster. The result was a song of real musical power and lyrical poignancy that did Eddie's original vision proud. "Pretty good song actually, in the end," concedes Foster. "Once Eddie stuck that bit in, everybody started to take it more seriously. Oddly enough, it started to sound more like what

Jack had been talking about when he first brought the idea in. There was a dangerous moment when it might have gone in a lighter direction, which would have ruined it."

Of his composition 'Ghost Division', Jack says "Basically a social comment. It's about the city and it's just another look at it, another angle." Foster: "That's a damn good song. I like that. It's again a thing that Jack originated. The elongated melody is very good. Having the melody twice as many bars long as you would normally have and that chorus which is mono-chordal, that was a very interesting thing to do. From a musicological point of view, it's fascinating."

Of the album closer 'O+N', Jack recalls, "I had this thought about what it would be like (if) I left the planet earth on a rocket ship and it just didn't go to the moon, it went into space and it just went on and on and on. There was no returning to earth. It just went on and on and on. One day it would fall to earth and blow up or run out of petrol or whatever or get hit by a meteor." Though Jack's vision was cosmic, it had its origins in modest Walworth, as Foster recalls: "There was some weird arts place next to the studio where we used to go in the cafe and there were big banners hanging from the building that said 'O + N'. I don't know what they were. And there were other letters, something plus something. Loads of weird shit like that.

"Jack and Kenny were working out all these odd ideas. God knows what it all meant in the end. Whatever, it came out pretty good. Pretty good guitar bits on there. Main thing I remember about that is that Kenny wanted to get a really kind of awful, wasted vocal sound so we were walking around shouting and screaming to try and get that vocal quality. I shouted myself hoarse encouraging him. It was quite funny. I think he got it in the end. He does sound quite croaky."

The feelings about the finished album among its participants are mixed. "It was pretty good," says Foster. "They all seemed pretty happy with it. That was the main thing. I'd come up with what was requested: an album by The Creation. It sounded like them. They were all happy with it. That's it. My job was done." Foster's predecessor as Creation producer, Shel Talmy, says, "I've heard it. Eddie sent me a copy. I don't think it was that good. I don't Eddie thought it was that good either. I'd have done it a lot better. I think the whole thing sucked, quite frankly. It was not recorded well. It just wasn't good. It could have been done lots better.

"They continued to write great songs. Eddie still continues to write great songs. They may not be necessarily totally of today but they're still great songs as far as I'm concerned. I have heard that during the making of that they were back to feuding like crazy yet again and stuff and I gather nobody was there to act as the captain of the ship: 'Let's get on guys, let's get this thing together.' So what you have is kind of a disjointed group of things that are done but they don't really sound necessarily like they were finished, or even from the same band for that matter."

"Not as good as the single," opines McGee of the album. "I thought the single was great. If it had been 24-year-old kids that were great-looking, they'd have been huge. It was a great version of Brit-pop really, made by 50 year-old guys. I think there is a real division of songwriting on that album. The EP 'Creation', Eddie wrote that, no matter what it says in the brackets. Those three songs were written by Eddie and Eddie definitely was the real writer of the band. Then it ended up a lot of the rest of the album wasn't written by Eddie. The album was a bit of hit-and-miss but when Eddie was writing the songs or he'd an involvement in the songwriting, it was a lot better."

"Don't like it," is Eddie's simple summary of 'Power Surge'. "It's too depressing. One dirge after another." Jack says, "I think it's 80 per cent. It could have been better but it's pretty good." For Bob, "the vocals were too laid-back, for the Sixties type of thing. You had to strain your ears. You never got a definition. You couldn't define the vocal too much, or enough. I prefer the old stuff where you could hear the singer, hear what he was singing. The vocals were laid into the music too much for me. The producer, his interpretation was not the same."

Rod Siebke: "Ed said to me that it was becoming overproduced. It was just overdub on overdub on overdub. It was really a case of, 'We've got 24 tracks and we're going to use 'em'." Foster doesn't feel the album was overproduced, claiming there were a variety of different layering types employed. "Things that had more bits in them were worked on more," says Foster. "Things that were more straightforward, the idea was just to capture the power of it. Certainly, things like 'Power Surge' and 'Shock Horror', they're the ones that fall in-between because they were very tightly arranged and produced to produce the effect of a big powerful thing going on. There are other tracks which are very orchestrated in that way for other reasons and there are tracks that are very straightforward: 'Let's just cut this and then put some mad bits on it.' "

Of the allegation that the production made the group sound a bit like a modern indie band, McGee says, "Maybe because of the budget and the studio and stuff like that. That might have been what that (was about), but

I think the songs were there. The songs that Eddie wrote were definitely there." Jack: "If you're trying to create a sound of 1966, I don't think that would have been possible. Everybody had moved on that far. Our techniques had improved and we had so much more in our head, in our system, music-wise. You're not going to produce 1966 35 years later. It's not there. You're talking about kids of 21 and you're talking guys of 50. They are changed people. And so we left (it) with Joe because we trusted him and we knew Joe was a good guy."

Considering its piecemeal and fractious genesis, 'Power Surge', is a record of a remarkably high standard. Its also an amazingly young-sounding recording. Revivals of rock bands are so often characterised by a certain deflation in musical energy levels which served to cancel out the increased technical proficiency the musicians have gained in the interim. 'Power Surge', however, has – in spades – that youthful pizzazz and vigour missing from other reunion projects: no unsuspecting listener would have known that 'Power Surge' was recorded by men in their fifties rather than people just out of their teens.

There are some fine individual performances, with Kenny singing strongly (especially on the title track), Eddie contributing some sparkling guitar parts and Jack – as though to silence the doubters who found his live work inconsistent – drumming imaginatively and powerfully throughout. The album's faults start with the fact that it is slightly too dramatic overall, with a spectacular and larger-than-life feel attempted on too many songs. Notwithstanding the comments above about the retention of a youthful rock'n'roll vigour after such a long absence, not everything should be an epic. Another track of the uncomplicated, down-to-earth nature of 'That's How I Found Love' would have helped leaven things.

Another shortcoming is that at times the band – and/or Foster – seem too determined to fit in with the orthodoxies of indie rock: rhythm-guitar parts are blurred and continuous instead of stabbed, a general shimmering, out-of-focus soundscape and the endless snotty confrontationalism of the vocals. Yet though 'Power Surge' is far from a classic record, to set it into some sort of context – and to unapologetically bring up that hoary old Who comparison again – it was a far more listenable affair than the (then) last Who album 'It's Hard'. It was also far more imaginative, especially in terms of the lyrics, than the contemporaneous Oasis album, '(What's The Story) Morning Glory'.

It was an album of great potential and indicated that the band had a future. Unfortunately, it is not merely musical competence which dictates whether or not a band is a going concern. "I think what happened really was it that was another example that us lot just couldn't all get on together" says Eddie, "and I don't suppose we'd have stayed civil enough at that time to make a second album."

I n July 1995, *Record Collector* magazine published a feature on The Creation by John Reed. The feature was intended to coincide with the projected release date of the re-formed Creation's new studio album. It's a measure of just how tortuous, fractious and elongated that recording process became that the album did not appear for almost a year after that issue of *Record Collector* had hit the stands. By that time, a Creation with Eddie – who clearly finished the album through gritted teeth – was a lost cause. Kenny proceeded to do what was unthinkable and/or pointless to many: continue The Creation without Eddie Phillips.

A post-album release gig was arranged at London's Dingwalls, with Tony Barber standing in. Of course, to Kenny there was no reason why it should be pointless to continue the group without Eddie: he had done just that in 1968 and had both recorded some good material and made healthy amounts of money. This, though, wasn't 1968, and if Eddie had been an extremely important component of The Creation's sound in the Sixties he was an irreplaceable part 30 years later.

"It was pretty grim," says Siebke of the gig. "Of all of 'em, that was grim." It confirmed his feeling that the whole Creation reunion project should have been a short, sharp burst: "It should have been no more than a year: in there, done it, forget it. But it went on and on. In the end it got to such a state, that very last gig at Dingwalls, everything was so secretive. You've got Bob coming out and having a word with me, Jack creeping out and having a word with me about different things. It's really strange. It wasn't a band."

"Crap," is Bob's assessment of the Dingwalls gig. "That was the end. I said, 'That's it, I'm not doing that again.' Again, I saw it through to its conclusion. I went along and met Tony Barber and we had a couple of rehearsals, for what they were worth, and I thought 'This is not going to do anything'. Really hoping Eddie might see sense. I thought that it wasn't doing any damage to The Creation. So I just went along with it and it was awful. I remember (saying) in the car park (afterwards), 'Kenny just give me my money 'cos I've got to get going'."

Though Kenny and Jack seemed to be of the opinion that the band were viable without Eddie, Bob found himself thinking identical thoughts to those he'd experienced on the German/Swiss tour of 1967 when he concluded that there was no hope for the band without their recently departed guiding light. "I said, 'Well that's it, I'm not bothering no more'," he says. "What's the point? If Eddie falls out, he knows that it's not the same. It's like if the Beatles appear and Lennon says, 'Hang on, I'm not bothering' but McCartney would say, 'Well I'll carry on anyway'."

Though Jack says there was no decision between he and Kenny to finally call a day on the Creation, the fact that there was no further Creation activity implies that – unlike in the Sixties – this time the departures of Eddie and Bob were assumed, even if subconsciously, by the remaining members to be an obstacle the group could not survive. Jack recalls, "Nobody sits down and makes a decision. Everything just slowly happens. And of course Kenny fell down and died."

Jack implies that Kenny might have still been trying to continue the Creation's name had he lived: "He would always keep things going. He would be out there today, hustling and bustling, trying to do something. He would when he was 90. He loved the band and loved singing and he loved rock music." However, the fact that at the time of his death Kenny was talking about relocating to America to pursue songwriting suggests that he had abandoned hopes of further Creation activity.

So ended The Creation's second coming. Alan McGee – who had made that second coming possible only to see it crumble into a heap of squabbles and recriminations – would not have been human if he hadn't felt hacked off by the situation. Did he think that they were being a bit ungrateful to him and Creation Records? "Yeah but I just thought, 'Well, they're The Creation – I'll wear it'," McGee says. "I like them. They're good guys and they're a great band. Ultimately, I'm quite liberal about my attitude towards musicians: it's like, let them be what they want to be and if they want to be self-indulgent or they want to be intensely left-field with their approach to making a record, I'm going to allow it."

How did the album sell? McGee: "I honestly don't know. Probably 10,000 copies maybe around the world." Asked if that figure was disappointing, McGee emphatically says no: "We didn't expect to sell any of them. We were just putting that out because it was The Creation and if it sold one or it sold 20,000 it was a result. We were just making a statement: It was ten years of Creation, recording an album by The Creation. It was really like, 'Let's see if it comes out good'. I don't think they did fall flat on their faces but then again I just think we were a completely different label to the rest of the music business. One of my greatest successes is Kevin Rowland's 'My Beauty'; it sold about 20,000 records worldwide but I'm castigated from pillar to post. It's supposedly the downfall of my record label, Creation, but you know what? That's one of the most beautiful records anybody's ever made. So to be honest I don't really judge things on commerciality. I base things on 'Do I still play it five years later?'"

McGee is ambivalent on the issue of whether he would have been prepared to finance another album. "I don't know now," he says. "The Creation lives on through them and in a weird way it lives on in spirit though having a publishing company and a studio and a management company all inspired by their group. You can't read too much into it: it's a brilliant name and they were a brilliant group and they influenced an idea that I had which was merging punk rock and psychedelia and they kind of gave us a benchmark for sound. But I think Creation developed as a label over the 17 years it was around, from that into something else anyway. It became a much more mainstream rock'n'roll label by the end of it."

Having made that fairytale transition from fan to financier of their music, how does McGee think it panned out? Was it all worth it? "Yeah. I don't reach for the record and play it. I haven't played it in the last five years, actually. But I'm glad I did it. Joe really enjoyed doing it. It's a payback to them really: they had inspired us and we gave them a chance." A chance, of course, they did not take.

For Bob, the project had started unravelling at an early stage, leaving him with a feeling of *déjà vu*. "I thought, 'Ohhh, here we go again'.." he says. "It went through the whole process again. I made a point of going to the first rehearsal studio, that I would look, listen and just watch all over again. And I watched it all happen again. This was to convince myself that I do remember things as it was the first time round. It was just a reincarnation of that: here we go. It's frustration again. Kenny wanted to do it overnight. It's almost as if he knew what was round the corner."

"It was nice to meet the guys and make some music with them again but we was a band that because of our personalities we would always argue," says Eddie. "It was inevitable. We was never a band that could actually get on well as people all the time. That's probably why we kicked it off musically because we turned a lot of our frustration, we took it out on the music." That, this time round, the blame couldn't be pinned on Bob for the band's upheavals is not merely Bob's opinion. Siebke: "Bob tried to keep everyone happy. He was a really nice bloke. 'Whatever you want to do, I'll do it.' That was his attitude."

Shortly after the release of 'Power Surge', June Clark went into a record store on Bleeker Street, New York. She had started a new life in America in the Seventies and had lost contact with the members of The Creation. "They were playing a record in the store and it struck me that it sounded just like The Creation used to sound," says Clark. "I said to the guy behind the counter, 'Whose record is this?' He said, 'Creation'. I said, 'Creation or The Creation?' He said, 'No, Creation'. And I said, 'Can I see that please?' I looked at it, I read it, I couldn't believe it. And I bought it.

"It was them. I recognised it. Nothing else sounds like Eddie. Nothing else sounds like The Creation. I knew nothing about the reunion,. I was stunned when I read that. 'God, these guys have gone from that to playing at the Royal Albert Hall with Oasis.' And Alan McGee being so impressed with The Creation that he named his record label Creation Records. I couldn't believe it."

In 1997, Kenny Pickett had finally lain the ghost of The Creation, even if it wasn't of his own volition. A musical career was still very much on his mind, however. Continuing to be a heating engineer (Glen Colson: "He hated being called a plumber") for the rest of his working life was not on the agenda. He was making plans to move to Nashville to write songs with his old friend Billy Bremner. "Very serious," says Glen Colson. "He was definitely planning on doing that. I think he thought that he could earn a living out there songwriting. Country and Western. He loved it. He used to listen to country music all day. His other big hero was Fats Domino. He'd sit and cry if he heard a Fats Domino record."

For Kenny, this move was planned as his salvation from the life into which he had been sidetracked. "He was incredibly frustrated," says Glen Colson. "Unfulfilled really." On 10 January 1997, before he could make his Nashville dream a reality, Kenny Pickett died, leaving behind a son, a stepson and a stepdaughter. The cause of death remains unknown. Glen Colson: "He was just doing 'Johnny B Goode' on stage as an encore and he just fell over flat on his face dead. They did loads of tests and they couldn't find out (why)... The pathologist told his brother that one in so many hundred people die and they can't work out why.

"I know he had narcolepsy. He did that quite a few times on me. You'd be talking to him and he'd fall fast asleep. I don't know whether that had anything to do with his death." Colson concludes of his friend, "He was just a nice, pleasant guy. Very bright, very literary." Jack, in touch with

Kenny right up until the end, has ambivalent but warm comments about the man for whom he once held such bitter feelings over his 1966 dismissal but who he, ironically, sided with in the acrimonious disagreements surrounding the Nineties reunion. Jack: "Kenny's a number one man. He could be a bit of a bugger at times (but) he was a good guy."

Kenny's death brought about one final Creation reunion. At his wake, a band composed of Bob on vocals, Eddie on guitar, Jack on drums and John Dalton on bass performed a few numbers, including 'Painter Man'. Ironically, it was a highly creditable performance. Rod Siebke goes as far as to say, "The very final gig that I saw that was anything approaching the old line-up was at Ken's wake."

By the time of his death, Kim Gardner had also lain the ghost. With rock'n'roll evidently out of his system, he was the proprietor of the English themed pub The Cat and Fiddle, located in Los Angeles, first on Laurel Canyon Boulevard, then Sunset Boulevard. It was, by all accounts, a place that was heaving, with several music celebrities propping up the bar on any given night.

In 1999, Johnny Byrne hooked up again with The Creation member to whom he had become closest in his brief stint as their tour manager back in '67. Invited as a guest of honour to an American *Space: 1999* fan convention, he visited Kim at the pub. "We went down to the Strip, saw Kim and it was absolutely wonderful," Byrne recalls. "I was astonished at what a mad, successful place he had there."

On 24 October 2001, Kim Gardner died of cancer of the throat. June Clark, who had re-established contact with the members of the band whose fan club she had once run following their appearance in *Ugly Things* magazine, says of Kim, "He was a good guy. He was a good friend to me. Very sweet person. Had a lovely family life. Very happy. A total alcoholic, unfortunately." Kim left behind two daughters, one of whom – Eva – is a professional bassist.

For a while after the final dissolution of The Creation, Jack Jones carried on his cabaret singing career. However, he eventually began winding down his cabaret work through a mixture of his own volition and circumstances outside his control. Jack: "A lot of things come into play. You got to remember, back in the Sixties and the Seventies you could go out and work every night. There was gigs everywhere. Now when you got into the Eighties, you had the influence of disco, you had the influence of people getting up and doing it themselves (karaoke), that sort of crap, and basically that took over.

"Well, once that takes over, then people stop booking acts. You can see the writing on the wall and Annie was fed up. All the cabaret clubs are shutting down. They were becoming discotheques so that limited the work. And basically you get to an age where bombing up and down the country is hard work. So I decided eventually I would settle down."

Bob Garner continues to this day the cabaret/comedy career he began in 1977. Over the years, his show – in which he is billed as Bobby Grand – has become more and more comedy-oriented. "Like Joe Brown, that sort of cheeky kid next door," is how he describes it.

This is something which might surprise those who remember him as the rock singer with the smouldering good looks, as well as those who knew him in his personal life as a rather diffident character. Bob: "It's very dry... That sort of eyes-into-the-forehead sort of thing. I suppose I've learnt how to do it over the years. I've worked with some really good people. From Freddie Starr. On the cabaret circuit that I've been on for years, there's been some great comics, your Bernard Mannings. When I did Blackpool, (I saw) Colin Crompton. They still do the clubs where I am now, Stan Boardman, Mick Miller and that."

Another cheeky chappie from English musical history whose style informs Bob's act is George Formby. Bob: "It's flavoured that way but it's tongue-in-cheek as well. If you do it light-heartedly – 'This is only a bit of fun' – people respond to it. The knack is that I can play the ukulele. Make it sound like George Formby. It's a fascinating instrument. People say, 'How do you manage to get that much out of a little thing like that?' So if you're capable of playing the ukulele as George Formby, people appreciate it. They're all little party pieces. I've learnt that from watching your Dickie Henderson and all the rest of them from years ago. You go on and you have little showstoppers and party pieces and don't make too much of it... A personality thing."

Post-'Power Surge', Eddie Phillips began performing as a local one-man band. "I was putting down some bass, drum and piano tracks, taking them out and playing guitar to them. Then I started singing a bit and that really took off," he says. "It was mad. I was playing to three or four hundred people at a time. Places like Broxbourne Civic Centre. That scale of venue."

Eddie's box-office appeal increased further in 1996 after Bob informed him that the word was out that the makers of the long-running British rural soap opera *Emmerdale* were looking for songs. A rock'n'roll/country band called The Woolpackers were then featuring in the storylines and songs were required for them to play in order to cash in on the then-current line-dance craze. The individual in charge of the mission to find the songs was none other than Simon Cowell, then working for BMG but subsequently to become famous as the acid-tongued judge of TV talent programmes *Pop Stars*, *Pop Idol* and *American Idol*.

Surprisingly, Eddie has a soft spot for Cowell. "He's okay, Simon," he says. "In fact, I've got a lot of respect for him because he knows what he likes and what's good and he doesn't beat about the bush. You know exactly where you are with him. I'd much rather deal with a person like that than have someone say something to you in front of your face and then say something completely different behind your back. If I took a song in and he liked it, he'd say he liked it and yet if I took a song and he didn't like it, equally he'd say he didn't like it. Instantly, you knew exactly where you were."

Bob had written a song called 'Line Dancing' which he thought was ideal for the Woolpackers and Eddie recorded a demo of it in his home studio. Eddie also recorded a demo for a song he had written around three years previously called 'Hillbilly Rock, Hillbilly Roll' which he also thought might be suitable for the project. He had previously issued this song (as 'Hillbilly Rock') in 1994 as the title track to a cassette-only album sold at his gigs. For once, luck was shining on Eddie. "He took my song with his song into BMG Records," he says of Bob, "but they picked my song as the A-side. So I thought, 'Well I'll go 50-50 with Bob on it because it was his idea to go up there and take it in.'" Bob's song became the B-side of the single.

The Woolpackers' rendition of Eddie's catchy country anthem featured in the programme, much to the delight of Eddie's other half. "She's watched *Emmerdale* ever since it first started. She's a big fan." Not only that, but the Woolpackers' version (on which neither Eddie or Bob played) went to Number 5 in the UK charts, the highest chart placing in their home country for any record with which Eddie or Bob had been associated. "There we were 35 years down the line and we had a Top 5 record," Eddie marvels.

The song subsequently became a staple of his live act: "Even if I go out and play it now, all these people get up and do these dances to it. It's lovely." Not so lovely was the financial consequences of the hit. Just after the single's release, an unusually bitter-sounding Bob spoke to *Ugly Things* about how Jack and Kenny had reneged on the royalties split agreement for 'Power Surge' and exulted, "The bittersweet (thing) is that

Eddie and I have gone up in the charts this week and we can tell 'em both 'Up yours'." However, his exultation was to be short-lived. Bob and Eddie discovered that the small print of their respective publishing contracts with Creation Records dictated that their advances from the label be repaid out of any subsequent songwriting activity. Bob: "So when I wrote 'Line Dancing' for the Woolpackers, I gave them the publishing for that and the first eight thousand pound went to clear off that advance. So how does that feel? Because it was a block thing: should any one of you write a song, we have the publishing and the advance will be taken out of that."

1998 saw the third UK Creation compilation (not counting augmented reissues or Edsel's mini-album 'Painter Man') in the shape of Demon's 'Our Music Is Red With Purple Flashes'. This was the best one yet, a (for once) chronologically arranged mopping up of everything then known to have been released by the group in its Sixties incarnation except for 'Sylvette'.

In 1999 'Making Time' was used on the soundtrack of the movie *Rushmore* while that same year, and by complete coincidence, the first domestic Creation album was released in the States. In fact, two albums.

'Making Time' and 'Biff Bang Pow' were the first releases on the now defunct Retroactive Records, yet American fans who had been waiting a long time for a Creation collection at better than import prices expressed disgust that the band's small *oeuvre* was spread across two CDs padded out with mono and stereo mixes of several tracks. Ed Strait, the Retroactive staffer who supervised the project, pleads innocence, claiming Shel Talmy made it a condition of licensing The Creation's material to Retroactive that they release two CDs' worth of material.

"It was decided that we do this as two separate records because we didn't know what the market would bear in the United States for a double, 30-dollar Creation package at that time," explains Strait. The mono and stereo mixes were forced on him by necessity: Talmy seemingly wasn't completely familiar with The Creation's catalogue because he didn't realise there wasn't enough material to fill two CDs. Strait: "I was a little worried once we got the list of all these tapes so that's when I came up with the (idea of) 'Let's do monos and stereos', 'cos I had heard before that with the Shel Talmy stuff there was a lot of differences between them because there'd been all the rumours about The Who and everything. There are some different guitar parts and things like that. I still have stereo and mono things that weren't included because the quality was bad, some that had some mistakes in them when we did the mastering and stuff we just couldn't use."

Strait adds, "I would have liked to have found other stuff. I was hoping that there would be some gems unearthed and I was a little disappointed that all that we really found was that instrumental. And I was glad to find the alternate lyrics on 'Life Is Just Beginning': Mike Stax had mentioned it in *Ugly Things*." The instrumental Strait refers to is 'Instrumental #1', making its first appearance anywhere. Two alternate versions of 'Life Is Just Beginning', one without strings, the other with an additional verse, also saw the light of day for the first time. Strait also had the initiative to seek out live cuts: 'Making Time' included live versions of 'I'm A Man', 'Making Time' and 'That's How Strong My Love Is' (the latter previously released on the French Eva album 'The Sound Of The Sixties', all three from *Beat Beat Beat*), while 'Biff Bang Pow!' featured live takes of 'Painter Man' and 'Try And Stop Me', also from *Beat Beat Beat*.

"There were video copies floating around," Strait explains, "so we just took it off a video and transferred. (It was) recorded in mono anyway." Additionally, 'Making Time' included a Creation rarity in 'Ostrich Man' with a pulsing intro, although the rest of the track is the same take as the familiar versions: "We chose the best-sounding version from what we had transferred to DAT," says Strait. "I was unaware of a different intro."

Another criticism levelled against the two Retroactive CDs was that the songs were not in chronological sequence. "I was trying to sell both volumes," says Strait. "In order to beef up both volumes I was trying to balance out the quality of the material." How well did the two discs sell? Strait: "They did great, all things considered, in that the companies were going through two or three changes through this whole thing where the backers pulled out and then we had to find the original investors, then try to regroup. So we were with four distribution companies in (this) period. At one point in time it was the only thing that was keeping everything afloat through the Christmas season of '99. So for a reissue on a small label with spotty distribution it was doing really well.

"Volume 1 outsold volume 2 because of 'Making Time' being used in the *Rushmore* film. Volume 1 probably sold 15-20,000 and volume 2 probably in the 8-10,000 range. Eddie and Bob were the ones I spoke to. I sent product to everybody and Jack sent me some signed picture of him from back then. They were glad to have it out but probably not that pleased that the money was going through Shel, although I think they've reconciled themselves with that and I think they were compensated for it, but it wasn't like we did a royalty thing to them directly. I think they're not resentful of him but maybe that they wish they hadn't signed that away. In the Seventies there was some sort of document signed that assigned everything to Shel later on when nobody thought it had any real value."

In 2002 and 2003, Eddie worked on a new solo album. Originally his intention had been to resurrect that great lost Creation album recorded for Polydor/Jet. The Eighties drum sound he now found so objectionable was to be replaced by a new drum track and new bass parts were to be supplied by Bob. (With Kenny's vocal track, this would have been three-quarters of the way toward a full album by The Creation's original line-up but Eddie would not countenance overdubs by Jack to complete the line-up.)

The album would have been completed by the song 'Red With Purple Flashes', a number inspired by that famous quote which Eddie had finally got round to completing in 2001 after a 35-year gestation. Eddie: "I got the idea for it years ago. I thought 'I should write a song about this' and I started writing a couple of verses. I never ever did anything with it. I had a way it went I've always known. Ridiculous (to have) a song in your head for years. I do literally do that. I've got probably four or five songs now which I could sit down if I wanted to and write."

As the album progressed, however, it mutated into far more of an Eddie Phillips solo project than a Creation album. By mid-2003, he was saying, "I've got four songs off the Eighties album which I'm thinking of using: 'Lay The Ghost', 'Psychedelic Rose', 'Radio Beautiful' and 'United'." Eddie had suddenly hit a writing streak. "(I'm) writing a lot of new stuff and as I'm finishing one song I'm getting ideas for another one, so this thing is becoming a little bit open-ended at the minute," he said. "I've written eight new songs and I've got ideas for another two and if I finish those two then I might not use those four from the Eighties sessions, I might use two of them.

"Some of the tracks I've recorded are very long. I haven't given one minute's thought to what's commercial or what's not. I've just done this music and the song as I think it should be done. If it lasts six minutes, it lasts six minutes, if it lasts two minutes, it lasts two minutes. It shall probably just be my album. I (asked) Bob if he had any ideas or anything but he hasn't come up with anything so maybe it's not his way of thinking now." Bob laughed when the latter point was put to him. "I didn't know he was doing an album," he said. "He said to me, 'I've got some tracks (I've) done at home'. He certainly didn't say to me, 'This is for an album.' Now and again, he'll say 'Have you got some ideas?' because we've been writing these country line dance songs and stuff but he certainly never said to me have I got any songs to put on an album. If he's doing the vocals on it, it's unnecessary for me to be around."

Once again, Eddie had taken a Sixties approach to the album. "I've had my head there and one foot there right the way through this project," he says. "I've literally gone out the way to try and get back to that style of playing and that style of thinking, even with lyrics. To sort of write as was. Although there's a couple of songs on there which stand up as today's kind of songs, it's all done really with (the attitude that) if people know me, that might be what they're expecting."

Perhaps it was just as well that Eddie got sidetracked from his original album plans. In 2004, there was – at last – a happy ending to the saga of the Polydor/Jet Creation sessions when Eddie agreed a deal with Cherry Red Records to issue the album spawned by them. It was scheduled for a summer 2004 release.

'Red With Purple Flashes' was premiered in New York in November 2001 when The Creation made their live American debut at the Cavestomp Festival, following an invitation from sometime Bruce Springsteen sidekick Steve Van Zandt. The line-up was Eddie and Bob plus Tony Barber on bass and Kevin Mann on drums. (Barber took the mic for the performance of 'I Am The Walker'.) "Eddie likes New York as a city," says Bob. "I wasn't surprised that he wanted to do it and go there, I was surprised that he wanted to do it as in Creation. But he was quite insistent that Jack wasn't doing it, so again I just nodded and went, 'Okay'."

Bob recalls The Creation's American debut as a triumph. "We had three or four rehearsals...and I hadn't done anything since the Mean Fiddler, and Eddie as well, so it was like, learn all over again. The amount of rehearsals that we had added up to about three hours, if that, and we went on there for an hour and 15 minutes and to listen to Eddie – the noise after all these years that he got out of that guitar, and it wasn't his amplifier, we had to use what was there, I thought was amazing. Really was. He should be remembered for that."

The Creation were introduced on stage by Van Zandt, who told the crowd that they were the band he had always wanted to come ever and play but assumed were beyond his reach. Bob was amazed by Van Zandt's knowledge about the group. "He knew all the words to the songs," he says. "He asked me about 'Through My Eyes'. He said, 'That's my favourite record'. I'm thinking to myself, 'This is a guy in America.' I said,

'Have you got it?' He said, 'Have I got it?' and he just stood there and told me all the words. When we came off, he said, 'You guys, what are you doing when you go back?' I said, 'Well, we all go our separate ways'. He said, 'This is a crime, this is a crime.' And he just stood there absolutely gobsmacked. He said, 'I've never, ever seen anybody get so much out of one guitar. He should be out among the Townshends and the Hendrixes'."

The Creation made quite a splash. June Clark: "They did get a write-up in the *New York Times*. I was really shocked because the *New York Times* doesn't usually write anything up unless they feel it's significant. They don't waste their time because they've got everybody begging on their doorstep. For reviews and artistic comment, culturally the *New York Times* carries a lot of weight in this city."

Eddie enjoyed the extra wallop given the sound by having a young rhythm section and he and Bob employed the same line-up for six more North American gigs in September 2002.

However, after that either Barber or Mann would usually be unavailable when other gigs were mooted. At one point Eddie was thinking of approaching Tony McCarroll and Paul McGuigan, once the rhythm section of Oasis, with a view to employing them.

Such is The Creation's legend that in 2003 Courtney Love – widow of Kurt Cobain – tried to get Phillips to play on a session of hers.

Having tired of "bombing up and down the country", Jack Jones, decided in the Nineties that the musical part of his professional life was at an end and opted for running a convenience store that incorporates video rental and an off-licence. "I'm just seeing how this goes," he says. In conversation, he gives the impression of trying to overcome the gruffness and confrontationalism so often bequeathed to men by a working-class upbringing. On more than one occasion, he dismissed the bickering in The Creation's ranks as typical of "guys". He no longer has any contact with the two surviving members of the original band, although doesn't rule out a reunion providing there was a "decent offer".

Like most musicians, though, he can't get music out of his system completely and still does the occasional singing gig. "I don't want to go on 'til I'm 80 years old singing in clubs but if something comes along I'll do it," he says. "Good fun and it keeps you young." He also continues to whack the skins now and again: "I've still got my drums and do the odd gig just to keep my hand in and I enjoy it."

Bob Garner continues to ply his very successful cabaret trade. He is proud of the classic records with which he was involved but seems equally proud of the fact that, bar brief periods, he has always been able to make a living from showbusiness. It was for that reason, he says, that he was able to accept with stoicism the fact that the magnificent Creation compositions for which he was jointly responsible did not become hits in his home country. "That's like asking have I got a chip on me shoulder," he says. "Am I going to carry this weight? No, myself I've always had the ability to sort of close that door and walk away. It just didn't happen. I haven't got a grudge. Otherwise I wouldn't be able to do what I've done for a living ever since, doing a grotty pub or a social club. My main concern was staying in the entertainment business. There's success at all levels, really."

There seems to be an element of rationalisation here, given the title of his song about Smiley – 'Nobody Wants To Know'. Perhaps he's changed his attitude toward The Creation's misfortunes in the interim. He certainly seems to have changed in other ways, if we are to believe people who have attested to the fact that he was a manipulative and self-centred character in the Sixties. Those who know Bob now – some of them the same people – say that he is a pleasant and helpful character with no particular 'side' to him. (For the record, it was Bob who, via a circuitous route, put the author in touch with Jack, who was unlikely to say nice things about him.)

Eddie Phillips gives the impression of being torn between settling into his dotage and maintaining his artistic ambitions. He said in 2002 that his excitement about making his solo album was ridiculous at his time of life. Yet one of the most gifted guitarists of his generation – especially one who has not had the ego-gratifying and therefore ambition-blunting acclaim of contemporaries like Clapton, Page and Beck – cannot quell his impulse to create. That impulse also seems to have overcome the aversion to the music industry brought about by the horrific litany of bad luck and disappointment he experienced in his solo career let alone during his time with The Creation.

This may be something to do with a changing world. Though Eddie is still interested in a conventional record deal, he is also happily aware that the advent of avenues of self-manufacture and self-distribution opened up by the age of CD-burning and the Internet now virtually guarantees he need never again experience the disappointment of putting his heart and soul into a musical project only to see it go to waste through failure to interest a record company in issuing it. Perfectly willing as he is to do occasional gigs under The Creation banner with Bob, he continues to derive most of his income from his solo show.

Though driving a vehicle for a living was something he was able to give up in the Seventies, transport is to some extent in his blood: his hobby is tending to vintage cars. Eddie retains the friendly but over-sensitive nature June Clark referred to, so much so that the skeletons in The Creation's cupboard (extremely minor and mundane though they are) brought up by research for this book made him rather agitated. He felt the book should concentrate on the positive aspects of The Creation and asked not to be quoted on one specific subject. Happy despite all the disappointments he's endured in his musical career, he says the planet may be in bad shape but it's "still great to be on it".

Eddie feels he has to be careful with his Creation activities, not wanting the sole reason for his appeal to be nostalgia. This presumably explains his apparent ambivalence about continuing Creation work. Bob: "I was talking to him the other day. We were saying, 'Should we do a little bit more or not?' and I'm always saying to Eddie, 'You've got to down tools and get on with it if that's what you're gonna do.' I think he still wants to do it, it's just that he's safe with what he's got. He says 'I'm getting old' and all that business. I said, 'You're not frightened of dying, are you?' He feels if he did it and then he dropped dead the day after, was it worth it? I said, 'Well of course it would be'."

Not that there's much chance of The Creation being something easily dismissible as a nostalgia turn. "When you listen to The Searchers and everything else, it still sounds like it was," points out Bob. "It's from the Sixties and that's where you can put your finger on it. But with The Creation stuff, there's still young bands trying to do the same thing today so it still sounds okay. You can't put a time on it. The amount of bands on the bill with us all over America that played Creation songs…"

This, of course, is the consequence of The Creation having been ahead of their time. "I think we were the ones who got the first door banged in our face," says Bob. "Eddie, in recent years, has said to me, 'If you think about the things that we were doing on the stage and the amount of acts that have taken up those ideas.' Eddie was definitely the first on the violin bow for a start. Jimmy Page – no way. Jimmy got it off Eddie. And the strobe, the smoke thing. We had a tape loop with sitars on just playing a continual loop on a tape, just went round and round and round. I suppose now they call it sampling. We just sampled a little bit of the Indian stuff off one of George Harrison's things and let that go round and round. Even the graffiti – you never saw graffiti on walls before 'Painter Man'. I'm not saying we started it, but we were the first ones to do art on stage."

Of course, first doesn't necessarily mean best. However, Shel Talmy – who has been at the helm of more classic records than most producers have had hot dinners – is in no doubt about the aesthetic brilliance of the band whose career he oversaw. "You are talking to somebody who thinks that The Creation was one of the great bands of all time," he states. "I like virtually everything they ever recorded." This coupling of innovation and excellence accounts for the fact that The Creation continue to possess a relevance to both their own generation (although even most fans of their vintage discovered them retrospectively) and to young kids for whom fine melodies, great musicianship and a certain anti-conventional *frisson* will always have an importance.

More than 35 years after the surviving members of the group dispersed to – they thought – live out the rest of their lives in anonymity as a bus driver, a baker (maybe) and a Tesco bureaucrat, they are still sought out for interviews and/or performances related to the two years they traded under the name of The Creation.

"Eddie and myself and Jack, we're living antiques," says Bob. "I'm a big fan of George Formby: I listen to the records, I'm in the Society, I read as much as I can and I get all bits of information and it's the same thing again. Young people wanting to read and hear things from the Sixties, especially people who were trying to innovate something, (were) quite underground, didn't make it, whatever." He sums up, "We were trying to push the boundaries. We were young people, saying 'Let's stretch things here'."

Though there were many fine moments on their comeback album 'Power Surge' and though 'A Spirit Called Love' was a good single, it was their recorded output of 1966-68 that made The Creation beloved of so many young musicians and music buffs. It is astonishing to contemplate the fact that their considerable reputation is built on roughly two dozen songs, the sum total of their recorded output during those two years. This section attempts to analyse the 25 separate songs recorded (though not all released) in that period in ascending order of merit, according to the author. Alternate versions and live recordings are not included.

25 UNCLE BERT

Probably the last self-composed Creation track to be recorded has a nice, stuttering riff, a good, straining melody and an intermittently infectious party atmosphere that all deserve better than the mean-spirited lyric that accompanies them and consigns this grotesque tale of a flasher to the status of the least of all Sixties Creation recordings.

24 SYLVETTE

Originally known as 'Instrumental 2', this is patently the backing for a version of 'Leaving Here', a very good Holland-Dozier-Holland song urging men to treat their womenfolk better ('Hey, fellas, have you heard the news/Yeah, the women in this town have been misused') that had also been recorded by fellow Talmy protégés The Who – though their version was not released for many years. It's as characterless as you would expect a recording which was intended to have an overdubbed vocal to be. Yet Eddie does coax interesting feedback and some intriguing liquid noises from his instrument. Had Kenny added one of his wheezy and passionate vocals, this could have ended up as the definitive reading of 'Leaving Here'. A wasted opportunity.

23 INSTRUMENTAL #1

Marginally more noteworthy than 'Sylvette' because it's not recognisably the backing to a known song, and because it has the slightly monotonous feel of a track in which featureless gaps have been left for the insertion of a vocal, so is therefore probably the basic track to a lost Creation original. Apart from that and the fact that it's even mildly exciting in places as an instrumental, there are no particular stimulating features – violin bow work, feedback, etc – to make it deserving of much attention.

22 BONY MORONIE

Whoever is responsible for it (Bob, Kim, Herbie Flowers or someone else), this track's basswork – a constantly interesting, coiling background presence – is the best thing on an unremarkable recording. Otherwise, there's nothing to make you want to hear this perfunctory run-through of one of Larry Williams' less remarkable songs ever again.

21 HEY JOE

Billy Roberts' adaptation of an old folk story was filtered through the consciousness and styles of many artists in the mid Sixties before arriving at what is widely considered its definitive reading by the Jimi Hendrix Experience (which itself owed much to Tim Rose's unusually sultry take on it). As the members of The Creation first heard it from the Experience and as Eddie was such a big fan of Hendrix, it was inevitable that their version would effectively be a cover of their cover. Thus we have a nondescript, almost note-for-note copy (including the guitar solo and spooky falsetto harmonies) of the reading by that famed power trio, with the one exception of the country-flavoured spoken-word bridging segment. If we'd never heard the Hendrix version, we'd think this was an excellent track – but if that had never existed, neither would this.

20 LIKE A ROLLING STONE

Bob Garner always seems to be stumbling over the words on this version of Bob Dylan's classic, seeming to not quite get them right but with his amendments not quite decipherable either. This only adds to the insubstantial feeling of the recording (despite the dramatic, high backing vocals during the chorus). Dylan's malicious original is imperishable. Since Jimi Hendrix's mournful take on the song was intriguing but inessential, The Creation's perfunctory cover of that was never going to be anything more than dispensable. Competent but utterly second-hand.

19 OSTRICH MAN

That 'Ostrich Man' covers the same territory as The Kinks' broadsides against bourgeois conformity 'Well Respected Man', 'Mr Pleasant' and 'Plastic Man' is appropriate: Eddie here sometimes sounds like Ray Davies in his unusually parodic delivery. Kenny's anti-conservative lyric is no worse than that of The Beatles' 'Nowhere Man', which was probably its main inspiration. Unfortunately Kenny Pickett's whimsical, socially-conscious lyric is not as powerful as an angry Pickett protest song like 'Making Time', despite that latter song's lack of focus:

Living your life with half closed eyes
Seeing a world that's living on lies
Pull down your shades and close out day
Hide long enough and it might go away
Ostrich man
In the sand
World's going 'round and 'round
I stand still as can be
I'll hide inside myself
No one will ever see me

The faults of this almost generic Sixties piece of straight-bashing are compounded by relatively nondescript instrumentation – which even the pretty tones of a harpsichord don't alleviate – and a slightly dreary chorus.

18 I AM THE WALKER

'I Am The Walker' has a great pounding intro: guitar, drums, piano, and cymbal all gradually joining in an imitation of a pair of hobnail boots marching on concrete.

I saw a man standing by the river
He had a dog wrapped in a bag
I thought the dog would be thrown in the river
But it was wrapped because it was bald

The strange opening verse gives way to a slinky, swaying chorus:
I hear the walker
The telephone talker
I see the man hanging on to the phone

That pleasing pounding takes us into the next chorus:
Down at the pet shop, selling a parrot
Somebody told me the parrot could talk

I went along to hear what it was saying
But it was sold, so I went for a walk

And then, after more hobnail-bootery, the song circles back on itself.
That's when I found I was down by the river
Seeing a man with a dog in a bag.
I thought the dog would be thrown in the river
But it was wrapped because it was bald

The song is a little less interesting aesthetically than it is structurally –
and the chorus is utterly opaque – but on balance one feels pleased to have
heard this track as it gradually decreases in pace and drama with a
classical-style piano winding it gently to a close and a Fifties sci-fi flying-
saucer effect whooshing across the soundscape.

17 SWEET HELEN

In the first verse of this latter-day Creation track, as backing harmonies
coo sweetly and a cello (or mellotron set to cello) zigzags lugubrious
tones, Kenny enunciates:
A girl that I knew
Came out of the blue
Yesterday
She sat down by me
Put her hand on my knee
In a way
That started my blush
While matching the blush
On her face

Kenny's lyric is cleverly olde-worlde and courtly and the
instrumentation – though a basic rock set-up – suitably dandified, largely
due to Nicky Hopkins' frilly piano work. The marching chorus sounds
more like a rock song but still retains that antediluvian air:
Then sweet Helen thought again
She could have her pick of many men
Some of them were tall
Some of them were small
Some of them were just like me

Kenny's clever, intricate internal rhymes continue in verse two:
Then I suppose
She looked down her long nose
At me
I put my hand on her shoulder
And I'd almost told her
That she
Would look lovely in white
And someday she might
Marry me

The song is let down slightly by a somewhat lazy third verse:
She picked up her shawl
And stood very tall
In her shoes
A well-bred young man
Then gave her his hand
And they blew
They walked from the room
As much bride and groom as they knew

In addition to the caveat about the third verse, it would have been nice to have seen this given a more ornate treatment. It's a track superbly suited to harpsichord, chamber strings and other antiquated instrumentation. But one mustn't quibble. The song has a wistful air and there is, endearingly, no discernible resentment on the part of the narrator at the fickleness of his beloved but, instead, almost amusement. A track that proves that though The Creation with Ronnie Wood could never have been as substantial a band as they were with Eddie Phillips, they were still capable of making very good music.

16 COOL JERK

The Capitols' 'Cool Jerk' – a number about a man who cannot believe there is a better proponent of the titular dance than he – is a good song so the fact that the version by The Creation at the very peak of their powers (mid-1967) is a very diverting couple of minutes should not be too much of a surprise. (They recorded two other, far more lacklustre, covers the same day but they worked much harder on 'Cool Jerk' and it shows.)

Nicky Hopkins produces a nifty, lapel-grabbing, stentorian piano opening. An explosive entrance from Kim's bass then takes us into a track that is utterly infectious, something assisted by relentless handclaps. It's an almost guilty pleasure. When Bob – as in the original – prompts the different instruments to take a bow, such hammy, old-fashioned showbiz stuff is almost ludicrous for a band so utterly space-age, but they do it so well. And when the song swings into that 'Can ya do it, can ya do it' quicktime refrain, it's wonderful. Bright, fresh and seamless, this is a recording that is as pleasing on the ears as is chocolate on the tongue.

15 MERCY MERCY MERCY

A song written by Joe Zawinul, originally recorded by jazzer Cannonball Adderley and made famous by the Buckinghams. The Creation's version is remarkably soulful. It's also extraordinarily smooth, swinging from chorus to verse to middle eight and back again in an exquisite display of flawless professionalism. Like 'Cool Jerk', you know it's inessential – and that feeling is intensified by the uncertainty about whether it's even The Creation that recorded it – but you can't help wanting to hear it again as soon as it's over.

If it had been done by, say, Cliff Bennett and the Rebel Rousers we would accept it as what it is: a corking good interpretation of someone else's song. Because it's The Creation, we have an immediate resistance to it, perceiving it as something beneath the band, which colours our listening. Yet, in a sense, the assumption that covers like this were not real Creation is erroneous. It's certainly not representative of recorded Creation but there was also The Creation the live band, for whom material like this was part and parcel of what they did – especially in the early days when they only had a couple of original songs to their name and had to pad out their set with other people's compositions.

Kenny gets the lyric slightly wrong, rendering 'My baby, she may not a-look' (As in: 'like one of those bunnies out of a Playboy Club') as 'My baby, she's made out of love' – but who cares when he never sang more passionately or movingly than he does throughout this joyous recording?

14 THE GIRLS ARE NAKED

See them all by the strip club door
Twenty men, or maybe more
Pay their money and they take a chance
The girls are naked and they dance

With that opening verse, Kenny Pickett – penning his first Creation original without the assistance or presence of Eddie Phillips – puts the band triumphantly back on form following a dry patch, writing-wise, after Eddie's departure. Not only is it a lyric of brilliant descriptive precision, it is an act of some daring. This was mid-1968, a time when such near-the-knuckle material as the sexual desperation-engulfed gloom of strip joints did not feature in mainstream pop records.

Businessmen in polished shoes
That come to cheer and clap and boo
Delighted faces in the dark
The girls are naked and they dance

The lovelessness of the atmosphere of such establishments is underscored by a matter-of-fact musical accompaniment and prosaic structure (the only preamble to the start of the lyric is a few bashes from Jack). There is no riff as such, merely a dense, mid-tempo chunky supporting shape. Only the la-la harmonies behind Kenny's lead vocal provide anything in the way of adornment in a thoroughly enjoyable but grim recording.

13 FOR ALL THAT I AM

'For All That I Am' is extremely similar in sentiment to The Kinks' 'Days', which was released at around the same time. However, there is here a mythical air absent in Ray Davies' composition: the lyric mentioning 'castles of longing from the dream-maker's hand' and 'playgrounds of fantasy and strings of desire', the quasi-Gregorian backing chants and Ronnie's fuzz-toned guitar lines all lend a surreal urgency and drama. Nonetheless, the song's soul roots are evident, making for a hybrid that places it halfway between the band's soul covers like 'Mercy Mercy Mercy' and psychedelia such as 'Through My Eyes'. Immaculately crafted and very agreeable.

12 IF I STAY TOO LONG

'If I Stay Too Long' sounds exactly like an 'album track', one of those passages of a long player which makes no particularly profound impression on the listener the first couple of times but whose subtle merits gradually become impressed upon the listener through 'enforced' exposure. In the case of 'If I Stay Too Long' these merits turn out to be considerable, even if they're not fast-working enough to be the kind of thing that can propel a song into the hit parade.

The lyric details the thoughts of a man approaching his lover's house, rehearsing what he is about to say to her, with succeeding verses a further step in both his thought processes and his physical journey. On the chorus, the sound swells impressively – hugely, even – with the mass slowly building and spreading enunciation of the title phrase like the pattern created by an unfolding fan, each fan-leaf a different tone and pitch. Indeed, the whole song builds with exquisite subtlety, a tambourine being introduced here, the organ being mixed up there.

There is no conventional break with the spotlight on an individual instrument. Instead, we have a mosaic composed of a whirling guitar pattern, swelling organ and massed voices cooing almost spookily. Bob's 'Don't be worried about a thing' doesn't quite work as a closing line, sitting oddly with the self-doubt that has preceded it, but otherwise this is a strong, moody piece of work, even if it had no business ever being a single.

11 TRY AND STOP ME

Comparisons between The Creation and The Who are as misguided as they are tedious. However, it has to be observed that – probably through accident, not design – the B-side of The Creation's debut single sounds (and this is no bad thing, remember) like contemporaneous Who from first to last: listen to Jack's opening warm, smooth tom-toms roll and Eddie's ringing, brittle chords. Even Bob's belligerent basslines put one in mind of John Entwistle. Kenny, meanwhile, trills as sweetly as Roger Daltrey was apt to on early Who material, only differing in pitch: Kenny's vocal is so high that it sounds like he'll be grasping for an asthmatic's inhaler at any minute.

This dismissal of a clinging lover is nothing very remarkable – its conventionality makes it sound more of a Mark Four record than a Creation one – but with its passable riff and tune and high-quality singing (especially at the close) it's a perfectly diverting way to spend two minutes 26 seconds.

10 BIFF BANG POW

The Creation were not a mod band but this breathless track has Modernism written all over it. From the references to then-contemporary media figures like Adam West's Batman and James Bond to its use of colloquial phrases like 'You know the score' to its colour- and action-evoking title to its relentless, bristling, youthful snap, it is the sonic equivalent of the roundel, the red, white and blue target symbol so beloved of the mod. The only thing that keeps it from achieving the status of true greatness is the fact that the riff played by the rhythm section is a hand-me-down from 'My Generation'. The star of the show is Jack who – aside from executing a brilliant roll before each use of the title phrase – is a man whose sticks are a blur of activity at all junctures, helping give the song its aura of boyish, sharp-dressed zest.

9 MIDWAY DOWN

Hats off to the band: right from the moment this track opens with a typically classy bit of bass work from Kim and is followed by some razor-sharp guitar from Ronnie and a rat-a-at-tat from Jack, then proceeds to explore the larger-than-life terrain – what Eddie once described as "way out pop...with feeling" – of previous Creation recordings, it's like a seamless segue from old Creation to new. Only the absence of truly virtuoso guitarwork betrays that this is a band with its vital ingredient (to be more specific, vital member) missing. That and, of course, the fact that the song is supplied by outside sources.

Some purists might quibble over the fact of a band who once wrote classic songs now reduced to being dependent on others for material and certainly it is natural to feel less admiration for a merely well-delivered cover than for a self-generated song of similar quality. But a great record is a great record. John Wonderling's superb melody and lyric are done justice in spades by a punch-packing Creation band performance.

Kim's relentless, brawny bass work – a couple of times isolated as the other instruments drop out as though to emphasise its quality – seems to hold the recording together, allowing Ronnie Wood and Jack to provide sterling accompaniment while Kenny delivers one of the vocal performances of his life, despite it being an octave below the range in which he was most comfortable. You can virtually taste the cotton candy and smell the elephants in this utterly evocative, classy and slightly menacing depiction of a carnival and its bizarre attractions.

8 NIGHTMARES

Kenny's (first time round) parting legacy to The Creation is the flipside of Bob's more celebratory exploration of the LSD experience in 'Through My Eyes'. The intro sees Eddie producing creeping, trebly noises via tapped harmonics against a background of ghostly harmony singing. Some violin-bow work materialises as well as delicate piano work before

Kenny's lyric – through Bob's voice – of sweaty paranoia kicks in:

Faces, places move around your mind
Ideas come cruel, ideas come kind
Mind in a state of constant confusion
And your brain has suffered an illusion

The chant of 'La, La, La, La, La, La' that follows each line is half-jaunty and half-sinister, like the jeering of psychopathic clowns. Jack's broiling drums take the song into a killer of a chorus. The rising cry of 'Nightmares!' is stretched out to four syllables, with Jack executing panoramic sweeps across the kit before each repeat.

As ever during this period, Kenny's lyric is half-great, half-lazy, but the final verse is very strong:

Touch on the brow by unseen hands
Petrified to where you stand
Death comes never shedding a tear
Wake up shouting, sweating with fear

A great track whose richly sinister air is in no way undermined by the band's perennial pop smarts showing in an attractive melody and hugely singable chorus.

7 TOM TOM

Another instantly catchy Eddie riff – in possession of that booming quality that comes with an amp cranked up to the max – opens proceedings.

Tom Tom ba-na-na-na-na
Run, run get your gun
Tom Tom ba-na-na-na-na
Bang, bang spoil the party

A raised key and an adroitly used hi-hat instantly increase the excitement factor as Bob goes into the first verse:

Tom Tom the piper's son
Kissed the girls and made them run
Run far away from the mirror Mary
Hope Sleeping Beauty scared the fairy

And so it goes on, a litany of fairy-tale characters and fable scenarios, joined together in no particularly coherent manner but sung with such conviction by Bob, accompanied with such aplomb by Eddie's sparkling Hendrix-esque lead guitarwork and Jack's thumping rhythm work as to make it seem weighty. It is the latter two who take the instrumental break, engaging in call-and-response.

After a final verse bulging with pantomime grotesqueries there is a respite, some pulsing feedback and then a fade of the chorus first line, sung in near-falsetto and treated with echo, thus injecting an unexpected twist at the very close.

An example of precisely what it was The Creation were capable of at their very peak, effortlessly constructing a classic recording from a glorified doodle – the very definition of rock class.

6 THROUGH MY EYES

A great burbling bass run opens proceedings, followed by a mile-high, keening Eddie guitar riff. Bob's lyric – and the minor-chord melody – have that half-celebratory and half-menacing tone that characterised much psychedelia. The last word of each line is echoed, as though a hostile crowd is mocking the narrator:

If you could see through my eyes (Ey-yies)
You would get a big surprise (Ey-yies)
Things you haven't noticed before (Fo-ore)
Things you haven't seen I'm sure (Su-ure)

A slow, languid chorus follows to the background of exquisite effects: a semi-spooky, semi-soothing atmosphere created by the echo given the cooing, almost monk-like chorus.

Ohhhhhhh ohhhh my eyes
Ohhhhhhh ohhhh my eyes
Through my eyi-yi-yies
Through my eyes

The instrumental break sees the gratifying re-emergence of that colossal guitar. Hopkins' piano bobs and shimmies throughout a recording that is a dark treat.

5 MAKING TIME

What a debut! Eddie pounds put out that razor-sharp riff – one of those riffs so simple that one wonders why nobody ever thought of it before – and Jack performs a roll across the tom-toms and we are into one of the most remarkable entrées imaginable.

Making time
Shootin' a line

For people to believe in
Things you say
Gone in a day
Everybody leavin'
Everybody leavin'
Why do we have to carry on?
Always singing the same old song.
Same old song
Same old song

It's a bellyache – and a scattershot, stream-of-consciousness one at that, with good lines followed by lazy rhyme-makers – but the general point is made: Kenny is stating that the destiny decreed for him by the powers-that-be is not acceptable. This is hammered home by Eddie, swinging effortlessly back and forth between that insistent lead riffing and choppy rhythm stuff, and some fine drumming from Jack, who maintains an imaginative, pulsating tattoo throughout. As the second verse begins, a tambourine kicks in, building the drama.

Tellin' lies
Closin' your eyes
Makin' more excuses
Pullin' the wool
Actin' the fool
People have their uses
People have their uses

Another chorus, then comes that famous bowed solo. Eddie's initial swipes are counterpointed against a more conventional picked progression but, as the instrumental break progresses, the bow takes over. While Bob plays some looping basslines in the background, Eddie's bow work runs through the gamut, one second sounding like a saw against a solid object, the next taking on the tone of a cello, the next squealing feedback, the next shimmering almost prettily.

Finally, the bowed guitar 'shoves' the conventionally played guitar aside: as the song swings back into the riff again for the final act, it is the bow that is playing it, as it will for the remainder of the record. Yet another ratcheting up of the drama occurs when Kenny raises keys brilliantly for the third verse:

Looking f-o-o-r
An open door

Never takin' chances.
Take your pick
Makes you sick! (A line veritably spat out)
Seekin' new advances
Seekin' new advances
Why do we have to carry on?
Always singing the same old song

The track ends with more shimmeringly dissonant trickery via the violin bow.

It's not perhaps quite as good as many Creation fans – or Eddie, who considers it definitive early Creation – imagine it to be but 'Making Time' is a quite extraordinary and powerful slab of music.

4 PAINTER MAN

Unlike on 'Making Time', the riff of the Creation's second single, and most famous song, is played with a violin bow from the beginning. It is a riff with more body than the debut's, a pleasantly fat, grinding affair almost like a cello progression. While Hopkins tinkles away in the background, Kenny tells us in a nasally tone:

Went to college, studied art
To be an artist, make a start
Studied hard, gained my degree
But no one seemed to notice me-e-ee

Instantly, it is obvious that this is a stronger lyric than 'Making Time', more focused and logical. It is also highly unusual: how inimical a phrase like 'gained my degree' was to rock'n'roll at the time (or now, come to that). Similarly, when the song rises for the terse but forceful chorus, how unusual it is that it is not to celebrate – or lament – love:

Painter man, painter man
Who would be-ee a painter man?
Painter man, painter man
Who would be-ee a painter man?

Jack's drums shadow Kenny's voice, nailing each word of the chorus into the listener's mind.

As the group swing into the next verse, a protesting squeal can be heard from Eddie's abused guitar:

Tried cartoons and comic books
Dirty postcards, woman's books

Here was where the money lay
Classic art has had its day

A stupendous bowed solo from Eddie follows the second chorus, a razor-sharp, twirling, growling, churning affair rising to a thrilling crescendo.

As with a strangely high percentage of Pickett lyrics, the third verse is the laziest, as though he'd satisfied himself that he'd done well with the first couple:

Do adverts for TV,
Household soap and brands of tea.
Labels all around tin cans,
Who would be a painter man?

Shouldn't 'Do adverts' be 'I do adverts'? And wouldn't 'Labels that go around tin cans' be better than 'Labels all around tin cans'? However, before we can brood on that, we are into another slammed chorus, followed by a respite featuring collective 'La la la' chanting set against some clever, pulsing work on guitar. A last chant of half of the chorus, a final repeat of the bowed riff and the track ends in a performance of catgut squalling that impertinently approximates part of Nat King Cole's empathically non-squalling 'Mona Lisa'.

A superb record – to these ears, superior to 'Making Time' – that is just about perfect from beginning to end. Unless 'Can I Join Your Band' – recorded without Kenny's participation – counts, 'Painter Man' is the greatest testament to the worth of the original line-up of The Creation.

3 LIFE IS JUST BEGINNING

The Creation's foray into Pepperland could so easily have been a disaster. Ornamentation being added to rock recordings as an afterthought is, naturally, a minefield. The brass and string sections on the Pretty Things' third album 'Emotions', for instance, are so obviously an artificial graft as to be cringe-making. However, despite the fact that its classical string arrangements are an embellishment unforeseen at the time of its recording, 'Life Is Just Beginning' is a triumph: no-one would have known that band and strings did not play together if the band hadn't blown the gaffe on themselves.

Not that the track is a triumph merely because you can't 'see the join'. The recording is exquisite. It starts with a beautiful string motif which gives way to a fade-in of the band's collective voices chanting the title phrase. As Bob begins singing the verse – in whose background an ornate piano is just audible – his voice is treated to give it an electronic-transmission quality:

When I think of all the things I've done
In my younger days
Not knowing what was right from wrong
And life's terrible ways
In my younger days

A key and tempo shift occurs, then:
There's so many things to do
That's why I'm telling you

And then we are into a lilting, soothing chorus:
Li-i-i-i-i-i-i-fe's just beginning, beginning
Li-i-i-i-i-i-i-fe's just beginning
Life is just beginning for me
Life is just beginning for me

All through this and the succeeding verses and choruses, a lovely, churning string arrangement is taking place, not so much behind the vocal as with it and through it. There is nothing artificial about the strings, which are weaved into the song in a completely organic way. Massive credit has to go to Talmy and whoever wrote the string parts.

This is what classical rock should be like. A track that is – dare one say it – as good as anything on 'Sgt Pepper's Lonely Hearts Club Band'.

2 CAN I JOIN YOUR BAND

'Can I Join Your Band' opens with one of Eddie's greatest licks. Picked, not strummed, it's a wonderful proud, chest-out, arms-swinging affair. As is the chorus, sung against ululating background harmonies:

Can I join your band?
Go on parade
With my new guitar
My coat is suede
Can I join your band?
I'm a hippie guy
Always stoned and eight miles high

The background harmonies become mournful – though the tempo doesn't slacken – as the protagonist begins recounting his sad life in the verses:

My daddy was a soldier
Played the fife and drums
Left mummy and the children
Starving in the slums
Pinched my granddad's savings
Bought a new guitar
Set off to join a brass band
Someday be a star

After another imploring, technique-boasting chorus, the song switches into double time as the protagonist's request is answered:

There's a vacant situation
We'll accept your application
Learn to march and to play
Ready for that special day

The pace slackens for an instrumental break in which Hopkins plays piano progressions alongside Eddie's wobbly catgut swipes, the progression joined on the last bars by powerchord crashing from Eddie. The pace quickens again and that proud ascending riff makes a reappearance, this time with Kim shadowing on the bass.

The drums drumming, fifes fifing
Played the jubilee
The only drag about it was they didn't take me
Three days heartbreaking, watched them out of sight
Round the party came the guard; the old man could be right

After another chorus, 'Can I join your band?' is repeated over and over again, with a set of harmonies intertwining with a set of overdubs. This collective falsetto repetition becomes, by the end, like a church choir. Meanwhile, the tempo is picking up. The band begin hurtling towards the climax, Eddie's blurred guitar strum and Jack's furious drumming brilliantly in unison as they press their feet down ever harder on the accelerator. The music stops dead. A pause, then a crash of instrumentation and gentle feedback brings to a close a recording of utterly galvanising, endlessly intriguing perfection.

1 HOW DOES IT FEEL TO FEEL (US VERSION)

Chances are, if we had never heard the take released in the States, we would accept the UK version of this song as the band's masterpiece. However, once having had our senses delighted by the feedback and catgut-scrape inferno of the US version, the UK one can't help but sound tame.

As soon as the opening, booming snare and bass drum combination kicks this song off, and the elongated swipes of bow on guitar strings push it forward, one knows to take it seriously. This is a magnum opus in which every bar, every note, is marked by a flawlessness that is utterly deliberate and intended: the sound of an artist exulting in the fact that he is at the peak of his powers and cruising on a once-in-a-lifetime synchronism of accumulated technical proficiency, in-born artistic instinct and hunger to prove his artistic worth in the world. That point where an artist is in The Zone.

It is a track in good company. The very effortless, larger-than-life immaculacy that informs The Creation's 'How Does It Feel To Feel' is exactly the quality possessed by The Rolling Stones' 'Gimme Shelter', The Who's 'Won't Get Fooled Again', Bob Dylanís 'Like A Rolling Stone' and the Small Faces' 'Tin Soldier'. It is that good.

This is a track where the members of the band each hit an individual peak which itself ensures a collective peak. Jack's drumming is stupendous in its brutality and epic nature. Kim's thrumming basswork adds a vital menacing tone. Bob's lyric is dazzling. And Eddie's guitarwork is among the finest ever recorded.

The song starts like a sequel to 'Nightmares', with the protagonist beset by fears in the small hours. A backing chant jeers the title:

(How does it feel?)
When the day is over?
(How does it feel?)
When the dark comes down?
(How does it feel?)
When your room is black as sin
(How does it feel?)
When you're scared by the dark.
How does it feeeeel to feel?

The musical backdrop as these tormented musings continue is appropriately heavy. The sheer distortion of this track is staggering. It positively groans with it, every switch into a new verse, every key change, every tempo shift is almost always attended by a screech from guitar strings, a squeal of feedback, a break-up of sound through over-amplification, a wince-making but wonderful squeal of catgut against guitar-string. This is weal-raising stuff. And yet at no point does the distortion overwhelm the melody or the backing harmonies or the wondrous visions created by Bob's words:

(How does it feel?)
When the shadow moves you
(How does it feel?)
Rustles by your bed
(How does it feel?)
When it finally holds you
(How does it feel?)
When you're thinkin' you're dead.
How does it feeeeel to feel?

After that creepy second verse comes the track's *coup de grace*: Eddie's bowed guitar solo. Just as Hendrix, Townshend, Page and Beck can lay claim to recording performances that involve unprecedented and unrepeated guitarwork, so Eddie can point to this track to stake his claim for a plinth in the pantheon of axe heroes with a solo which procures from the guitar noises never heard before or since. The sounds his strings produce in the instrumental break – and other places – are spindly, shivering, delicate things that one would simply not expect to arise from the connection of catgut and guitar string.

The result is simply awe-inspiring. Bob's lyric, meanwhile, culminates in a blissful final verse where the morning has banished the demons:

(How does it feel?)
When you wake in the morning
(How does it feel?)
Feeling sun in the shade
(How does it feel?)
When you slide down a sunbeam
(How does it feel?)
Bursting clouds on your way
(How does it feel?)
Now that the night is over
(How does it feel?)
I'll never sleep again
How does it feeeeel to feel?

This phantasmagoric masterpiece is, in the first place, the sound of young men striving for – and achieving – great art. Ultimately, it is far more than that. It is the clincher for the argument that The Creation are one of history's truly great rock bands.

CHAPTER 8

APPENDIX 1: IN THE SPIRIT OF

I n the spirit of this book, a brief mention of half a dozen other bands who did not achieve the commercial success the quality of their records merited but who became a cult, name-to-drop act as a consequence.

THE ACTION

Exact London contemporaries of the Creation. Originally a mod band, they were produced by George Martin, who imparted to their records his trademark glossy sound. Vocalist Reg King had an even more asthmatic style than Kenny Pickett and applied it initially to creamy smooth covers of soul numbers like 'Since I Lost My Baby' and subsequently to excellent band compositions like the life-affirming anthem 'Never Ever'. The group's peak recordings are collected on the Edsel compilation 'Action Packed'.

A slight change in personnel led to a profound change in sound, with the group riding the tide of progressive rock (when that term meant hard rock instead of Emerson, Lake and Palmer-style bombast). The results can be heard on the Reaction Recordings CD 'Rolled Gold'. It's intermittently enjoyable but not, to these ears, completely convincing. By the time they had mutated into Mighty Baby, the band had all but spoiled the memories of their original pop flash with utterly uninteresting Grateful Dead-style workouts.

BIG STAR

Their artistically negligible 'In the Street' was the theme tune to the TV comedy series *That Seventies Show* but don't hold that against Memphis' Big Star. Their albums '#1 Record' (1972) and 'Radio City' (1974) were excellent power-pop collections (albeit tinged with a rock element). Mainman Alex Chilton and drummer Jody Stephens also recorded a third album on which Chilton abandoned melody for experimentation. It was unreleased at the time, has been subsequently issued as – among other titles – 'Third' and is massively overrated. The anthemic 'September Gurls' from 'Radio City' should have been a huge hit. As with Boney M's royalties-generating cover of ' Painter Man' years after The Creation had dribbled to a disillusioned close, 'September Gurls' was subsequently covered by a far more successful act, appearing in 1986 on the Bangles' 'Different Light' album which topped the US charts.

GRIN

Nils Lofgren achieved a modicum of success in the mid Seventies as a solo rocker (and subsequently as Bruce Springsteen's lead guitarist) but his glory days – artistically speaking – were spent in a superb three-piece from Washington DC called Grin who released four albums from 1971-74, all of which feature Lofgren's amazing knack for melodies so sweet you could taste them, heartbreaking so-happy-they're-sad lyrics and a guitar talent as mellifluous as any of his generation. All are recommended but the band's peak was '1+1' (1972), a great lost classic that should have sealed the band's superstardom but went nowhere.

THE KOOBAS

Perhaps not a great group but one feels almost obliged to mention Scousers The Koobas, so intertwined are they in the story of the Creation. Manager Tony Stratton-Smith later admitted that he foolishly allowed his heart to rule his head over this band, pouring money and energy into them long after it was apparent that they would never become stars. Indeed, it may have been his very loyalty to them that sealed the Creation's fate: if Stratton-Smith and The Creation had not fallen out over his diverting of Creation profits to the promotion of the Koobas and The Creation had retained his considerable managerial nous, who knows what might have happened?

As with The Action, The Koobas became less interesting as they became more progressive. The handful of singles they recorded in the mid-Sixties are pretty good (although not generally self-written): material like 'Sweet Music' and 'Gypsy Fred' are rather novel in their mixture of melody and brutal rhythm, not so much power pop as glam stomp several years before its time. Those singles and the tracks of their sole album – self-written and lacking their melodic edge – can be found on the Beat Goes On CD 'Koobas'.

THE MISUNDERSTOOD

Despite journeying to England to record in 1966 and being championed by a very young John Peel, this American garage band turned psychedelic rock outfit never did break through. Perhaps the fuzz-tone freakouts lacing their fine melodies was what prevented mainstream success. There have been subsequent competent recordings using the band's name but with only one original member. The reader is advised to stick to the music collected as 'Before The Dream Faded' on Cherry Red.

THE SMOKE

A staggeringly brilliant band. As with The Creation, only the Germans were intelligent enough at the time to give them hits. Known chiefly in this country for the banned-by-the-BBC single 'My Friend Jack' – an LSD anthem which referred to the user's habit of ingesting the drug on a cube of sugar – there was in fact far more to them than that one semi-hit. They were an ensemble with a punch-packing but utterly melodic sound fronted by exceptionally talented vocalist Mick Rowley. Almost everything they recorded was self-composed and ranged from pop to soul to psychedelia. Unlike the Creation, they even got to record a proper album in the Sixties, the brilliant 'It's Smoke Time'. Everything they recorded can be found on the Sanctuary 2-CD set 'High In A Room'.

This discography endeavours to list every legally commercially available Mark Four, Creation and Eddie Phillips-related release from the UK, the US and Germany. Releases from other territories are noted if of particular importance.

Singles reissues are only listed for the UK.

Only significant Various Artists compilations are noted such as ones featuring the first album appearance of a previously single-only track.

The discography attempts to cover as many releases related to the other Creation personnel as possible although, in the cases of some ex-members (Ronnie Wood especially), listing their entire post-Creation catalogue would not be appropriate or practical.

Bootlegs are not included.

KEY
CREDITED ARTIST

Month and year of release
Format of release
A-side or title of release
B-side (if applicable)
Extra tracks (if applicable)
Country of issue
Label
Tracklisting (if applicable)
Notes

* First instance of a Creation song being commercially available in any territory

THE MARK FOUR

May 1964

Single

Rock Around The Clock

Slow Down

-

UK

Mercury

THE MARK FOUR

August 1964

Single

Try It Baby

Crazy Country Hop

-

UK

Mercury

THE MARK FOUR

August 1965

Single

Hurt Me If You Will

I'm Leaving

-

UK

Decca

THE MARK FOUR

February 1966

Single

Work All Day (Sleep All Night)

Going Down Fast

-

UK

Fontana

THE CREATION

June 1966

Single

Making Time*

Try and Stop Me*

-

UK

Planet

THE CREATION

June 1966

Single

Making Time

Try and Stop Me

-

USA

Planet

THE CREATION

July 1966

Single

Making Time

Try and Stop Me

-

West Germany

Hit-Ton

THE CREATION

October 1966

Single

Painter Man*

Biff Bang Pow*

-

UK

Planet

THE CREATION

October 1966

Single

Painter Man

Biff Bang Pow

-

USA

Planet

THE CREATION

? 1966

EP

Making Time

-

-

France

Disques Vogue

Making Time/Biff Bang Pow/Try and
Stop Me/Sylvette*

Only Sixties appearance of Sylvette anywhere

THE CREATION
? 1967

3. Single

4. Painter Man

5. Biff Bang Pow

6. -

7. West Germany

8. Hit-Ton

THE CREATION
? 1967

Single

Can I Join Your Band*

Tom Tom*

-

Belgium

Disques Vogue

-

Possibly the first appearance of both tracks
Disc pressed in France

THE CREATION
June 1967

Single

If I Stay Too Long*

Nightmares*

-

UK

Polydor

THE CREATION
June 1967

Single

If I Stay Too Long

Nightmares

-

USA

Decca

THE CREATION
July 1967

Single

Tom Tom

Nightmares*

-

West Germany

Hit-Ton

-

THE CREATION
? 1967

Album

We Are Paintermen

-

-

West Germany

Hit-Ton

Cool Jerk*/Making Time/Through
My Eyes*/Like A Rolling Stone*/
Can I Join Your Band/Tom Tom/
Try And Stop Me/If I Stay Too
Long/Biff Bang Pow/Nightmares/
Hey Joe*/Painter Man

First appearances of Cool Jerk, Like A
Rolling Stone, Hey Joe and probably
Through My Eyes.
First album appearances of all tracks.

THE CREATION
? 1967

Single

How Does It Feel To Feel
(UK Version)*

If I Stay Too Long

-

West Germany

Hit-Ton

THE CREATION
October 1967

Single

Life Is Just Beginning*

Through My Eyes

-

UK

Polydor

THE CREATION
November 1967

Single

How Does It Feel To Feel*
(US Version)

Life Is Just Beginning

-

USA

Decca

THE CREATION

? 1968

Single

Cool Jerk

Life Is Just Beginning

-

West Germany

Hit-Ton

THE CREATION

February 1968

Single

How Does It Feel To Feel
(UK Version)

Tom Tom

-

UK

Polydor

THE CREATION

April or May 1968

Single

Midway Down*

The Girls Are Naked*

-

UK

Polydor

-

Possibly first appearance of both sides

THE CREATION

? 1968

Single

Midway Down

The Girls Are Naked

-

West Germany

Hit-Ton

THE CREATION

? 1968

Single

Bony Moronie*

Mercy Mercy Mercy*

-

West Germany

Hit-Ton

Possibly first appearance of both sides

A-side misspelt 'Bonney Moroney'

THE CREATION

? 1968

Single

For All That I Am*

Uncle Bert*

-

West Germany

Hit-Ton

-

Possibly first appearance of both sides

THE CREATION

? 1968

Album

Best Of The Creation

-

-

West Germany

Pop Schallplatten

Bony Moronie/Uncle Bert/Life Is Just
Beginning/How Does It Feel To Feel
(UK version)/Mercy Mercy
Mercy/The Girls Are Naked/For All
That I Am/Midway Down/Tom
Tom/Cool Jerk/Painter Man/
Making Time

First album appearance of Bony Moronie,
Uncle Bert, Life Is Just Beginning. How Does
It Feel To Feel (UK version), Mercy Mercy
Mercy, The Girls Are Naked, For All That I
Am, Midway Down

THE CREATION

July 1973

Album

'66-'67

-

-

UK

Charisma

Making Time/Life Is Just
Beginning/If I Stay Too
Long/Through My Eyes/Hey
Joe/Painter Man/Cool Jerk/How
Does It Feel To Feel (UK
version)/Try And Stop Me/I Am The
Walker*/Can I Join Your Band/
Tom Tom

First ever UK Creation album
First appearance of I Am The Walker
Only Eddie Phillips tracks chosen
Reissued on bootleg as If I Stay Too Long on
"Planet Records"

THE CREATION
September 1973
Single
Making Time
Painter Man
-
UK
Charisma

EDDY PHILLIPS
? 1976
Single
Limbo Jimbo
Change My Ways
-
UK
Charisma
-
A-side is reggae version of Painter Man with
new lyric

EDDIE PHILLIPS
? 1977
Single
City Woman
Duckin' And Weavin'
-
West Germany
Casablanca

EDDIE PHILLIPS
? 1977
Single
City Woman
Duckin' And Weavin'
-
USA
Casablanca

THE CREATION
November 1977
Single
Making Time
Painter Man
-
UK
Raw

KENNEDY EXPRESS
June 1979
Single
Little Lolita
Stop Stop Stop
-
UK
Jet
-
Eddie Phillips and Kenny Pickett project

KENNEDY EXPRESS
? 1980
Single
Is There Life On Earth
Stop Stop Stop
Little Lolita
UK
Jet
-
Eddie Phillips and Kenny Pickett project

VARIOUS ARTISTS
? 1980
Album
Mersey Sounds
-
-
UK
Decca
-
Includes first album appearance of
The Mark Four's Hurt Me If You Will

EDDIE AND THE PLAYERS

? 1981

Single

Space Invaders

Penny Arcade

-

USA

Plantation

-

Eddie Phillips project

THE CREATION

? 1982

Single

Alpha Beta*

Man In The Mist*

-

France

Trema

-

Eddie Phillips is the only member of Creation personnel on these tracks.

THE CREATION

? 1982

Album

We Are Paintermen

-

-

West Germany

Outline/Line

Cool Jerk/Making Time/Through My Eyes/Like A Rolling Stone/Can I Join Your Band/Tom Tom/Try and Stop Me/If I Stay Too Long/Biff Bang Pow/Nightmares/Hey Joe/ Painter Man

Reissue

THE CREATION

September 1982

Album

How Does It Feel To Feel

-

-

UK

Edsel

How Does It Feel To Feel (US version)/Life Is Just Beginning/Through My Eyes/Ostrich Man*/ I Am the Walker/Tom Tom/The Girls Are Naked/Painter Man/Try and Stop Me/Biff Bang Pow/Making Time/ Cool Jerk/For All That I Am/Nightmares/Midway Down/Can I Join Your Band

First appearance of Ostrich Man
First album appearance of How Does It Feel To Feel (US version)

THE CREATION

? 1982

Album

Re-Creation – The Rest Of The Creation

-

-

West Germany

Outline/Line

Life Is Just Beginning/Midway Down/The Girls Are Naked/Sylvette/Ostrich Man/How Does It Feel To Feel (US version)/Bony Moronie/Mercy Mercy Mercy/For All That I Am/Uncle Bert/I Am The Walker/How Does It Feel To Feel (UK version)

First album to feature both versions of 'How Does It Feel To Feel'.

THE MARK FOUR/ THE CREATION

? 1983

Album

The Mark Four/The Creation

-

-

France

Eva

Biff Bang Pow/Rock Around The Clock/Try It Baby/Hurt Me If You Will/Work All Day (Sleep All Night)/Tango/Nightmares/Like A

371

Rolling Stone/Slow Down/Crazy Country Hop/I'm Leaving/Going Down Fast/Baby What's Wrong/Sylvette

Includes first ever album appearances of Rock Around The Clock, Slow Down, Try It Baby, Crazy Country Hop, I'm Leaving, Work All Day (Sleep All Night), Going Down Fast, Sylvette

Baby What's Wrong and Tango are by the unrelated group The Mark Five

VARIOUS ARTISTS

? 1983

Album

The Sound Of The Sixties

-

-

France

Eva

First appearance of The Creation's That's How Strong My Love Is (live TV, 1966)

THE CREATION

February 1984

Album

We Are Paintermen

-

-

West Germany

Line

Cool Jerk/Making Time/Through My Eyes/Like A Rolling Stone/Can I Join Your Band/Tom Tom/Try and Stop Me/If I Stay Too Long/Biff Bang Pow/Nightmares/Hey Joe/Painter Man

Reissue

THE CREATION

February 1984

Album

The Singles Collection

-

-

West Germany

Line

Making Time/Try And Stop Me/Painter Man/Biff Bang Pow/Tom Tom/Nightmares/ How Does It Feel To Feel (UK version)/If I Stay Too Long/Cool Jerk/Life Is Just Beginning/ Midway Down/The Girls Are Naked/ Bony Moronie/Mercy Mercy Mercy/For All That I Am/Uncle Bert

Features all Creation A and B-sides released in West Germany during the Sixties.

THE CREATION

May 1984

Single

Making Time

Uncle Bert

-

UK

Edsel

EDWIN PHILLIPS

? 1985

12-inch single

Life On Earth

Life On Earth (radio mix)

Life On Earth (instrumental)

Germany

T-Mac

THE MARK FOUR

? 1985

EP

Live At The Beat Scene Club

-

-

UK

Bam Caruso

Hurt Me If You Will/Got My Mojo Working/That's How Strong My Love Is

Selection from The Mark Four's 1985 reunion Limited edition promo of 500 copies only

SPECTRUM

October 1985

Single

All Or Nothing (Traditional)

All Or Nothing (Contemporary)

-

UK

Phoenix

-

Eddie Phillips appears on record
Also released as a 12-inch single with the
same tracks

VARIOUS ARTISTS

1986

Album

Dedicated – The Mod Live Aid Album

-

-

UK

Phoenix

-

Eddie Phillips appears on track
Spectrum Jam
Live album, recorded December 1985

THE CREATION

April 1987

Single

A Spirit Called Love*

Making Time*

-

UK

Jet

-

Making Time is a re-recording
Kenny Pickett and Eddie Phillips are only
Creation personnel on the recordings

THE CREATION

April 1987

12-inch single

A Spirit Called Love

Making Time

Mumbo Jumbo*

UK

Jet

THE CREATION

? 1988

Album

The Creation Collection

-

-

West Germany

Line

Painter Man/Biff Bang Pow/If I Stay
Too Long/Can I Join Your Band/Tom
Tom/Nightmares/Mercy Mercy
Mercy/Bony Moronie/Midway
Down/The Girls Are Naked/For All
That I Am/Uncle Bert/Cool Jerk/
Life Is Just Beginning/Making
Time/Try And Stop Me/How Does It
Feel To Feel (UK version)/Hey
Joe/Through My Eyes/Ostrich Man/
I Am The Walker

First Creation compact disc.

THE BRITISH
INVASION ALLSTARS

April 1990

Album

Regression

-

-

UK

Promised Land

Train Kept A Rollin'/My
Generation/Route 66/The House Of
The Rising Sun/Let It Rock/Tobacco
Road/Nadine/Summertime
Blues/Sweet Little Rock And
Roller/Hang On Sloopy.

Personnel: Eddie Phillips, Don Craine, Keith
Grant, Jim McCarty, Ray Phillips.

THE CREATION

August 1990

Album

How Does It Feel To Feel

-

-

UK

Edsel

How Does It Feel To Feel (US
version)/Life Is Just
Beginning/Through My Eyes/Ostrich
Man/I Am the Walker/Tom Tom/The
Girls Are Naked/Painter Man/Try
and Stop Me/Biff Bang Pow/Making
Time/Cool Jerk/For All That I
Am/Nightmares/Midway Down/Can
I Join Your Band/Uncle Bert/Like A

Rolling Stone/If I Stay Too Long/
Hey Joe
CD reissue with extra tracks

EDDIE PHILLIPS
October 1990

Album

Riffmaster Of The Western World

-

-

UK

Promised Land

Riffmaster/Spirit Called Love/How
Does It Feel To Feel/Hi Heel
Sneakers/The Jimi Hendrix
Trilogy/Midnight Hour/Teacher,
Teacher/Riffmaster Of The Western
World/Mumbo Jumbo

Mumbo Jumbo is the same recording as
featured on the Spirit Called Love 12-inch
single. Other Creation songs are
re-recordings.

THE BRITISH
INVASION ALLSTARS
August 1991

Album

United

-

-

UK

Promised Land

United/Gimme Some Lovin'/Bad
Penny/Heavy Weather/Shakin' All
Over/Shapes Of Things/Green
Onions/Mona/Talkin' 'Bout You/I
Can Tell/Promised Land/I'm A
Man/Little Egypt

Personnel: Eddie Phillips, Don Craine,
Matthew Fisher, Keith Grant, Jim McCarty,
Ray Phillips, plus guest appearances by Mick
Green, Phil May, Dick Taylor.

THE MARK FOUR/
THE CREATION
? 1992

Album

The Mark Four/The Creation

-

-

France

Eva

Biff Bang Pow/Rock Around The
Clock/Try It Baby/Hurt Me If You
Will/Work All Day (Sleep All
Night)/Tango/Nightmares/Like A
Rolling Stone/Slow Down/Crazy
Country Hop/I'm Leaving/Going
Down Fast/Baby What's
Wrong/Sylvette

CD reissue

THE CREATION
April 1993

Album

Painter Man

-

-

UK

Edsel

Painter Man/Making Time/Biff Bang
Pow/Life Is Just Beginning/How
Does It Feel To Feel (US
version)/Bony Moronie/Mercy
Mercy Mercy/Sweet Helen*

First appearance of Sweet Helen

THE CREATION
October

1993

Album

Lay The Ghost

-

-

UK

Cohesion

Batman Theme-Biff Bang Pow*/Try
And Stop Me*/Life Is Just
Beginning*/I'm A
Man*/Nightmares/If I Stay Too
Long*/Hey Joe*/Making Time*/Tom
Tom*/Through My Eyes*/That's
How Strong My Love Is*/Lay The
Ghost*/How Does It Feel To
Feel*/Painter Man*

Creation reunion gig, recorded live at the
Mean Fiddler in 1993.

STEADY EDDIE AND THE COWBOY OUTFIT

? 1994

Album

Hillbilly Rock

-

-

UK

None listed

Dixie Medley/Sea Cruise/That'll Be The Day/Halfway To Paradise/Hillbilly Rock/Singing Cowboy/Cajun Baby/Hot Dog/Burning Love/Hoochie Coochie Man/Laredo/The Jimi Hendrix Trilogy/Midnight Special/Don't/Duelling Banjos

Eddie Phillips project
Cassette-only format available only at Eddie Phillips gigs
The Jimi Hendrix Trilogy is the same recording as featured on the Riffmaster Of The Western World album.

THE YARDBIRDS EXPERIENCE

March 1994

Album

The Yardbirds Experience

-

-

UK

Promised Land

White Knight/Whole Lotta Love/Riffmaster/Glimpses Of God/Shapes Of Things/Lavender Down/Communication Breakdown/Train Kept A Rollin'/How Does It Feel To Feel/Heavy Weather/Tobacco Road/Southbound/Jimi Hendrix Trilogy

Personnel: Jim McCarty, Noel Redding, Eddie Phillips, Ray Phillips, Don Craine, Keith Grant with guests Matthew Fisher, Phil May, Eddie Edwards, Ray Majors
Features remixed British Invasion Allstars recordings (1, 4, 5, 6, 8, 10, 11) and remixed Eddie Phillips solo recordings (3. 9, 13). Released in the US as The Yardbirds Experience British Thunder (1996)

THE CREATION

July 1994

Single

Creation*

Shock Horror*

-

UK

Creation

-

Studio reunion of original Creation line-up.

THE CREATION

July 1994

CD single

Creation

Shock Horror

Power Surge*

UK

Creation

THE CREATION

June 1996

Album

Power Surge

-

-

UK

Creation

Creation/Power Surge/Someone's Gonna Bleed*/Shock Horror/That's How I Found Love*/Killing Song*/Nobody Wants To Know*/City Life*/English Language*/Free Men Live Forever*/Ghost Division*/O+N*

Studio reunion of original Creation line-up.

THE CREATION

October 1998

Album

The Complete Collection Volume 1: Making Time

-

-

USA

Retroactive

Making Time (mono)/Try And Stop Me (mono)/How Does It Feel To Feel (US version – mono)/Tom Tom (mono)/Nightmares (mono)/If I Stay Too Long (mono)/How Does It Feel to Feel (UK version – stereo)/For All That I Am (mono)/Uncle Bert (mono)/Cool Jerk (mono)/Bony Moronie (mono)/Ostrich Man* (mono)/I Am the Walker (mono)/For All That I Am (stereo)/ Nightmares(stereo)/How Does It Feel To Feel (UK version – stereo)/Instrumental #1*/I'm A Man (live)*/That's How Strong My Love Is (live)/Making Time (live)*

Joint first ever Creation album release in USA.
First appearance of Instrumental #1 alternate Ostrich Man with different introduction, I'm A Man (live) and Making Time (live)

THE CREATION

October 1998

Album

The Complete Collection Volume 2: Biff Bang Pow!

-

-

USA

Retroactive

Biff Bang Pow (mono)/Painter Man (mono)/Life Is Just Beginning (mono)/Through My Eyes (mono)/Midway Down (mono)/The Girls Are Naked (mono)/Can I Join Your Band (mono)/Sweet Helen (mono)/Hey Joe (mono)/Like a Rolling Stone (mono)/Mercy Mercy Mercy (mono)/Sylvette (stereo)/Biff Bang Pow (stereo)/Painter Man (stereo)/Can I Join Your Band (stereo)/Midway Down (stereo)/Life Is Just Beginning Alternate Take 1 (stereo)*/Life Is Just Beginning Alternate Take 2 (mono)*/Painter Man (live)*/ Try And Stop Me (live)*

Joint first ever Creation album release in USA. First appearances of Life Is Just Beginning Alternate Take 1, Life Is Just Beginning Alternate Take 2, Painter Man (live)/Try And Stop Me (live)

THE CREATION

April 1998

Album

Our Music Is Red – With Purple Flashes

-

-

UK

Diablo/Demon

Making Time/Try And Stop Me/Painter Man/Biff Bang Pow/If I Stay Too Long/Nightmares/Cool Jerk/Like A Rolling Stone/I Am The Walker/Can I Join Your Band/Hey Joe/Life Is Just Beginning/Through My Eyes/How Does It Feel To Feel (US version)/How Does It Feel To Feel (UK version)/Tom Tom/Midway Down/The Girls Are Naked/Bony Moronie/Mercy Mercy Mercy/For All That I Am/Uncle Bert/Ostrich Man/Sweet Helen

THE CREATION

? 1999

Album

We Are Paintermen

-

-

Germany

Repertoire

Cool Jerk/Making Time/Through My Eyes/Like A Rolling Stone/Can I Join Your Band/Tom Tom/Try And Stop Me/If I Stay Too Long/Biff Bang Pow/Nightmares/Hey Joe/Painter Man/How Does It Feel To Feel (US version)/Sylvette/I Am The Walker/Ostrich Man/Sweet Helen/Life Is Just Beginning (alternate take)/For All That I Am (Stereo)/Midway Down (Stereo)/Hurt Me If You Will/ I'm Leaving/Work All Day (Sleep All Night)/Going Down Fast

Reissue with extra tracks.
Includes Mark Four material

THE CREATION

July 2002

Album

Best Of The Creation

-

-

Germany

Repertoire

Bony Moronie/Uncle Bert/Life Is Just Beginning/How Does It Feel To Feel (UK version – mono)/Mercy Mercy Mercy/The Girls Are Naked/For All That I Am/Midway Down/Tom Tom/Cool Jerk/Painter Man/Making Time/Like A Rolling Stone/Can I Join Your Band/Sylvette/Biff Bang Pow/Nightmares/Can I Join Your Band/Life Is Just Beginning/How Does It Feel To Feel (UK version – stereo)/Rock Around The Clock/Slow Down/Crazy Country Hop/Try It Baby

Reissue with extra tracks
Includes Mark Four material

BOB GARNER
THE MERSEYBEATS

On Stage – live EP (1964)

LEE CURTIS & THE ALL-STARS

It's Lee – album (1965),
Nobody But You – single (1965).

SMILEY

Penelope b/w I Know What I Want – single (1972)

KIM GARDNER

Appears as a permanent band member on recordings by:

The Birds

Santa Barbara Machine Head

Ashton Gardner & Dyke

RONNIE WOOD

Appears as a permanent band member on recordings by :

The Birds

The Jeff Beck Group

The Faces

The Rolling Stones

CREATION-RELATED UNRELEASED RECORDINGS

All the recordings below are known to be in existence.

BOBBY LEE AND THE TRAVELLERS

Radcliffe Recording Services Acetate 1961

Eddie Phillips-written instrumental

Pointed Toe Shoes (?)

JIMMY VIRGO AND THE BLUE JACKS

City Of London studio acetates 1963

Say Mama

Brand New Cadillac

THE MARK FOUR

City Of London studio acetates 1964

Crazy Country Hop

Slow Down

THE MARK FOUR

Regent Sound studio acetate 1964

You Be My Baby

Sick And Tired

MEN OF STEEL

Eddie Phillips promotional solo single 1978

Hail Superman b/w Keep On Movin' To The Music (Jet)

KENNY PICKETT

Kenny Pickett promotional solo single 1980

Got A Gun

THE MARK FOUR

Live at the Beat Scene Club 18/1/85; unreleased songs

I'm A Man

That's Who Strong My Love Is

Shame Shame Shame

Hurt Me If You Will

The House Of The Rising Sun

Around And Around

Mona

Hoochie Coochie Man

Walking The Dog

In The Midnight Hour

Painter Man

Johnny B Goode

Got My Mojo Working

EDDIE PHILLIPS

The Mitra

Album

Recorded 1982-1985(?)

Tracklisting: Alpha Beta/The Void/Man In The Mist/Ocean Of Storms/Ramon Ramon/Enigma/ Ave/Human Human/Between Two Worlds/Light Of The Worlds

The album from whose sessions the 1982 Trema single Alpha Beta b/w Man In The Mist (credited to The Creation) was released. It is not known if a final track-listing or running sequence was ever settled on.

THE CREATION

Untitled

Album

Recorded 1985-1987

Tracklisting: Lay The Ghost/Doing It My Way/Radio Beautiful/Psychedelic Rose/A Spirit Called Love/Making Time/Far From Paradise/ United/Mumbo Jumbo/White Knight

The album from whose sessions the 1987 Jet singles tracks A Spirit Called Love, Making Time (re-recording) and Mumbo Jumbo were released.
Kenny Pickett and Eddie Phillips are only Creation personnel on the recordings.
Possibly additional versions of some tracks produced by Nick Lowe in existence.
It is not known if a final track-listing or running sequence was ever settled on.

THE CREATION

Mean Fiddler 6/7/93 – soundcheck recordings

Lay The Ghost

Making Time

THE CREATION

Power Surge Outtakes (1995)

Out Of My Mind

Bald Eagle

AND FINALLY...

There are several German Creation TV appearances in existence.
There are possibly some BBC Radio Creation session recordings in existence. They definitely appeared on at least one edition of *Saturday Club* in the Sixties and recorded a session for Mark Radcliffe in 1994

Also available from
cherry red books

Rockdetector
'THRASH METAL
ry Sharpe-Young
covers, 460 pages
£14.99 in UK
N 1-901447-09-X

Rockdetector
A-Z of DOOM, GOTHIC &
STONER METAL
Garry Sharpe-Young
Paper covers, 455 pages
£14.99 in UK
ISBN 1-901447-14-6

Rockdetector
A-Z of '80s ROCK
**Garry Sharpe Young
& Dave Reynolds**
Paper covers, 752 pages,
£17.99 in UK
ISBN 1-901447-21-9

Rockdetector
OZZY OSBOURNE
**THE STORY OF THE
OZZY OSBOURNE BAND
(AN UNOFFICIAL
PUBLICATION)**
Garry Sharpe-Young
Paper covers 368 pages
£14.99 in UK
ISBN 1-901447-08-1

Rockdetector
ACK SABBATH
SAY DIE 1979-1997
ry Sharpe-Young
covers 448 pages
£14.99 in UK
N 1-901447-16-2

Rockdetector
A-Z of BLACK METAL
Garry Sharpe-Young
Paper covers 416 pages
£14.99 in UK
ISBN 1-901447-30-8

Rockdetector
A-Z of DEATH METAL
Garry Sharpe-Young
Paper covers 416 pages
£14.99 in UK
ISBN 1-901447-35-9

Rockdetector
A-Z of POWER METAL
Garry Sharpe-Young
Paper covers 512 pages
£14.99 in UK
ISBN 1-901447-13-8

Available on DVD
RED WITH PURPLE FLASHES
The Creation Live (CRDVD 53)

This is a unique document of the band's reformation concerts in the early 1990s.

*The band's most successful line-up - Kenny Pickett, Eddie Phillips, Bob Garner and Jack Jones -
give frank assessments of their feelings in the run-up to the featured 1993 concert,
their first show together in over 25 years.
Also featured on the DVD is a full-length concert from 1995.*

*The DVD can be purchased in all good record stores,
or via the Cherry Red Records website
www.cherryred.co.uk*

PSYCHEDELIC ROSE
THE GREAT
LOST CREATION ALBUM

The Creation
(CDMRED 256)
Available July 2004

Track listing:

1. Lay The Ghost
2. Psychedelic Rose
3. Radio Beautiful
4. United
5. Doing It My Way
6. Making Time
7. Far From Paradise
8. White Night
9. Spirit Called Love
10. Spoken word extract from book
Our Music Is Red - With Purple Flashes:
The Story Of The Creation by Sean Egan, read by Joe Foster.
11. CD-Rom enhanced video track 'Painter Man'

*Available from all good record stores,
distributed by Pinnacle, or via mail order from
Cherry Red with Visa, Mastercard or Switch.
Call 0044 (0)207 371 5844 for details,
email info@cherryred.co.uk or write to:
Cherry Red, Unit 17, 1st Floor, Elysium Gate West,
126-128 New Kings Road, London SW6 4LZ
CD prices including post and packaging*

£9.95 UK £10.45 Europe £10.95 Rest of World

RED WITH
PURPLE FLASHES

the CREATION

LIVE

Indie Hits 1980-1989

The Complete UK Independent Chart (Singles And Albums)

Compiled By Barry Lazell

Paper covers, 314 pages, £14.99 in UK

Cor Baby, That's Really Me!

(The New Millennium Hardback Edition)

John Otway

Hardback, 192 pages and 16 pages of photographs £11.99 in UK

All The Young Dudes, Mott the Hoople and Ian Hunter The Biography

Campbell Devine

Paper covers, 448 pages and 16 pages of photographs £14.99 in UK

Embryo - A Pink Floyd Chronology 1966-1971

Nick Hodges and Ian Priston

Paper covers, 302 pages and photographs throughout £14.99 in UK

Johnny Thunders In Cold Blood

Nina Antonia

Paper covers, 270 pages and photographs throughout £14.99 in UK

Songs In The Key Of Z

The Curious Universe of Outsider music Irwin Chusid

Paper covers, 311 pages, fully illustrated £11.99 in UK

The Legendary Joe Meek The Telstar Man

John Repsch

Paper covers, 350 pages plus photographs, £14.99 in UK

Random Precision Recording the Music of Syd Barrett 1965-1974

David Parker

Paper covers, 320 pages and photographs throughout £14.99 in UK

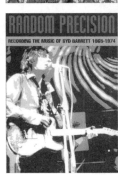

Also available from Cherry Red Books

Those Were The Days

Stefan Granados

An Unofficial History of the Beatles' Apple Organization 1967-2002

Paper covers, 300 pages including photographs £14.99 in UK

The Rolling Stones: Complete Recording Sessions 1962-2002

Martin Elliott

Paper covers, 576 pages plus 16 pages of photographs £14.99 in UK

Goodnight Jim Bob – On The Road With Carter The Unstoppable Sex Machine

Jim Bob

Paper covers, 228 pages plus 16 pages of photographs £12.99 in UK

Our Music Is Red - With Purple Flashes: The Story Of The Creation

Sean Egan

Paper covers, 378 pages plus 8 pages of photographs £14.99 in UK

Bittersweet: The Clifford T Ward Story

David Cartwright

Paper covers, 352 pages plus 8 pages of photographs £14.99 in UK

The Spirit Of Wimbledon: Footballing Memories Of The Dons 1922-2003

Niall Couper

Paper covers, 288 pages and photographs throughout £14.99 in UK

CHERRY RED BOOKS

We are always looking for interesting books to publish.
They can be either new manuscripts or re-issues of deleted books.
If you have any good ideas then please
get in touch with us.

CHERRY RED BOOKS
a division of Cherry Red Records Ltd.
3a Long Island House,
1–4 Warple Way,
London W3 0RG.

E-mail: iain@cherryred.co.uk
Web: www.cherryred.co.uk